Children of Depressed Parents

Mechanisms of Risk and Implications for Treatment

Edited by
Sherryl H. Goodman
and Ian H. Gotlib

AMERICAN PSYCHOLOGICAL ASSOCIATION
WASHINGTON, DC

Published by
American Psychological Association
750 First Street, NE
Washington, DC 20002
www.apa.org

To order
APA Order Department
P.O. Box 92984
Washington, DC 20090-2984
Tel: (800) 374-2721, Direct: (202) 336-5510
Fax: (202) 336-5502, TDD/TTY: (202) 336-6123
Online: www.apa.org/books/
Email: order@apa.org

In the U.K., Europe, Africa, and the Middle East, copies may be ordered from
American Psychological Association
3 Henrietta Street
Covent Garden, London
WC2E 8LU England

Typeset in Goudy by AlphaWebTech, Mechanicsville, MD

Printer: Sheridan Books, Ann Arbor, MI
Cover designer: NiDesign, Baltimore, MD
Technical/Production Editor: Jennifer Powers

The opinions and statements published are the responsibility of the authors, and such opinions and statements do not necessarily represent the policies of the American Psychological Association.

Library of Congress Cataloging-in-Publication Data

Children of depressed parents : mechanisms of risk and implications for treatment / edited by Sherryl H. Goodman and Ian H. Gotlib.
    p. cm.
  Includes bibliographical references and index.
    ISBN 1-55798-875-7 (hbk. : alk. paper)
    1. Children of depressed persons—Mental health. 2. Parent and child. 3. Adjustment (Psychology). I. Goodman, Sherryl H. II. Gotlib, Ian H.

RC537 C469 2001
618.92'89—dc21   2001046426

British Library Cataloguing-in-Publication Data
A CIP record is available from the British Library.

Printed in the United States of America
First Edition

CONTENTS

CONTRIBUTORS

Sharon B. Ashman, Center on Human Development and Disability, University of Washington, Seattle

William R. Beardslee, Children's Hospital, Judge Baker Children's Center, Harvard Medical School, Boston, MA

Elisa Bronfman, Department of Psychiatry, Children's Hospital, Harvard Medical School, Boston, MA

Bruce E. Compas, Department of Psychology, University of Vermont, Burlington

Mary Ellen Copeland, Brattleboro, VT

Betsy Davis, Oregon Research Institute, Eugene

Geraldine Dawson, Center on Human Development and Disability, University of Washington, Seattle

Amy M. Duhig, Department of Psychology, University of South Florida, Tampa

Tiffany M. Field, Touch Research Institute, Department of Pediatrics, University of Miami Medical School, Miami, FL

Judy Garber, Department of Psychology and Human Development, Vanderbilt University, Nashville, TN

Tracy R. G. Gladstone, Children's Hospital, Judge Baker Children's Center, Harvard Medical School, Boston, MA

Sherryl H. Goodman, Department of Psychology, Emory University, Atlanta

Ian H. Gotlib, Department of Psychology, Stanford University, Stanford, CA

Constance Hammen, Department of Psychology, University of California at Los Angeles

Hyman Hops, Oregon Research Institute, Eugene

Gary Keller, Otter Creek/Matrix Associates, Burlington, VT

Bonnie Klimes-Dougan, Department of Psychology, Catholic University of America, Washington, DC

Adela M. Langrock, Department of Psychology, University of Vermont, Burlington

Karlen Lyons-Ruth, Department of Psychiatry, Cambridge Hospital, Harvard Medical School, Cambridge, MA

Amy Lyubchik, Department of Psychiatry, Cambridge Hospital, Harvard Medical School, Cambridge, MA

Nina C. Martin, Department of Psychology and Human Development, Vanderbilt University, Nashville, TN

Mary Jane Merchant, Otter Creek/Matrix Associates, Burlington, VT

Vicky Phares, Department of Psychology, University of South Florida, Tampa

Marian Radke-Yarrow, Scientist Emeritus, National Institute of Mental Health, Bethesda, MD

Sir Michael Rutter, Institute of Psychiatry, London, United Kingdom

Lisa Sheeber, Oregon Research Institute, Eugene

Judy Silberg, Department of Human Genetics, Virginia Institute for Psychiatric and Behavioral Genetics, Virginia Commonwealth University, Richmond

M. Monica Watkins, Department of Psychology, University of South Florida, Tampa

Rebecca Wolfe, Department of Psychology, Harvard University, Cambridge, MA

Children of Depressed Parents

1

INTRODUCTION

IAN H. GOTLIB AND SHERRYL H. GOODMAN

Depression is among the most common psychiatric disorders in adults. Rates of depression are higher in women than in men: One in 5 women and 1 in 10 men can expect to develop a clinically significant episode of depression at some point in their lives (Blehar & Oren, 1995; Kessler, in press). Depression is also a highly recurrent disorder: Over 80% of depressed individuals have more than one depressive episode (Belsher & Costello, 1988). In fact, more than 50% of depressed individuals have been found to relapse within 2 years of recovery (e.g., Keller & Shapiro, 1981); individuals with three or more previous episodes of depression may have a relapse rate as high as 40% within only 12 to 15 weeks after recovery (Keller et al., 1992; Mueller et al., 1996). Moreover, data suggest that individuals who have experienced a depressive episode do not return to completely asymptomatic functioning following the episode, but rather, continue to experience subclinical levels of depressive symptoms. Finally, depression may be particularly prevalent during women's childbearing years (Robins et al., 1984) and among women with young children (Brown & Harris, 1978). These data converge to suggest that a large number of young children are exposed repeatedly to maternal depression and consistently to subclinical depressive symptoms (Boland & Keller, in press). There is little question that this exposure has adverse consequences.

We should be concerned about the functioning of children of depressed parents for a number of reasons. First, depression is highly heritable. Second, infants born to mothers who are depressed during pregnancy may be exposed to neuroendocrine abnormalities, reduced blood flow to the fetus, poor health behaviors, or antidepressant medications. Third, many of the symptoms of depression are incompatible with, or preclude, good parenting. Thus, feeling sad or blue, experiencing loss of interest or pleasure in one's usual pursuits, loss of energy, low self-esteem, poor concentration, indecisiveness, and hostility and irritability all make it difficult for parents to be responsive to the needs of their children and to be good role models for healthy social and emotional functioning. Fourth, the lives of children with depressed parents may be particularly stressful.

Given this context, therefore, it is not surprising that young children of depressed parents have high rates of psychiatric disorder. Indeed, estimates of psychiatric disorder among children of depressed parents range from 41 to 77% (e.g., Beardslee, Schultz, & Selman, 1987; Goodman, Adamson, Riniti, & Cole, 1994; Orvaschel, Walsh-Ellis, & Ye, 1988; Weissman et al., 1987). Even among children of unipolar depressed parents (which arguably has a weaker genetic component), rates of psychiatric disturbance, including depression, oppositional or conduct disorder, anxiety disorders, and alcohol or drug use and dependency, exceed 40%. Moreover, negative effects of maternal depression on children have been documented across a wide age range, from infancy through adolescence. For example, (compared to offspring of nondepressed controls, infants of depressed mothers have been found to be more fussy, to obtain lower scores on measures of mental and motor development, and to have more difficult temperaments and less secure attachments to their mothers. Toddlers of depressed mothers have been found to react more negatively to stress and to be delayed in their acquisition of effective self-regulation strategies. Relative to control children, school-aged children and adolescents whose mothers are depressed have been found to have more school problems, to be less socially competent, and to have lower levels of self-esteem and higher levels of behavior problems (for recent reviews of these literatures, see Cummings & Davies, 1994; Gotlib & Goodman, 1999; and Gotlib & Lee, 1996).

Researchers recently have attempted to move beyond an examination of the relatively simple question of whether children of depressed mothers are at risk for abnormal development, and have begun to identify factors that are associated with this risk. Despite this shift in focus, however, we know relatively little about why and how these children are at risk—that is, we do not have an adequate understanding of the mechanisms that underlie the risk for these adverse outcomes.

Risk might be transmitted through several mechanisms. For example, risk for depression may be transmitted genetically from mother to child. Alternatively, dysfunctional neuroregulatory systems in the children may interfere with emotion regulation processes, leading to increased risk for depression. These dysfunctional neuroregulatory systems may be inherited, or they may be acquired, either prenatally through *in utero* hazards or postnatally as a function of inadequate parental support of the infants' maturing neurophysiological systems. Other possible mechanisms for the intergenerational transmission of risk for depression involve interpersonal or cognitive processes. Depressed parents, for example, may serve as maladaptive role models for their children and as inadequate social–emotional partners. They may also model negative cognitive functioning for their children (see Goodman & Gotlib, 1999, for an extended discussion of these possibilities). The stressful context of the lives of children in families with depressed parents may contribute significantly to the development of psychopathology in the children.

Not only are discussions of these potential mechanisms relatively rare, but they are also not found in a single source. The purpose of this volume is to bring together perspectives from diverse theoretical approaches to understanding the transmission of risk for psychopathology in children of depressed parents. Typically, each mechanism focuses on one particular limited age period (e.g., infancy, early childhood, adolescence). Because we believe that it is important to try to account for the transmission of risk for psychopathology over the course of development, we have also tried to structure this volume to achieve this goal. This book provides opportunities to explore integrative approaches to understanding the transmission of risk and to examine clinical implications of these approaches for prevention and treatment of psychopathology in general and of depression more specifically.

In developing and organizing this book, we wanted to cover the major approaches to examining possible processes involved in the intergenerational transmission of risk for depression. We also wanted to ensure that this volume would be relevant and of interest to researchers and clinicians alike. To meet these objectives, we made several requests of the contributors to this volume. We invited the authors to focus on possible mechanisms or moderators of the transmission of risk for depression from parent to child and to discuss how and why, or under what circumstances, parental depression increases children's risk for the disorder. We also encouraged the contributors to take a developmental perspective in writing their chapters. Finally, we asked all of the authors to elaborate on the clinical implications of their work for prevention and intervention. Indeed, to emphasize the clinical relevance of the research described in this volume, we asked all of the authors to include a section in their chapters entitled *Implications for Clinicians*. This common focus not only underscores the link between research and clinical practice, but also serves to enhance continuity across the chapters.

The chapters contained in Part I deal with mechanisms that might underlie the transmission of risk for psychopathology from depressed parent to child. Silberg and Rutter (chapter 2, this volume) describe the importance of environmentally and genetically mediated risks to the children of depressed parents. They discuss the interplay of nature and nurture, including gene–environment correlations and interactions, in increasing children's vulnerability to depression and to other disorders. Ashman and Dawson (chapter 3, this volume) discuss the mechanisms through which inadequate early parenting by depressed mothers may contribute to abnormalities in the development of their children's psychobiological systems involved in emotion expression and regulation. Field (chapter 4, this volume) focuses on the effects of depression occurring during pregnancy, discussing the impact of prenatal exposure to elevated levels of norepinephrine and cortisol and lower levels of dopamine. She describes how this exposure might contribute to neonatal psychobiological dysregulation, which then is exacerbated by inadequate stimulation and arousal modulation from the mothers.

Lyons-Ruth, Lyubchik, Wolfe, and Bronfman (chapter 5, this volume) argue that depressed parents engage in inadequate early parenting, which, in the context of problematic family relationship patterns, increases the likelihood of insecure attachment. They then discuss insecure attachment as a risk factor for the subsequent development of psychopathology. Garber and Martin (chapter 6, this volume) describe research with older children of depressed parents. They postulate that depressed parents model negative cognitions, engage in dysfunctional parent–child relationships, and expose their children to stressful life events. All of these mechanisms are hypothesized to increase the risk for the development of negative cognitions in their children, which imparts a vulnerability for the development of depression and other forms of psychopathology. Radke-Yarrow and Klimes-Dougan (chapter 7, this volume) describe multiple, co-acting factors through which depressed parents might influence the emergence of various forms of psychopathology and other adverse developmental courses. In this context, they place special emphasis on normal development in contributing to this process. Finally, Hammen (chapter 8, this volume) discusses the formulation that children of depressed parents experience highly stressful environments, which may set into play additive or interactive processes that contribute to the subsequent development of psychological problems.

Whereas these authors focus on potential mechanisms underlying the transmission of risk, the authors of the chapters contained in Part II examine possible moderators that might help explain how it is that a significant subset of offspring of depressed parents do not develop psychopathology. The three chapters in this section, therefore, deal with moderators of the association between parental depression and child outcomes. We invited the authors to help us to understand the factors that are related to better or worse outcomes among children with depressed parents. Inherent in the emphasis on moderators is the notion of multiple risk factors, which is important for at least two reasons. First, it is unlikely than any single risk factor, including parental depression, accounts for large proportions of the variance in child outcomes. Second, studying parental depression as the single predictor of child outcome ignores individual differences among the children, as well as differences in the contexts within which children are developing. Therefore, we gave three sets of moderators primary consideration: (a) the role of the family (Phares, Duhig, and Watkins, chapter 9, this volume), (b) children's coping processes and adaptation (Compas, Langrock, Keller, Merchant, and Copeland, chapter 10, this volume), and (c) gender (Sheeber, Davis, and Hops, chapter 11, this volume).

Phares and her co-authors elaborate on the role of three family influences on the association between parental depression and child functioning: the co-parenting dyad, the parent–child dyad, and the sibling dyads. They propose that children of depressed parents who are also exposed to psychopathology in the other parent, to psychopathology in siblings, or to high levels of familial conflict, are likely to have elevated levels of psychological difficulties. Compas and his colleagues provide an in-depth exploration of the influence of children's coping responses on the association between parental depression and the development of psychopathology in the children. They present empirical findings suggesting that children's coping responses may mediate the association between exposure to the stressful environments characteristic of depressed parents and the emergence of child psychopathology. In the third chapter in this section, Sheeber and her co-authors provide a comprehensive review of the literature concerning gender-specific vulnerability to depression. They propose a diathesis-stress model to explain the greater likelihood of depression in adolescent girls than boys that also involve the constructs of coping and modeling.

Part III of this book contains two chapters. In the first, Gladstone and Beardslee (chapter 12, this volume) summarize the empirical clinical work that has been conducted with offspring of depressed parents. These authors provide an overview of the findings from empirically based interventions for children with depressed parents, and they make recommendations for further research on both prevention and intervention. In the final chapter, we draw connections across the chapters, highlighting common themes that emerged in the discussions of mechanisms and moderators of the transmission of risk from depressed parent to child. We also discuss clinical implications of these connections for prevention and intervention and outline what we believe are important questions that should guide future research in this area. It is our fervent hope that the discussions in this book concerning both the mechanisms through which the risk for depression is transmitted from depressed parents to their children and the factors that may alter the likelihood that these children will experience an episode of depression will lead researchers and clinicians alike to focus on reducing this risk and developing programs that may prevent the occurrence of this debilitating disorder in the offspring of depressed parents.

REFERENCES

Beardslee, W. R., Schultz, L. H., & Selman, R. L. (1987). Level of social–cognitive development, adaptive functioning, and *DSM–III* diagnoses in adolescent offspring of parents with affective disorders: Implications for the development of the capacity for mutuality. *Developmental Psychology, 23,* 807–815.

Belsher, G., & Costello, C. G. (1988). Relapse after recovery from unipolar depression: A critical review. *Psychological Bulletin, 104,* 84–96.

Blehar, M. C., & Oren, D. A. (1995). Women's increased vulnerability to mood disorders: Integrating psychobiology and epidemiology. *Depression, 3,* 3–12.

Boland, R. J., & Keller, M. B. (in press). Course and outcome of depression. In I. H. Gotlib & C. L. Hammen (Eds.), *Handbook of depression: Research and treatment.* New York: Guilford Press.

Brown, G. W., & Harris, T. (1978). *Social origins of depression.* New York: Free Press.

Cummings, E. M., & Davies, P. T. (1994). Maternal depression and child development. *Journal of Child Psychology and Psychiatry, 35,* 73–112.

Goodman, S. H., Adamson, L. B., Riniti, J., & Cole, S. (1994). Mothers' expressed attitudes: Associations with maternal depression and children's self-esteem and psychopathology. *Journal of the American Academy of Child and Adolescent Psychiatry, 33,* 1265–1274.

Goodman, S. H., & Gotlib, I. H. (1999). Risk for psychopathology in the children of depressed mothers: A developmental model for understanding mechanisms of transmission. *Psychological Review, 106,* 458–490.

Gotlib, I. H., & Goodman, S. H. (1999). Children of parents with depression. In W. K. Silverman & T. H. Ollendick (Eds.), *Developmental issues in the clinical treatment of children* (pp. 415–432). Boston: Allyn & Bacon.

Gotlib, I. H., & Lee, C. M. (1996). Impact of parental depression on young children and infants. In C. Mundt, M. J. Goldstein, K. Hahlweg, & P. Fiedler (Eds.), *Interpersonal factors in the origin and course of affective disorders* (pp. 218–239). London: Royal College of Psychiatrists.

Keller, M. B., Lavori, P. W., Mueller, T. I., Endicott, J., Coryell, W., Hirschfeld, R. M. A., & Shea, T. (1992). Time to recovery, chronicity, and levels of psychopathology in major depression: A 5-year prospective follow-up of 431 subjects. *Archives of General Psychiatry, 49,* 809–816.

Keller, M. B., & Shapiro, R. W. (1981). Major depressive disorder: Initial results from a one-year prospective naturalistic follow-up study. *Journal of Nervous and Mental Disorders, 169,* 761–768.

Kessler, R. C. (in press). The epidemiology of depression. In I. H. Gotlib & C. L. Hammen (Eds.), *Handbook of depression: Research and treatment.* New York: Guilford Press.

Mueller, T. I., Keller, M. B., Leon, A. C., Solomon, D. A., Shea, M. T., Coryell, W., & Endicott, J. (1996). Recovery after 5 years of unremitting major depressive disorder. *Archives of General Psychiatry, 53,* 794–799.

Orvaschel, H., Walsh-Ellis, G., & Ye, W. (1988). Psychopathology in children of parents with recurrent depression. *Journal of Abnormal Child Psychology, 16,* 17–28.

Robins, L. N., Helzer, J. E., Weissman, M. M., Orvaschel, H., Gruenberg, E., Burke, J. D., Jr., & Regier, D. A. (1984). Lifetime prevalence of specific psychiatric disorders in three sites. *Archives of General Psychiatry, 41,* 949–958.

Weissman, M. M., Gammon, G. D., John, K., Merikangas, K. R., Warner, V., Prusoff, B., & Sholomskas, D. (1987). Children of depressed parents: Increased psychopathology and early onset of major depression. *Archives of General Psychiatry, 44,* 847–853.

I

MECHANISMS OF RISK

2

NATURE–NURTURE INTERPLAY IN THE RISKS ASSOCIATED WITH PARENTAL DEPRESSION

JUDY SILBERG AND MICHAEL RUTTER

It has long been established that the children of depressed parents have a substantially increased risk of developing a variety of psychopathological disorders (Cooper & Murray, 1997; Downey & Coyne, 1990; Hammen, 1991; Radke-Yarrow, 1998; Rutter, 1966, 1989; Rutter & Quinton, 1984). Parental depressive disorder constitutes a significant risk indicator for psychopathology in children. A key question pertains to the nature of the processes mediating the risk. Does it derive from parental depression as such or from other risk factors with which parental depression happens to be associated? Does the raised rate of disorder in the children reflect genetic mediation? Alternatively, do the risks derive from the suboptimal rearing environments that depressed parents tend to provide for the children, so that the risks are environmentally rather than genetically mediated? Moreover, to what extent are the environments that depressed parents provide related to the genes

We are most grateful to Lindon Eaves and Patrick Sullivan for many helpful suggestions. This research was supported by National Institute of Mental Health Grant MH-55557 and the Carman Trust for Scientific Research.

13

for depression? Do the modes of risk mediation vary according to the type of parental depression or the type of psychopathology in the children? In this chapter, we consider the evidence on these issues from the perspective of research strategies using genetic designs.

We note the need to consider different patterns of depression and then to consider the findings on the increased rate of a range of disorders in the offspring of depressed parents and in the families more generally. We then proceed to review the evidence from quantitative and molecular genetic research. We recognize that parental depression provides both environmentally and genetically mediated risks for the children. We then discuss the processes involved in the nature–nurture interplay with respect to gene–environment correlations and interactions, and we conclude by considering the clinical implications.

PATTERNS OF DEPRESSION

One of the difficulties in any consideration of depressive disorders is that the phenomenon of depression is so pervasive (Maj & Sartorius, 1999). Depression is a defining symptom of major psychiatric conditions that can be of psychotic intensity, but it is also a nonspecific symptom associated with most forms of psychopathology, and it is a normal response to strong feelings of psychological loss. A further complication is that it is very common for depressive disorders to be accompanied by personality difficulties and by drug and alcohol problems (Klein, Kupfer, & Shea, 1993; Merikangas, Angst, Eaton, & Canino, 1996). Accordingly, in considering the effects on children of parental depression, one must ask the extent to which the risks derive from the depression as such or from the associated comorbid conditions. Much research has been based on cross-sectional comparisons of individuals who do or who do not have depressive disorder. In that connection, it is relevant to note that probably a quarter to a third of women suffer from a clinically significant major depressive disorder during their lifetime (Kendler & Prescott, 1999).

Moreover, depression shows a strong tendency to recur (Judd, 1997), and this applies as much to depressive disorders beginning in childhood as to those that begin in adult life. Follow-up studies of children with major depressive disorders have shown a high rate of recurrence during the adult years (Harrington, Fudge, Rutter, Pickles, & Hill, 1990; Weissman et al., 1999). It has generally been supposed that depressive disorders beginning in childhood tend to be more severe; but long-term follow-up studies have shown that only a tiny proportion of the recurrences in adult life involve bipolar affective disorders (which is a severe variety as judged by both recurrence risk and social impairment). Although depression is a recurrent disorder, there is huge individual variability in the extent to which it interferes with social functioning over time. Many people have a single episode of depression, whereas others are chronically handicapped by repeated episodes (Duggan, Sham, Minne, Lee, & Murray, 1998). Recurrence is more likely when depression is accompanied by personality disorder (Quinton, Gulliver, & Rutter, 1995).

In the epidemiology of depression, two features stand out. First, the incidence of major depressive disorder rises markedly during the period of adolescence (Kessler, 2000). The available evidence suggests that the rise is related to the onset of puberty (Angold, Costello, & Worthman, 1998), and it seems that the main stimulus derives from the hormonal changes rather than from the alterations in body shape (Angold, Costello, & Erkanli, 1999). It is not likely that the sex hormones directly cause depression but, rather, that hormonal changes in some way increase the underlying predisposition (Frank & Young, 2000; Holsboer, 1999).

The second epidemiological feature is that depressive disorders are more common in female than male individuals, the sex difference being evident, however, only from about the time of puberty (Kessler, 2000; Nolen-Hoeksema & Girgus, 1994; Rutter, 1986). The causes of this difference between the sexes in incidence have received considerable attention over the years, but no firm conclusions have been reached. It may be noteworthy, however, that the sex difference appears to diminish markedly in old age (Bebbington, 1996, 1998; Bebbington et al., 1998).

Numerous studies have shown a high comorbidity between depression and generalized anxiety disorders (Andrews, 1996; Merikangas et al., 1996), and twin studies have shown that the genetic liability for the two disorders is largely the same (Eley & Stevenson, 1999; Kendler, 1996; Silberg, Rutter, & Eaves, 2001; Thapar & McGuffin, 1997). There is also substantial comorbidity between depression and substance abuse involving both alcohol and drugs (Merikangas et al., 1996). The available evidence suggests that this reflects both genetic and environmental mediation (Silberg, Rutter, D'Onofrio, & Eaves, 2001). Family studies suggest that they do not reflect genetic predisposition (Maier & Merikangas, 1996). Few studies have explored the extent to which the environmental risk factor is the same or different for these various disorders that are comorbid with depression. Some evidence suggests that the type of stressful life event may differ between depression and anxiety, with loss events more important for depression and danger events more important for anxiety conditions (Brown, Harris, & Eales, 1996).

Another feature of depression that should be taken into account concerns the rise in the frequency of depressive disorders among younger people over the last half century (Fombonne, 1995). Although it is not possible entirely to rule out the possibility that the rise is artifactual, arising from memory differences (because the data largely derive from retrospective reports), it seems unlikely that this wholly accounts for the rise. Moreover, suicide rates have risen in young male individuals over the same time period, although they have been falling in older age groups, with a less consistent change in young female individuals (Diekstra, Kienhorst, & de Wilde, 1995). Clearly, such a rise must reflect some type of environmental influence and, moreover, one that probably applies predominantly to younger age groups.

The first episode of major depression may bring about changes that predispose the individual to recurrence, even in the absence of further environmental precipitants—the so-called *kindling effect* (Kendler, Thornton, & Gardner, 2000; Post, 1992).

FAMILY STUDIES

Numerous family studies, both those using as a starting point depressive disorders in children and those based on depressive disorders in adults, have shown an increased familial loading for depressive disorders in first degree relatives. In a meta-analysis, Sullivan, Neale, and Kendler (2000) focused on high-quality family studies and concluded that the odds ratio comparing families of cases and controls was 2.84 (with 95% confidence limits of 2.3 to 3.5). Harrington (1993; Harrington et al., 1997) showed that the increased familial loading for depressive disorders was diagnosis specific, was most marked with respect to depressive disorders occurring in multiple relatives, and was greatest when depressive disorder in the child probands was diagnosed according to stringent criteria. Familial loading did not vary substantially according to the age of onset of the disorder, but when depression began in childhood rather than adolescence, it was more likely that the familial loading in relatives would include antisocial problems as well as depression.

PSYCHOPATHOLOGICAL DISORDERS IN THE CHILDREN OF DEPRESSED PARENTS

An important advance in family studies has been the use of prospective longitudinal designs in which the emergence of disorders in the offspring of affectively ill parents and of parents without affective disorder have been compared (Rutter, Silberg, O'Connor, & Simonoff, 1999b). The findings have confirmed the psychopathological risks for the children associated with parental depression, but they have also emphasized several important features. First, the risks seem to be greatest when parental depression is accompanied by personality disorder (Rutter & Quinton, 1984). The finding is important in view of the extensive evidence of the frequency with which depressive conditions are associated with personality disorders (Klein et al., 1993). Second, the risks to the children are at least as high when the parent has a unipolar depressive disorder as when he or she has a bipolar affective disorder (Hammen, 1991; Radke-Yarrow, 1998). That is relevant because the genetic evidence suggests that the heritability of bipolar disorders is greater than that for unipolar disorders (see below).

Third, the increased rate of disorder in the children extends far more broadly than depression (Lapalme, Hodgins, & LaRoche, 1997; Warner, Weissman, Mufson, & Wickramaratne, 1999; Weissman, Warner, Wickramaratne, Moreau, & Olfson, 1997; Wickramaratne & Weissman, 1998). Thus, the increased risk for conduct disorder in the children is about as great as that for depressive disorders. Fourth, Warner et al.'s (1999) three-generation study suggested that the risk mediation may operate differently for depression than for disruptive behavior disorders in the offspring. Both depression in parents and depression in grandparents was associated with an increased risk of depression in the offspring (a finding that is consistent with genetic mediation). However, depression in parents but not grandparents was associated with an increased risk for disruptive disorder (suggesting the possibility of environmental risks in the home). The risk for anxiety disorders (usually with an onset in childhood) and for dependence on drugs or alcohol (generally starting either in early adolescence or early adult life) was similarly increased. The implication is that effects on parenting may create the risk for disruptive behavior but that genetic factors also play a role in depressive disorders. However, it has yet to be determined whether the association between conduct problems and depression is genetically or environmentally mediated.

Fifth, many researchers (Adrian & Hammen, 1993; Daley et al., 1997; Hammen, 1991; Harrington, 1996; Rutter, 1989, 1990; Weissman & Paykel, 1974) have shown that parental depression is accompanied by alterations in family function that are likely to constitute an environmental risk for the children. For example, researchers have indicated the frequency with which parental depression has adverse effects on children associated with impaired parenting (Davenport, Zahn-Waxler, Adland, & Mayfield, 1984; Downey & Coyne, 1990; Radke-Yarrow, 1998). Depressed mothers have been described as more insensitive and inattentive and less psychologically available to their children (Cox, Puckering, Pound, & Mills, 1987; Goodman & Brumley, 1990). A parenting style characterized by hostility, irritability, and enmeshment (Parker, Tupling, & Brown, 1979) has been shown to be an important risk factor for childhood depression (Davenport et al., 1984; Hammen et al., 1987; Weissman & Paykel, 1974), and low parental warmth and overprotectiveness are predicted by a history of parental psychopathology (Kendler, Myers, & Prescott, 2000). In addition, parental depression is associated with increased family discord and scapegoating of the children, family break-up, a range of associated stresses and adversities, widespread interpersonal relationship problems, associated excessive drinking and drug misuse, and general social disadvantage.

QUANTITATIVE GENETIC STUDIES

Most evidence regarding the relative strength of genetic and environmental influences on the underlying propensity to depressive disorders derives from twin studies. In essence, the design relies on the fact that members of monozygotic (MZ) twin pairs share all their genes whereas dizygotic (DZ) pairs share on average just half (see Eley, 1999). Because of this, the difference between MZ and DZ pairs in the extent to which they also share a particular trait or disorder can be used to infer the extent to which genetic factors are influential. This inference is warranted, however, only if one can assume that there is no difference between MZ and DZ pairs in their experiences of environments that predispose to the trait or disorder (the *equal environments assumption* [EEA]). The EEA does not require that MZ and DZ pairs are treated similarly (obviously they are not with respect to features such as being dressed alike), but only that, insofar as there are experiential differences between MZ and DZ pairs, these do not affect the trait or disorder being studied. A violation of the EEA leads to spuriously inflated estimates of heritability.

Geneticists have usually assumed that the EEA is justified (Kendler & Gardner, 1998; Kendler, Neale, Kessler, & Eaves, 1994), but recent evidence from studies of both children (Silberg et al., 1999) and adults (Kendler, Karkowski, & Prescott, 1999b; Kendler, Neale, Kessler, Heath, & Eaves, 1993) shows that it is not in the case of depression. That is because of the genetic influence on a tendency to experience stressful life events (i.e., MZ twins differ from DZ twins in being more similar in their exposure to life events carrying psychological threat), and because such life events have an environmentally mediated effect on depression (i.e., the difference within MZ pairs in their experience of stressful life events is systematically associated with their propensity to depression). A consideration of both the concepts and the empirical evidence leads to the conclusion that the EEA is invalid for many multifactorial psychiatric disorders (Rutter, Pickles, Murray, & Eaves, 2001). This means that part of the difference between MZ and DZ pairs is due to environmental, rather than genetic, influences and that the true genetic effect is somewhat less than the heritability estimate indicates.

Although we cannot quantify the extent of this inflation of genetic effects precisely, it is unlikely to affect significantly the conclusions on genetic effects. Thus, even if genetic effects in fact contribute 35% rather than 45% to depression in children of depressed parent, the theoretical and practical implications would remain the same. Note, however, that violation of the EEA would be more important for the study of specific measured environmental factors. That is because it is usual for the effects of any single environmental factor or any single gene to be small (Rutter, 2000a). The main impact generally comes from combinations of risk factors (Rutter, 2000b). It is true that several other assumptions are relevant to twin analyses (see Rutter, Silberg, O'Connor, & Simonoff, 1999a; Rutter et al., 2001), but most do not threaten significantly the twin strategy, although they do have implications for the ways in which findings are interpreted (see below). We discuss the findings from twin studies with these caveats in mind.

Moldin (1999), Craddock and Jones (1999), and Sullivan et al. (2000) reviewed the findings from studies of depression in adults; Eley (1999) and Rutter et al. (1999b) summarized the findings from studies with children and adolescents. Sullivan et al. used a quantitative meta-analytic approach to the more rigorous twin studies and estimated that the genetic effect on major depression accounted for 36% of the variance, the 95% confidence limits being narrow (26–42%). Because measurement error is included in the environmental effect, this estimate is certainly misleadingly low. Violation of the EEA means that the estimate is too high. It seems reasonable to assume that these two biases probably roughly balance each other out and, therefore, that the genetic effects, although substantial, are far from overwhelming. They are, however, probably greater in the case of bipolar affective disorder (Craddock & Jones, 1999).

The findings on children and adolescents are not directly comparable because most of them are based on accounts of symptoms rather than clinically significant disorder. Nevertheless, the genetic estimates are of the same general order. Two additional features of the results are evident. First, the four studies that have looked for possible age effects have all found that genetic influences on depression are stronger during adolescence than in childhood (Eley & Stevenson, 1999; Murray & Sines, 1996; Silberg et al., 1999; Thapar & McGuffin, 1994). The same may be true of anxiety symptoms, at least in girls (Eley & Stevenson, 1999; Feigon, Waldman, Levy, & Hay, in press; Topolski et al., 1997; Topolski et al., 1999) although this has not been found in all studies (Eaves et al., 1997; Thapar & McGuffin, 1995). Second, on the whole, genetic effects have been found to be stronger for parent-reported symptoms than child-reported symptoms (see, e.g., Eaves et al., 1997). One might suppose that this is due to a lower reliability for child reports, but this has not proved to be the case with anxiety (Topolski et al., 1999).

MOLECULAR GENETIC FINDINGS

To date, no positive molecular genetic findings with either major depression or bipolar disorder have been consistently replicated, although there are several promising leads (Craddock & Jones, 1999; Moldin, 1999). In view of the interest in the probable role of the serotonin "system" in major depression (Maes & Meltzer, 1995; Stanford, 1996), attention has particularly focused on the sequence of variation in the serotonin transport gene coding region (e.g., Lesch et al., 1996). However, studies using the transmission disequilibrium test [TDT] have generally not associated or shown linkages with the serotonin transporter gene; Geller & Cook, 1999; Kirov et al., 1999). Mouse studies have produced positive findings for a region on chromosome 1 with respect to emotionality (Flint, 1997; Talbot et al., 1999). The relevance of these findings for humans has yet to be established, but the search continues for susceptibility genes for neuroticism as the personality trait that seems to predispose to depression and anxiety disorders.

ENVIRONMENTALLY MEDIATED PSYCHOSOCIAL RISKS

A key strength of genetically sensitive designs is that they enable a more rigorous testing of hypotheses regarding environmentally mediated risks. Several designs may be used for this purpose. One strategy is to determine whether the difference within MZ twins for the environmental risk factor correlate with parallel variations within the pair in depression (or whatever form of psychopathology is being studied; Pike, Reiss, Hetherington, & Plomin, 1996). The logic is that because MZ twins share all of their genes (and therefore all combinations of genes), any within-pair difference has to represent environmental mediation. The two main methodological issues that have to be dealt with are (a) the possibility that the association represents rating bias if both the risk factor and the psychopathology derive from information from the same informant and (b) the possibility that the causal influence runs from the child to the environmental risk factor rather than the reverse. The solution to the first problem lies in using different informants for the independent and dependent variable or using combined data sources. The best solution to the second problem lies in the use of longitudinal data; if they are not available, more indirect approaches may be used.

Using multivariate analyses of twin data, researchers have shown that negative life events carry a significant risk for depression in both children (Rutter, 2000a; Silberg et al., 1999) and adults (Kendler et al., 1999b). Evidence that family negativity predisposes people to depression is weaker (Pike, McGuire, Hetherington, Reiss, & Plomin, 1996). A second strategy has been to focus on events that involve no genetic influence. Kendler, Karkowski, and Prescott (1999a) found that a lack of genetic influence generally coincided with the concept of independent events, and Silberg, Rutter, Neale, and Eaves (2001) showed that events free of genetic influence did have a significant association with depression in adolescent twins. A third approach is to use cross-twin, cross-trait bivariate analyses in which the environmental risk factor is treated as a phenotype. In this way, the association between the environmental phenotype and depression can be assessed for the extent to which it represents environmental, rather than genetic, mediation. Using this approach, Kendler et al. (1999b) showed a significant environmental effect of life events on depression in adults.

Studies with adoptive families may also be used to provide a test of environmentally mediated risks (Rutter et al., 2001), although they have the disadvantage that adopting families are chosen in such a way as to keep environmental risks to a minimum (Rutter et al., 1999a). Cadoret, Troughton, Merchant, and Whitters (1990) used this approach, and they found that the adverse environments associated with antisocial behavior and substance misuse carried environmentally mediated risks for depressive symptoms. However, the strategy has not been used in other studies, and it has not been used in relation to environmental risk factors for depression. An offspring of twins design also has many strengths for distinguishing between the true environmental risk factors for depression and those that are merely secondary consequences of genetic liability transmitted from parent to child (Rutter et al., 2001). Despite its utility, the children of twins design has yet to be used for this purpose in relation to depression.

NATURE–NURTURE INTERPLAY

There are three types of nature–nurture interplay (Rutter & Silberg, in press). First, passive gene–environment correlations reflect the fact that parents pass on their genes to their children and also create the environments in which children are raised. Passive correlations arise when, as is often the case, the genetic influences are correlated with the environments created by parents. In other words, the parents who pass on susceptibility genes to some extent tend to be the same parents who create risk environments for their children.

Active, or evocative, gene–environment correlations are different in that they pertain to the effects on the environment generated by individuals themselves, rather than by their parents. The psychosocial influences that predispose to depression for which there is good evidence are those that pertain to either the loss of an important close confiding relationship or humiliation or entrapment in a conflictual social relationship (Rutter, 2000a, 2000b). Because all of these involve dyadic interactions of one kind or another, a child's own interpersonal style probably makes it more or less likely that he or she will experience stressful interactions and relationships. That is what is meant by the term *evocative*. Thus, someone with an abrasive manner is likely to elicit negative responses in other people. The term *active* is slightly different in that it refers to the tendency of people to put themselves in risk situations, rather than to the effects that they elicit in other people. Thus, by the way they behave, people may find themselves unemployed or performing unskilled labor.

Gene–environment interactions are different yet again in that they describe the situation whereby genetic effects vary according to environmental circumstances and vice versa. They can take many forms, but three types serve to illustrate the variety. First, it is a universal finding of all psychosocial risk studies that there is enormous individual variation in how people respond to stress and adversity (Rutter, 1999, 2000c). One of the ways in which genes may operate is through affecting people's sensitivity to environmental hazards. That is, the genetic liability operates through an increased reactivity to risk environments. That probably does apply to depression (see below). Second, the interaction may work in the opposite direction. In other words, when adverse environmental influences are maximal, the effects of individual differences in genetic liability may be less influential. There is very little indication that this is so in the case of depression, but it may be so for intelligence (Rowe, Jacobson, & van den Oord, 1999). This form of interaction is likely to come about when the genetic effects operate through mechanisms that are relatively independent of environmental circumstances and where environmental influences do not involve any substantial genetically influenced individual variation in response.

Third, the interactions may involve individual differences in response to treatment. With virtually all treatments (either pharmacological or psychological) there are marked individual variations; some people respond very well, some not at all, and some are even made worse by the same interventions that are beneficial for others. In the field of drug treatments, the recognition that genetic factors may be crucially important in such individual variation has led to the development of a field that has come to be called *pharmacogenetics* (Evans & Relling, 1999). Treatment efficacy clearly could be greatly improved if one could identify in advance those persons most likely to respond well and those for whom the treatment is unlikely to make any difference or might even make things worse. Potentially, molecular genetic findings could provide such information, but the science must advance a good deal before that becomes practically possible.

In the sections that follow, we discuss the nature–nurture interplay in relation to gene–environment correlations and interactions.

Passive Gene–Environment Correlations

The usual way in which passive correlations have been tested has been through across-twin, across-trait twin analyses. In essence, the logic lies in treating individual differences in environmental risk provision as a phenotype, in the same way that the psychopathology (in this case depression) is a phenotype. The question then is whether the patterns of MZ and DZ twin correlations indicate that the genetic influences on the one coincide with those on the other. This has been done, for example, with respect to the co-occurrence of depression and the provision of adverse parenting (Kendler, Sham, & MacLean, 1997). In order to focus on the intergenerational transmission of risks, the environmental phenotype must concern the environments provided for the children, rather than the environments experienced by the parents. The latter has been the focus of extensive research (e.g., in relation to life events; Kendler & Karkowski-Shuman, 1997). Because of the substantial comorbidity between depression and personality disorders and between depression and substance misuse, it is crucial that the study of passive correlations should extend to these comorbid features and not be restricted to depression. Unfortunately, very little research has done this.

Active or Evocative Gene–Environment Correlations

Active and evocative correlations have been investigated in several different ways. In many respects, the adoption design provides the best approach. Thus, psychopathology in the biological parent is used as the index of genetic risk and the rearing environment provided by the adopting parents as the environmental risk (O'Connor, Deater-Deckard, Fulker, Rutter, & Plomin, 1998). With respect to antisocial behavior, O'Connor et al. (1998) found that genetically at-risk adopted children experienced more negative parenting from their adoptive mothers and that, to an important extent, this was a function of their own disruptive behavior. The findings also showed that this effect of the child's behavior on the rearing environment applied just as much to those who were not genetically at risk. The decisive variable seems to be the qualities of the child's behavior irrespective of the extent to which it is genetically or environmentally influenced. So far as we are aware, this approach has not been used with respect to gene–environment correlations as they apply to depression. We also note that the strategy is severely constrained in that the adoptive parents are selected on the basis that they are likely to provide a safe environment (Rutter et al., 1999a; Rutter et al., 2001; Stoolmiller, 1999).

An alternative approach is provided by the twin design, as outlined above. Several independent studies of both children (Silberg et al., 1999; Thapar, Harold, & McGuffin, 1998) and adults (Kendler & Karkowski-Shuman, 1997) have shown significant overlap between the propensity to depression and the liability to negative life events. The implication is that there is something about the ways in which people behave that tends to predispose them to negative life experiences. The Virginia Twin Study of Adolescent Behavioral Development (VTSABD) findings also suggested that this mechanism may well play a role in the rising rate of depression among adolescent girls (Silberg et al., 1999). That is because genetic influences increase in girls during this age period when the genetic liability to depression overlaps with life events that in turn are associated with the rise in depression. Much the same applies to the family study data that show associations between the familial loading for depression and the familial loading for negative life events (McGuffin, Katz, & Bebbington, 1987), although a recent study has not replicated this (Farmer et al., 2000).

Longitudinal studies that examine the extent to which the psychopathology in childhood predisposes people to negative life experiences in adult life provide yet another strategy (Champion, Goodall, & Rutter, 1995; Rutter, Champion, Quinton, Maughan, & Pickles, 1995). Although this effect has been found to be much greater for disruptive behavior, it also exists in cases of emotional disturbance in middle childhood. Although studies of this kind cannot show the extent to which this effect derives from genetically influenced behavior, the findings do indicate that people's own behavior serves to shape their interpersonal experiences.

A modification of this approach is to examine the extent to which the rate of negative life experiences remains high both before and after the onset of the depressive disorder. Because psychosocial researchers have tended to focus on the role of life events in the precipitation of disorder, few data are available on this comparison. Those that are available do not apply specifically to depression, but they do suggest that disorders in children are associated with an increase in negative life events both before and after onset (Sandberg, Rutter, Pickles, McGuinness, & Angold, 2001). Studies of adults, too, suggest that depression may generate negative life events that could contribute to the chronicity of the disorder (Cui & Vaillant, 1997). The issues here go beyond gene–environment correlations because people's influence on the environments they experience may arise from behaviors that are themselves largely environmentally influenced. However, an understanding of causal processes requires that the mechanisms of transmission be identified and their operations understood.

GENE–ENVIRONMENT INTERACTIONS

One advantage of using adoption designs in the study of gene–environment interactions is the clear differentiation between genetic risk and environmental risk (because they concern different families); the parallel disadvantage is that the number of individuals experiencing both is usually small. The approach has shown the existence of interaction effects in relation to antisocial behavior, whereby those who are genetically at risk are most vulnerable to the risks associated with a disruptive discordant environment (Rutter, Giller, & Hagell, 1998). So far, the same approach has not been used with depression. Twin studies may also be used to look for interactions. Kendler et al. (1995) used an indirect approach; they used the pattern of MZ–DZ correlations to infer which individuals were most genetically at risk and then related this to the likelihood that those with the greatest genetic risk would experience major depression. A significant interaction was found, suggesting that part of the way in which genetic liability works is through increased sensitivity to environmental stressors.

Silberg et al. (1999, 2001) addressed the same question more directly in relation to depression and anxiety in adolescent girls. One of the problems of the twin design is that it is very difficult to identify interaction effects if there are also gene–environment correlations. Accordingly, we, as researchers, focused on what happened with life events that involved no genetic influence. We found a significant gene–environment interaction involving genetically influenced sensitivity to environmental stressors. We used a complementary approach in the same study by taking parental anxiety or depressive disorder as an index of genetic risk (even though this includes long-standing environmental risks) and then testing whether life events had an effect in its absence. However, there was a significant effect of life events on adolescent depression in the presence of parental emotional disorder, again suggesting a genetically influenced susceptibility to stressors. So although life events did not have an effect in the absence of parental emotional disorder, parental emotional disorder had an effect even in the absence of life events. It seems that the effects of parental emotional disorder are not confined to their role in increasing sensitivity to life events. That does not necessarily mean that the effects are independent of the environment, because the same finding could reflect the operation of long-standing environmental adversities as well as more direct genetic effects.

IMPLICATIONS FOR CLINICIANS

When evaluating the full range of findings from genetic research and from research designs that address the issues of nature–nurture interplay, we must consider the clinical implications as they apply particularly to the risks for children associated with parental depressive disorder.

Seven main messages can be derived from the findings. First, genetic mediation is involved for some of the psychopathological risks to the children associated with parental depressive disorder. This risk route is likely to be strongest when dealing with the intergenerational associations between bipolar disorder in the parent and bipolar disorder in the child. Most instances of depressive disorder in parents do not take this form and, even when they do, the risks to the children are far from confined to bipolar disorders. Genetic mediation is likely to be least when dealing with the association between parental depressive disorder and nondepressive forms of psychopathology in the children, such as conduct disorder. Environmental mediation of risks seems likely to predominate in this circumstance, although this has yet to be shown empirically. The associations between unipolar depressive disorders in parents and anxiety or depressive disorders in the children are intermediate with respect to the relative importance of genetic factors. Genetic mediation is likely to play some part, but environmental effects are also operative and the genetic contribution is probably not as strong as for bipolar disorders.

Second, the findings on gene–environment correlations and interactions indicate the importance of indirect genetic effects. That is, to an important extent, genetic influences are involved in the psychopathological risks to the children because genetic factors increase the probability that children experience risk environments and that they are more sensitive to such environmental hazards. The implication is important because it means that the genetic effects are open to environmental manipulation. A better understanding of the mechanisms involved in these indirect effects should provide the means for effective intervention by interrupting the indirect causal chain, thereby, reducing the indirect genetic impact that comes about through correlations and interactions of environmental risks.

Third, it is likely that, at least with unipolar disorders, most of the genetic effects operate through personality traits of one kind or another. The construct of neuroticism or emotionality seems to describe best the characteristics that are likely to be implicated, but many issues remain unresolved. For example, high emotionality seems to provide some protection against antisocial behavior (Rutter et al., 1998), yet conduct problems predispose individuals to depressive symptoms in adult life, especially in women (Moffitt, Caspi, Rutter, & Silva, 2001; Rutter et al., 1997). On the face of it, this seems contradictory (the test being whether or not conduct disorder and depression to some extent share the same genetic liability, a question that has yet to be tackled systematically), so how do the risk and protective processes operate? Similarly, the concept of neuroticism focuses on emotional hyper-responsiveness and susceptibility to environmental stressors, but cognitive attributional styles occupy a central role in many theories of depression (Teasdale & Barnard, 1993). Is the focus on social cognitions and attributional style misdirected (see, e.g., Roberts & Kendler, 1999), or are there interconnections between emotionality and social cognition that are as yet ill-defined and ill-understood?

Fourth, genetic studies have been highly informative by providing rigorous tests of environmental mediation. Evidence available so far indicates the importance of environmentally mediated risks in relation to the associations between negative life events and depression and between family negativity and antisocial behavior. Family negativity probably also carries an increased risk for depression, but the effects are less strong than those for disruptive behavior. Genetic studies clearly have the potential for sorting out which putative environmental risk factors do actually provide environmentally mediated risks and which ones only appear to do so because they are associated with genetic mediation. Knowledge of this kind would be hugely helpful in avoiding interventions that waste time because they focus on risk features that do not actually carry much environmentally mediated risk, even though their name suggests that they do. Unfortunately, few genetic studies have attempted to do this in any systematic way, and such studies are much needed.

Fifth, the findings also indicate that much of the psychopathological risk to the children associated with parental depression is likely to derive as much from disorders associated with depression (such as personality disturbances or drug and alcohol misuse) as from the depressive disorder as such. This means that, at least insofar as the risks to the children are concerned, we cannot assume that alleviation of the depression necessarily reduces the psychopathological risks. Indeed, this has been the conclusion insofar as treatment studies have looked at this matter (Cooper & Murray, 1997). From both research and clinical perspectives, it is most important that more is learned about the ways in which these patterns of comorbidity arise, as well as about the ways in which they generate environmentally mediated risks. It is also important to understand that the comorbidity may well play a role in genetic mediation. To the extent that personality features are central in the genetic vulnerability to depression, the presence of at least some forms of personality disorder may be crucial, because that is what they reflect.

Sixth, identification of gene–environment correlations, and more broadly person–environment correlations, serves as a reminder that, in thinking about prevention, we need to pay as much attention to the origins of risk factors as to their impact on children. Thus, interventions have tended to focus on improving children's social problem-solving skills, helping them deal better with stress circumstances, or improving their level of social support (Haggerty, Sherrod, Garmezy, & Rutter, 1994). Such interventions are certainly worthwhile, but we also must appreciate that children have an increased likelihood of experiencing psychosocial risks because of the ways that their parents behave, the patterns of interaction in the family, and the parental shaping of children's experiences. We need to think about how to intervene higher up the causal chain by making it less likely that depressed parents create risky environments for their children. To do that more effectively, however, we must improve our understanding of the mechanisms by which these effects come about. To date, most of the research has been concerned with showing the existence of gene–environment correlations, and it has been much less concerned with the careful delineation of the causal mechanisms that underlie the correlations. The latter area constitutes a priority for future research.

Finally, the role of genetic influences in increased susceptibility to environmental stress and adversity has certain implications. There is a temptation, in this connection, to conclude that we should concentrate all our intervention efforts on this most vulnerable group. It may well be sensible to devote some forms of intervention to this group, but it is necessary to appreciate that, even when there is an identifiable risk factor that greatly multiplies the risk, a high proportion of the children suffering psychopathology are in the low-risk groups. That is because it is extremely unusual for any vulnerability factor, however strong, to account for all the variations in susceptibility and because there are many more children from a lower risk background than from a high-risk one (Rutter et al., 1998). Although relatively fewer of the children at low risk develop psychopathology, in absolute terms they constitute many of those who suffer simply because they far outnumber the high-risk children. Considerations of this kind as well as the dimensional (rather than categorical) operation of most risk factors have led public health epidemiologists to argue that prevention almost always should involve a degree of total population coverage, as well as (sometimes instead of) a focus on high-risk subgroups (Holland & Stewart, 1997; Rose, 1992). The more important message from identification of gene–environment interactions concerns the possible leads that it provides for an understanding of the causal risk and protective processes.

The identification of interactions constitutes the beginning of the research enterprise and not the end of it (Rutter & Pickles, 1991). Knowing that there is an interaction is, in itself, not very useful in identifying the causal mechanism, but it is hugely helpful in indicating where to focus attention in seeking to elucidate what is involved in the causal processes that underlie individual differences in risk susceptibility.

REFERENCES

Adrian, C., & Hammen, C. (1993). Stress exposure and stress generation in children of depressed mothers. *Journal of Consulting and Clinical Psychology, 61*, 354–359.

Andrews, G. (1996). Comorbidity and the general neurotic syndrome. *British Journal of Psychiatry, 168*, 76–84.

Angold, A., Costello, E. J., & Erkanli, A. (1999). Pubertal changes and depression in girls. *Psychological Medicine, 29*, 1043–1053.

Angold, A., Costello, E. J., & Worthman, C. M. (1998). Puberty and depression: The roles of age, pubertal status and pubertal timing. *Psychological Medicine, 28*, 51–61.

Bebbington, P. (1996). The origins of sex differences in depressive disorder: Bridging the gap. *International Review of Psychiatry, 8*, 295–332.

Bebbington, P. (1998). Sex and depression. *Psychological Medicine, 28*, 1–8.

Bebbington, P., Dunn, G., Jenkins, R., Lewis, G., Brugha, T., Farrell, M., & Meltzer, H. (1998). The influence of age and sex on depressive conditions: Report from the National Survey of Psychiatric Morbidity. *Psychological Medicine, 28*, 9–10.

Brown, G. W., Harris, T. O., & Eales, M. J. (1996). Social factors and comorbidity of depressive and anxiety disorders. *British Journal of Psychiatry, 168*(Suppl. 30), 50–57.

Cadoret, R. J., Troughton, E., Merchant, L. M., & Whitters, A. (1990). Early life psychosocial events and adult affective symptoms. In L. Robins & M. Rutter

(Eds.), *Straight and devious pathways from childhood to adulthood* (pp. 300–313). Cambridge, England: Cambridge University Press.

Champion, L. A., Goodall, G., & Rutter, M. (1995). Behavioural problems in childhood and stressors in early adult life: I. A 20-year follow-up of London school children. *Psychological Medicine, 25,* 231–246.

Cooper, P. J., & Murray, L. (1997). The impact of psychological treatments of postpartum depression on maternal mood and infant development. In L. Murray & P. J. Cooper (Eds.), *Postpartum depression and child development* (pp. 201–220). New York: Guilford Press.

Cox, A. D., Puckering, C., Pound, A., & Mills, M. (1987). The impact of maternal depression on young children. *Journal of Child Psychology and Psychiatry, 28,* 917–928.

Craddock, N., & Jones, I. (1999). Genetics of bipolar disorder. *Journal of Medical Genetics, 36,* 585–594.

Cui, X.-J., & Vaillant, G. E. (1997). Does depression generate negative life events? *Journal of Nervous and Mental Disease, 185,* 145–150.

Daley, S. E., Hammen, C., Burge, D., Davila, J., Blair, P., Lindberg, N., & Herzberg, D. S. (1997). Predictors of the generation of episodic stress: A longitudinal study of late adolescent women. *Journal of Abnormal Psychology, 106,* 251–259.

Davenport, Y. B., Zahn-Waxler, C., Adland, M. C., & Mayfield, J. (1984). Early child-rearing practices in families with a manic-depressive parent. *American Journal of Psychiatry, 141,* 230–235.

Diekstra, R. F. W., Kienhorst, C. W. M., & de Wilde, E. J. (1995). Suicide and suicidal behaviour among adolescents. In M. Rutter & D. J. Smith (Eds.), *Psychosocial disorders in young people: Time trends and their causes* (pp. 686–761). Chichester, England: John Wiley & Sons.

Downey, G., & Coyne, J. C. (1990). Children of depressed parents: An integrative review. *Psychological Bulletin, 108,* 50–76.

Duggan, C., Sham, P., Minne, C., Lee, A., & Murray, R. (1998). The family history as a predictor of poor long-term outcome in depression. *British Journal of Psychiatry, 173,* 527–530.

Eaves, L. J., Silberg, J. L., Meyer, J. M., Maes, H. H., Simonoff, E., Pickles, A., Rutter, M., Neale, M. C., Reynolds, C. A., Erikson, M. T., Heath, A. C., Loeber, R., & Truett, T. R. (1997). Genetics and developmental psychopathology: II. The main effects of genes and environment on behavioral problems in the Virginia Twin Study of Adolescent Behavioral Development. *Journal of Child Psychology and Psychiatry, 38,* 965–980.

Eley, T. (1999). Behavioral genetics as a tool for developmental psychology: Anxiety and depression in children and adolescents. *Clinical Child and Family Psychology Review, 2,* 21–36.

Eley, T. C., & Stevenson, J. (1999). Exploring the covariation between anxiety and depression symptoms: A genetic analysis of the effect of age and sex. *Journal of Child Psychology and Psychiatry, 40,* 1273–1284.

Evans, W. E., & Relling, M. V. (1999). Pharmacogenomics: Translating functional genomics into rational therapeutics. *Science, 286,* 487–491.

Farmer, A., Harris, T., Redman, K., Sadler, S., Mahmood, A., & McGuffin, P. (2000). Cardiff Depression Study: A sib pair study of life events and familiality in major depression. *British Journal of Psychiatry, 176,* 150–155.

Feigon, S. A., Waldman, I. D., Levy, F., & Hay, D. A. (in press). Genetic and environmental influences on separation anxiety disorder symptoms and their moderation by age and sex. *Behavior Genetics.*

Flint, J. (1997). Freeze! *Nature Genetics, 17,* 250–251.

Fombonne, E. (1995). Depressive disorders: Time trends and possible explanatory mechanisms. In M. Rutter & D. J. Smith (Eds.), *Psychosocial disorders in young people: Time trends and their causes* (pp. 544–615). Chichester, England: John Wiley & Sons.

Frank, E., & Young, E. (2000). Pubertal challenges and adolescent challenges. In E. Frank (Ed.), *Gender and its effects on psychopathology* (pp. 85–102). Washington, DC: American Psychiatric Press.

Geller, B., & Cook, E. H. (1999). Serotonin transporter gene (HTTLPR) is not in linkage disequilibrium with prepubertal and early adolescent bipolarity. *Biological Psychiatry, 49,* 1230–1233.

Goodman, S. H., & Brumley, H. E. (1990). Schizophrenic and depressed mothers: Relational deficits in parenting. *Developmental Psychology, 26,* 31–39.

Haggerty, R. J., Sherrod, L. R., Garmezy, N., & Rutter, M. (1994). *Stress, risk and resilience in children and adolescents: Processes, mechanisms and interventions.* New York: Cambridge University Press.

Hammen, C. (1991). *Depression runs in families: The social context of risk and resilience in children of depressed mothers.* New York: Springer Verlag.

Hammen, C., Gordon, D., Burge, D., Adrian, C., Jaenicke, C., & Hiroto, D. (1987). Maternal affective disorders, illness, and stress: Risk for children's psychopathology. *American Journal of Psychiatry, 144,* 736–741.

Harrington, R. C. (1993). Child and adult depression: A test of continuities with data from a family study. *British Journal of Psychiatry, 162,* 627–633.

Harrington, R. (1996). Family–genetic findings in child and adolescent depressive disorders. *International Review of Psychiatry, 8,* 355–368.

Harrington, R., Fudge, H., Rutter, M., Pickles, A., & Hill, J. (1990). Adult outcome of childhood and adolescent depression: I. Psychiatric status. *Archives of General Psychiatry, 47,* 465–473.

Harrington, R., Rutter, M., Weissman, M., Fudge, H., Groothues, C., Bredenkamp, D., Pickles, A., Remde, R., & Wickramaratne, P. (1997). Psychiatric disorders in the relatives of depressed probands: I. Comparison of prepubertal, adolescent and early adult onset cases. *Journal of Affective Disorders, 42,* 9–22.

Holland, W. W., & Stewart, S. (1997). *Public health: The vision and the challenge.* London: Nuffield Trust.

Holsboer, F. (1999). Clinical neuroendocrinology. In D. S. Charney, E. J. Nestler, & B. S. Bunney (Eds.), *Neurobiology of mental illness* (pp. 149–161). New York: Oxford University Press.

Judd, L. L. (1997). The clinical course of unipolar major depressive disorders. *Archives of General Psychiatry, 54,* 989–991.

Kendler, K. S. (1996). Major depression and generalised anxiety disorder: Same genes, (partly) different environments—Revisited. *British Journal of Psychiatry, 168*(Suppl. 30), 68–75.

Kendler, K. S., & Gardner, C. O. (1998). Twin studies of adult psychiatric and substance dependence disorders: Are they biased by differences in the environmental experience of mono- and dizygotic twins in childhood and adolescence? *Psychological Medicine, 28,* 625–633.

Kendler, K. S., Karkowski, L. M., & Prescott, C. A. (1999a). The assessment of dependence in the study of stressful life events: Validation using a twin design. *Psychological Medicine, 29,* 1455–1460.

Kendler, K. S., Karkowski, L. M., & Prescott, C. A. (1999b). Causal relationship between stressful life events and the onset of major depression. *American Journal of Psychiatry, 156,* 837–841.

Kendler, K. S., & Karkowski-Shuman, L. (1997). Stressful life events and genetic liability to major depression: Genetic control of exposure to the environment? *Psychological Medicine, 27,* 539–547.

Kendler, K. S., Kessler, R. C., Walters, E. E., MacLean, C., Neale, M. C., Heath, A. C., & Eaves, L. J. (1995). Stressful life events, genetic liability, and onset of an episode of major depression in women. *American Journal of Psychiatry, 152,* 833–842.

Kendler, K. S., Myers, J., & Prescott, C. A. (2000). Parenting and adult mood, anxiety, and substance use disorders in women: An epidemiological, multi-informant, retrospective study. *Psychological Medicine, 30,* 281–294.

Kendler, K. S., Neale, M. C., Kessler, R. C., & Eaves, L. J. (1994). Parental treatment and the equal environments assumption in twin studies of psychiatric illness. *Psychological Medicine, 24,* 579–590.

Kendler, K. S., Neale, M. C., Kessler, R., Heath, A., & Eaves, L. (1993). A twin study of recent life events and difficulties. *Archives of General Psychiatry, 50,* 789–796.

Kendler, K. S., & Prescott, C. A. (1999). A population-based twin study of lifetime major depression in men and women. *Archives of General Psychiatry, 56,* 39–44.

Kendler, K. S., Sham, P. C., & MacLean, C. J. (1997). The determinants of parenting: An epidemiological, multi-informant, retrospective study. *Psychological Medicine, 27,* 549–563.

Kendler, K. S., Thornton, L. M., & Gardner, C. O. (2000). Stressful life events and prior episodes in the aetiology of major depression in women: An evaluation of the "kindling" hypothesis. *American Journal of Psychiatry, 157,* 1243–1251.

Kessler, R. C. (2000). Gender differences in major depression: Epidemiological findings. In E. Frank (Ed.), *Gender and its effects on psychopathology* (pp. 61–84). Washington, DC: American Psychiatric Press.

Kirov, G., Rees, M., Jones, I., MacCandless, F., Owen, M. J., & Craddock, N. (1999). Bipolar disorder and the serotonin transporter gene: A family-based association study. *Psychological Medicine, 29*, 1249–1254.

Klein, M. H., Kupfer, D. J., & Shea, M. T. (1993). *Personality and depression: A current view*. New York: Guilford Press.

Lapalme, M., Hodgins, S., & LaRoche, C. (1997). Children of parents with bipolar disorder: A meta-analysis of risk for mental disorders. *Canadian Journal of Psychiatry, 42*, 623–631.

Lesch, K. P., Bengel, D., Heils, A., Sabol, S. Z., Greenberg, B. D., Petri, S., Benjamin, J., Muller-Reible, C. R., Hamer, D. H., & Murphy, D. L. (1996). A gene regulatory region polymorphism alters serotonin transporter expression and is associated with anxiety-related personality traits. *Science, 274*, 1527–1531.

Maes, M., & Meltzer, H. Y. (1995). The serotonic hypothesis of major depression. In F. E. Bloom & D. J. Kupfer (Eds.), *Psychopharmacology: The fourth generation of progress* (pp. 933–944). New York: Raven Press.

Maier, W., & Merikangas, K. (1996). Co-occurrence and co-transmission of affective disorders and alcoholism in families. *British Journal of Psychiatry, 168*(Suppl. 30), 93–100.

Maj, M., & Sartorius, N. (Eds.). (1999). *Depressive disorders*. Chichester, England: Wiley.

McGuffin, P., Katz, R., & Bebbington, P. (1987). Hazard, heredity and depression: A family study. *Journal of Psychiatric Research, 4*, 365–375.

Merikangas, K. R., Angst, J., Eaton, W., & Canino, G. (1996). Comorbidity and boundaries of affective disorders with anxiety disorders and substance misuse: Results of an international task force. *British Journal of Psychiatry, 168*(Suppl. 30), 58–67.

Moffitt, T. E., Caspi, A., Rutter, M., & Silva, P. A. (2001). *Sorting out differences in antisocial behavior: Findings from the first two decades of the Dunedin longitudinal study*. New York: Cambridge University Press.

Moldin, S. (1999). Report of the NIMH's Genetics Workgroups: Summary of Research. *Biological Psychiatry, 45*, 559–602.

Murray, K. T., & Sines, J. O. (1996). Parsing the genetic and nongenetic variance in children's depressive behavior. *Journal of Affective Disorders, 38*, 23–34.

Nolen-Hoeksema, S., & Girgus, J. S. (1994). The emergence of gender differences in depression during adolescence. *Psychological Bulletin, 115*, 424–443.

O'Connor, T. G., Deater-Deckard, K., Fulker, D., Rutter, M., & Plomin, R. (1998). Early adolescence: Antisocial behavioral problems and coercive parenting. *Developmental Psychology, 34*, 970–981.

Parker, G., Tupling, H., & Brown, L. B. (1979). A parental bonding instrument. *British Journal of Medical Psychology, 52*, 1–10.

Pike, A., McGuire, S., Hetherington, E. M., Reiss, D., & Plomin, R. (1996). Family environment and adolescent depression and antisocial behavior: A multivariate genetic analysis. *Developmental Psychology, 32*, 590–603.

Pike, A., Reiss, D., Hetherington, E. M., & Plomin, R. (1996). Using MZ differences in the search for non-shared environmental effects. *Journal of Child Psychology and Psychiatry, 37*, 695–704.

Post, R. (1992). Transduction of psychosocial stress into neurobiology of recurrent affective disorder. *American Journal of Psychiatry, 149*, 999–1010.

Quinton, D., Gulliver, L., & Rutter, M. (1995). A 15–20 year follow-up of adult psychiatric patients: Psychiatric disorder and social functioning. *British Journal of Psychiatry, 167*, 315–323.

Radke-Yarrow, M. (1998). *Children of depressed mothers.* New York: Cambridge University Press.

Roberts, S. B., & Kendler, K. S. (1999). Neuroticism and self-esteem as indices of the vulnerability to major depression of women. *Psychological Medicine, 29*, 1101–1109.

Rose, G. (1992). *The strategy of preventive medicine.* Oxford, England: Oxford Medical Publications.

Rowe, D. C., Jacobson, K. C., & van den Oord, J. C. G. (1999). Genetic and environmental influences on vocabulary IQ: Parental education level as a moderator. *Child Development, 70*, 1151–1162.

Rutter, M. (1966). *Children of sick parents: An environmental and psychiatric study* (Institute of Psychiatry Maudsley Monographs No. 16). London: Oxford University Press.

Rutter, M. (1986). The developmental psychopathology of depression: Issues and perspectives. In M. Rutter, C. Izard, & P. Read (Eds.), *Depression in young people: Developmental and clinical perspectives* (pp. 3–30). New York: Guilford Press.

Rutter, M. (1989). Psychiatric disorder in parents as a risk factor for children. In D. Shaffer, J. Philipe, & N. B. Enzer (Eds.) with M. M. Silverman & V. Anthony (Associate Eds.), *Prevention of mental disorders, alcohol and other drug use in children and adolescents* (Office for Substance Abuse Prevention Monograph 2, pp. 157–189). Rockville, MD: Office for Substance Abuse Prevention, U.S. Department of Health & Human Services.

Rutter, M. (1990). Commentary: Some focus and process considerations regarding effects of parental depression on children. *Developmental Psychology, 26*, 60–67.

Rutter, M. (1999). Resilience concepts and findings: Implications for family therapy. *Journal of Family Therapy, 21*, 119–144.

Rutter, M. (2000a). Negative life events and family negativity. In T. Harris (Ed.), *Where inner and outer worlds meet: Psychosocial research in the tradition of George W. Brown* (pp. 123–149). London: Routledge.

Rutter, M. (2000b). Psychosocial influences: Critiques, findings and research needs. *Development and Psychopathology, 12*, 375–405.

Rutter, M. (2000c). Resilience reconsidered: Conceptual considerations, empirical findings, and policy implications. In J. P. Shonkoff & S. J. Meisels (Eds.), *Handbook of early childhood intervention* (2nd ed., pp. 651–682). New York: Cambridge University Press.

Rutter, M., Champion, L., Quinton, D., Maughan, B., & Pickles, A. (1995). Understanding individual differences in environmental risk exposure. In P. Moen, G. H. Elder, Jr., & K. Lüscher (Eds.), *Examining lives in context: Perspectives on the ecology of human development* (pp. 61–93). Washington, DC: American Psychological Association.

Rutter, M., Giller, H., & Hagell, A. (1998). *Antisocial behavior by young people.* New York: Cambridge University Press.

Rutter, M., Maughan, B., Meyer, J., Pickles, A., Silberg, J., Simonoff, E., & Taylor, E. (1997). Heterogeneity of antisocial behavior: Causes, continuities and consequences. In R. Dienstbier & D. W. Osgood (Eds.), *Nebraska Symposium on Motivation: Vol. 44. Motivation and delinquency* (pp. 45–118). Lincoln: University of Nebraska Press.

Rutter, M., & Pickles, A. (1991). Person–environment interactions: Concepts, mechanisms and implications for data analysis. In T. D. Wachs & R. Plomin (Eds.), *Conceptualization and measurement of organism—environment interaction* (pp. 105–141). Washington, DC: American Psychological Association.

Rutter, M., Pickles, A., Murray, R., & Eaves, L. (2001). Testing hypotheses on specific environmental causal effects on behavior. *Psychological Bulletin, 127,* 291–324.

Rutter, M., & Quinton, D. (1984). Parental psychiatric disorder: Effects on children. *Psychological Medicine, 14,* 853–880.

Rutter, M., & Silberg, J. (in press). Gene–environment interplay in relation to emotional and behavioral disturbance. *Annual Review of Psychology.*

Rutter, M., Silberg, J., O'Connor, T., & Simonoff, E. (1999a). Genetics and child psychiatry: I. Advances in quantitative and molecular genetics. *Journal of Child Psychology and Psychiatry, 40,* 3–18.

Rutter, M., Silberg, J., O'Connor, T., & Simonoff, E. (1999b). Genetics and child psychiatry: II. Empirical research findings. *Journal of Child Psychology and Psychiatry, 40,* 19–55.

Sandberg, S., Rutter, M., Pickles, A., McGuinness, D., & Angold, A. (2001). Do high threat life events really provoke the onset of psychiatric disorder in children? *Journal of Child Psychology and Psychiatry, 42,* 523–532.

Silberg, J., Pickles, A., Rutter, M., Hewitt, J., Simonoff, E., Maes, H., Carbonneau, R., Murrelle, L., Foley, D., & Eaves, L. (1999). The influence of genetic factors and life stress on depression among adolescent girls. *Archives of General Psychiatry, 56,* 225–232.

Silberg, J., Rutter, M., D'Onofrio, B., & Eaves, L. (2001). *Genetic and environmental risk factors in adolescent substance use.* Manuscript submitted for publication.

Silberg, J. L., Rutter, M., & Eaves, L. J. (2001). Genetic and environmental influences on the temporal association between early anxiety and later depression in girls. *Biological Psychiatry, 49*, 1040–1049.

Silberg, J., Rutter, M., Neale, M., & Eaves, L. (2001). Genetic moderation of environmental risk for depression and anxiety in adolescent girls. *British Journal of Psychiatry, 179*, 116–121.

Stanford, S. C. (1996). Prozac: Panacea or puzzle? *Trends in Pharmacological Science, 17*, 150–154.

Stoolmiller, M. (1999). Implications of the restricted range of family environments for estimates of heritability and nonshared environment in behavior–genetic adoption studies. *Psychological Bulletin, 125*, 392–409.

Sullivan, P. F., Neale, M. C., & Kendler, K. S. (2000). Genetic epidemiology of major depression: Review and meta-analysis. *American Journal of Psychiatry, 157*, 1552–1562.

Talbot, C. J., Nicod, A., Cherny, S. S., Fulker, D. W., Collins, A. C., & Flint, J. (1999). High-resolution mapping of quantitative trait loci in outbred mice. *Nature Genetics, 21*, 305–308.

Teasdale, J. D., & Barnard, P. J. (1993). *Affect, cognition and change: Re-modelling depressive thought.* Hove, England: Erlbaum.

Thapar, A., Harold, G., & McGuffin, P. (1998). Life events and depressive symptoms in childhood—Shared genes or shared adversity? A research note. *Journal of Child Psychology and Psychiatry, 39*, 1153–1158.

Thapar, A., & McGuffin, P. (1994). A twin study of depressive symptoms in childhood. *British Journal of Psychiatry, 165*, 259–265.

Thapar, A., & McGuffin, P. (1995). Are anxiety symptoms in childhood heritable? *Journal of Child Psychology and Psychiatry, 36*, 439–447.

Thapar, A., & McGuffin, P. (1997). Anxiety and depressive symptoms in childhood—A genetic study of comorbidity. *Journal of Child Psychology and Psychiatry, 38*, 651–656.

Topolski, T. D., Hewitt, J. K., Eaves, L., Meyer, J. M., Silberg, J. L., Simonoff, E., & Rutter, M. (1999). Genetic and environmental influences on ratings of manifest anxiety by parents and children. *Journal of Anxiety Disorders, 13*, 371–397.

Topolski, T. D., Hewitt, J. K., Eaves, L. J., Silberg, J. L., Meyer, J. M., Rutter, M., Pickles, A., & Simonoff, E. (1997). Genetic and environmental influences on child reports of manifest anxiety and symptoms of separation anxiety and over-anxious disorders: A community-based twin study. *Behavior Genetics, 27*, 15–28.

Warner, V., Weissman, M. M., Mufson, L., & Wickramaratne, P. J. (1999). Grandparents, parents and grandchildren at high risk for depression: A three-generation study. *Journal of the American Academy of Child and Adolescent Psychiatry, 38*, 289–296.

Weissman, M., & Paykel, E. (1974). *The depressed woman: A study of social relations*. Chicago: University of Chicago Press.

Weissman, M. M., Warner, V., Wickramaratne, P. J., Moreau, D., & Olfson, M. (1997). Offspring of depressed parents: Ten years later. *Archives of General Psychiatry, 54*, 932–940.

Weissman, M. M., Wolk, S., Goldstein, R., Moreau, D., Adams, P., Greenwald, S., Klier, C. M., Ryan, N. D., Dahl, R. E., & Wickramaratne, P. (1999). Depressed adolescents grown up. *Journal of the American Medical Association, 281*, 1707–1713.

Wickramaratne, P. J., & Weissman, M. M. (1998). Onset of psychopathology in offspring by developmental phase and parental depression. *Journal of the American Academy of Child and Adolescent Psychiatry, 37*, 933–942.

3

MATERNAL DEPRESSION, INFANT PSYCHOBIOLOGICAL DEVELOPMENT, AND RISK FOR DEPRESSION

SHARON B. ASHMAN AND GERALDINE DAWSON

Researchers studying the effects of maternal depression on child development have consistently found associations between maternal depression and adverse child outcomes (Downey & Coyne, 1990; Goodman & Gotlib, 1999; Murray & Cooper, 1997; Radke-Yarrow, 1998). A range of adverse outcomes for these children has been documented at various points in development, from infancy through adolescence. Compared to the offspring of nondepressed mothers, neonates of depressed mothers exhibit higher cortisol and norepinephrine levels, poorer orientation, abnormal reflexes, and less optimal levels of excitability, withdrawal, and irritability (Abrams, Field, Scafidi, & Prodromidis, 1995; Lundy et al., 1999). During interactions with their mothers, infants of depressed mothers display more frequent negative

The writing of this chapter and the research reported herein were supported by National Institute of Mental Health Grant No. MH47117. We wish to gratefully acknowledge the women and infants who participated in this study. Cathy Brock, Liliana Lengua, Jan St. John, Dick McDonald, Julie Osterling, Al Ross, Sally Shuh, and numerous student research assistants made important contributions to this work.

37

emotions and fewer positive emotions, vocalize less, and have lower activity levels (Dawson, Frey, Self, et al., 1999; Field, 1995). Research also demonstrates that infants of depressed mothers, on average, have poorer mental and motor development and higher levels of emotional and attachment difficulties (Murray & Cooper, 1997). Preschool children of depressed mothers have been reported to have lower social competence and more internalizing and externalizing behavior problems (Field et al., 1996; Gross, Conrad, Fogg, Willis, & Garvey, 1995). Finally, compared to children of nondepressed mothers, school-aged and adolescent children of depressed mothers have more difficulties relating to peers, higher rates of depression and anxiety, and increased rates of disruptive behavior problems (Radke-Yarrow, 1998).

Although a great deal of research has assessed negative child outcomes associated with maternal depression, relatively less research effort has attempted to address the mechanisms by which children of depressed mothers develop a vulnerability to depression and other behavioral problems. In this chapter, we focus on one set of such contributing factors involved in the transmission of risk from depressed mothers to their offspring. We hypothesize that children of depressed mothers are at risk for negative outcomes, including depression, in part because of the effects of inadequate early parenting on the development of children's psychobiological systems related to emotion expression and regulation. Alterations in these systems are reflected in changed levels of cortical activity, autonomic reactivity, and stress hormone secretion. We discuss the known or hypothesized brain systems related to each of these psychobiological indices and how the early social environment may affect their functioning. In addition, we present data from our own and others' research studies that demonstrate the relation between maternal depression and alterations in child behavior and psychobiology, and we examine how such alterations may increase a child's vulnerability to depression.

CORTICAL ACTIVITY: THE PREFRONTAL CORTEX

In this section, we discuss the role of the prefrontal cortex in emotion regulation and expression and how the early social environment, particularly parenting, may affect the functioning of the prefrontal cortex.

Functional and Developmental Considerations

The prefrontal cortex has long been recognized as important for emotional and social behavior. Studies of frontal lobe lesions in animals and humans and of brain activity based on functional neuroimaging and electroencephalographic (EEG) recording have suggested that prefrontal cortical activity plays an important role in emotion regulation and expression. With respect to emotion expression, human and animal research on frontal lobe lesions have shown that the left and right frontal regions mediate the expression of different types of emotions. Left frontal lobe lesions tend to result in depression and catastrophic reactions, whereas right frontal lobe lesions tend to result in apathy or euphoria (Gainotti, 1969, 1972; Heller, 1990; Robinson & Benson, 1981; Robinson, Kubos, Starr, Reo, & Price, 1984; Robinson & Stetela, 1981). Additional support for the differential mediation of specific emotions by the left and right frontal regions comes from research on frontal EEG activity during the expression of different emotions (Davidson, Ekman, Saron, Senulis, & Friesen, 1990; Davidson & Fox, 1988, 1989; Dawson, Panagiotides, Grofer Klinger, & Hill, 1992; Finman, Davidson, Colton, Straus, & Kagan, 1989). These studies demonstrate that relative left frontal activation occurs during the expression of "approach" emotions, such as joy and interest, and relative right frontal activation occurs during the expression of "withdrawal" emotions, such as distress and fear. This result has been replicated in studies of adults, children, and infants.

Research has also associated frontal EEG asymmetries with individual differences in emotion expression, and some investigators have speculated that these differences indicate an individual's propensity to experience approach as opposed to withdrawal emotions (Davidson & Fox, 1988; Fox, 1991). For example, Davidson (1987) observed adults' EEG patterns in response to emotional films and found associations between positive or negative emotional valence and relative left or relative right frontal lobe activation, respectively. Research has extended this finding to infants and children. Davidson and Fox (1989) found that infants with relative right frontal activation during a baseline condition were more likely to cry during separation from their mothers. Similarly, Finman et al. (1989) found an association between relative right frontal activation and a predisposition toward withdrawal emotions. They reported that, compared to uninhibited peers, behaviorally inhibited children displayed greater resting right frontal asymmetry.

Whereas the above research links asymmetric frontal activation with the valence (happy vs. sad) of emotions, Dawson and colleagues (in press) has associated generalized frontal EEG activity with emotional intensity. This research demonstrated that, when compared to a baseline condition, both left and right frontal regions displayed increased activation when infants were separated from their mothers, a condition in which all the infants expressed intense emotion. The subtle asymmetry between left and right frontal activation was superimposed on this generalized increase. In addition, some research suggests that the right parietal region may be associated with the level of autonomic arousal accompanying emotions. Heller (1990) has theorized that when arousal is high, such as during the expression of happiness or anxiety, right parietal activation is high, and when arousal is low, such as during sad or calm emotions, right parietal activation is low. Support for this theory can be found in a variety of investigations, including studies of right parietal brain damage and measures of right parietal brain activation and blood flow in depressed patients (see Heller, 1990, for a review). For example, individuals with right parietal brain damage demonstrate activity and attention deficits similar to those seen in depressed patients. In addition, studies of brain activation and blood flow in depressed patients have found reduced activity in the right parietal region (Flor-Henry, 1979; Uytdenhoef et al., 1983). Heller speculated that this decreased right parietal activation may be associated with a general reduction in cerebral and autonomic arousal in depressed patients.

In addition to its role in emotion expression, the prefrontal cortex plays an important role in emotion regulation (Davidson, 2000; Fox, 1994). Research indicates that brain damage to the prefrontal cortex often results in difficulties in regulating emotional responses (Anderson, Bechara, Damasio, Tranel, & Damasio, 1999; Fuster, 1989). In addition, individuals with frontal lesions demonstrate distractibility (Hécaen, 1964), perseverative behavior and thinking (Fuster, 1989), and difficulties in directing and sustaining attention (Luria, 1966/1980) and in monitoring temporal sequences (Milner, Petrides, & Smith, 1985). Furthermore, many specialized prefrontal functions support emotion regulatory behaviors. These functions include the ability to inhibit inappropriate responses, to guide one's behavior on the basis of internal representations (Goldman-Rakic, 1987), to monitor complex temporal sequences, and to form generalizable mental representations related to expectancies for reward and punishment (Damasio, 1995; Goldman-Rakic, 1987; B. M. Jones & Mishkin, 1972).

Some researchers have theorized that the previously described frontal lobe EEG asymmetries index different emotion regulation strategies (Dawson, 1994; Dawson, Panagiotides, et al., 1992; Kinsbourne & Bemporad, 1984; Tucker & Williamson, 1984). These investigators have suggested that left frontal activation reflects active, organized regulation and coping schemes, such as expressive language, that involve engagement of the external environment. At the same time, they have suggested that right frontal activation reflects disruption in ongoing activity and withdrawal from the environment. This view is consistent with a perspective on emotion offered by Campos, Campos, and Barrett (1989), who maintained that emotions reflect establishment or disruption of relations between the person and the environment. Thus, positive emotions, such as happiness, involve striving toward a goal, and negative emotions, such as sadness, involve relinquishing of striving toward a goal.

Frontal lobe development occurs gradually throughout infancy, early childhood, and adolescence (Huttenlocher & Dabholkar, 1997). Rapid postnatal synaptogenesis appears to correspond with the emergence of early frontal skills, such as mastery of the delayed response task, which some have hypothesized to be one of the earliest tasks mediated by the prefrontal cortex (Diamond & Goldman-Rakic, 1989). During this early period of rapid brain development, infants also acquire other important regulatory abilities, including the ability to selectively attend to relevant stimuli and to perceive temporal contingencies between their own actions and external stimuli (Aslin, Pisoni, & Jusczyk, 1983; Watson, 1979). By the second half of the first year, the infant engages in more intentional and planned behaviors mediated by the acquisition of skills such as means–end schemas, anticipatory responses, and complex sequences of gaze that permit shared attention and social referencing. These new skills assist the infant in better regulating his or her emotions (Bruner, 1977; Campos, Barrett, Lamb, Goldsmith, & Sternberg, 1983; Klinnert, Campos, Sorce, Emde, & Svejda, 1983; Piaget, 1954; Scaife & Bruner, 1975; Stern, 1985).

The protracted developmental course of the prefrontal cortex, extending throughout infancy, childhood, and adolescence, allows for many opportunities for experience to shape the development of frontal lobe neural circuitry and functions. Specifically, experience may influence patterns and responsiveness of neural circuits, a process that has been referred to as *ontogenetic sculpting* (Kolb, 1989). In this process, experience selectively reinforces and amplifies some neural networks and eliminates others. Edelman (1987, 1989) and others (e.g., Black, T. A. Jones, Nelson & Greenough, 1998; Hebb, 1949; Huttenlocher, 1994; Kolb, 1989) have suggested that the reinforcement of specific neural connections occurs in response to repeated and intense environmental stimulation. Out of this process emerge ordered groups of neurons—neural maps—that stabilize and become less susceptible to change over time. When neural maps are stabilized, encounters with similar stimuli preferentially activate the previously selected group of neurons (Edelman, 1989). In this manner, a caretaker's pattern of responding to infant behaviors and emotional responses may facilitate or impede the development of emotion regulation by selectively reinforcing specific neural connections. In the next two sections, we discuss evidence suggesting that the early social environment, especially parenting, influences the development of emotion regulation and the developing psychobiological activity that underlies emotion regulation.

Environmental Influences on Development

Children learn how to express and regulate emotions through interactions with parents, siblings, teachers, peers, and others who play a significant role in their lives (Denham, 1998). At various points in children's development, some individuals may have a more prominent influence than others. For instance, early in life, parents are typically the primary caretakers and are generally most influential in constructing their child's experience. As children grow and enter into other environments, such as school, peers and teachers have an important impact. We concentrate here on the parental role in the socialization of emotion regulation and expression.

Research demonstrates that parents socialize emotion expression and regulation in their children using several mechanisms, including modeling, coaching, and contingency (Denham, 1998; Malatesta, Culver, Tesman, & Shepard, 1989; Malatesta & Haviland, 1982). This socialization begins as early as infancy (Malatesta & Haviland, 1982; Tronick, 1989) and continues throughout childhood. Parents model emotion expression and regulation through their own patterns of behavior. They reveal the emotional significance of specific situations and demonstrate ways to display and cope with those emotions (Denham, 1998). For instance, a child may learn about the expression of anger and sadness when witnessing an argument between his or her parents. Parents may also directly coach emotional expression in their children by discussing the emotional experience of a character in a story. Finally, parents influence the development of emotion regulation in their children by their contingent responses to children's affective displays (Denham, 1998). Parents react to their children's emotional communications, and the way they react may facilitate or impede the development of emotion regulation (Tronick, 1989). Furthermore, mothers model facial expressions for their infants and respond contingently to changes in infants' facial expressions with changes in their own facial expressions (Malatesta & Haviland, 1982).

Impact of Maternal Depression

Parental psychopathology, specifically maternal depression, may interfere with a child's development of emotion regulation in two important and related ways. First, a depressed mother may not provide a positive role model for emotional expression and may not facilitate emotion regulation through sensitive and responsive caretaking. Second, the mother's depressed behavior patterns may influence emotional regulation development by modulating the psychobiological systems that mediate the expression and regulation of emotion.

Evidence for ineffective modeling of emotional expression and facilitation of emotion regulation in depressed mothers comes from observations of mother–infant interactions. These investigations have demonstrated differences in the interaction styles of depressed and nondepressed mothers. For example, compared to nondepressed mothers, depressed mothers tend to express positive emotions less frequently and to express negative emotion more frequently, talk less, and disengage more during face-to-face interactions with their infants (Cohn & Tronick, 1989; Cohn, Mataias, Tronick, Connell, & Lyons-Ruth, 1986; Field, 1986, 1995; Field et al., 1988). In addition to this more withdrawn pattern of interaction, some depressed mothers have been observed to have an "intrusive" style of interacting with their infants (Cohn et al., 1986; Hart, Field, del Valle, & Pelaez-Nogueras,

1998; N. A. Jones, Field, Fox, Davalos, et al., 1997). Intrusive behaviors, which tend to overstimulate the infant, include such behaviors as poking, tickling, restraining, directing the infants' attention, and abruptly offering or withdrawing a toy (Hart et al., 1998). This interaction style may occur more frequently when depressed mothers interact with boys (Hart et al., 1998). Finally, studies have found that, compared to nondepressed mothers, depressed mothers are less sensitively attuned to their infants (Donovan, Leavitt, & Walsh, 1998; Murray, Fiori-Cowley, Hooper, & Cooper, 1996). For example, Donovan et al. (1998) reported that elevated symptoms of maternal depression, especially cognitive symptoms, predict decreased sensitivity to infants' cries.

During these mother–infant interactions, infants of depressed mothers have been found to display affect and behaviors similar in some ways to their mothers' affect and behaviors. The infants appear withdrawn, vocalize less, have reduced activity levels, and display less positive and more negative affect (Cohn et al., 1986; Dawson, Frey, Self, et al., 1999; Field, 1995). This "depressed" style of interaction generalizes to interactions with nondepressed adult strangers (Field et al., 1988). Field (1986) has speculated that infants of depressed mothers mirror their mothers' depressed behaviors and, subsequently, develop a "depressed" style of interacting, which they generalize to interactions with others. In contrast, Tronick and Gianino (1986) have proposed a "mutual regulation model" in which the mother's failure to respond contingently to the infant's other-directed regulatory signals results in poorly coordinated interactions and increased negative affect for the infant. After repeated, unsuccessful attempts to engage the unresponsive parent, the infant withdraws and becomes increasingly reliant on less mature, self-regulatory strategies (e.g., thumb-sucking, rocking, gaze aversion) to cope with the negative feelings. Thus, it appears that the infant abandons "approach" regulation strategies, such as signaling the mother, in favor of "withdrawal" regulation strategies.

Research has suggested that depressed mothers' interactions with their infants influence not only the regulatory behaviors of their children, but also the psychobiological systems underlying those behaviors (Dawson, Frey, Self, et al., 1999). Several studies have documented a relation between maternal depression and infants' frontal electrical brain activity. Specifically, investigators have found that infants of depressed mothers exhibit reduced left frontal electrical brain activity during a baseline condition and during playful interactions with their mothers and a familiar adult (Dawson, Frey, Panagiotides, Osterling, & Hessl, 1997; Dawson, Frey, Panagiotides, et al., 1999; Dawson, Grofer Klinger, Panagiotides, Hill, & Spieker, 1992; Field, Fox, Pickens, & Nawrocki, 1995; N. A. Jones, Field, Fox, Lundy, & Davalos, 1997).

During a condition designed to elicit negative affect (separation from mother), Dawson, Grofer Klinger, Panagiotides, Hill, and Spieker (1992) found that infants of mothers with depressive symptoms exhibited both reduced distress and greater left frontal EEG activation. This finding is consistent with Tronick and Gianino's (1986) mutual regulation model, in which maternal depression results in the infant's reliance on more self-directed regulatory strategies. In other words, when experiencing negative emotions, the infant does not try to elicit the mother's attention because the depressed mother does not respond contingently to her child's distress in prior situations. Some evidence suggests that this pattern of results is amplified when the infant is also insecurely attached to the mother (Dawson, Grofer Klinger, Panagiotides, Spieker, & Frey, 1992).

We have hypothesized that the atypical frontal electrical brain activity observed in infants of depressed mothers is mediated, in part, by the depressed mother's behaviors with her infant. There is ample evidence that maternal depression influences maternal behaviors (Cohn & Tronick, 1989; Cohn et al., 1986; Field, 1986, 1995; Field et al, 1988). Other factors that may contribute to the atypical brain activity found in infants of depressed mothers include genetic effects and prenatal exposure to maternal depression. In fact, N. A. Jones et al. (1998) reported atypical frontal brain activity in newborns of mothers with depressive symptoms only 24–72 hours after birth. In addition, other research demonstrates that neonates of depressed mothers exhibit higher cortisol and norepinephrine levels, poorer orientation, abnormal reflexes, and less optimal levels of excitability, withdrawal, and irritability (Abrams et al., 1995; Lundy et al., 1999). These prenatal effects may operate in an additive fashion with effects related to maternal depression during the postnatal period, including maternal behavior, to influence frontal brain activity.

Dawson and her colleagues (1997) attempted to address the question of prenatal versus postnatal associations between maternal depression and infant brain activity by comparing infants of mothers who experienced depression only after the child's birth (postnatal only group) to infants of mothers who experienced both prenatal and postnatal depression. Both groups of infants of depressed mothers displayed reduced left frontal EEG activity, and both groups differed significantly from the nondepressed group, but they did not differ from each other. The finding of atypical frontal EEG asymmetry in infants in the postnatal only group suggests that exposure to prenatal maternal depression is not necessary for infants to exhibit atypical brain activity. Furthermore, in a multiple regression in which number of months of postnatal maternal depression was accounted for, the number of months of prenatal maternal depression did not predict infant frontal EEG patterns. After reversing the order of these two variables in the regression equation, prenatal months were marginally predictive of infant frontal EEG ($p < .10$), and postnatal months remained a significant predictor. Postnatal months of maternal depression were a stronger predictor of infant frontal EEG patterns than prenatal months.

This study indicates that maternal depression during the postnatal months is associated with atypical patterns of infant frontal brain activity; however, it does not directly address whether the depressed mother's behaviors mediate the relation between maternal depression and infant frontal brain activity. To address this question more directly, Dawson (1999) observed mother–infant interactions outside the psychophysiological laboratory and tested whether the observed mother behaviors mediated the relation between maternal depression and infant frontal EEG asymmetry. Four types of mother behaviors were coded: affection, negativity, scaffolding, and insensitivity. Compared to nondepressed mothers, depressed mothers engaged more frequently in insensitive behaviors, which included tickling, poking, frequent noncontingent initiation by the mother of physical contact and responding to the infant's bid for attention by either physically holding the infant or dismissing the infant (withdrawing, moving the infant away, or by terminating or rejecting contact; Dawson, 1999).

Path analyses were conducted to examine whether depressed mothers' insensitive behaviors mediated the relation between maternal depression and infant frontal EEG asymmetry. Two hierarchically nested models were compared using chi-square goodness-of-fit tests. In the first model, researchers estimated the direct relations between maternal depression and infant EEG and between maternal depression and maternal insensitivity. Both these paths were found to be significant ($p < .05$). In the second model, the mediating path from maternal insensitivity to infant EEG was added. All paths in this model were significant, and the addition of the mediator did not significantly improve the model fit (Dawson, 1999). These results support a partial mediation hypothesis, in which mediation by mothers' behaviors accounts for part but not all the variance in infant frontal EEG asymmetry.

Interestingly, when this analysis was repeated using only the infants of mothers without prenatal depression (postnatal only group), the results supported a mediation model. In this model, the direct path from maternal depression to infant EEG became nonsignificant after the addition of the path from mother's level of insensitivity to infant EEG. Mediation was not supported in the prenatal group (Dawson, 1999). This result provides support for the hypothesis that the mother's behaviors toward her infant, particularly insensitive behaviors, influence not only the infant's regulatory behaviors, but also frontal brain activity, which may be related to those behaviors. Specifically, high maternal insensitivity was found to be associated with reduced left frontal brain activation. That mediation was not supported for infants of mothers depressed during the prenatal period suggests that a different mechanism may be operating in the transmission of risk related to maternal depression from prenatally depressed mothers to their infants. This mechanism, reflected in the direct association between maternal depression and infant frontal brain activity, may relate to genetic or intrauterine factors.

STRESS RESPONSES: AUTONOMIC ACTIVITY
AND STRESS HORMONE LEVELS

In this section, we discuss the relation between maternal depression and infant and child stress responses as reflected in autonomic activity and stress hormone levels.

Functional and Developmental Considerations

The principle of homeostasis underlies both autonomic activity and stress-related endocrine activity. Stressful events activate both the sympathetic and parasympathetic components of the autonomic nervous system. The sympathetic nervous system mobilizes the body to respond to the stressor in various ways (e.g., by increasing heart rate). To restore homeostasis, the parasympathetic nervous system reacts to slow down physiological processes, such as increased heart rate. Parasympathetic activity is often measured using *vagal tone*, a measure of the neural control of the heart by the 10th cranial nerve. Vagal tone is evaluated by quantifying the amplitude of the respiratory sinus arrhythmia using heart rate data from an electrocardiogram (Porges, Doussard-Roosevelt, & Maiti, 1994). Stress-related hormonal responses are mediated by the hypothalamic-pituitary-adrenal (HPA) axis, which activates in response to stress and leads to the secretion of cortisol, the primary peripheral stress hormone. Stress-related hormonal responses, such as the secretion of cortisol, also restore homeostasis through negative feedback loops.

Researchers have linked individual differences in emotion expression and regulation with specific variations in heart rate, vagal tone, and HPA axis activity (Boyce, Barr, & Zeltzer, 1992; Fox, 1994; Fox & Fitzgerald, 1990; Gunnar, 1992). For example, Kagan and colleagues (Kagan, 1982; Kagan, Reznick, Clarke, Snidman, & Garcia-Coll, 1984) reported an association between high and stable heart rate and behavioral inhibition. Porges et al. (1994) reported correlations between vagal tone and autonomic reactivity, emotion expression, and self-regulation. Higher vagal tone was associated with larger autonomic responses, greater facial expressivity in 5-month-old infants, and higher soothability in 3-month-old infants. Finally, negative emotions have been associated with activation of the HPA axis stress response (Stansbury & Gunnar, 1994).

Stansbury and Gunnar (1994) have suggested that increased activity of the HPA axis in response to stress is associated with a lack of control of the stressor and decreased availability of coping resources rather than to negative emotional valence per se. For example, rats exposed to inescapable electric shocks exhibit significantly higher corticosterone levels than rats exposed to avoidable shocks (Weiss, 1971), and the presence of a familiar social group attenuates the adrenocortical response of squirrel monkeys subjected to maternal separation (Levine & Wiener, 1988). Over time, the absence of effective coping resources and strategies may affect the development of stress responses.

Environmental Influences on Development

Parent–infant interactions play an important role in the development of effective self-regulatory strategies and, consequently, may influence the development of the infant's ability to regulate stress responses. Moreover, evidence from both animal and human studies suggests that the effects of these early interactions may persist well beyond infancy into adulthood.

An extensive animal literature describes the effects of early environmental events on the modulation of the HPA response to stress. In rats, early postnatal handling has been found to result in a decreased glucocorticoid response to stress (Francis et al., 1996; Meaney, Aitken, van Berkel, Bhatnagar, & Sapolsky, 1988), and prolonged maternal separation (3 hours or more) has been shown to lead to elevated glucocorticoid levels in response to stress (Kuhn, Pauk, & Schanberg, 1990; Kuhn & Schanberg, 1998; Pihoker, Owens, Kuhn, Schanberg, & Nemeroff, 1993). Longitudinal studies have shown that these effects can persist into adulthood (Ladd, Owens, & Nemeroff, 1996; Plotsky & Meaney, 1993). Recent research suggests that these effects result from early alterations in glucocorticoid receptor expression in brain regions, such as the frontal cortex and hippocampus, that influence negative feedback regulation of HPA axis activity (Francis et al., 1996). Evidence suggests that early handling leads to increased receptor expression and increased negative feedback efficacy, whereas early separation yields the opposite response (Francis et al., 1996).

Recent findings also provide suggestive evidence that maternal behaviors can influence HPA axis responsiveness. Francis et al. (1996) have reported a significant negative correlation between the frequency of maternal behaviors, such as licking, grooming, and arch-backed nursing, and the magnitude of corticosterone responses to stress. In addition, Suchecki, Rosenfeld, and Levine (1993) have demonstrated that specific maternal behaviors, such as feeding and stroking, can weaken the adrenocortical response to maternal deprivation. In mother-deprived rat pups, feeding has been shown to inhibit corticosterone secretion and stroking to suppress ACTH secretion. Research suggests that the attenuating effects of these behaviors are specific to maternal stimuli, as opposed to nonspecific social stimuli (Stanton & Levine, 1990).

Research with nonhuman primates (squirrel monkeys and rhesus macaques) has also demonstrated increases in HPA responses to stress following maternal separation. In a review of psychoendocrine responses to disruptions in the mother–infant relationship in nonhuman primates, Levine and Wiener (1988) described plasma cortisol elevations in response to maternal separation in squirrel monkeys and rhesus macaques and found them to be significantly and positively correlated with the duration of maternal separation. For these nonhuman primates, the presence of a familiar social group or visual access to the mother during separation was found to buffer the endocrine effects of disruptions to mother–infant relationships. This finding provides evidence that the availability of coping resources, such as a stable, predictable environment or ability to vocalize to the mother, can attenuate the adrenocortical response to stress.

Although it would be unethical to conduct such studies on human infants, naturalistic forms of early deprivation sometimes occur in human populations. One such tragic case occurred in Romania, where orphanage children experienced significant deprivation before their adoption into homes in Europe, Canada, and the United States. In a follow-up study, Gunnar and Chisholm (1999) found that, similar to animal models of early deprivation, early institutional rearing had lasting effects on stress hormone levels. Approximately 6 years after adoption, children who had experienced 8 or more months of institutional rearing displayed significantly higher salivary cortisol levels compared to sex, age, and socioeconomically matched controls and compared to children who had experienced 4 or fewer months of institutional life. In addition, longer exposure to deprivation was associated with higher evening cortisol levels, and secure attachment moderated the effects of institutional rearing.

Secure attachment also played a moderating role in the relation between salivary cortisol levels and behavioral inhibition in 18-month-old children. Nachmias, Gunnar, Mangelsdorf, Parritz, and Buss (1996) exposed inhibited and uninhibited toddlers to a novel situation and found that only the inhibited toddlers, who were also insecurely attached to their mothers, displayed significant elevations in salivary cortisol. In a similar study, Gunnar, Brodersen, Nachmias, Buss, and Rigatuso (1996) found that attachment security buffers the cortisol response of more fearful 15-month-olds to inoculation distress. Fearful toddlers who were also insecurely attached displayed elevated cortisol levels. These studies provide evidence for the importance of sensitive, responsive caretaking early in life in the modulation of the HPA axis.

Impact of Maternal Depression

Animal and human research demonstrating the long-term impact of early life stress on stress response systems raises the question: Do less profound forms of early stress, such as exposure to maternal depression, also have long-term consequences for the regulation of stress responses? In our research, we have hypothesized that maternal depression may be stressful for infants in several ways and, consequently, may lead to disruptions in the development of stress responses. First, given that maternal depression affects how mothers behave with their infants, infants may experience a depressed mother's behaviors as stressful. Second, the depressed mother's inability to model effective self-regulatory strategies and to provide regulatory assistance may increase the stressful nature of mother–infant interactions by not providing the infant with effective coping strategies in distressing situations. Third, given the episodic nature of depression, the infant may experience the mother's behaviors as less stable and predictable, and evidence from animal models suggests that unpredictable caretaking can affect stress responses (Coplan et al., 1996).

Few data exist on the effects of maternal depression on children's stress responses, but the available evidence so far provides support for the above hypotheses. In one study, Field et al. (1988) examined infant heart rate, vagal tone, and cortisol levels during mother–infant interactions. The infants of depressed mothers had higher heart rate, lower vagal tone, and higher cortisol levels than infants of nondepressed mothers, suggesting that infants of depressed mothers experienced interactions with their mothers as stressful. In addition, during the interactions, infants of depressed mothers displayed more frequent "depressed" behaviors, such as gaze aversion, decreased physical activity, fewer facial expressions, and fewer vocalizations.

Dawson and her colleagues have investigated the association between maternal depression and children's stress responses by examining autonomic activity of 13–15-month-old infants of depressed and nondepressed mothers (Dawson et al., in press). The infants' heart rates were recorded during a baseline condition and during two social conditions, which consisted of playing with the mother and playing with a familiar adult. Compared to infants of nondepressed and subthreshold depressed mothers, infants of mothers with major depression exhibited elevated heart rates across all conditions. These results are consistent with past studies demonstrating that infants of depressed mothers tend to exhibit higher arousal levels as reflected in higher heart rates, especially during social interaction, than do infants of nondepressed mothers.

In a longitudinal study conducted by Hessl and colleagues (Hessl et al., 1996), salivary cortisol levels were measured in these same children when they were 3½ years of age, both at baseline and in response to a mild laboratory stressor. At baseline, preschool children of depressed mothers had higher salivary cortisol levels than children of nondepressed mothers (Hessl et al., 1996). Furthermore, because animal research (e.g., Ladd et al., 1996; Plotsky & Meaney, 1993) shows that early life stress may lead to long-term disruptions in HPA responses to stress, analyses were conducted that explored the relation between maternal depression during specific years of the child's life and the child's stress hormone responses. Results indicated that the number of months of prenatal depression was the best predictor of preschool children's baseline cortisol levels (Dawson, 1999). This finding is not surprising considering that maturity of the central nervous system (CNS) during the early postnatal life of a rat pup corresponds approximately to the CNS maturity of a 24-week gestational age human fetus (Graham, Heim, Goodman, Miller, & Nemeroff, 1999). Although these results are tentative and require replication, they suggest that human psychobiological systems (like animal systems) may have sensitive periods in terms of the influences of early life stress, such as maternal depression, on their functioning.

SUMMARY

In this chapter, we have posited that children of depressed mothers are at risk for negative outcomes in part because of the effect of depressed mothers' behaviors on early developing psychobiological systems related to emotion expression and regulation. Research findings suggest that, as early as infancy and the neonatal period, maternal depression is associated with disturbances in behavior and psychobiology. Compared to infants of nondepressed mothers, infants with depressed mothers display less optimal behaviors, including greater irritability and withdrawal, lower activity levels, and more negative facial expressions. In terms of their psychophysiology, these infants exhibit reduced left frontal electrical brain activity and increased autonomic activity, especially during social interactions. Evidence suggests that depressed mothers' behaviors, especially insensitive behaviors, may partially account for these effects. Thus, infants of depressed mothers may not only experience more negative affect than other infants, they may also lack appropriate parental support to develop adaptive regulatory strategies to cope with distressing emotions. These factors, taken together, may operate to increase risk for developing depression as well as other emotional problems later in life.

IMPLICATIONS FOR CLINICIANS

Because research has demonstrated that maternal depression is associated with negative behavioral and physiological outcomes as early as the neonatal period, the need for early interventions to prevent negative outcomes is quite substantial. Prenatal depression screening by health care professionals may be one way to reduce negative outcomes. Identifying depressed mothers during the prenatal period and connecting them with mental health services may mitigate both prenatal and early postnatal risks associated with maternal depression. In addition, physiological markers, such as atypical EEG activity and elevated cortisol levels, may permit early identification of children who are most at risk for negative outcomes, and these children may be appropriate targets for early intervention. Field (1998) has proposed several possible interventions for at-risk mother–child dyads, including massage therapy for infants, music therapy and massage therapy for mothers, and interaction coaching for mothers. She reported that infants who received massage therapy cried less, had lower salivary cortisol levels, and spent more time in active awake states than infants with depressed mothers who had not received such therapy. Mothers who received music and massage therapies had attenuated atypical frontal EEG activation. In addition, mothers who received interaction coaching became more animated and sensitive to their infants' signals than depressed mothers who had not received such coaching. These results are promising, but more effort is needed to assure the most optimal outcomes for children of depressed mothers. It is likely that early interventions are most beneficial when coupled with psychotherapy and medication to treat the mother's depression.

FUTURE DIRECTIONS

This chapter has presented psychobiological factors involved in the transmission of risk from depressed mother to offspring, but the challenge of future research is to integrate these factors with other contributing factors in order to develop a more comprehensive model of risk. Such factors may include aspects of the mother–child relationship (e.g., attachment), maternal behaviors, contextual risk factors (e.g., marital conflict), genetic influences, and aspects of the prenatal environment. In a recent article, Goodman and Gotlib (1999) have proposed one such integrative model. The research reported in this chapter takes a step toward testing more complex theoretical models, but much research remains to be done. In addition, because not all children of depressed mothers develop negative outcomes, researchers should examine resilience in this population. What are the moderators of risk? How do protective factors interact with risk factors to yield positive outcomes? These analyses are important for gaining a comprehensive understanding of risk and resilience in children of depressed mothers, and, ultimately, for designing effective intervention programs.

REFERENCES

Abrams, S. M., Field, T., Scafidi, F., & Prodromidis, M. (1995). Newborns of depressed mothers. *Infant Mental Health Journal, 16*(3), 233–239.

Anderson, S. W., Bechara, A., Damasio, H., Tranel, D., & Damasio, A. R. (1999). Impairment of social and moral behavior related to early damage in human prefrontal cortex. *Nature Neuroscience, 2,* 1032–1037.

Aslin, R. M., Pisoni, D. B., & Jusczyk, P. W. (1983). Auditory development and speech perception in infancy. In P. H. Mussen (Series Ed.) & M. M. Haith & J. J. Campos (Vol. Eds.), *Handbook of child psychology: Vol. 2. Infancy and developmental psychobiology* (4th ed., pp. 573–687). New York: Wiley.

Black, J. E., Jones, T. A., Nelson, C. A., & Greenough, W. T. (1998). Neuronal plasticity and the developing brain. In J. D. Noshpitz (Series Ed.), & N. E. Alessi, J. T. Coyle, S. I. Harrison, & S. Eth (Vol. Eds.), *Handbook of child and adolescent psychiatry: Vol. 6. Basic psychiatric science and treatment* (pp. 31–53). New York: John Wiley & Sons.

Boyce, W. T., Barr, R. G., & Zeltzer, L. K. (1992). Temperament and the psychobiology of childhood stress. *Pediatrics, 90,* 483–486.

Bruner, J. S. (1977). Early social interaction and language acquisition. In H. R. Schaffer (Ed.), *Studies in mother–infant interaction* (pp. 271–289). London: Academic Press.

Campos, J. J., Barrett, K. C., Lamb, M. E., Goldsmith, H. H., & Sternberg, C. R. (1983). Socioemotional development. In M. M. Haith & J. J. Campos (Eds.), P. H. Mussen (Series Ed.), *Handbook of child psychology: Vol 2. Infancy and developmental psychobiology* (pp. 783–915). New York: Wiley.

Campos, J. J., Campos, R. G., & Barrett, K. C. (1989). Emergent themes in the study of emotional development and emotion regulation. *Developmental Psychology, 25,* 394–402.

Cohn, J. F., Mataias, R., Tronick, E. Z., Connell, D., & Lyons-Ruth, D. (1986). Face-to-face interactions of depressed mothers and their infants. In E. Z. Tronick & T. Field (Eds.), *Maternal depression and infant disturbance* (pp. 31–45). San Francisco: Jossey-Bass.

Cohn, J. F., & Tronick, E. Z. (1989). Specificity of infants' response to mothers' affective behavior. *Journal of the American Academy of Child and Adolescent Psychiatry, 28,* 242–248.

Coplan, J. D., Andrews, M. W., Rosenblum, L. A., Owens, M. J., Friedman, S., Gorman, J. M., & Nemeroff, C. B. (1996). Persistent elevations of cerebrospinal fluid concentrations of corticotropin-releasing factor in adult nonhuman primates exposed to early-life stressors: Implications for the pathophysiology of mood and anxiety disorders. *Proceedings of the National Academy of Sciences, USA, 93,* 1619–1623.

Damasio, A. R. (1995). On some functions of the human prefrontal cortex. In J. Grafman, K. J. Holyoak, & F. Boller (Eds.), *Annals of the New York Academy of Sciences: Vol. 769. Structure and functions of the human prefrontal cortex* (pp. 241–251). New York: New York Academy of Sciences.

Davidson, R. J. (1987). Cerebral asymmetry and the nature of emotion: Implications for the study of individual differences and psychopathology. In R. Takahashi, P. Flor-Henry, J. Gruzelier, & S. Niwa (Eds.), *Cerebral dynamics, laterality, and psychopathology* (pp. 71–83). New York: Elsevier.

Davidson, R. J. (2000). Affective style, psychopathology, and resilience: Brain mechanisms and plasticity. *American Psychologist, 55,* 1196–1214.

Davidson, R. J., Ekman, P., Saron, C., Senulis, R., & Friesen, W. V. (1990). Approach–withdrawal and cerebral asymmetry: I. Emotional expression and brain physiology. *Journal of Personality and Social Psychology, 58,* 330–341.

Davidson, R. J., & Fox, N. A. (1988). Cerebral asymmetry and emotion: Development and individual differences. In S. Segalowitz & D. Molfese (Eds.), *Developmental implications of brain lateralization* (pp. 191–206). New York: Guilford Press.

Davidson, R. J., & Fox, N. A. (1989). Frontal brain asymmetry predicts infants' response to maternal separation. *Journal of Abnormal Psychology, 98*, 127–131.

Dawson, G. (1994). Frontal electroencephalographic correlates of individual differences in emotional expression in infants: A brain systems perspective on emotion. *Monographs of the Society for Research in Child Development, 59*(2–3, Serial No. 240), 135–151.

Dawson, G. (1999, August). *The effects of maternal depression on children's emotional and psychobiological development.* Paper presented at a National Institutes of Health Conference on Parenting, Bethesda, MD.

Dawson, G., Ashman, S. B., Hessl, D., Spieker, S., Frey, K., Panagiotides, H., & Embry, L. (in press). Autonomic and brain electrical activity in securely- and insecurely-attached infants of depressed mothers. *Infant Behavior and Development.*

Dawson, G., Frey, K., Panagiotides, H., Osterling, J., & Hessl, D. (1997). Infants of depressed mothers exhibit atypical frontal brain activity: A replication and extension of previous findings. *Journal of Child Psychology and Psychiatry, 38*, 179–186.

Dawson, G., Frey, K., Panagiotides, H., Yamada, E., Hessl, D., & Osterling, J. (1999). Infants of depressed mothers exhibit atypical frontal electrical brain activity during interactions with mother and with a familiar, nondepressed adult. *Child Development, 70*, 1058–1066.

Dawson, G., Frey, K., Self, J., Panagiotides, H., Hessl, D., Yamada, E., & Rinaldi, J. (1999). Frontal electrical brain activity in infants of depressed mothers: Relation to variations in infant behavior. *Development and Psychopathology, 11*, 589–605.

Dawson, G., Grofer Klinger, L., Panagiotides, H., Hill, D., & Spieker, S. (1992). Frontal lobe activity and affective behavior of infants of mothers with depressive symptoms. *Child Development, 63*, 725–737.

Dawson, G., Grofer Klinger, L, Panagiotides, H., Spieker, S., & Frey, K. (1992). Infants of mothers with depressive symptoms: Electroencephalographic and behavioral findings related to attachment status. *Development and Psychopathology, 4*, 67–80.

Dawson, G., Panagiotides, H., Grofer Klinger, L., & Hill, D. (1992). The role of frontal lobe functioning in the development of self-regulatory behavior in infancy. *Brain and Cognition, 20*, 152–175.

Denham, S. A. (1998). *Emotional development in young children.* New York: Guilford Press.

Diamond, A., & Goldman-Rakic, P. S. (1989). Comparison of human infants and rhesus monkeys on Piaget's AB task: Evidence for dependence on dorsolateral prefrontal cortex. *Experimental Brain Research, 74*, 24–40.

Donovan, W. L., Leavitt, L. A., & Walsh, R. O. (1998). Conflict and depression predict maternal sensitivity to infant cries. *Infant Behavior and Development, 21*, 505–517.

Downey, G., & Coyne, J. (1990). Children of depressed parents: An integrative review. *Psychological Bulletin, 108*, 50–76.

Edelman, G. M. (1987). *Neural Darwinism: The theory of neuronal group selection.* New York: Basic Books.

Edelman, G. M. (1989). *The remembered present: A biological theory of consciousness.* New York: Basic Books.

Field, T. (1986). Models for reactive and chronic depression in infancy. In E. Z. Tronick & T. Field (Eds.), *Maternal depression and infant disturbance* (No. 34, pp. 47–60). San Francisco: Jossey-Bass.

Field, T. (1995). Infants of depressed mothers. *Infant Behavior and Development, 18,* 1–13.

Field, T. (1998). Maternal depression effects on infants and early interventions. *Preventive Medicine, 27,* 200–203.

Field, T., Fox, N. A., Pickens, J., & Nawrocki, T. (1995). Right frontal EEG activation in 3- to 6-month old infants of depressed mothers. *Development and Psychopathology, 31,* 358–363.

Field, T., Healy, B., Goldstein, S., Perry, S., Bendall, D., Schanberg, S., Zimmerman, E., & Kuhn, C. (1988). Infants of depressed mothers show "depressed" behavior even with non-depressed adults. *Child Development, 59,* 1569–1579.

Field, T., Lang, C., Martinez, A., Yando, R., Pickens, J., & Bendell, D. (1996). Preschool follow-up of infants of dysphoric mothers. *Journal of Clinical Child Psychology, 25*(3), 272–279.

Finman, R., Davidson, R. J., Colton, M. B., Straus, A. M., & Kagan, J. (1989). Psychophysiological correlates of inhibition to the unfamiliar in children (Abstract). *Psychophysiology, 26*(4A), S24.

Flor-Henry, P. (1979). On certain aspects of the localization of the cerebral systems regulating and determining emotion. *Biological Psychiatry, 14,* 677–698.

Fox, N. A. (1991). If it's not left, it's right: Electroencephalograph asymmetry and the development of emotion. *American Psychologist, 46,* 863–872.

Fox, N. A. (Ed.). (1994). The development of emotion regulation: Biological and behavioral considerations. *Monographs of the Society for Research in Child Development, 59*(2–3, Serial No. 240).

Fox, N. A., & Fitzgerald, H. E. (1990). Autonomic function in infancy. *Merrill–Palmer Quarterly, 36*(1), 27–52.

Francis, D., Diorio, J., LaPlante, P., Weaver, S., Seckl, J. R., & Meaney, M. J. (1996). The role of early environmental events in regulating neuroendocrine development: Moms, pups, stress, and glucocorticoid receptors. In C. F. Ferris & T. Grisso (Eds.), *Annals of the New York Academy of Sciences: Vol. 794. Understanding aggressive behavior in children* (pp. 136–152). New York: New York Academy of Sciences.

Fuster, J. M. (1989). *The prefrontal cortex: Anatomy, physiology, and neuropsychology of the frontal lobe.* New York: Raven Press.

Gainotti, G. (1969). Reactions "catatrophiques" et manifestations d'indifférence au cours des atteintes cerebrais ["Catastrophic" reactions and manifestations of indifference during cerebral disorders]. *Neuropsychologia, 7,* 195–204.

Gainotti, G. (1972). Emotional behavior and hemispheric side of lesion. *Cortex, 8,* 41–55.

Goldman-Rakic, P. S. (1987). Circuitry of primate prefrontal cortex and regulation of behavior by representational memory. In F. Plum (Ed.), *Handbook of physiology: Section 1. The nervous system. Vol. 5. Higher functions of the brain* (pp. 373–417). Bethesda, MD: American Physiological Society.

Goodman, S. H., & Gotlib, I. H. (1999). Risk for psychopathology in the children of depressed mothers: A developmental model for understanding mechanisms of transmission. *Psychological Review, 106,* 458–490.

Graham, Y. P., Heim, C., Goodman, S. H., Miller, A. H., & Nemeroff, C. B. (1999). The effects of neonatal stress on brain development: Implications for psychopathology. *Development and Psychopathology, 11,* 545–565.

Gross, D., Conrad, B., Fogg, L., Willis, L., & Garvey, C. (1995). A longitudinal study of maternal depression and preschool children's mental health. *Nursing Research, 44*(2), 96–101.

Gunnar, M. R. (1992). Reactivity of the hypothalamic-pituitary-adrenocortical system to stressors in normal infants and children. *Pediatrics, 90,* 491–497.

Gunnar, M. R., Broderson, L., Nachmias, M., Buss, K., & Rigatuso, J. (1996). Stress reactivity and attachment security. *Developmental Psychobiology, 29*(3), 191–204.

Gunnar, M. R., & Chisholm, K. C. (1999, April). *Effects of early institutional rearing and attachment quality on salivary cortisol levels in adopted Romanian children.* Poster session presented at the biennial meeting of the Society for Research in Child Development, Albuquerque, NM.

Hart, S., Field, T., del Valle, C., & Pelaez-Nogueras, M. (1998). Depressed mothers' interactions with their one-year-old infants. *Infant Behavior and Development, 21,* 519–525.

Hebb, D. O. (1949). *The organization of behavior: A neuropsychological theory.* New York: Wiley.

Hécaen, II. (1964). Mental symptoms associated with tumors of the frontal lobe. In J. M. Warren & K. Akert (Eds.), *The frontal granular cortex and behavior* (pp. 335–352). New York: McGraw-Hill.

Heller, W. (1990). The neuropsychology of emotion: Developmental patterns and implications for psychopathology. In N. L. Stein, B. Leventhal, & T. Trabasso (Eds.), *Psychological and biological approaches to emotion* (pp. 167–211). Hillsdale, NJ: Erlbaum.

Hessl, D., Dawson, G., Frey, K., Panagiotides, H., Self, J., Yamada, E., & Osterling, J. (1996, May). *A longitudinal study of children of depressed mothers: Psychobiological findings related to stress.* Poster session presented at the National Institute of Mental Health Conference for Advancing Research on Developmental Plasticity, Chantilly, VA.

Huttenlocher, P. R. (1994). Synaptogenesis in human cerebral cortex. In G. Dawson & K. W. Fischer (Eds.), *Human behavior and the developing brain* (pp. 137–152). New York: Guilford.

Huttenlocher, P. R., & Dabholkar, A. S. (1997). Developmental anatomy of prefrontal cortex. In N. A. Krasnegor, G. R. Lyon, & P. S. Goldman-Rakic (Eds.), *Development of the prefrontal cortex* (pp. 69–83). Baltimore, MD: Paul H. Brookes.

Jones, B. M., & Mishkin, M. (1972). Limbic lesions and the problem of stimulus reinforcement association. *Experimental Neurology, 36,* 362–377.

Jones, N. A., Field, T., Fox, N. A., Davalos, M., Lundy, B., & Hart, S. (1998). Newborns of mothers with depressive symptoms are physiologically less developed. *Infant Behavior and Development, 21,* 537–541.

Jones, N. A., Field, T., Fox, N. A., Davalos, M., Malphurs, J., Carraway, K., Schanberg, S., & Kuhn, C. (1997). Infants of intrusive and withdrawn mothers. *Infant Behavior and Development, 20*(2), 175–186.

Jones, N. A., Field, T., Fox, N. A., Lundy, B., & Davalos, M. (1997). EEG activation in 1-month-old infants of depressed mothers. *Development and Psychopathology, 9,* 491–505.

Kagan, J. (1982). Heart rate and heart rate variability as signs of temperamental dimension infants. In C. E. Izard (Ed.), *Measuring emotions in infants and children* (pp. 38–66). Cambridge, England: Cambridge University Press.

Kagan, J., Reznick, J. S., Clarke, C., Snidman, N., & Garcia-Coll, C. (1984). Behavioral inhibition to the unfamiliar. *Child Development, 55,* 2212–2225.

Kinsbourne, M., & Bemporad, B. (1984). Lateralization of emotion: A model and the evidence. In N. A. Fox & R. J. Davidson (Eds.), *The psychobiology of affective development* (pp. 259–291). Hillsdale, NJ: Erlbaum.

Klinnert, M. D., Campos, J., Sorce, J., Emde, R. N., & Svejda, J. (1983). Emotions as behavior regulators: Social referencing. In R. Plutchik & H. Kellerman (Eds.), *Emotion: Theory, research, and experience. Vol. 2. Emotions in early development* (pp. 57–86). New York: Academic Press.

Kolb, B. (1989). Brain development, plasticity, and behavior. *American Psychologist, 44,* 1203–1212.

Kuhn, C. M., Pauk, J., & Schanberg, S. M. (1990). Endocrine responses to mother–infant separation in developing rats. *Developmental Psychobiology, 23,* 395–410.

Kuhn, C. M., & Schanberg, S. M. (1998). Responses to maternal separation: Mechanisms and mediators. *International Journal of Developmental Neuroscience, 16*(3/4), 261–270.

Ladd, C. O., Owens, M. J., & Nemeroff, C. B. (1996). Persistent changes in corticotropin-releasing factor neuronal systems induced by maternal deprivation. *Endocrinology, 137,* 1212–1218.

Levine, S., & Wiener, S. G. (1988). Psychoendocrine aspects of mother–infant relationships in nonhuman primates. *Psychoneuroendocrinology, 13*(1–2), 143–154.

Lundy, B. L., Jones, N. A., Field, T., Nearing, G., Davalos, M., Pietro, P. A., Schanberg, S., & Kuhn, C. (1999). Prenatal depression effects on neonates. *Infant Behavior and Development, 22*(1), 119–129.

Luria, A. R. (1980). *Higher cortical functions in man.* New York: Basic Books. (Original work published 1966)

Malatesta, C. Z., Culver, C., Tesman, J. R., & Shepard, B. (1989). The development of emotion expression during the first two years of life. *Monographs of the Society for Research in Child Development, 54*(1–2, Serial No. 219).

Malatesta, C. Z., & Haviland, J. M. (1982). Learning display rules: The socialization of emotion expression in infancy. *Child Development, 53*, 991–1003.

Meaney, M. J., Aitken, D. H., van Berkel, C., Bhatnagar, S., & Sapolsky, R. M. (1988). Effect of neonatal handling on age-related impairments associated with the hippocampus. *Science, 239*, 766–768.

Milner, B., Petrides, M., & Smith, M. L. (1985). Frontal lobes and the temporal organization of memory. *Human Neurobiology, 4*, 137–142.

Murray, L., & Cooper, P. J. (1997). Postpartum depression and child development. *Psychological Medicine, 27*, 253–260.

Murray, L., Fiori-Cowley, A., Hooper, R., & Cooper, P. (1996). The impact of postnatal depression and associated adversity on early mother–infant interactions and later infant outcome. *Child Development, 67*, 2512–2526.

Nachmias, M., Gunnar, M., Mangelsdorf, S., Parritz, R. H., & Buss, K. (1996). Behavioral inhibition and stress reactivity: The moderating role of attachment security. *Child Development, 67*, 508–522.

Piaget, J. (1954). *The construction of reality in the child.* New York: International University Press.

Pihoker, C., Owens, M. J., Kuhn, C. M., Schanberg, S. M., & Nemeroff, C. B. (1993). Maternal separation in neonatal rats elicits activation of the hypothalamic-pituitary-adrenocortical axis: A putative role for corticotropin-releasing factor. *Psychoneuroendocrinology, 18*(7), 485–493.

Plotsky, P. M., & Meaney, M. J. (1993). Early, postnatal experience alters hypothalamic corticotropin-releasing factor (CRF) mRNA, median eminence CRF content and stress-induced release in adult rats. *Molecular Brain Research, 18*, 195–200.

Porges, S. W., Doussard-Roosevelt, J. A., & Maiti, A. K. (1994). Vagal tone and the physiological regulation of emotion. *Monographs of the Society for Research in Child Development, 59*(2–3, Serial No. 240), 167–186.

Radke-Yarrow, M. (1998). *Children of depressed mothers: From early childhood to maturity.* Cambridge, England: Cambridge University Press.

Robinson, R. G., & Benson, D. F. (1981). Depression in aphasic patients: Frequency, severity, and clinical-pathological correlations. *Brain and Language, 14*, 282–291.

Robinson, R. G., Kubos, K. L., Starr, L. B., Reo, K., & Price, T. R. (1984). Mood disorders in stroke patients: Importance of location of lesion. *Brain, 107*, 81–93.

Robinson, R. G., & Stetela, B. (1981). Mood change following left hemispheric brain injury. *Annals of Neurology, 9*, 447–453.

Scaife, M., & Bruner, J. S. (1975). The capacity for joint visual attention in the infant. *Nature, 253*, 265–266.

Stansbury, K., & Gunnar, M. R. (1994). Adrenocortical activity and emotion regulation. *Monographs of the Society for Research in Child Development, 59*(2–3, Serial No. 240), 108–134.

Stanton, M. E., & Levine, S. (1990). Inhibition of infant glucocorticoid stress response: Specific role of maternal cues. *Developmental Psychobiology, 23*, 411–426.

Stern, D. (1985). *The interpersonal world of the infant.* New York: Basic Books.

Suchecki, D., Rosenfeld, P., & Levine, S. (1993). Maternal regulation of the hypothalamic-pituitary-adrenal axis in the infant rat: The roles of feeding and stroking. *Developmental Brain Research, 75*, 185–192.

Tronick, E. Z. (1989). Emotions and emotional communication in infants. *American Psychologist, 44*, 112–119.

Tronick, E. Z., & Gianino, A. F. (1986). The transmission of maternal disturbances to the infant. In E. Z. Tronick & T. Field (Eds.), *Maternal depression and infant disturbance* (pp. 5–11). San Francisco: Jossey-Bass.

Tucker, D. M., & Williamson, P. A. (1984). Asymmetric neural control systems in human self-regulation. *Psychological Review, 91*, 185–215.

Uytdenhoef, P., Portelange, P., Jacquy, J., Charles, G., Linkowski, P., & Mendlewicz, J. (1983). Regional cerebral blood flow and lateralized hemispheric dysfunction in depression. *British Journal of Psychiatry, 143*, 128–132.

Watson, J. S. (1979). Perception of contingencies as a determinant of social responsiveness. In E. B. Thoman (Ed.), *The origins of the infant's social responsiveness* (pp. 33–64). Hillsdale, NJ: Erlbaum.

Weiss, J. M. (1971). Effects of coping behavior with and without a feedback signal on stress pathology in rats. *Journal of Comparative and Physiological Psychology, 77*, 22–30.

4

PRENATAL EFFECTS OF MATERNAL DEPRESSION

TIFFANY M. FIELD

The maternal depression literature over the past 15 years has generally reported that a mother's depressive interaction with her young infant is a source of negative effects on the infant. Several studies have noted growth and developmental delays for infants whose mothers remained depressed for at least the first 6 months of the infants' life. These studies highlighted the need for very early interventions. Short-term mood inductions for the mothers and more comprehensive day care and home visit interventions for the mothers and infants were then studied. More recent research on chronically depressed mothers suggests that infants of depressed mothers may be affected as early as birth. These findings highlight the need for even earlier prenatal interventions. Even newborns born to depressed mothers appeared to have a profile of "depressive" behavior and physiology and a pattern of neurotransmitter–neurohormone activity that mimicked their mothers' profile, suggesting maternal depression effects on the fetus. Although the *Diagnostic and*

I wish to thank the infants and parents who participated in these studies as well as the research assistants who helped with the data collection. This research was supported by National Institute of Mental Health (NIMH) Merit Award Research Grant MH46586 and NIMH Senior Research Scientist Award MH00331.

Statistical Manual of Mental Disorders (4th ed.; *DSM–IV*; American Psychiatric Association, 1994) does not feature a diagnosis for infant depression, chronic maternal depression effects may appear as early as the prenatal period. Because most chronically depressed women are unwilling to take medications during pregnancy, psychology is challenged to find alternative preventive treatments. This literature also highlights the importance of genetic studies including adoption and twin research to assess potential genetically mediated risk factors for newborn depression.

Whereas about 10% of nonrisk community samples experience clinical depression in the postpartum period, in at least one sample less than 2% of women experienced depression continuing past 6 months, and 80% of them recovered relatively quickly without treatment and without significantly affecting their infants' development (Campbell & Cohn, 1997). However, in communities with other risk factors such as poverty, significant numbers of women are chronically depressed (Field, 1995). For this group, maternal depression appears to affect prenatal, neonatal, and infant development.

The purpose of this chapter is to review studies on this high-risk group including early intervention studies that may help inform clinicians' referrals. Most of the studies on this high-risk population were conducted by our group and therefore are presented in detail. However, studies from other labs are also briefly reviewed whenever relevant or if they served as models for our studies. In most of these studies the mothers were chronically depressed (dysthymic) as well as having other risk factors including low socioeconomic status (SES). In some studies the mothers were adolescent, another notable risk factor for maternal unavailability to infants. These risk factors are potential confounds. However, the depressed and nondepressed mothers came from the same SES and age groups, so depression was an additional factor for the group labeled *depressed* and seemingly the only way in which the depressed and nondepressed groups differed.

In most of the studies reviewed, *depression* was defined as protracted state of low mood or dysthymia, typically determined by the Beck Depression Inventory (BDI; Beck et al., 1961) or Center for Epidemiological Studies Depression Scale (CES-D; Radloff, 1977) combined with a diagnostic interview (often the Diagnostic Interview Survey [DISC]). Although these measures have been noted to be significantly correlated (Wilcox, Field, Prodromidis, & Scafidi, 1996), more mothers have been classified as depressed on the basis of the BDI or CES-D alone and not the DISC, which suggests that combining one of these with the diagnostic interview yields false positives. Differential diagnosis is one of the primary methodological difficulties conducting research with this population. Other problems include noncompliance with the treatment and the research assessment process, which probably relates to those other risk factors including poverty, minority status, lack of education and learned helplessness of the women, and in some cases age.

This review starts with research conducted 15 years ago when interactions between young infants and their mothers were the primary focus of the research field on depressed mothers and their infants. Soon thereafter, many laboratory studies were conducted on the infants' affect perception and production using face and voice stimuli to determine maternal depression effects on the infant's emotional development. Next the review turns to newborn studies in which investigators attempted to explore the infants' contribution to the disturbed mother–infant interactions. Because the newborns were showing behavioral, physiological, and hormonal patterns that mimicked their mothers' patterns, the research turned to the prenatal period and differences in fetal actions and responses to stimulation. The longitudinal research that highlighted the need for intervention at all stages from the prenatal period across infancy is then reviewed. This research suggests that different types of maternal depression may result in different infant outcomes and may require different interventions. The chapter concludes with a review of early intervention studies showing that maternal depression effects can be ameliorated in at least the short term.

MOTHER–INFANT INTERACTIONS

Fifteen years ago, the primary focus in the field of maternal depression effects was the interactions between the mothers and their young infants. In 1983 Cohn and Tronick published one of the first studies on the effects of maternal depression on young infants. In this study they simulated maternal depression by having mothers show a still-face during a brief face-to-face interaction with their infant. Using this technique they were able to document negative effects of very brief periods of simulated maternal depression on infants of nondepressed mothers. The infants showed significantly greater amounts of protest behavior followed by distress behavior. In 1984 Field used this simulated maternal depression technique with infants of naturally depressed mothers. The infants of depressed mothers did not react with protest and distress in the same way that the infants of nondepressed mothers did in the Cohn and Tronick (1983) study. Instead, the infants showed inattentive behavior and flat affect. These findings suggested that the infants of depressed mothers had already become accustomed to this type of unresponsive, emotionally unavailable behavior and therefore did not protest or show distress behavior. Field (1984) described the infants of depressed mothers as mirror images of their mothers.

Many subsequent studies by Cohn, Tronick, Lyons-Ruth, Field, and their colleagues engaged the mothers and infants in a mother–infant interaction context at the optimal time for those interactions, namely when the infants were between the ages of 3 and 6 months. The depressed mothers were documented as being unresponsive, noncontingent, and emotionally unavailable. The infants were similarly inactive and were less facially and vocally expressive. The interactions were measured for many time series phenomena such as the mothers and infants being in similar or different states, the synchrony of their behaviors, and the synchrony of behaviors and heart rates. Whereas the nondepressed mothers and their infants appeared to be having smooth, harmonious interactions in which the infants were quickly learning rudimentary conversation rules, the face-to-face interactions of the depressed mothers and their infants were choppy, uncoordinated and unpleasant to observe (Field et al., 1988). The mothers' and infants' elevated heart rates and stress hormones (salivary cortisol) suggested that they were being stressed by their interactions together. Parenthetically, the stressful nature of their interactions may explain why significantly fewer depressed mothers (25% vs. 66%) breastfeed their infants (Campbell & Cohn, 1997).

Laboratory Studies on Affect Perception and Production

Soon after the mother–infant interaction studies became popular, some investigators turned to laboratory studies of mothers' emotional expressions and infants' perception and production of facial and vocal expressions. These studies on affect perception and production suggested that (a) depressed mothers exhibited fewer positive faces and fewer animated faces and voices (Raag et al., 1997); (b) infants of depressed mothers produced more sad and angry faces and showed fewer expressions of interest (Pickens & Field, 1993b), (c) they also showed a preference for sad faces and voices as expressed by greater looking time at videotaped models that looked and sounded sad (Pickens & Field, 1993b), which might relate to sad expressions being more familiar to them; (d) they also displayed less accurate matching of happy facial expressions with happy vocal expressions as early as the neonatal period (Lundy, Field, & Pickens, 1997), and (e) during a "mother holding doll" situation, 1-year-old infants of depressed mothers showed less protest behavior, suggesting a continuity of flat affect across the first year (Hart, Field, DelValle, & Letourneau, 1998).

Field summarized this early research on depressed mother–infant interactions and limited affect in a model entitled *psychobiological attunement* (Field, 1985). In this model, depressed mothers were seen as emotionally unavailable to their infants and therefore unable to provide adequate stimulation and arousal modulation. External regulation, in this model, is required from caregivers for infants to develop adequate self-regulation. Tronick and Gianino (1986) developed a similar model entitled *mutual regulation*. Much of this early research was summarized in a volume edited by Tronick and Field (1996) called *Maternal Depression and Infant Disturbance*. This absence of maternal regulation may have contributed to the dysregulation noted in these young infants, and the infants' dysregulation in turn could have also derived from prenatal influences.

Infant Depression Emerges at the Newborn Stage

Attempts were then made to explore the infants' contributions to the disturbed mother–infant interactions. Recent data revealed that many infants of chronically depressed mothers were affected prenatally (or genetically) and showed different behavior as early as birth. These behavior differences at birth may in turn contribute to the interaction disturbances that had been documented in the literature. Infants of depressed mothers were noted to have a profile of dysregulation as early as the neonatal period. This dysregulation profile could be characterized by (a) limited responsivity on the Brazelton Neonatal Behavior Assessment Scale (Brazelton, 1973). and limited attentiveness and responsiveness to facial expressions (Abrams, Field, Scafidi, & Prodromidis, 1995; Lundy et al., 1997), fussiness and inconsolability (Whiffen & Gottlib, 1989; Zuckerman, Als, Bauchner, Parker & Cabral, 1990), excessive indeterminate (disorganized) sleep and elevated stress hormones (norepinephrine and cortisol) at the neonatal period (Lundy et al., 1999) and (b) relative right frontal EEG activation at 1 week (Jones, Field, Lundy, Davalos, & Fox 1997), which has been associated with depression in adults (Henriques & Davidson, 1990) and negative affect, withdrawn, inhibited behavior, fear, and anxiety in infants and children (Fox, 1994; Fox et al., 1995).

This dysregulation was noted to continue across the first year of infancy and was characterized by (a) relative right frontal EEG activation at 1 month (Jones, Field, Lundy, et al., 1997) and at 3 months (Field, Fox, Pickens, Nawrocki, & Soutullo, 1995) and stability of these patterns from 3 months to 3 years (Jones, Field, Davalos, & Pickens, 1997); (b) limited responsivity to facial expressions (Field, Pickens, Fox, Nawrocki, & Gonzalez, 1995); (c) lower vagal tone, or heart rate variability, and signs of neurological delays at 6 months (Field, 1992); and (d) limited play and exploratory behavior, inferior Bayley mental and motor development scores at 2 months (Whiffen & Gotlib, 1989) and at 12 months (Hart et al., 1998; Hay, 1997), and delayed growth at 12 months (Hay, 1997).

Compared to the performance of infants born to nondepressed mothers, lesser performance on the Brazelton Neonatal Behavior Assessment Scale by the newborns of depressed mothers included less optimal scores on the orientation cluster, less developed motor tone, lower activity levels, greater irritability, less robustness and endurance, unavailability, lethargy, and more stress behaviors during the examination (Abrams et al., 1995; Lundy et al., 1997). Specifically, on the orientation items, these infants did not localize the sound of a shaken rattle or track a moving bell as well as the newborns of nondepressed mothers. Their minimal response to inanimate versus animate stimuli suggests that they may have higher sensory thresholds and require the more arousing animate stimuli for optimal responding. Less responsive newborn behaviors contribute to early interaction disturbances inasmuch as

Brazelton orientation scores have been related to later interaction behaviors (Field, 1992, 1995). They were also less attentive and less expressive during a neonatal procedure involving modeling exaggerated faces for them and coding their looking behavior and their mimicry (Lundy et al., 1997). Decreased motor tone and lower activity levels on the "depressed" cluster and less robustness are perhaps not surprising given that lower activity level, lethargy, and unavailability were the behaviors frequently reported for 3-month-old infants of depressed mothers. The infants of depressed mothers also had elevated stress hormones (cortisol and norepinephrine levels; Lundy et al., 1999) and indeterminate sleep patterns at the newborn stage (Jones et al., 1998). The elevated stress hormones of infants were similar to their mothers' elevated stress hormones and could explain their behavior differences. Their excessive indeterminate sleep (sleep that is difficult to code) is disconcerting given the findings of Sigman and Parmelee (1989), suggesting an inverse relationship between the amount of indeterminate sleep during the neonatal period and IQ scores at 12 years.

Fetuses of Depressed Mothers Differ

Because the infants of the depressed mothers showed behavioral, physiological, and hormonal patterns that mimicked their mothers' patterns as early as the neonatal stage, research turned to the prenatal period. These newborn studies highlighted the need to identify chronically depressed mothers during pregnancy and evaluate the behavior of their fetuses. The findings that the neonates' biochemical profile matched their depressed mothers' prenatal biochemical profile (elevated norepinephrine and cortisol and lower dopamine levels during the third trimester of pregnancy) implied prenatal effects (Lundy et al., 1999).

In a subsequent study, chronically depressed mothers were identified during the second trimester of pregnancy (Dieter, Field, Hernandez-Reif, & Emory, 2001), and their levels of catecholamine and cortisol were assayed. Once again, a similar pattern was noted. At this time fetal ultrasounds were also observed for activity level and the fetal responses to vibrotactile stimuli (a vibrator briefly stimulating the mothers' abdomen during prescribed ultrasound sessions). The fetuses of the depressed mothers were more active (spent more time moving) during the second trimester (specifically at the 6th month; see Figure 4.1), and the ultrasonographers estimated their weight to be significantly lower. Their responses to the vibrotactile stimuli were also more active. One possible explanation for this hyperactivity in fetuses of depressed mothers is their mothers' relative inactivity, which creates the need for self-stimulation. Regression analyses suggested that 37% of the variance in fetal activity could be accounted for by scores on the CES-D depression scale and the State–Trait Anxiety Inventory (STAI; Speilberger, Gorusch, & Lushene, 1970).

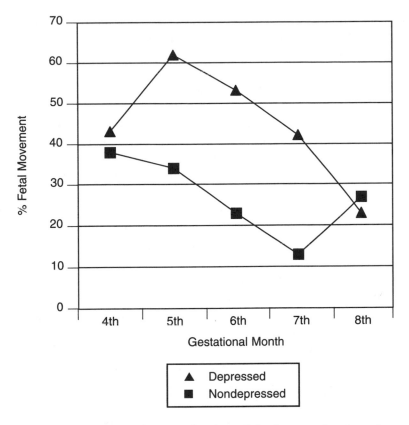

Figure 4.1. Fetal movement by gestational month in depressed and nondepressed mothers.

Several research studies summarized in a volume called *Fetal Development: A Psychobiological Perspective* (edited by Lecanuet, Fifer, Krasnegor, & Smotherman, 1995) suggest that significant amounts of learning occur prenatally. Research by DeCasper and Fifer (1980), for example, illustrates that newborns preferred their mother's voice to the voices of other women and particularly when it was electronically altered to sound as if the newborn was again in the womb as opposed to hearing the mother's unamplified voice. These data were not surprising given the data of DeCasper and Fifer (1980) showing that newborns discriminated a Dr. Seuss story that they had heard prenatally from another that they had not heard prenatally. They would suck harder or less hard depending on the conditions of the experiment to hear the preferred familiar Dr. Seuss story "To Think That I Saw It on Mulberry Street" (DeCasper & Fifer, 1980).

More direct evidence for fetal learning comes from studies on habituation, the most primitive form of learning. A stimulus is applied, typically a vibrotactile stimulus using a vibrator, to the pregnant woman's abdomen. The fetus first moves in response to that stimulus, and after repeated presentations of the stimulus, the fetus pays less attention or stops responding, having "habituated" the stimulus or having learned that it is not relevant. Several researchers have documented evidence of habituation by the fetus, including Lecanuet et al. (1995).

Fetal behavior is also predictive of later temperament. In a study by DiPietro and her colleagues (DiPietro, Hodgson, Costigan, Hilton, & Johnson, 1996) on fetuses of mothers experiencing depressed mood, movement and heart rate could predict 20–60% of the variation in infant temperament. Fetal recordings were made at six points during prenatal development, and then the infants' mothers completed temperament questionnaires at 3 and 6 months after birth. Babies who were more active in utero were more irritable and active on the temperament assessments. Babies who had irregular sleep–wake patterns in utero also showed sleep problems at 3–6 months. Even small changes in the mother's mood in that study seemed to directly affect fetal activity.

The mechanism by which these effects are transmitted is unclear. The mother's activity level, heart rate, and intrauterine hormones may all be involved. Some offspring of depressed women may be more vulnerable to the impact of environmental factors such as these because of some underlying genetic predisposition (Kendler, Neale, Kessler, Heath, & Eaves, 1992). The possibility that maternal depression effects are genetically mediated has been raised by many researchers (McGuffen, Owen, O'Donovan, Thapar, & Gottesman, 1994; Plomin, DeFries, McClearn, & Rutter, 1997; Rutter et al., 1997). To verify, this requires genetic research strategies such as twin and adoptee designs. In the interim, the data from the fetal research and the ultrasound study on fetuses of depressed mothers highlighted the need for studying profiles of early dysregulation in the infants that might relate to their prenatal experience and might help explain their less optimal early interaction behavior.

DYSREGULATION IN THE EARLY STAGES OF INFANCY

Relative Right Frontal EEG Activation

Assessments of EEG asymmetry have revealed a pattern of relative right frontal EEG activation in chronically depressed adults (Henriques & Davidson, 1990). In studies on depressed mothers, both the mothers and their infants showed relative right frontal EEG when the infants were 3 months old (Field, Grizzle, et al., 1996), when they were 1 month old (Jones, Field, Lundy, et al., 1997), and even as early as 1 week of age (Jones et al., 1998). An earlier study by Dawson, Klinger, Panagitotides, Hill, and Spieker (1992) had revealed this phenomenon at 18 months. Relative right frontal EEG at 1 month was also related to indeterminate sleep patterns and negative affect at the neonatal period (Jones et al., 1998). That the depressed mothers showed relative right frontal EEG activation is not surprising, but the appearance of this pattern in infants as young as 1 week was unexpected given the supposed plasticity of brain development during the first several months of life. The literature had suggested that the frontal cortex was very slow to develop and would not be expected to reveal patterns of this kind until at least age 6 months. In addition, this pattern appeared to be stable in infants of depressed mothers, at least from 3 months to 3 years of age (Jones, Field, Davalos, & Pickens, 1997).

Lower Vagal Tone

Lower vagal tone has been reported for 3- to 6-month-old infants of depressed mothers (Field, 1995). The developmental increase in vagal tone that occurred between 3 and 6 months for infants of nondepressed mothers did not occur for the infants of depressed mothers. Lower vagal tone at 6 months was correlated with fewer vocalizations and facial expressions during interactions (which was not surprising given the activation of facial expressions and vocalization by the vagus) and less optimal neurological scores, suggesting a lesser degree of autonomic development and control by infants of depressed mothers.

Lower vagal tone has also been noted in infants of depressed mothers during their interactions with both their mothers and nondepressed strangers (Field et al., 1998). Vagal tone could be responsive to contextual factors such as stress and changes in attention during interactions. Contextual demands could be different for infants of depressed and nondepressed mothers. For example, depressed mothers are notably less expressive, and their infants may become more agitated in their attempts to elicit more responsivity. It is not clear whether the differences reflect a neuroregulation difference determined by the complexity of genetics and previous experience with the mother or whether the differences reflect different demands placed on the two groups in the interaction situation. The absence of a developmental increase in vagal tone in the infants of depressed mothers could relate to cumulative effects of maternal depression, including the continuing elevated norepinephrine levels noted in these infants.

Another complex finding emerged in a study in which both facial expressions and vagal tone were recorded (Pickens & Field, 1993b). In that study, interest and joy expressions were significantly correlated with vagal tone in infants of nondepressed mothers. However, for infants of depressed mothers, more negative behaviors, including gaze aversion and sad and angry expressions, were positively correlated with vagal tone. Although the significance of lower vagal tone is not entirely understood, higher vagal tone is typically associated with better performance on attention and learning tasks. The lower vagal tone in the infants of depressed mothers may be related to the lesser attentiveness and limited performance on cognitive tasks noted later in infancy and during the preschool years (Field, 1998).

Negative Longer Term Outcomes

Negative longer-term outcomes have been reported when mothers remain depressed over the first 6 months of infancy (Field, 1995). Some suggest that approximately 10% of infants are affected because approximately 10% of 25-to 44-year-old mothers are depressed during the first 6 months of their infants' lives (O'Hara, 1997). Others, as already mentioned, suggest that whereas about 10% of community samples experience clinical depression during the postpartum period, less than 2% of women remain depressed after 6 months (Campbell & Cohn, 1997). The 10% prevalence figure was based on a diagnosis of depression including depressed mood and several other *DSM–IV* symptoms and in samples that were low risk for other factors. In samples identified by depressed symptoms alone and featuring other risk factors such as poverty, the chronicity of depression appears to be more prevalent. For example, in one of our samples 75% of the postpartum depressed mothers remained depressed when their children were 3 years old (Field, 1998).

Most of the longer term outcome studies have involved single time point studies of preschool and grade school aged children of depressed mothers. The general conclusion of this literature is that the children of depressed mothers have internalizing and externalizing problems and that these often affect school performance as well as lead to more serious problems such as conduct disorder.

Recent longitudinal studies have shown a relationship between earlier and later problems. For example, in the work of Dale Hay (1997) the evolution of problems can be clearly seen from the very early infancy stage when the infants of depressed mothers appeared to have problems regulating attention and emotion; they showed dysregulated arousal and attention and less awareness of contingencies. This is not surprising inasmuch as the mothers showed "choppy" attention and were not contingently responsive. The infants could not perform object permanence tasks at age 9 months, and this inability persisted at age 18 months. Ultimately, by age 4 years the children in the Hay study showed lower cognitive scores. Hay also reported that male individuals seemed to be more vulnerable, and she ascribed this to the slower development of hemispheric regulation. Others as well have noted inferior performance for boys (Murray & Cooper, 1997a).

In a similar longitudinal study by Field and her colleagues (Field, 1998), 6-month-old infants whose mothers had been depressed for their first 6 months experienced growth and developmental delays at 1 year of age. At that age they also had neurological soft signs, showed less exploratory behavior, had lower mental and motor scale scores, and were at lower weight percentiles than infants of nondepressed mothers (Field, 1995). The same infants showed nonempathetic behavior in a laboratory situation in which the mothers feigned being hurt (Jones, Field, Davalos, et al., 1997). Ultimately, at the preschool stage they showed conduct disorderlike behaviors (Field, 1995).

Some researchers consider the first 6 months as a critical or sensitive period for the development of social–emotional and cognitive behavior. Early learning has become more valued as researchers have discovered how sophisticated the newborn is, for example, the newborn's preference for his or her mother's voice (DeCasper & Fifer, 1980) and face, (Field, Cohen, Garcia, & Greenberg, 1984), their imitative abilities (Field, Healy, Goldstein & Guthertz, 1990; Meltzoff & Moore, 1983), and their very early learning of the basic conversation skills during face-to-face interactions (Tronick, Als, Adamson, Wise, & Brazelton, 1977). These skills highlight the amount of learning that happens during the early infancy period. Murray and Cooper (1997b) consider that the mother's most important ability is sustaining the infant's attention and involvement. They suggest that by 4–5 months of age the infant's attentiveness and information processing have been highly influenced by the mother's interaction behavior and that this allows for attentiveness and information processing of the wider social and nonsocial environment. This attentiveness and habituation of nonsocial tasks at 4–5 months is thought to be predictive of later IQ. Thus, the depressed mother's social and emotional unavailability limits the infant's development. Irritability and sleep disturbances are other problems that have been noted in infants of depressed mothers that would conceivably affect their development (Field, 1984; Murray & Cooper, 1997b; Zuckerman et al., 1990).

When we assessed our longitudinal follow-up sample, 75% of the mothers with high scores on the BDI (Beck et al., 1961) at the neonatal period had high BDI scores again at the 3-year follow-up (Field, 1998). Their preschool age children at this time continued to show interaction problems, they scored in the clinical range on the externalizing and internalizing factors of the Child Behavior Checklist (Achenbach & Edelbrock, 1994) as rated by their mothers, they had elevated cortisol levels, and they were viewed by their mothers as vulnerable (Bendell et al., 1994). Early infancy predictors that contributed to this outcome variance included ratings of the infants' interactions and their vagal activity at 3 months (Field, Yando, et al., 1996). In addition to the continuity of interaction patterns, stability was noted in the infants' relative right frontal EEG activation from 3 months to 3 years (Jones, Field, Davalos, et al., 1997). The 3-year-olds with greater relative right frontal EEG activation showed more inhibited behavior in strange object–strange person situations, and they showed nonempathetic behavior during their mothers' display of simulated distress (crying) behavior. Two styles of nonempathetic behavior were noted including passive–withdrawn (ignoring the mother's distress) and angry–aggressive nonempathetic behavior (e.g., in shouting at the "distressed" mother or kicking her). Although depressed mothers have been noted to rate their children more negatively perhaps because of their own depression, their ratings in this case were consistent with the behavior ratings by objective observers.

Regression analyses yielded some reliable markers of the mothers' continuing depression (mothers remaining depressed across the first 6 months; Field, 1998). These included the mothers' relative right frontal EEG activation at 3 months (explaining 31% of the variance) and their newborns' lower vagal activity and serotonin (5HIAA) and elevated norepinephrine and cortisol levels (51% of the variance in the mothers' continuing depression with lower vagal activity and serotonin being signs of depression). These variables were then used to identify mothers and infants who needed early intervention. More accurate estimation of infant outcome was also based on the depressed mothers' interaction style.

DIFFERENT OUTCOMES FOR INFANTS OF DIFFERENT INTERACTION STYLE MOTHERS

Analyses of depressed mother–infant interactions have identified two different styles of interactions that might differentially affect the infants' development (Cummings & Davies, 1994; Field et al., 1990). Although depressed mothers' interaction behavior was typically withdrawn (Field, 1998), some depressed mothers showed intrusive interaction behavior (Cohn, Matias, Tronick, Connel, & Lyons-Ruth, 1986; Field et al., 1990). The withdrawn mothers demonstrated affectively restricted behaviors. They typically turned away from their infants, adopted a "slouched back" posture, and verbalized in an expressionless tone of voice with little facial expression. In severe cases, this interaction pattern was seen for 75% of the interaction time.

Intrusive mothers were noted to be involved with their infants to the point of interfering (Egeland, Pianta, & O'Brian, 1993), overstimulating them by poking and jabbing them, talking loudly and exhibiting anger, and showing high levels of irritability (Lyons-Ruth, Zoll, Connell, & Grunebaum, 1986; Weissman & Paykel, 1974). Some associated this pattern with greater covert hostility, affectivity, and more interference with infants' goal-directed activity (Lyons-Ruth et al., 1986). Others described this behavior as overstimulation and physical intrusiveness (Malphurs, Larrain, et al., 1996; Panaccione & Wahler, 1986).

The reports on the behavior differences of the infants of intrusive and withdrawn mothers were conflicting. Cohn and his colleagues (1986) reported that withdrawn mothers spent approximately 80% of their time disengaged from their infants and responded only to distressed infants. Intrusive mothers showed anger and irritation or roughly handled their infants 40% of the time. The infants of intrusive mothers protested less than 5% of the time but spent 55% of the time avoiding their mothers. On the other hand, infants of withdrawn mothers protested 30% of the time and watched their mothers less than 5% of the time. In contrast, data from Field and her colleagues (1990) indicated that infants of withdrawn mothers were inactive and spent a majority of their time looking around, whereas infants of intrusive mothers fussed a large proportion of the time.

These different maternal interaction styles also appear to differentially affect male and female infants. In at least one study boys appeared to be more vulnerable than girls to the withdrawn state; one hypothesis is that the mothers' regulatory support was missing (Weinberg & Tronick, 1998). Girls, in contrast, seemed to be more vulnerable to the intrusive type interaction, perhaps because it interfered with their exploratory activities. Independent of the infants' gender, however, the long-term outcomes appeared to be less favorable for infants of withdrawn mothers (Field, 1998). In early infancy they had less optimal interaction behavior, and in later infancy their Bayley Mental Scale scores were lower.

Fox and Davidson's (1984) theories on approach–withdrawal emotions and their corresponding relative left–right frontal EEG activation suggest that infants of intrusive mothers might show different asymmetry patterns than infants of withdrawn mothers. If infants' EEG asymmetry tends to mimic their mothers', as it did in the Field, Fox, et al. (1995) and Jones et al. (1998) studies, and given that angry, intrusive behaviors are an approach emotion, one would expect infants of intrusive mothers to show greater relative left frontal EEG activation patterns. In contrast, infants of withdrawn mothers might be expected to show greater relative right frontal EEG activation. In a recent study, these different interaction styles (intrusive–overstimulating and withdrawn–understimulating) were assessed in 3-month-old infants and their mothers during their face-to-face interactions (Jones, Field, Fox, Davalos, Malphurs, et al., 1997). Behavioral assessments were made at 3, 6, and 12 months. The results indicated that infants of withdrawn mothers showed less-optimal interaction behavior, displayed greater relative right frontal EEG activation at 3 months, and had lower Bayley Mental Scale scores at 1 year. Infants of intrusive mothers, in contrast, had higher dopamine levels and greater relative left frontal EEG activation (see Figure 4.2).

We then looked retrospectively at the neonatal and fetal ultrasound data on this sample to determine whether there were any differences between the infants of intrusive and withdrawn mothers as early as the neonatal and prenatal periods. Although the mothers from both groups had been diagnosed as dysthymic and had equivalently high BDI scores, the intrusive mothers had higher dopamine levels. Retrospective analyses of the ultrasound videotapes of the fetuses suggested both lower and higher than normal activity levels. The fetuses of the withdrawn depressed mothers (classified as withdrawn on the basis of their interaction behaviors with their 3-month-old infants) had lower activity levels, and the fetuses of intrusive mothers

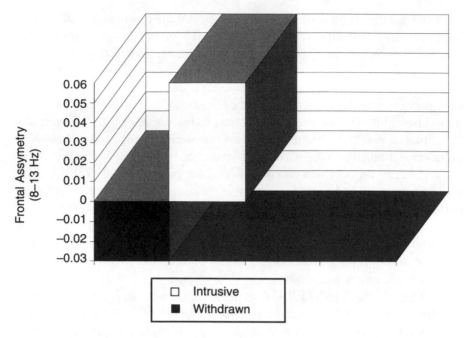

Figure 4.2. Frontal asymmetry scores of 3-month-old infants of intrusive and withdrawan mothers.

had higher activity levels. As neonates they were showing greater relative right frontal or greater relative left frontal EEG activation, again depending on the interaction style of their mothers (greater relative right frontal EEG activation for infants of withdrawn mothers and greater relative left frontal EEG activation for infants of intrusive mothers). The newborns of withdrawn mothers had lower Brazelton orientation and motor scores along with higher depression scores, and their dopamine levels were lower.

The elevated dopamine in the intrusive mothers and their infants is perhaps not surprising given that dopamine is an activating neurotransmitter. It has been considered a pivotal neurotransmitter in Rogeness, Javors, and Pliszka's (1992) model of children's psychiatric disorders. In that model, which was based on a fairly extensive database on multiple kinds of children's disorders, high norepinephrine and high dopamine are typically associated with normal, extraverted, high-energy traits. However, children with elevated norepinephrine and dopamine but low serotonin levels (5HIAA) often have externalizing problems. High norepinephrine accompanied by low dopamine is associated with anxious, inhibited, depressed behavior. Withdrawn mothers who themselves showed lower activity levels and less responsivity to social stimulation along with greater relative right frontal EEG activation (associated with inhibition and withdrawn behavior) had infants with lower dopamine levels.

Weiss, Demetrikopoulos, West, and Bonsall (1996) have developed an animal model (in the rat) linking the noradrenergic and dopaminergic systems in depression. They have suggested that although numerous observations indicate that norepinephrine is important in therapy and the pathogenesis of depression, basic research implicates dopamine much more than norepinephrine in depression-related behavioral responses including dampened motor activity and hedonic responses. In their animal model of stress-induced behavioral depression, they have traced depressive symptoms to abnormal activity (hyperresponsivity) of the locus coeruleus neurons, which then release galanin from the locus coeruleus access terminals, thus inhibiting (hyperpolarizing) dopamine neurons in the ventral tegmentum from mediating depression-related behavioral changes.

Thus, the elevated norepinephrine levels and the depressed dopamine levels in the withdrawn mothers relative to the intrusive mothers suggest a greater degree of depression, at least depression that dampens activity levels and hedonic responses. The intrusive mothers (and their infants) may experience a stress-induced increase in dopamine, but prolonged and repeated stress would more likely lead to decreased dopamine levels (which might explain the pattern seen in the withdrawn mothers and infants). This neurotransmitter pattern of elevated norepinephrine and depressed dopamine in the infants during the neonatal period might also explain their depressed activity, their less than optimal responses to social stimulation on the Brazelton Scale, and their greater relative right frontal EEG activation. Any early neurotransmitter effects would be compounded by the mothers' interactive behavior.

It is unclear why maternal depression may take these two different forms, withdrawn and intrusive. The different styles may derive from different neurotransmitter profiles, as already mentioned, and from different temperament and personality styles with an approach–withdrawal orientation to life much as in the extroverted–introverted or the externalizer internalizer dimensions discussed by Eysenck (1967). It could be that these mothers experience different emotions (anger in the case of the intrusive mothers and sadness in the case of withdrawn mothers) and that they have developed different coping-with-depression styles, such as has been termed in the psychotherapy literature *anger out* versus *anger in* or in the coping literature as *active coping* versus *passive coping*. These could also be different types of pathology, as in the old nomenclature *reactive–endogenous* with different biological substrates (e.g., the noradrenergic–dopaminergic neurotransmitter interaction). They could also reflect different degrees of severity, with the intrusive behavior happening at an earlier stage of depression and the withdrawn stage occurring later as learned helplessness and more vegetative symptoms such as psychomotor retardation and anhedonia develop. It is also possible that the intrusive style occurs more often in younger depressed mothers than in older ones. Although the intent of this research is not to determine the origins of these different styles but rather their effects on the infant, some stronger impressions about their origins may become apparent in future research. Nonetheless, the existing data suggest that these styles are stable (at least across the first years of life; Jones, Field, Davalos, et al., 1997) and that they are characteristic of these mothers' interactions not only with their infants but also with their husband or boyfriends (Hart, Field, Jones, & Yando, 1999).

Knowing the differences between infants of intrusive and withdrawn mothers may suggest intervention strategies that correspond to the mother's interaction profile. For example, the interaction coaching study just discussed demonstrated that coaching instructions given to depressed mothers were effective only when the mother's specific style of interaction was considered (Malphurs, Larrain, et al., 1996). Specifically, mothers showing a profile of overstimulating and intrusive behavior elicited positive infant responses only when they were instructed to "imitate your infant" or to "slow down and be less intrusive." The overstimulating mothers did not elicit positive infant responses when they were instructed to "keep your infant's attention." In contrast, mothers who showed understimulating and withdrawn behavior elicited positive infant responses from the coaching instruction asking them to "get their attention" and did not benefit from the instruction to imitate their infant. This study showed that intervention techniques had to be tailored to the interaction profile of the mother to elicit positive responses in the infant.

HEURISTIC MODEL

As already mentioned, the model that we had derived from the earlier research on depressed mother–infant interactions suggested that depressed mothers were emotionally unavailable to their infants and therefore were unable to provide adequate stimulation and arousal modulation. In this model, called *psychobiological attunement* (Field, 1985, 1992, 1995), external regulation is required from caregivers for infants to develop adequate self-regulation, as was the case in the similar model entitled *mutual regulation* advanced by Tronick and Gianino (1986).

However, recent data suggest that infants of chronically depressed mothers have an even greater need for external regulation because they are "dysregulated" as early as the neonatal period. Their sympathetically aroused state (elevated norepinephrine and cortisol levels) may contribute to their disorganized behavior on the Brazelton Scale, their excessive indeterminate sleep, and their greater relative right frontal EEG activation during the neonatal period. The infants' sympathetic arousal would be further compounded by inadequate stimulation and arousal modulation from their mothers. Whether the mothers had a withdrawn (understimulating) or intrusive (overstimulating) interaction style, their stimulation would be inadequate. Animal data suggest that inadequate stimulation could contribute to the infants' neurotransmitter (elevated norepinephrine) and neuroendocrine (elevated cortisol) imbalance (Kraemer, Ebert, Lake, & McKinney, 1984). The infants may have developed withdrawn behavior (flat affect and low activity level) or hyperactive behavior (irritable affect and high activity level) as stimulus barriers to block the inappropriate stimulation from their mothers, hence avoiding further sympathetic arousal. This profile of dysregulation in biochemistry (elevated cortisol and norepinephrine), physiology (lower vagal tone and greater relative right frontal EEG activation), and sleep–wake behavior (excessive indeterminate sleep) may contribute to the externalizing and internalizing behaviors noted at the preschool stage and the disproportionate incidence of depression, conduct disorder, and aggression and inadequate self-regulation reported in older children of depressed mothers.

The more recent data on different interaction styles suggest that we might need to modify this model further because in a more evenly balanced sample of intrusive and withdrawn mothers the data show a better development (at least better interaction behaviors and one year Bayley Mental Scores) in the infants of intrusive depressed mothers. This may result from more verbal stimulation from their intrusive mothers or the greater approach behavior (exploratory behavior) shown by the intrusive mothers' infants themselves. The infants of intrusive mothers may thus be less dysregulated, enabling them to modulate their mothers' excessive stimulation. Alternatively (as suggested by animal stress models), these infants' accelerated development may relate to stress. Research is needed to determine how these two maternal interaction styles differentially affect the development of infants, how the infants' dysregulation interacts with the maternal behavior effects, and ultimately, what types of interventions these findings might suggest. Studies on newborns of depressed mothers that noted inferior Brazelton Scores and behavioral, physiological and biochemical characteristics that were similar to those of their depressed mothers (including flat affect, greater relative right frontal EEG activation, elevated norepinephrine and cortisol levels) suggested that the infants were affected prenatally by their mothers' depression (or a genetic predisposition that would be difficult to evaluate at this time), highlighting the need for very early intervention (Lundy et al., 1999).

IMPLICATIONS FOR CLINICIANS

For many mothers who experience postpartum depression, the depression subsides in the first few months after delivery. In one of our studies, mothers who were depressed during the first few months of their infants' life but were no longer depressed by 6 months had infants whose development was normal at 1 year (Field, 1992). In contrast, mothers who remained depressed over the infants' first 6 months of life had infants who developed a depressed style of interacting and later at 1 year showed inferior mental and motor development performance and were at lower growth percentiles (particularly weight percentiles). Maternal depression persisted for 75% of that sample, and the children eventually had externalizing or internalizing behavior problems at the preschool stage (Field, 1995). Identifying those mothers who would remain depressed is extremely important because their infants, as already mentioned, began to show growth and developmental delays at 1 year, suggesting that they needed early intervention. Behavioral markers of chronic depression have been unreliable, but physiological and biochemical markers may be more promising. In our longitudinal study, recall that 51% of the variance in continuing depression (mothers still being depressed at 6 months) could be explained by variables collected at 3 months. These included the mothers' relative right frontal EEG asymmetry, which explained 31% of the variance. The variables that explained the remaining 20% of the variance included low vagal tone and serotonin and elevated norepinephrine and cortisol levels. This profile was considered a promising way of identifying mother–infant dyads who needed intervention. Finding cost-effective interventions was then the next problem.

Short-Term Interventions

At least 50% of women who experience postpartum depression have been found to refuse treatment (O'Hara & Swain, 1996). Women with postpartum depression have also been noted to refuse antidepressants such as fluoxetane (Cooper, Murray, Hooper, & West, 1996). Although some hormone treatments have been effective postnatally, including transdermal estrogen (Gregoire, Kumar, Everitt, Henderson, & Studd, 1996) and oral estrogen (Sichel, Cohen, Robertson, Ruttenberg, & Rosenbaum, 1996), which are intended to decrease the rate of estrogen change and prevent an impact on dopaminergic and serotonergic neuroreceptors, women have been reluctant to take hormones, particularly during pregnancy.

This reluctance to use mood-altering drugs highlights the need to find other interventions to improve the mother's mood and thereby improve her interactions with her infant. Depressed mothers' most common parenting problems include their depressed state, their withdrawn behavior, and their lesser sensitivity to their infants' emotional cues. The mothers' depressed affect (mood) is a problem because the infants do not receive feedback for their own behavior, and the mothers' depressed behavior also serves as a model for the infant developing depressed behaviors. A parsimonious intervention, then, would focus on these common problems. Altering the mother's mood state may help change her behavior at least during interactions with her infant. Mood alteration techniques that have been used to decrease mothers' depressed affect include relaxation and massage therapy and music mood induction. In a study using relaxation and massage therapy techniques, positive effects occurred following both therapies, although better results were noted for the massage therapy group. Following a 30-minute massage, the mothers' depressed mood, anxiety levels, and salivary cortisol levels (stress hormones) decreased. A shift away from greater relative right frontal EEG activity was also noted in another study that provided massage therapy (Jones & Field, 1999). Chronically depressed adults have shown greater relative right frontal EEG activation, which remains even after their behavioral symptoms are in remission (Henriques & Davidson, 1990), suggesting that this pattern would be difficult to alter. After a 4-week period of two massages per week, the mothers were significantly less depressed and their urinary cortisol levels were lower, suggesting stable decreases in anxiety, depression, and stress.

Similar effects have been noted for music mood induction (Field et al., 1998). After only 20 minutes of music (a selection of 5 rock music pieces), 10 of the 12 depressed adolescent mothers showed an attenuation of greater relative right frontal EEG activation, moving toward symmetry or toward greater relative left frontal EEG activation. The two adolescent mothers whose EEG pattern did not change claimed that they did not enjoy rock music. When their favorite music (classical) was played, they too experienced a shift toward symmetry. Although it is not clear how long-lived these effects are, it was surprising that the greater relative right frontal EEG activation, thought to be a marker of chronic depression, could be altered by only 20 minutes of music or massage.

Infant massage therapy was also used to enhance the mothers' sensitivity to their infants' cues and to improve the infants' mood state. Depressed adolescent mothers giving their infants a massage were compared to depressed mothers rocking their infants for 15-minute periods for 12 days over a 6-week period (Field, Grizzle, et al., 1996). During the session, the massaged infants spent more time in active alert states than the rocked infants, and they cried less. After the massage they had lower salivary cortisol levels, suggesting lower stress levels. They also spent less time in an active awake state after the session, suggesting that massage may be more effective than rocking for inducing sleep. The rocked infants slept during the rocking and then woke up when it was over, and the massaged infants were awake during the massage and slept when it was over. After the 6-week follow-up period, the massaged infants gained more weight than the rocked infants and they improved on emotionality, sociability, soothability temperament dimensions, and face-to-face interaction ratings. They also showed decreased urinary stress hormones, including cortisol and catecholamines (norepinephrine, epinephrine), and increased serotonin levels.

More recently, pregnancy massage was given to depressed women to reduce their stress hormones (catecholamines and cortisol) and decrease their obstetric and postnatal complications (Field, unpublished data). Following a protocol of twice-weekly massage sessions during the third trimester, the women were less depressed and had lower norepinephrine, epinephrine, and cortisol levels. In addition, they experienced less sleep disturbance, had less back and leg pain, and fewer obstetric and postnatal complications including prematurity.

Interaction coaching is another technique for altering the mother's sensitivity to her infant's cues and for improving mother–infant interactions. Maternal imitation is one of the most effective interaction coaching techniques (Field, 1977). In one study depressed mothers were given an interaction technique instructing them to imitate their infants (Pickens & Field, 1993a). Their pacing became slower whereas their contingent responsivity increased. When asked to get their infants' attention, the depressed mothers played more games and displayed more positive affect. In another study these techniques were differentially effective for both intrusive and withdrawn depressed mothers (Malphurs, Larrain, et al., 1996). Instructions to imitate the infants were most effective in optimizing the interactions of intrusive mothers, whereas instructions to elicit the infants' attention were more effective with the withdrawn mothers.

For the mothers' touching behavior, for example, the intrusive mothers' touching decreased during the imitation session, and the withdrawn mothers' touching increased during the attention-getting, game-playing session. The infants' facial expressions, in turn, were more frequent during the imitation session in the case of the infants of intrusive mothers, and infant facial expressions increased during game-playing in the case of the infants of withdrawn mothers.

The technique of having mothers massaging their infants during their face-to-face interactions was also used, because depressed mothers are noted to touch their infants less frequently (Malphurs, Raag, Field, Pickens, & Pelaez-Nogueras, 1996). When they do touch, it is typically more negative (e.g., poking, punching, and pinching). To demonstrate the effectiveness of touching, both depressed and nondepressed mothers were asked to show a still-face and remain quiet and unexpressive (Pelaez-Nogueras, Field, Hossain, & Pickens, 1996). The mothers were then asked to massage their infants' legs as they retained the still-face position. Adding the massage led to increased infant smiling and decreased infant gaze aversion, particularly in the depressed mother–infant dyads.

Introducing infants of depressed mothers to a nondepressed adult was also expected to alter their interaction behavior (Field et al., 1988). Unfortunately, however, the infants showed a generalized depressed mood state with nondepressed adults. Because this might be related to the nondepressed adult not being a mother herself, the infants of depressed mothers were introduced to nondepressed mothers, and the interactions of depressed mothers with nondepressed infants were observed (Martinez et al., 1996). These interactions were relatively ineffective because the infants' behavior changed very little, whether they were depressed infants interacting with nondepressed mothers or infants of nondepressed mothers interacting with depressed mothers. Even though the infants of nondepressed mothers appeared to be trying harder with the depressed mothers, the depressed mothers looked much the same whether they were with their own or another mother's infant. However, the depressed mothers did not negatively affect the infants of nondepressed mothers.

Introducing infants of depressed mothers to nondepressed teachers who were familiar (they were the infants' teacher and primary caregiver), in contrast, improved the infants' interaction behaviors (Pelaez-Nogueras, Field, Cigales, Gonzalez, & Clasky, 1995). They showed more positive facial expressions and vocalizations. Fathers have been known to buffer negative effects (Goodman, Brogan, Lynch, & Fielding, 1993; Radke-Yarrow, Cummings, Kuczynski, & Chapman, 1985). Infants of depressed mothers have been shown to interact more optimally with their fathers (Hossain, Field, Pickens, & Gonzalez, 1995). In the Hossain et al. study, the fathers showed more positive facial expressions and vocalizations than the mothers did, and, in turn, the infants of depressed mothers showed more positive facial expressions and vocalizations. These data suggest that nondepressed fathers and nondepressed infant nursery teachers can compensate for the negative effects of depressed mothering. In a similar way, the employment of depressed mothers may protect their infants from these negative effects (Cohn et al., 1986). Finally, the Cambridge treatment trial by Cooper and Murray (1997) has been notably effective in decreasing the mothers' depression and enhancing the mother–infant relationship. The different components (including counseling and cognitive–behavioral and psychodynamic interventions) were equally effective in reducing the mothers' depression. However, none of the interventions affected the children's behavioral problems or attachment ratings.

Long-Term Interventions

Comprehensive intervention programs for depressed mother–infant dyads are rare. One of the biggest problems in working with depressed mothers is finding them an educational–vocational experience that might attenuate their depression and finding their infants substitute caregiving so that they in turn, would have less exposure to their mothers' depressive behavior. Toward that end, we arranged a social–educational–vocational rehabilitation program for the mothers and a free day care for the infants in a model infant nursery in a local public vocational high school (Field, 1998). Although this kind of intervention had not been tried with depressed mothers, we had successfully used similar intensive interventions with nondepressed teenage mothers (Field, Widmayer, Ignatoff, & Stringer, 1982). In addition, the program included those effective mood inductions already discussed including music mood induction, relaxation therapy, massage therapy, infant massage, and interaction coaching. In this program, which specifically targeted depressed teenage mothers, the mothers attended vocational high school in the mornings and participated in social and vocational rehab activities and aerobics in the afternoons, and their infants received all-day model day care on a daily basis for 3 months. The mothers also spent approximately 1 hour per day in the infant nursery helping the teachers take care of their infants.

In the first part of this study we developed a risk index for identifying those mothers who would remain depressed and need intervention in order to prevent infant depression. Behavioral, psychophysiological, and biochemical assessments were made at the neonatal, 3- and 6-month periods on a sample of depressed mothers, 75% of whom were expected in the absence of intervention to continue being depressed by the infants' 6th month. We used a regression model for the predictor variables from the neonatal and 3-month assessments to identify those mothers who would remain depressed at 6 months.

A sample of 160 depressed mothers and 100 nondepressed mothers and their infants were monitored over the first 6 months to assess the infants' development and to identify potential markers from the first 3 months that predict chronic depression in the mothers. The markers were then used to identify a second sample of chronically depressed mothers as candidates for an intervention. In the longitudinal sample, a syndrome of dysregulation was noted in the infants including lower Brazelton scores, more indeterminate sleep and elevated norepinephrine and epinephrine at the neonatal period, right frontal EEG activation, lower vagal tone, and negative interactions at the 3- and 6-month periods. As already noted, a group of variables contributed to 51% of the variance in the mothers' continuing depression including the mothers' relative right frontal EEG activation and their newborns' lower vagal tone and serotonin and elevated norepinephrine and cortisol levels. In the second sample identified by these markers, depressed mothers and their infants received the 3-month intervention and were compared to depressed and nondepressed control groups.

Although the intervention mothers continued to have higher depression scores than the nondepressed mothers, their interaction behavior became significantly more positive and their biochemical values and vagal tone approximated the values of the nondepressed control group. The infants in the intervention (day care) group also showed more positive interaction behavior, better growth, fewer pediatric complications, and normalized biochemical values, and by 1 year they had superior Bayley mental and motor scores. Thus, chronically depressed mothers could be identified and this relatively cost-effective intervention attenuated the typical delays noted in growth and development in their infants even though the mothers' depression scores remained high, and like other intensive intervention programs (Field et al., 1982), the positive effects on the infants may have disappeared after the intervention program ended.

SUMMARY

Most of the early literature focused on problematic interactions of post-partum depressed mothers and infants. Most of these mothers' depression was limited to the postpartum period, and the effects on their infants were relatively short-term. In the samples of depressed mothers who were at high risk because of other factors (including poverty, minority status, lack of education, being a teenage mother, learned helplessness, and noncompliance), the mother's depression appeared to be chronic, and the effects on the infants started during the prenatal period. Soon after birth, these infants were showing lower activity levels, less responsivity to social stimulation, indeterminate sleep, relative right frontal EEG activation, and elevated stress hormones (norepinephrine and cortisol), patterns that were generally similar to those noted in their depressed mothers. We refer to this profile of behavior–physiology–biochemistry as *dysregulation*, a pattern that appeared to persist across infancy and into preschool.

In our model of psychobiological attunement, we suggested that the infants of chronically depressed mothers had an even greater need for external regulation because they were dysregulated as early as the neonatal period, and they were disadvantaged by their depressed mothers being emotionally unavailable and therefore unable to provide adequate stimulation and arousal modulation. Whether the depressed mothers had a withdrawn (understimulating) or intrusive (overstimulating) interaction style, their stimulation appeared to be inappropriate. In turn, the infants developed withdrawn behavior (flat affect and low activity levels) or hyperactive behavior (irritable affect and high activity level) that apparently served as stimulus barriers to block the inappropriate stimulation from their mothers, hence avoiding further sympathetic arousal. This stimulus-blocking behavior may persist as a pattern and be manifested as externalizing and internalizing behaviors noted at the preschool stage. Further research is needed to determine how these two maternal interaction styles differentially affect the development of their infants, how the infants' dysregulation interacts with maternal behavior effects, and ultimately what types of interventions these findings suggest. The example we presented on the differential response to interaction coaching techniques highlights the importance of this problem. The interaction coaching instructions to imitate the infants were most effective in optimizing the interactions of intrusive mothers, whereas instructions to keep the infants' attention were more effective with the withdrawn mothers. Mood induction techniques may similarly need to be tailored to the different types of depressed mothers.

Another significant problem that has confounded the research and is troublesome for the clinician is this high-risk population's noncompliance with treatment. These women tend to be noncompliant not only in following up referrals for psychotherapy but also in taking their antidepressant medication. This poses a challenge for researchers and clinicians alike to develop alternative forms of therapy that may be more appropriate for this population.

Although some of the short-term interventions such as mood induction techniques and interaction coaching have been relatively effective, it is not clear that these effects can persist if the mother remains chronically depressed. Similarly, it may be necessary to provide alternative caregiving to infants of depressed mothers to insure that they are receiving adequate stimulation. As was noted, these infants fared better in nursery school and with their nondepressed fathers. Inasmuch as the effects of the mothers' chronic depression are already apparent at the neonatal stage, further research is needed to design effective therapies for the pregnant woman. Finding these women during pregnancy is still another problem inasmuch as they frequently do not seek prenatal care or attend prenatal clinics. At the very least, identification of these mothers at the time of delivery would be important to help prevent the confounding effects of the mothers' depressed behavior on the already dysregulated newborn. This problem, like many others in the field, may benefit most from the combined efforts of the researcher and clinician.

REFERENCES

Abrams, S. M., Field, T., Scafidi, F., & Prodromidis, M. (1995). Newborns of depressed mothers. *Infant Mental Health Journal, 16*, 231–235.

Achenbach, T., & Edelbrock, T. (1994). Child Behavior Checklist and related instruments. In M. E. Maruish (Ed.), *The use of psychological testing for treatment planning and outcome assessment* (pp. 517–549). New Jersey: Lawrence Erlbaum Associates.

American Psychiatric Association. (1994). *Diagnostic and statistical manual of mental disorders* (4th ed.). Washington, DC: Author.

Beck, A., Ward, C., Mendelson, M., Mach, J., & Erbaugh, J. (1961). An inventory for measuring depression. *Archives of General Psychiatry, 4*, 561–571.

Bendell, D., Field, T., Yando, S., Lang, C., Martinez, A., & Pickens, J. (1994). Depressed mothers' perception of their preschool children's vulnerability. *Child Psychiatry and Human Development, 24*, 183–190.

Brazelton, T. B. (1973). *The Neonatal Behavior Assessment Scale.* New York: Heineman.

Campbell, S., & Cohn, J. (1997). The timing and chronicity of postpartum depression: Implications for infant development. In L. Murray & P. Cooper (Eds.), *Postpartum depression and child development* (pp. 165–197). New York: Guilford Press.

Cohn, J. E., Matias, R., Tronick, E. Z., Connel, D., & Lyons-Ruth, K. (1986). Face-to-face interactions of depressed mothers and their infants. In E. Z. Tronick &

T. Field (Eds.), *Maternal depression and infant disturbance* (pp. 31–45). San Francisco: Jossey-Bass.

Cohn, J. E., & Tronick, E. Z. (1983). Three-month-old infants' reaction to simulated maternal depression. *Child Development, 54,* 185–193.

Cooper, P. J., & Murray, L. (1997). The impact of psychological treatments of postpartum depression on maternal mood and infant development. In P. J. Cooper & L. Murray (Eds.), *Postpartum depression and child development* (pp. 111–135). New York: Guilford Press.

Cooper, P. J., Murray, L., Hooper, R., & West, A. (1996). The development and validation of a predictive index for postpartum depression. *Psychological Medicine, 26,* 627–634.

Cummings, E. M., & Davies, P. T. (1994). Maternal depression and child development. *Journal of Child Psychology and Psychiatry, 35,* 73–112.

Dawson, G., Klinger, L. G., Panagitotides, H., Hill, D., & Spieker, S. (1992). Frontal lobe activity and affective behavior of infants of mothers with depressive symptoms. *Child Development, 63,* 725–737.

DeCasper, A. J., & Fifer, W. P. (1980). Of human bonding: Newborns prefer their mothers' voice. *Science, 208,* 1174–1176.

Dieter, J., Field, T., Hernandez-Reif, M., & Emory, G. (2001). *Preterm infants gain more weight following five days of massage therapy.* Manuscript submitted for publication.

DiPietro, J. A., Hodgson, D. M., Costigan, K. A., Hilton, S. C., & Johnson, T. R. (1996). Fetal neurobehavioral development. *Child Development, 67,* 2553–2567.

Egeland, B., Pianta, R., & O'Brian, M. (1993). Maternal intrusiveness in infancy and child maladaptation in early school years. *Development and Psychopathology, 5,* 359–370.

Eysenck, J. J. (1967). *The biological basis of personality.* Springfield, IL: Thomas.

Field, T. (1977). Effects of early separation, interactive deficits, and experimental manipulations on infant–mother face-to-face interaction. *Child Development, 48,* 763–839.

Field, T. (1984). Early interactions between infants and their postpartum depressed mothers. *Infant Behavior and Development, 7,* 537–540.

Field, T. (1985). Attachment as psychological attunement: Being on the same wavelength. In M. Reite & T. Field (Eds.), *Psychobiology of attachment* (pp. 415–454). New York: Academic Press.

Field, T. (1992). Infants of depressed mothers. *Development and Psychopathology, 4,* 49–66.

Field, T. (1995). Infants of depressed mothers. *Infant Behavior and Development, 18,* 1–13.

Field, T. (1998). Longitudinal follow-up of infants of depressed mothers. *Adolescence.*

Field, T., Cohen, D., Garcia, R., & Greenberg, R. (1984). Mother–stranger face discrimination by the newborn. *Infant Behavior and Development, 7,* 19–25.

Field, T., Fox, N., Pickens, J., Nawrocki, T., & Soutullo, D. (1995). Relative right frontal EEG activation in 3-to-6 month old infants of depressed mothers. *Developmental Psychology, 31*, 358–363.

Field, T., Grizzle, N., Scafidi, F., Abrams, S., Richardson, S., Kuhn, C., & Schanberg, S. (1996). Massage therapy for infants of depressed mothers. *Infant Behavior and Development, 19*, 107–112.

Field, T., Healy, B., Goldstein, S., & Guthertz, M. (1990). Behavior state matching and synchrony in mother–infant interactions of nondepressed versus depressed dyads. *Developmental Psychology, 26*, 7–14.

Field, T., Healy, B., Goldstein, S., Perry, S., Bendell, D., Schanberg, S., Zimmerman, E. A., & Kuhn, C. (1988). Infants of depressed mothers show "depressed" behavior even with non-depressed adults. *Child Development, 59*, 1569–1579.

Field, T., Martinez, A., Nawrocki, T., Pickens, J., Fox, N., & Schanberg, S. (1998). Music shifts frontal EEG in depressed adolescents. *Adolescence, 33*, 109–116.

Field, T., Pickens, J., Fox, N., Nawrocki, T., & Gonzalez, J. (1995). Vagal tone in infants of depressed mothers. *Development and Psychopathology, 7*, 227–231.

Field, T., Widmayer, S., Ignatoff, E., & Stringer, S. (1982). Developmental effects of an intervention for preterm infants of teenage mothers. *Infant Mental Health Journal, 3*, 11–18.

Field, T., Yando, R., Lang, C., Pickens, J., Martinez, A., & Bendell, D. (1996). Longitudinal follow-up of children of dysphoric mothers. *Journal of Clinical Child Psychology, 25*, 272–279.

Fox, N. A. (1994). Dynamic cerebral processes underlying emotion regulation. In N. A. Fox (Ed.), *The development of emotion regulation: Biological and behavioral considerations. Monographs for the Society for Research in Child Development* (pp. 21–38). Norwood, NJ: Ablex.

Fox, N. A., & Davidson, R. (1984). Hemispheric substrates of affect: A developmental model. In N. A. Fox & R. J. Davidson (Eds.), *The psychobiology of affective development* (pp. 218–224). Hillsdale, NJ: Erlbaum.

Fox, N. A., Rubin, K. H., Collins, S. D., Marshall, T. R., Coplan, R. J., Porges, S. W., Long, J. M., & Stewart, S. (1995). Frontal activation asymmetry and social competence at four years of age. *Child Development, 66*, 1770–1784.

Goodman, S. H., Brogan, D., Lynch, M. E., & Fielding, B. (1993). Social and emotional competence in children of depressed mothers. *Child Development, 64*, 513–531.

Gregoire, A. J. P., Kumar, R., Everitt, B., Henderson, A. F., & Studd, J. W. W. (1996). Transdermal estrogen for treatment of severe postnatal depression. *The Lancet, 347*, 930–933.

Hart, S., Field, T., DelValle, C., & Letourneau, M. (1998). Jealousy protests in infants of depressed mothers. *Infant Behavior and Development, 21*, 137–148.

Hart, S., Field, T., Jones, N. A., & Yando, R. (1999). Intrusive and withdrawn behaviors of mothers interacting with their infants and boyfriends. *Journal of Child Psychology and Psychiatry, 23*, 351–356.

Hay, D. F. (1997). Postpartum depression and cognitive development. In L. Murray & P. J. Cooper (Eds.), *Postpartum depression and child development* (pp. 85–110). New York: Guilford Press.

Henriques, J. B., & Davidson, R. J. (1990). Regional brain electrical asymmetries discriminate between previously depressed and healthy control subjects. *Journal of Abnormal Psychology, 99,* 22–31.

Hossain, Z., Field, T., Pickens, J., & Gonzales, J. (1995). Infants of "depressed" mothers interact better with their nondepressed fathers. *Infant Mental Health Journal, 15,* 348–357.

Jones, N. A., Field, T., Fox, N. A., Davalos, M., Malphurs, J., Carraway, K., Schanberg, S., & Kuhn, C. (1997). Infants of intrusive and withdrawn mothers. *Infant Behavior and Development, 20,* 177–178.

Jones, N., & Field, T. (1999). Right frontal EEG asymmetry is attenuated by massage and music therapy. *Adolescence, 34,* 529–534.

Jones, N., Field, T., Davalos, M., & Pickens, J. (1997). Brain electrical activity stability in infants/children of depressed mothers. *Child Psychiatry and Human Development, 28,* 326–339.

Jones, N., Field, T., Fox, N. A., Davalos, M., Lundy, B., & Hart, S. (1998). Newborns of mothers with depressive symptoms are physiologically less developed. *Infant Behavior and Development, 21,* 537–541.

Jones, N., Field, T., Lundy, B., Davalos, M., & Fox, N. (1997). EEG activation in one-month-old infants of depressed mothers. *Development and Psychology, 9,* 491–505.

Kendler, K. S., Neale, M. C., Kessler, R. C., Heath, A. C., & Eaves, J. (1992). A population-based twin study of major depression in women. *Archives of General Psychiatry, 49,* 257–266.

Kraemer, G. W., Ebert, M. H., Lake, C. R., & McKinney, W. T. (1984). Cerebrospinal fluid changes associated with pharmacological alteration of the despair response to social separation in rhesus monkeys. *Psychiatry Research, 11,* 303–315.

Lecanuet, J., Fifer, W. P., Krasnegor, N. A., & Smotherman, W. P. (1995). *Fetal development: A psychobiological perspective.* Hillsdale, NJ: Erlbaum.

Lundy, B., Field, T., & Pickens, J. (1997). Newborns of mothers with depressive symptoms are less expressive. *Infant Behavior and Development, 19,* 419–424.

Lundy, B., Jones, N., Field, T., Pietro, P., Nearing, G., Davalos, M., Schanberg, S., & Kuhn, C. (1999). Prenatal depression effects on neonates. *Infant Behavior and Development, 22,* 119–129.

Lyons-Ruth, K., Zoll, D. L., Connell, D., & Grunebaum, H. Y. (1986). The depressed mother and her one-year-old infant: Environment, interaction, attachment, and infant development. In E. Tronick & T. Field (Eds.), *Maternal depression and infant disturbance* (pp. 61–63). New York: Jossey-Bass.

Malphurs, J., Larrain, C. M., Field, T., Pickens, J., Pelaez-Nogueras, M., Yando, R., & Bendell, D. (1996). Altering withdrawn and intrusive interaction behaviors of depressed mothers. *Infant Mental Health Journal, 17,* 152–160.

Malphurs, J., Raag, T., Field, T., Pickens, J., & Pelaez-Nogueras, M. (1996). Touch by intrusive and withdrawn mothers with depressive symptoms. *Early Development and Parenting, 5,* 111–115.

Martinez, A., Malphurs, J., Field, T., Pickens, J., Yando, R., Bendell, D., DelValle, C., & Messinger, D. (1996). Depressed mothers' and their infants' interactions with non-depressed partners. *Infant Mental Health Journal, 17,* 74–80.

McGuffen, P., Owen, M. J., O'Donovan, M. C., Thapar, A., & Gottesman, I. I. (1994). *Seminars in psychiatric genetics.* London: Royal College of Psychiatrists.

Meltzoff, A. N., & Moore, M. K. (1983). Newborn infants imitate adult facial gestures. *Child Development, 54,* 702–709.

Murray, L., & Cooper, P. J. (1997a). The impact of postpartum depression on child development. *Psychological Medicine, 27,* 253–260.

Murray, L., & Cooper, P. J. (1997b). The role of infant and maternal factors in postpartum depression mother–infant interactions, and infant outcomes. In L. Murray & P. J. Cooper (Eds.), *Postpartum depression and child development* (pp. 111–135). New York: Guilford Press.

O'Hara, M. W. (1997). The nature of postpartum depressive disorders. In L. Murray & P. J. Cooper (Eds.), *Postpartum depression and child development* (pp. 3–31). New York: Guilford Press.

O'Hara, M. W., & Swain, A. M. (1996). Rates and risk of postpartum depression: A meta-analysis. *International Review of Psychiatry, 8,* 37–54.

Panaccione, V. F., & Wahler, R. G. (1986). Child behavior, maternal depression, and social coercion as factors in the quality of care. *Journal of Abnormal Child Psychology, 14,* 263–278.

Pelaez-Nogueras, M., Field, T., Cigales, M., Gonzalez, A., & Clasky, S. (1995). Infants of depressed mothers show less "depressed" behavior with their nursery teachers. *Infant Mental Health Journal, 15,* 358–367.

Pelaez-Nogueras, M., Field, T., Hossain, Z., & Pickens, J. (1996). Depressed mothers' touching increases infants' positives affect and attention in the still-face situation. *Child Development, 67,* 1780–1792.

Pickens, J., & Field, T. (1993a). Attention-getting vs. imitation effects on depressed mother–infant interactions. *Infant Mental Health Journal, 14,* 171–181.

Pickens, J., & Field, T. (1993b). Facial expressivity in infants of "depressed" mothers. *Developmental Psychology, 29,* 986–988.

Plomin, E., DeFries, J. C., McClearn, G., & Rutter, M. (1997). *Behavioral genetics.* New York: W. H. Freeman.

Raag, T., Malphurs, J., Field, T., Pelaez-Nogueras, M., Pickens, J., Martinez, A., Bendell, D., & Yando, R. (1997). Moderately dysphoric mothers behave more positively with their infants after completing the BDI. *Infant Mental Health Journal, 18,* 394–405.

Radke-Yarrow, M., Cummings, E. N., Kuczynski, L., & Chapman, M. (1985). Patterns of attachment in two and three-year olds in normal families and families with parental depression. *Child Development, 56,* 884–893.

Radloff, L. (1977). The CES-D scale: A self-report depression scale for research in the general population. *Applied Psychological Methods, 1,* 385–401.

Rogeness, G. A., Javors, M. A., & Pliszka, S. R. (1992). Neurochemistry and child adolescent psychiatry. *Journal of the American Academy of Child and Adolescent Psychiatry, 31,* 765–781.

Rutter, M., Maughan, B., Meyer, J., Pickels, A., Silberg, J., Simonoff, E., & Taylor, E. (1997). Heterogeneity of antisocial behavior: Causes, continuities, and consequences. In D. W. Osgood (Ed.), *Nebraska Symposium on Motivation: Vol. 44. Motivation and delinquency* (pp. 45–118). Lincoln: University of Nebraska Press.

Sichel, D. A., Cohen, L. S., Robertson, L. M., Ruttenberg, A., & Rosenbaum, J. F. (1996). Prophylactic estrogen in recurrent postpartum affective disorder. *Biological Psychiatry, 38,* 814–818.

Sigman, M., & Parmelee, A. (1989, January). *Longitudinal predictors of cognitive development.* Paper presented at the meeting of the American Association for the Advancement of Science, San Francisco.

Speilberger, C. D., Gorusch, T. C., & Lushene, R. E. (1970). *The State–Trait Anxiety Interview.* Palo Alto, CA: Consulting Psychologists Press.

Tronick, E. Z., Als, H., Adamson, O., Wise, S., & Brazelton, T. B. (1977). The infant's response to entrapment between contradictory messages in face-to-face interaction. *Journal of Child Psychiatry, 17,* 1–13.

Tronick, E. Z., & Field, T. (Eds.). (1996). *Maternal depression and infant disturbance.* San Francisco: Jossey-Bass.

Tronick, E. Z., & Gianino, A. F. (1986). The transmission of maternal disturbance to the infant. In E. Z. Tronick & T. Field (Eds.), *Maternal depression and infant disturbance* (New Directions for Child Development, No. 34, pp. 61–82). San Francisco: Jossey Bass.

Weinberg, M. K., & Tronick, E. Z. (1998). The impact of maternal psychiatric illness on infant development. *Journal of Clinical Psychiatry, 59,* 53–61.

Weiss, J. M., Demetrikopoulos, M. K., West, C. H., & Bonsall, R. W. (1996). An hypothesis linking the noradrenergic and dopagminergic systems in depression.

Weissman, M., & Paykel, E. (1974). *The depressed woman: A study of social relationships.* Chicago: University of Chicago Press.

Whiffen, V. E., & Gottlib, I. M. (1989). Infants of postpartum depressed mothers: Temperament and cognitive status. *Journal of Abnormal Psychology, 98,* 274–279.

Wilcox, H., Field, T., Prodromidis, M., & Scafidi, F. (1996). Correlations between the BDI and CES-D in a sample of adolescent mothers. *Adolescents, 33,* 565–574.

Zuckerman, B., Als, H., Bauchner, H., Parker, S., & Cabral, H. (1990). Maternal depressive symptoms during pregnancy, and newborn irritability. *Developmental and Behavioral Pediatrics, 11*, 190–194.

5

PARENTAL DEPRESSION AND CHILD ATTACHMENT: HOSTILE AND HELPLESS PROFILES OF PARENT AND CHILD BEHAVIOR AMONG FAMILIES AT RISK

KARLEN LYONS-RUTH, AMY LYUBCHIK,
REBECCA WOLFE, AND ELISA BRONFMAN

The interface between depression and the organization of attachment strategies has received much research attention. The demonstrated longitudinal relations between early attachment security and later adaptive interpersonal functioning highlight the importance of attachment security as an indicator of the developmental adequacy of early relationships. If a parent's depression interferes with the formation of a secure attachment relationship with the infant, then several adaptive outcomes in childhood are likely to be negatively affected (Weinfield, Sroufe, Egeland, & Carlson, 1999). In addition, the attachment literature has repeatedly documented the association between less sensitive and responsive parenting and increased rates of attachment insecurity among young children (for a meta-analytic review, see van IJzendoorn, 1995). Another extensive literature has documented that parental depression is also associated with a broad range of less optimal child socio-emotional outcomes, and depressed parents have been shown to display more problematic behaviors in interaction with their children (for a review, see Goodman & Gotlib, 1999). Therefore, both attachment and depression researchers have predicted that maternal depression would be associated with increased insecurity of infant attachment behaviors (e.g., Cummings & Cicchetti, 1990).

Human studies and recent neuroendocrine data from rat and primate studies also strongly suggest that key neurotransmitter and neuroendocrine systems involved in stress responses and mood regulation in infancy and early childhood should be related both to parental depression and to child attachment security. For example, alterations in neuroendocrine function in the hypothalamic-pituitary-adrenal (HPA) axis have been related to adult depression in humans (Amsterdam, Maislin, Gold, & Winokur, 1989) and to attachment disorganization in human infants (Hertsgaard, Gunnar, Erickson, & Nachmias, 1995; Spangler & Grossmann, 1993). Furthermore, when caregiving behavior is impaired among macaque mothers as a result of uncertainty about the ease of obtaining food, macaque infants develop enduring fearful behaviors and elevated levels of corticotropin-releasing factor that do not wane after a predictable food supply is reestablished (Coplan et al., 1996; Nemeroff, 1996). In addition, using a cross-fostering design with newborn rat pups, Francis, Diorio, Liu, and Meaney (1999) have recently demonstrated that both the quality of parent–pup interaction and the pup's associated physiological stress responses mediated by the HPA axis may be passed on intergenerationally, independent of genetic influence. These findings converge with findings from two- and three-generational human studies that have demonstrated the intergenerational transmission of attachment strategies (for a meta-analysis, see van IJzendoorn, 1995). Data from primate studies by Suomi, Kraemer, and others also document the influence of early nurturing conditions in setting up an enduring template for fearful behavioral responses, for HPA axis functioning, and for the coordination of neurotransmitter function (Boyce, Champoux, Suomi, & Gunnar, 1995; Clarke, 1993; Kraemer & Clarke, 1996). These findings are also beginning to be replicated among abused or neglected infants (e.g., Rogeness & McClure, 1996). Based on the accumulated primate data, Kraemer (1992) has argued that at birth the primate infant brain is designed as an open system that takes its organization from the organization of the caregiving environment.

Despite the many converging sources of evidence that parental depression affects caregiving and that caregiving conditions are related to the child's security of attachment and associated physiological responses to stressors, the evidence to date of an association between parental depression and child security of attachment is quite mixed.

In the remainder of this chapter, we consider the theoretical and methodological issues that may contribute to the current paradoxical state of the literature regarding parental depression and child attachment. We first briefly review the body of studies that have examined the parental depression–child attachment security link. We then consider two models of the parental depression–child insecure attachment relation, focusing on what we consider to be the most theoretically important third variable that potentially mediates the relation between parental depression and child attachment. This variable is the quality of the parent–child relationship, and, in particular, the adequacy of this relationship in regulating the child's fearful arousal.

We then present nationally representative survey data on the parenting correlates of depressive symptoms in mothers and fathers of children under age 3, data that describe the disparate parenting behaviors associated with depression. We discuss the possibility that clinical populations, including samples of depressed parents, are more likely to contain extremes of parental behavior that fall at opposite ends of various measurement dimensions. We argue further that this bipolarity of parental behavior poses methodological dilemmas for conventional strategies of data analysis and may artifactually attentuate statistical relations between depression and parenting and between parenting and attachment.

Finally, we integrate these findings with emerging results of attachment studies that demonstrate large differences in behavior between subgroups of parent–child dyads classified within the overall disorganized–controlling attachment classification. In some studies, these behavioral differences within the disorganized classification were larger than differences obtained between disorganized parents or children as a group and all nondisorganized individuals. For ease of reference, we have used the terms *hostile* or *helpless* to refer to the two parent–child subgroups that are emerging within the disorganized–controlling spectrum. For example, in our own study, one subgroup of parents displayed elevated rates of frightening, hostile, and intrusive behaviors as well as self-referential behaviors, whereas the other subgroup displayed elevated rates of withdrawing or subtly fearful behaviors, without accompanying hostile or threatening behavior. These different patterns of maternal behavior are described in more detail in a later section of the chapter on caregiving behaviors of mothers of disorganized infants.

Some evidence suggests that these hostile or helpless parenting organizations may be related, in turn, to the emergence of controlling–punitive or controlling–caregiving child attachment strategies by school age. On the basis of several recent studies, we argue that hostile-punitive parent–child dyads are much easier to discriminate on a variety of current measures, whereas helpless–fearful caregiving dyads may look adequate or even optimal on many measures compared to controls.

We conclude that helpless caregiving dyads may constitute an important subgroup in attachment-related studies of depressed parents, a sub-group that is currently underidentified and that further attenuates the obtained relations between child attachment and parental depression in the literature to date.

STUDIES OF THE RELATION BETWEEN PARENTAL DEPRESSION AND CHILD ATTACHMENT SECURITY

In a recent meta-analysis, van IJzendoorn, Schuengel, and Bakermans-Kranenburg (1999) analyzed the corpus of 16 published studies on the relationship between child disorganized attachment and parental depression and found only a small and nonsignificant effect size of .06. In addition, low socioeconomic status did not interact with parental depression to increase the relation between depression and disorganized attachment, indicating that the effect of depression on attachment security was similar over income levels. However, the effect size obtained in clinical samples of depressed mothers differed significantly from the effect size obtained in nonclinical samples.

When only clinical samples were considered, a significant relation between depression and attachment disorganization did emerge, although even in clinical populations the effect size of .13 was small. However, because the van IJzendoorn et al. (1999) meta-analysis focussed on correlates of disorganized attachment only, rather than insecure attachment more broadly, this effect size may be an underestimate (e.g., Frankel & Harmon, 1996; Murray, Fiori-Cowley, Hooper, & Cooper, 1996).

However, disorganized attachment behaviors, or their later analogue, the controlling attachment behaviors that emerge among disorganized infants during the preschool years, are the insecure behaviors that are consistently elevated in relation to parental clinical dysfunction (for a meta-analytic review, see van IJzendoorn, Goldberg, Kroonenberg, & Frenkel, 1992). Therefore, the relation between parental depression and child disorganized attachment behavior is the focus of this chapter. In addition, disorganized or controlling attachment behaviors are the only class of attachment behaviors that consistently predict clinical levels of child behavior problems (Lyons-Ruth, 1996; van IJzendoorn et al., 1999).

Studies that have reported significant relations between depression and attachment insecurity or disorganization have been those conducted with clinical samples in which depression was enduring (DeMulder & Radke-Yarrow, 1991; Frankel & Harmon, 1996; Lyons-Ruth, Connell, Grunebaum, & Botein, 1990; Murray et al., 1996; Teti, Gelfand, Messinger, & Isabella, 1995). Studies using self-report inventories in nonclinical populations, such as the National Institute of Child Health and Human Development (NICHD) study on day care, have not found significant relations (NICHD Early Child Care Research Network, 1997). Therefore, depression that is associated with "clinically significant interference with social or occupational functioning" (American Psychiatric Association, 1994, p. 163), an important criterion for the diagnosis of major depression, would seem to be the context in which parent–child attachment relationships may also be disturbed. Even in studies of samples meeting diagnostic criteria, however, research results are mixed, with DeMulder and Radke-Yarrow (1991), Frankel and Harmon (1996), and Seifer et al. (1996) failing to find a significant relation between child attachment and parental depression among mothers with unipolar depression. The relation between bipolar disorder and insecure attachment was significant in the DeMulder and Radke-Yarrow (1991) study, however, as was the relation between "double depression" (presence of both unipolar depression and chronic dysthymia) and insecure attachment in the Frankel and Harmon (1996) study.

It is also notable that DeMulder and Radke-Yarrow (1991) used a restricted sample selection strategy, specifying that the depressed mother had to be in a stable marriage at the time the study began. In addition, most families were very well-educated. This sampling strategy is likely to have selectively screened out those mothers whose depression most impaired their social and relational functioning, because depression has repeatedly been related to marital instability (Downey & Coyne, 1990).

Women in the Frankel and Harmon (1996) sample were also predominantly married and well-educated, with one-third of mothers classified as "in remission." In the authors' words, the sample "represents clinically depressed women in the community who experience diagnosable depressions and receive little or no treatment" (p. 295). Therefore, socioeconomically advantaged parents with stable marriages and episodic, but not chronic, depression may be more relationally skilled than most depressed women and therefore less likely to experience a sustained interference in functioning that affects their attachment relationships with their children.

In their recent meta-analysis of studies examining the relation between disorganized attachment and depression, van IJzendoorn et al. (1999) documented a significant difference in effect sizes between studies using the earlier developed infant attachment classification system and those using the MacArthur preschool classification system, with the infant system yielding more robust results. This finding may reflect a difference in the relation between maternal depression and child attachment disorganization by age, or it may reflect the need for continued refinement in the more recently developed preschool attachment assessment to reflect the range of behaviors encountered in clinical samples. Resolution of this issue awaits further research.

A "WEAK MODEL" OF RELATIONS BETWEEN PARENTAL DEPRESSION AND CHILD ATTACHMENT SECURITY

A number of variables are likely to partially mediate or moderate relations between parental depression and child attachment security. These include child characteristics, such as inhibited temperament or genetically mediated vulnerability to depression; parental characteristics, including gender role and temperamental qualities; and the stressful or beneficial characteristics of life contexts, including parent or child illnesses or separations, marital status, financial security, or social support. From a theoretical viewpoint, the quality of parent–child interaction should be particularly important in mediating relations between depression and child attachment. In fact, most of the contextual factors considered above would be viewed as affecting child attachment through their effects on the quality or frequency of parent–child interaction.

The potential contributions of individual genetic or biological vulnerability factors and of stressful or protective life conditions as potential mediators of relations between parental depression and child psychopathology have been reviewed extensively elsewhere and are not discussed further here (Goodman & Gotlib, 1999). Instead, we explore in more depth the parent–child interactive behaviors that have been related either to parental depression or child attachment because these behaviors are likely to mediate relations between parental depression and insecure child attachment.

In contrast to most models of the relations between parental depression and parental behavior, we do not assume that parental depression is the primary casual variable that acts through a variety of mechanisms to create poor child outcomes. In previous work, Lyons-Ruth (1995) noted the problems with the dominant view that parental depressive mood is a central causal contributor to the parent–child problems associated with parental depression. First, the less optimal parenting behaviors found in studies that compare well and depressed parents are also found among families with other parental diagnoses, such as anxiety disorders, substance abuse, or schizophrenia (Ledingham, 1990; Turner, Beidel, & Costello, 1987) and are also observed among parents with other serious stressors, such as medical illnesses (Breslau & Davis, 1986; Gordon, Burge, Hammen, Jaenicke, & Hiroto, 1989). There is little to suggest that the problematic relational behaviors observed in depression studies are specific to depression.

Second, the child outcomes associated with parental depression have not been specific to depression. Children of depressed parents show a range of maladaptive behaviors and psychiatric symptoms, similar to the children of parents with other psychiatric disorders or other severe personal or marital stressors (Downey & Coyne, 1990; Ledingham, 1990).

Third, problematic parenting behaviors, work-related difficulties, and child problem behaviors remain even after a clinical episode of major depression is in remission (Billings & Moos, 1986; Frankel & Harmon, 1996; Mintz, Mintz, Arruda, & Hwang, 1992; Richters & Pellegrini, 1989; Weinberg & Tronick, 1998; Weissman & Paykel, 1974). There is little to suggest, then, that problematic parenting closely tracks the mood changes associated with clinical depression, because considerable interepisode relational difficulties remain. Evidence continues to support the link between chronic depressive symptoms and parenting dysfunction (e.g., Hammen, Burge, & Stansbury, 1990; Lyons-Ruth, 1992), but depressive symptoms are elevated in a variety of clinical disorders, including anxiety disorders, conduct disorders, and substance abuse disorders, as well as in response to a variety of chronic stressors, including poverty (Ge, Conger, Lorenz, Shanahan, & Elder, 1995; Hammen et al., 1987; McLoyd, 1990). Therefore, the evidence is more consistent with the view that relational problems and generalized negative mood constitute a diathesis or vulnerability factor for episodes of clinical depression. This view received support from a recent study by Cadoret et al. (1996) of depressive diagnoses among adopted-away offspring of depressed parents. Adopted girls of depressed biological parents were more likely to develop clinical depression only if there was conflict in the adoptive family.

Further support of the view that parental depression may be, in part, a result of intergenerational family problems comes from several prospective longitudinal studies from middle childhood to early parenthood. These studies have independently replicated the finding that parent–child relational patterns in one generation are powerful predictors of similar patterns in the next generation (Caspi & Elder, 1988; Ge, Fan, & Wenk, 2000; Kremen & Block, 2000). In addition, longitudinal studies of the transition to parenting starting prior to the birth of the first child have found unexpectedly large proportions of variance in parenting behavior at 1 year explained by prenatal or early postnatal self-reported assessments of care received in childhood. Family relationship patterns in childhood continued to explain parenting behaviors at 1 year even after premarital personality and quality of the marital relationship were controlled (Belsky, Hertzog, & Rovine, 1986; Cox et al., 1985).

In the one study that specifically compared the relative contributions to observed parenting behaviors of depressive symptoms and of self-reported childhood patterns of care, earlier patterns of care accounted for both the parent's current depressive symptoms and the current maladaptive parenting behaviors associated with those symptoms, as well as a significant additional portion of variance in parenting not accounted for by depressive symptoms (Lyons-Ruth, 1992). Caspi and Elder (1988) concluded from their three-generational study that "attributing adult outcomes to proximal events ... is spurious because these effects derive from attributes of individuals, already evident in late childhood" (p. 135). Those attributes, in turn, were related to patterns of parent–child interaction in the first generation. This model of relations between depressive symptomatology and family process is displayed in Figure 5.1.

In this proposed "weak model" of the relations between parental depression and child maladaptation, we view maladaptive family interaction patterns in the first generation as a more powerful causal agent than second-generation clinically depressed mood in contributing to maladaptive family interaction patterns in the second generation. In addition, we view maladaptive family patterns in the family of origin as contributing causally both to clinical depression in the next generation and to maladaptive interaction patterns. In this view, the parent's depression does not cause the relational problems that contribute to child attachment insecurity or disorganization.

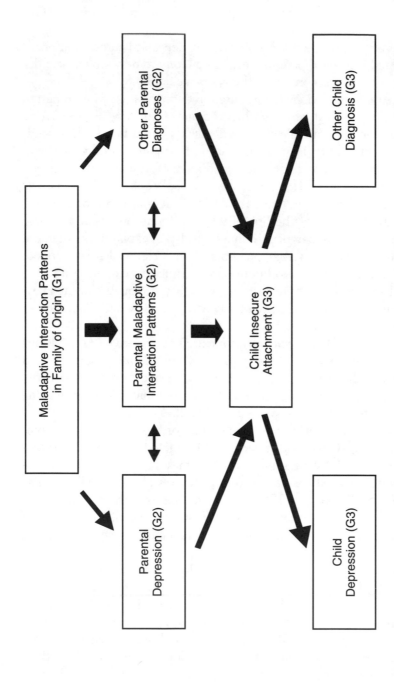

Figure 5.1. "Weak" Model of Relations Between Parental Depression, Parent–Child Interaction, and Child Attachment. From "Depressive Symptoms in Parents of Children Under Three: Sociodemographic Predictors, Current Correlates, and Associated Parenting Behaviors," by K. Lyons-Ruth, R. Wolfe, A. Lyubchik, and R. Steingard, in press, in N. Halfon, M. Schuster, & K. McLearn (Eds.), *The Health and Social Conditions of Young Children in American Families*, Cambridge, England: Cambridge University Press. Copyright by the Cambridge University Press. Reprinted by permission.

Instead, relational difficulties in the first generation predict relational difficulties in the second generation, thereby increasing the risk for both depression and attachment disorganization.

In the next sections, we explore what kinds of relational difficulties have been related both to parental depression and to the intergenerational transmission of attachment disorganization in very recent work.

PARENTING BEHAVIOR AMONG DEPRESSED PARENTS IN THE UNITED STATES: THE COMMONWEALTH SURVEY

As noted already, the literature to date on the parenting behaviors associated with parental depression indicates that parents who are depressed display a variety of less optimal caregiving behaviors compared to parents who are not depressed. Whether these differences are specific to depression or are related to parental stress or psychiatric problems more generally, the range of caregiving problems associated with a depressive diagnosis is quite broad, making it difficult to describe a single pattern of caregiving deviance associated with depression. For example, Zahn-Waxler and Kochanska (1990) described depressed mothers with young children as elaborating expressions of sadness in a laboratory role-play assessment and unnecessarily attributing their sadness to their children's behaviors in ways that were guilt-inducing for the child. In contrast, depressed parents are often described by clinicians as withdrawn, sad, and apathetic. Research results have also documented elevated levels of hostile, irritable behavior among depressed parents across child age and income levels (e.g., Lyons-Ruth, Zoll, Connell, & Grunebaum, 1986; Weissman & Paykel, 1974).

It remains unclear whether these differences in behavioral organization are associated with particular, as yet unmeasured, characteristics of depressed individuals, such as types of stressors experienced, cultural or ethnic factors, diagnostic subtypes or individual predispositions, or whether these several faces of depression are displayed at different times by the same individual.

A 1995 survey of parents of children under age 3 has explored the parenting behaviors correlated with increased depressive symptoms among both fathers and mothers of African American, Caucasian, and Hispanic ethnicity. These results again document the diverse array of parenting behaviors associated with depression, while also assessing their relation to socioeconomic status, ethnicity, and parental gender. We summarize these new epidemiological findings below and then turn to an examination of the hostile–helpless or frightened–frightening parenting behaviors associated with disorganization of infant attachment strategies.

In addition to the large number of smaller scale observational studies of parent–child interaction among depressed parents, the range of parenting problems associated with parental depressive symptoms has recently been explored in a nationally representative survey of 2,017 U.S. households with a child under age 3, commissioned by the Commonwealth Fund (Lyons-Ruth, Wolfe, Lyubchik, & Steingard, in press). The survey was designed to explore health and social conditions of young children in U.S. families (Halfon, Schuster, & McLearn, in press). The survey included 697 households in which the fathers were randomly selected as the interviewee and 1,320 households in which the mothers were selected to be interviewed. The sample was stratified and minority ethnic groups (Hispanic, African American) were oversampled to insure adequate sample sizes. All data analyses were weighted to correct for oversampling.

The size and representative nature of the survey added to the literature on parental depression by making it possible to examine the relation between depressive symptoms and parenting behaviors by socioeconomic level, ethnicity, and parental gender. The size and representativeness of the survey also made it possible to examine whether the socioeconomic factors often correlated with depressive symptoms explained any of the observed relations between depression and parenting behaviors. Such survey data do not have the strengths of direct observations of behavior or of more in-depth assessments of depressive symptoms. However, no large-scale epidemiologic data on depression and parenting have been available to anchor the myriad smaller scale research findings to a representative sample of parents with young children in the U.S. The Commonwealth Survey provides such a representative data set, making it possible to disentangle parenting behaviors that are correlates of parental depressive symptoms from parenting behaviors that are equally well explained by other aspects of the parent's sociodemographic profile.

The survey relied on five questions probing depressive symptoms taken from standard screening inventories for depression, inventories that focus on symptoms during the past week (e. g. CES-Depression Scale; Radloff, 1977). Parents were asked to rate how often the following depressive symptom statements applied to them during the past week: "I felt depressed," "I enjoyed life" (scored in reverse), "I had crying spells," "I felt sad," or "I felt that people disliked me." Response choices were "never," "rarely," "some of the time," and "most of the time." Endorsing "some of the time" or "most of the time" was considered a positive response to a given symptom statement.

Roughly 20% of mothers and 10% of fathers endorsed two or more of the five screening questions positively. These percentages corresponded to the prevalence of depressive symptoms needing clinical follow up among adults of parenting age found in other epidemiologic studies (e.g., Eaton & Kessler, 1981). Therefore, for categorized analyses, parents were classified "depressed" if two or more questions were answered positively.

To better communicate the quantitative findings, rates of depression or problematic parenting behaviors were also reported for three selected family profiles of interest to policy makers. Profile 1 consisted of a one-parent household with an income of less than $20,000 ($n = 289$); Profile 2 consisted of a two-parent household with an income of $30–40,000 ($n = 257$); and Profile 3 consisted of a two-parent household with an income greater than $60,000 ($n = 264$).

Socioeconomic and Prebirth Factors

The first class of survey responses analyzed included those aspects of the family's sociodemographic status and the parent's past experiences that were likely to have been in effect for some time prior to the birth of the child. The class of potential sociodemographic predictors included education, income, employment status, source of health insurance, receipt of government aid, single parenthood, teen parenthood, ethnicity (African American, Caucasian, Hispanic), and birth order of target child. Two types of stressful prebirth circumstances were also included in a separate step in the analysis. These were the parent's report of childhood experiences of emotional, physical, or sexual abuse and the parents' report of whether the pregnancy was wanted at that time.

Reiterating the results of previous epidemiologic surveys, the number of depressive symptoms endorsed was reliably related to most of the nine indicators of socioeconomic status, both for fathers and for mothers. When childhood abuse history and mistimed pregnancy were added to the significant sociodemographic predictors in a hierarchical multiple regression analysis, childhood abuse history predicted depressive symptoms independently of all sociodemographic indicators for both mothers and fathers. The odds of endorsing two or more depressive symptoms were 1.56 times higher for mothers and 2.23 times higher for fathers if they had experienced physical, sexual, or emotional abuse during childhood. Among mothers, 15% reported a childhood history of verbal or emotional abuse only and another 14% reported a history of physical or sexual abuse, for an overall rate of abuse of 29%. Among fathers, corresponding rates were 13% and 11%, or 24% overall (Lyons-Ruth et al., in press)

Positive and Negative Parenting Behaviors

The second set of multiple regression analyses examined whether the parents' depressive symptoms were related to their interactions with their young children, after controlling for all socioeconomic factors and stressful prebirth circumstances. The positive parent–child interactions that were examined included how frequently the parent cuddled, played with, read to, or sang or played music to the child. Parents were also asked whether they provided regular routines for the child regarding napping, mealtimes, and bedtimes. Conflict-related or limit-setting interactions were also examined, including how often the parent felt frustrated with the child; how often the parent yelled at the child; how often the parent spanked the child; and how often the parent hit, slapped, or shook the child.

For the parental behavior variables, analyses were conducted both on the multilevel frequency ratings for parental behaviors and on dichotomized versions of those variables (see text below for definitions of dichotomized variables). These analyses yielded similar results. Because of the small cell sizes for some parental behavior response categories, the odds ratios for the dichotomized parental behavior variables are reported here (see Lyons-Ruth et al., in press, for additional details of the analyses). The number of depressive symptoms was used to generate all odds ratios, so that the odds ratios refer to the increase in likelihood of a parental behavior that occurred with each additional depressive symptom endorsed by the parent.

When parents' positive interactive behaviors were analyzed, depressive symptoms emerged as an important predictor of mothers' lack of engagement in positive parenting behaviors. With all socioeconomic and prebirth factors controlled, the odds of a lack of daily routines for mealtimes, bedtimes, and naptimes rose by an average of 31% for each depressive symptom endorsed by mothers. The risk of reading to the child less than several times a week rose by 21%, and the risk of playing with the child less than once a day rose by 33%. The risk of engaging in low levels of two or more positive behaviors increased by 40% for each additional depressive symptom. These survey findings are notable additions to the literature because they explore key areas of parent–child interactions (play, reading, routines) that serve as the organizing foundation for the child's emerging critical competencies in social interaction, learning, and self-regulation.

Socioeconomic status and ethnicity also influenced mothers' positive engagement with their young children. Lower income mothers, teen mothers, and minority mothers (African American, Hispanic) reported engaging in fewer positive behaviors, independent of variance accounted for by depressive symptoms.

The contribution of maternal depression to decreased levels of positive interactions with the child across income levels is illustrated in Figure 5.2 in relation to the three profiles of American families.

Significant bivariate relations were also obtained between fathers' symptoms and positive parenting behaviors. However, in multivariate models, fathers' less positive parenting behaviors were better accounted for by socioeconomic factors than by depressive symptoms.

When conflict-related parent–child interactions were examined, depressive symptoms were an even more consistent predictor of parents' negative behaviors toward their children under age 3. With all 11 socioeconomic and prebirth variables controlled, the odds of a mother's feeling aggravated with her child twice a day or more, yelling at her child sometimes or often, spanking her child sometimes or often, or endorsing any one of the above negative behaviors rose by 32 to 39% with each additional depressive symptom endorsed. For fathers, the odds of ever hitting, slapping, or shaking the child increased by 47% for each depressive symptom reported, and the odds

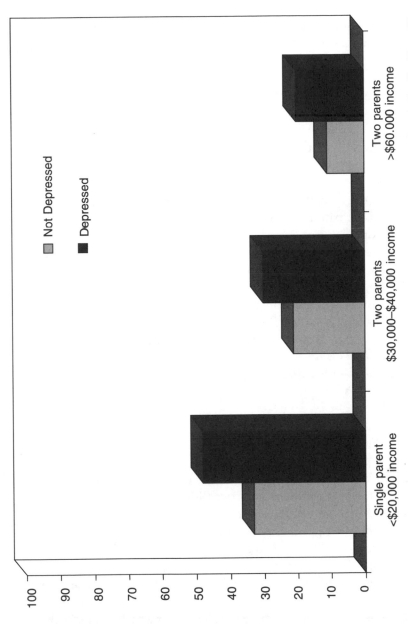

Figure 5.2. Percentage of Mothers Who Are Low on Two or More Forms of Positive Interaction, by Family Profile. From "Depressive Symptoms in Parents of Children Under Three: Sociodemographic Predictors, Current Correlates, and Associated Parenting Behaviors," by K. Lyons-Ruth, R. Wolfe, A. Lyubchik, and R. Steingard, in press, in N. Halfon, M. Schuster, & K. McLearn (Eds.), *The Health and Social Conditions of Young Children in American Families,* Cambridge, England: Cambridge University Press. Reprinted by permission.

of feeling aggravated with the child twice a day or more rose by 74%. These results are particularly dramatic because they pertain to parents' negative interactions with very young children.

In contrast to the previous findings regarding positive parental behaviors toward the child, socioeconomic and prebirth stressful events accounted for relatively little variance in conflict-related parental behavior once depressive symptoms were part of the model. In the multivariate analyses, number of depressive symptoms was the only variable associated with most forms of conflict-related interaction with the child, including (for both mothers and fathers) yelling, hitting, and overall negative interaction and (for mothers only) feeling aggravated with the child. For fathers, childhood abuse history also accounted for variation in feeling aggravated with the child after accounting for the variation associated with depressive symptoms. Income and ethnicity related only to the frequency of mother's spanking the child, after variance associated with depressive symptoms was accounted for (Lyons-Ruth et al., in press).

These are the first available data on an adequately large and representative sample of U.S. parents to demonstrate that previous associations in the research literature between low socioeconomic status or minority status and negative parental behaviors are mediated in large part by the level of the parents' current depressive symptoms (see also McLoyd, 1990). The demonstration that depressive symptoms are a more important correlate of irritable and punitive parenting behaviors than socioeconomic level is an important finding of the current survey. The contribution of parental depression to increased rates of one or more forms of negative interaction with the child across income levels is illustrated in Figure 5.3 in relation to the three profiles of American families described earlier.

THE TWO FACES OF PARENTAL DEPRESSION: SAME PARENT OR DIFFERENT PARENTS?

The Commonwealth Survey data, as well as data from smaller scale observational studies, describe at least two different faces of parental depression. Consistent with earlier descriptions in the literature, depressed parents were engaging in fewer positive and structuring interactions with the child; they were also more easily aggravated and more likely to lash out at the child verbally or physically than were nondepressed parents.

What remains unclear is whether a more withdrawn stance and a more irritable and punitive stance are alternative organizations of parenting displayed by different subgroups of depressed parents, or whether most depressed parents display all of these less optimal behaviors. For fathers, previous analyses had already revealed that increased negative behaviors were related to depressive symptoms, whereas variation in positive behaviors was not. To ad-

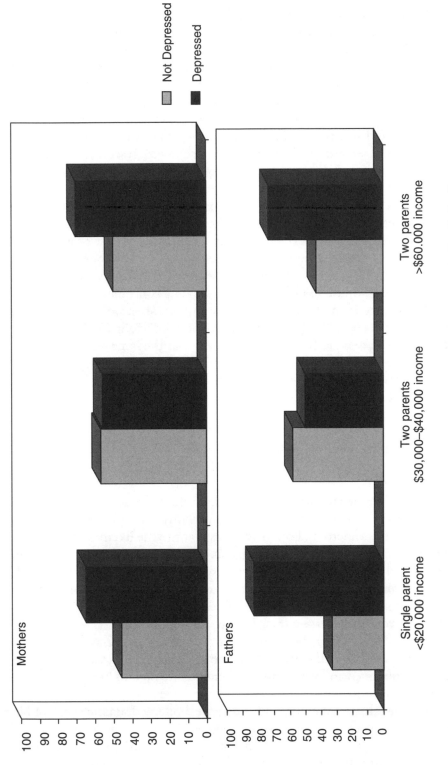

Figure 5.3. Percentage of Parents Who Display One or More Types of Negative Interaction, by Family Profile.

dress this question for mothers, an additional multiple regression analysis was conducted on the frequency of their depressive symptoms, entering first the set of decreased positive behaviors related to depressive symptoms, which included frequency of play, frequency of reading, and consistency of routines, and then entering the set of increased negative behaviors related to depressive symptoms, which included feeling aggravated, yelling, and spanking. If the same mothers were reporting both the negative and positive sets of behaviors related to depression, controlling for the association between a mother's decreased positive behaviors and her depression score should greatly attenuate the relation between the same mother's increased negative behaviors and her depression score.

As expected, the three positive behaviors negatively associated with maternal depressive symptoms—that is, frequency of play, frequency of reading, and consistency of routines—accounted for a significant proportion of variance in maternal depressive symptoms when entered as a block, $F(3, 990) = 13.07$, $p < .0001$. However, when the set of negative maternal behaviors was then added to the model, negative behaviors continued to account for unique variance in mother's depressive symptoms, after variance associated with decreased positive behaviors was accounted for, F chg $(3, 987) = 16.11$, $p < .0001$. This analysis for mothers confirms that the same depressed mothers are not reporting both decreased positive behaviors and increased negative behaviors. Instead, these two sets of behaviors are independently related to maternal depressive symptoms.

DEPRESSION, PARENTING, AND DISORGANIZED ATTACHMENT RELATIONSHIPS

The heterogeneity across individuals in the behaviors associated with depressive affect is consistent with the literatures on both stress responses and psychiatric symptoms. Both literatures point to the likelihood that stress and adversity may contribute to exaggerated behavioral differences between stressed individuals. Extensive studies of stress responses using animal models have highlighted the very different behavioral possibilities of fight or flight that emerge in response to stress, with freezing as a variant of flight in situations of extreme helplessness (e.g., Jansen, Nguyen, Karpitskiy, Mettenleiter, & Loewy, 1995). Using the group mean for aggressive behavior or fearful behavior among stressed animals would not capture the heterogeneity in the responses observed and would miss the underlying organizational principles of the behavior of different animals.

The psychiatric literature documents a similarly dramatic range of behavioral differences associated with different psychiatric disorders, ranging from the extremes of inhibition (e.g. catatonia, retarded depression) to the extremes of assaultiveness and criminality. These behavioral differences are also statistically linked to gender so that male individuals are greatly over-represented in diagnostic groups that include externalizing tendencies (e.g., attention deficit–hyperactivity disorder, conduct disorder, substance abuse, antisocial personality), whereas female individuals are overrepresented in several diagnostic groups that feature internalizing tendencies (e.g., depression, anorexia).

The same bimodality of behavioral organizations in response to adversity represented in the literatures on depression, stress, and psychopathology is now emerging in the attachment literature in relation to the disorganized attachment category. This bimodality is observed in relation to both parent and child behavior.

BEHAVIORAL DIFFERENCES WITHIN THE DISORGANIZED ATTACHMENT CATEGORY

Recent research is generating increasing evidence of at last two distinct subgroups within the disorganized attachment category during early childhood. Disorganized attachment strategies can first be identified at 12 months of age, when some infants display contradictory, apprehensive, undirected, or anomalous behaviors in the presence of the parent after the stress of a brief separation (e.g., starting toward mother smiling, then veering away from her; freezing for 20 seconds; aimless wandering in the vicinity of the parent; or falling on the floor and pointing at the ceiling while rolling back and forth in slow motion; see Main & Solomon, 1990, for detailed coding criteria). These disorganized attachment behaviors may occur in concert with other insecure behaviors that are part of an avoidant or ambivalent attachment strategy, resulting in a primary classification of disorganized attachment and a secondary classification of avoidant or ambivalent. Infants in this subgroup are hereafter referred to as *D-insecure*. However, disorganized behaviors may also be displayed in the context of behaviors that are usually part of a secure strategy, such as protesting separation, seeking contact with mother at reunion, and ceasing distress after being picked up. This disorganized subgroup is given a secondary classification of secure and is referred to as *D-secure*.

Lyons-Ruth, Repacholi, McLeod, and Silva (1991) reviewed studies that used the disorganized classification system while also reporting data on the secondary classifications for all disorganized infants. This review revealed that a majority of infants who were classified in the D category from low-risk middle-income samples displayed disorganized forms of secure strategies without marked avoidance or resistance. In contrast, a majority of infants from families with more serious psychosocial risk factors displayed disorganized forms of avoidant or ambivalent strategies (D-insecure). Analyses within a single low socioeconomic cohort have also confirmed that more severe psychosocial risk factors were associated with a relative increase in the proportion of D-insecure infant strategies, compared to D-secure strategies.

Sometime between 18 months of age and 6 years, with the cognitive developments of the preschool period, disorganized infants' attachment behaviors begin to become organized around the apparent goal of controlling the interaction with the attachment figure. Longitudinal studies from infancy to age 6 have confirmed that what had been a disorganized set of behaviors in infancy is likely to become an organized controlling attachment strategy by school entry (Main, Kaplan, & Cassidy, 1985; Wartner, Grossmann, Fremmer-Bombik, & Seuss, 1994). Controlling attachment behaviors have also been found to take two very different forms—one termed *controlling–punitive* and one termed *controlling–caregiving*. *Controlling–punitive behavior* is behavior in which the child attempts to take control of the relationship with the parent when attachment concerns are aroused through hostile, coercive, or more subtly humiliating behaviors. *Controlling–caregiving behavior* is behavior in which the child takes control by entertaining, organizing, directing, or giving approval to the parent.

In addition, Solomon, George, and De Jong (1995) found that some controlling 6-year-olds were extremely inhibited in play whereas another group played out frightening and chaotic scenes with no positive resolution. If the inhibited children could be induced to play, however, frightening and chaotic scenarios emerged. Solomon et al. further reported that children inhibited in play were more likely to be classified as *caregiving* whereas children with more chaotic play scenarios were more often classified as *punitive*. We speculate that the two disorganized infant subgroups mentioned earlier, D-secure and D-insecure, are early precursors, or anlagen, of the caregiving and punitive stances observed among controlling children at age 6. However, longitudinal data are not yet available to evaluate these postulated links between the two D subgroups in infancy and the two controlling subgroups during the preschool period. Like Main et al. (1985) and Solomon et al. (1995), we view these two disorganized–controlling patterns as different behavioral strategies for responding to a basic disruption in the regulatory function of the caregiving system that exposes the child to inadequately modulated fearful arousal.

CAREGIVING BEHAVIORS AMONG MOTHERS OF DISORGANIZED INFANTS: THE EMERGENCE OF DISTINCT PROFILES

Results from a number of studies using parental behavior measures have indicated that mothers of disorganized infants or controlling children demonstrate the least optimal interactive behaviors with their children (DeMulder & Radke-Yarrow, 1991; Lyons-Ruth et al., 1991; Main et al., 1985; Moss,

Parent, Gosselin, Rousseau, & St. Laurent, 1996; Stevenson-Hinde & Shouldice, 1995; Teti et al., 1995). In addition, all of the more distal correlates of disorganized or controlling behaviors, such as parental unresolved attachment classifications or parental psychosocial risk factors, point to a contribution of parent–infant interaction to the genesis of infant disorganization (see Lyons-Ruth & Jacobvitz, 1999; van IJzendoorn et al., 1999). However, it appears that parental behaviors other than those captured by Ainsworth's sensitivity scale (Ainsworth, Blehar, Waters, & Wall, 1978) must be investigated, because studies using that scale, in particular, have generated only a small association, albeit a reliable one, between parental behavior and infant disorganization (van IJzendoorn et al., 1999).

Along with others (Jacobvitz, Hazen, & Riggs, 1997; Schuengel, Bakermans-Kranenburg, & van IJzendoorn, 1999), we have explored Main and Hesse's (1990) hypothesis that the parent's frightened or frightening behavior is the distinctive element that is associated with disorganization of infant attachment strategies. Prior to the development of the Main and Hesse (1992) coding instrument for frightened or frightening behavior, however, our pilot work (Parsons, 1991) had led us to advance a broader regulatory hypothesis regarding the parental behaviors that would become disorganizing to the infant. Lyons-Ruth, Bronfman, and Parsons (1999) explored the hypothesis that appropriate parental response to the specific content of the infant's affective communications is the essential element that prevents the infant's excessive unregulated fearful arousal and associated behavioral disorganization. This view differed from the Main and Hesse (1990) hypothesis slightly in that it viewed infant fearful arousal as stemming either from particular parental behaviors (e.g., frightened or frightening behaviors) or from an absence of adequate parental regulatory responses. In this view, parental withdrawing behaviors or role-confused behaviors that leave the infant without adequate parental regulation of fearful affect would also be potentially disorganizing, whether or not the parent's own behaviors were directly frightened or frightening to the infant.

Whether investigators have coded frightened or frightening behaviors per se or have examined a broader inventory of parental disrupted affective communications, however, recent work suggests that two distinct profiles of mother–infant interaction may be associated with the disorganization of infant attachment strategies and that the two maternal profiles may be differentially linked to the two disorganized infant profiles (D-secure and D-insecure).

Lyons-Ruth, Bronfman, and Parsons (1999) used an atypical maternal behavior inventory that indexed the frequency of maternal withdrawing, negative–intrusive, role-confused, disoriented, and contradictory behaviors in response to infant cues, as well as the frightened or frightening behaviors included on the Main and Hesse (1992) coding inventory. As predicted, the frequency of atypical caregiving behaviors was significantly related to the infant's display of disorganized attachment behaviors ($r = .39, p < .01$). These atypical maternal behaviors, which were coded in the Ainsworth Strange Situation assessment (Ainsworth et al., 1978) which consists of a series of brief separations and reunions, demonstrated cross-situational stability in that they were significantly related to similar behaviors observed in an unstructured home observation. In addition, higher levels of atypical maternal behavior in the Strange Situation were associated with increased infant distress at home. Neither infant gender nor cumulative demographic risk was significantly related to maternal atypical behavior.

The more surprising finding, however, was that there were substantial differences in maternal behavior within the disorganized infant group, with mothers of D-insecure infants displaying significantly more atypical behaviors than mothers of D-secure infants, $t(22) = 2.49, p < .02$. In particular, mothers of D-insecure infants displayed significantly higher rates of both role confusion and negative–intrusive behavior than mothers of D-secure infants. In contrast, mothers of D-secure infants exhibited significantly higher rates of withdrawal than mothers of D-insecure infants (Lyons-Ruth, Bronfman, & Parsons, 1999). However, only the mothers of D-insecure infants differed significantly from mothers of organized infants in their rates of atypical behavior.

When examined separately, the frightened or frightening behaviors from the Main and Hesse protocol showed the same relation to infant disorganized attachment classification as did total atypical behavior. Mothers whose infants were classified D-insecure exhibited significantly more frightened or frightening behavior compared to mothers of organized infants and mothers of D-secure infants, whereas mothers of D-secure infants did not differ from mothers of organized infants in frequency of frightened or frightening behaviors.

Data from other studies have also suggested that parents in the D-secure subgroup may be harder to identify because their behaviors are withdrawing and inhibited rather than hostile, intrusive, frightened, or frightening. For example, Schuengel et al. (1999) examined the frightened or frightening behaviors of mothers classified as unresolved with respect to loss or trauma on the Adult Attachment Interview (George, Kaplan & Main, 1996). The *adult unresolved classification* is the theoretical analogue of the disorganized infant classification. As is the case for disorganized infants, unresolved mothers are also subclassified as unresolved-secure or unresolved-insecure, based on other characteristics of the parent's discourse during the interview. Contrary to prediction, mothers classified unresolved-secure displayed significantly less frightened or frightening behavior than did mothers judged fully secure. This finding converged with our finding that mothers of D-secure infants were more withdrawing in interaction and suggests some overall behavioral inhibition on the part of mothers classified as unresolved-secure. In contrast, unresolved-insecure mothers displayed the predicted elevation in frightened or frightening behavior. Jacobvitz et al. (1997) also found fewer frightened or frightening behaviors among unresolved-secure mothers than unresolved-insecure mothers.

This withdrawing or inhibited behavior pattern was statistically significantly discriminated in the Lyons-Ruth, Bronfman, and Parsons (1999) study when analyses were conducted on patterns of behavior across variables rather than on single variables. Mothers of D-secure infants were more likely than other mothers to exhibit a frightened-inhibited behavior pattern in which frightened behaviors were displayed at moderate but not extreme levels and in which there were no associated elevations in frightening, dissociated, or role-reversed behavior. In addition, mothers of D-secure infants were significantly more likely to display elevated rates of withdrawing behaviors, also without associated elevations in negative or frightening behavior (see Lyons-Ruth, Bronfman, & Atwood, 1999, and Lyons-Ruth, Bronfman, & Parsons, 1999, for details of these analyses).

The fearful-inhibited pattern of maternal behavior and the nonhostile withdrawn pattern together characterized 80% of the mothers of D-secure infants, compared to 29% of mothers of infants with organized attachment strategies and 20% of mothers of D-insecure infants, [Phi] = .44, $p < .005$, and [Phi] = .58, $p < .005$, respectively. Subsequent review of these behaviors on videotape revealed that many of the fearful or withdrawing maternal behaviors were displayed in response to the child's bids for proximity or contact. Therefore, the combined profile of subtly fearful or withdrawing but nonhostile maternal behaviors was termed *helpless–fearful regarding attachment*. The behaviors contributing to this profile are described in more detail in Lyons-Ruth, Bronfman, and Atwood (1999).

The subtle nature of the helpless–fearful profile of maternal behavior is important to note, however, as is the subtlety of many of the disorganized behaviors of D-secure infants. The maternal or infant behaviors that include negative affect are much easier to identify as maladaptive, yet recent data indicate that these behaviors characterize only one subgroup of the broader spectrum of mothers and infants who experience disorganized attachment relationships.

These data documenting two significantly different profiles of caregiving behavior among mothers of disorganized infants also converge well with the previously cited data on the two faces of maternal depression. It is also likely that the more punitive and aggravated behaviors of the irritable subgroups of depressed mothers are easier to identify than the relative absence of play, stimulation, and structure reported by mothers who are not also irritable.

Other data suggest that these difficulties in identifying problematic but non-hostile relationship patterns among high-risk mothers also extend to their children, particularly their female children.

Teti (1999), observing mother–child interactions among the two subgroups of controlling children at preschool age, noted that there were no reliable differences between the secure and caregiving groups, whereas punitive children were significantly more negative than both secure and caregiving children in emotional tone during interactions with mothers. In addition, punitive children differed marginally reliably from caregiving children on interest and involvement with mother. Murray, Woolgar, Briers, and Hipwell (1999) found similar large differences among school-age children of depressed parents in a nonattachment-oriented doll-play assessment. Girls of depressed mothers were coded as exhibiting the most optimal play characteristics, whereas boys of depressed mothers displayed the least optimal play. Both boys and girls of nondepressed parents received intermediate play scores. These data again suggest that one subgroup of at-risk children, here defined by child gender, may be successful in suppressing or controlling the expression of negative affect whereas among other at-risk subgroups the negative affects intrude into interactions with others, as well as into play representations of interactions.

It is plausible to speculate that female gender may be differentially related to caregiving forms of control whereas male gender may predispose to punitive forms of control. However, the small cell sizes that occur when controlling or disorganized groups are subdivided by gender has precluded any definitive test of this hypothesis. Data currently being analyzed in our lab indicate that as maternal behavior becomes more frightening or more withdrawing, gender differences in attachment behaviors emerge, with female infants more likely to be classified as secure, avoidant, or D-secure at 18 months of age and male infants more likely to display D-insecure behaviors (Lyons-Ruth, Bronfman, & Lyubchik, 2001).

All the difficulties noted above in distinguishing fully secure parent–infant dyads from D-secure or caregiving parent–child dyads, particularly among girls, may also contribute to the longitudinal pattern of findings obtained by Radke-Yarrow (1998). In that study, the children of unipolar depressed mothers were often classified as secure, but those secure children did quite poorly over time. In addition, the difficulties noted among these children began with disruptive behaviors observed as early as 1[½] to 3[½] years of age, roughly the same time that attachment was being assessed.

Although it would be tempting to conclude from the above findings that D-secure infants or controlling–caregiving children or girls of depressed mothers may be less at risk for negative outcomes, this conclusion is at odds with a large body of data. Compared to D-insecure infants, D-secure infants are at equal risk for a variety of negative outcomes, including elevated cortisol secretion to mild stressors in infancy (Spangler & Grossmann, 1993), elevated distress during interactions with mother at home (Lyons-Ruth, Bronfman, & Parsons, 1999), elevated hostile–aggressive behaviors towards peers in kindergarten and 2nd grade (Lyons-Ruth, Alpern, & Repacholi, 1993; Lyons-Ruth, Easterbrooks, & Cibelli, 1997), and elevated rates of controlling attachment patterns towards parents by age 6 (Main et al., 1985; Wartner et al., 1994). Controlling–caregiving children are also clearly at risk. When the more play-inhibited caregiving children observed by Solomon et al. (1995) were induced to engage in play, their play themes included fearful, chaotic, or bizarre elements, like those of controlling–punitive children. In addition, caregiving children, as well as punitive children, who were at elevated risk for behavior problems reported by both mothers and teachers (Solomon et al., 1995). Finally, no consistent gender differences in overall rates of behavior problems or psychopathology have emerged in the literature on children of depressed parents, so there is little reason to think that girls are at less risk than boys (e.g., Downey & Coyne, 1990; Goodman & Gotlib, 1999; Radke-Yarrow, 1998). Instead, the behaviors of some controlling or otherwise at-risk children may look better than average when interacting with their parents but worse than average in other assessment settings, including interactions with peers and teachers at school (Dumas, Gibson, & Albin, 1989). The accurate identification of parents and children in the D-secure subgroup gains additional importance because the attachment literature indicates that this subgroup of disorganized infants is likely to comprise the majority of disorganized infants in middle-income samples, which are the most widely studied samples (Lyons-Ruth et al., 1991). We conclude that the difficulty in documenting a consistent link between maternal depression and child disorganization, particularly in higher-income groups, may be partially a function of the difficulty in accurately identifying D-secure and caregiving children, as well as the difficulty in distinguishing the helpless–fearful maternal behaviors associated with those child adaptations.

IMPLICATIONS FOR CLINICIANS

Two major implications of the recent literature on depression and attachment were explored in this chapter. First, parental depression may be better modeled as a correlate, or even as a partial effect, rather than as a cause of intergenerationally transmitted, problematic family relationship patterns. As we discuss below, this shift in causal emphasis also implies a shift in treatment strategy. Second, disorganized child attachment behaviors, and the parent–child interactions associated with those patterns, may be composed of at least two dramatically different subgroups that differ more from one another than either group differs from the behavior patterns seen among nondisorganized parents and children. This increased variability complicates the clinical and research assessment of family interactions and of child attachment strategies. This variability also makes it unlikely that a single treatment approach is effective.

If clinically depressed mood is a partial correlate rather than a primary cause of many of the parenting difficulties associated with depression, then treating the depression alone is unlikely to ameliorate many of the parenting difficulties associated with depression. In studies documenting the less positive parenting practices of depressed parents, the depressed parents in many cases were already receiving medications and other standard forms of mental health care (e.g., Gordon et al., 1989; Teti et al., 1995; Weinberg & Tronick, 1998; Weissman & Paykel, 1974). Weinberg and Tronick observed that depressed mothers receiving treatment often reported improved mood even though their interactions with their infants remained significantly less positive than those of nondepressed controls. Therefore, intervention strategies for depressed parents should include both symptom relief, through medication or psychotherapy, and specific help with the stresses and problems of parenting (Lyons-Ruth, Wolfe, & Lyubchik, 2000).

Current developmental studies, both within and outside the attachment research tradition, converge on the view that parenting behaviors are influenced by relatively stable mental models of the parenting one received as a child. Even when these models are unsatisfactory to parents and consciously disavowed, they are grounded in early experience and strong emotions and tend to be repeated when alternative models are not available. Even when new models are provided, organized patterns of thinking and behavior change slowly and require extended periods of exposure to new models and reworking of old ways of interacting to become stable in the form of new parenting capabilities. Whereas psychiatric services are well-equipped to provide medication for depression, neither pediatric nor mental health services are currently well equipped to provide extended parenting help to parents with infants and young children. However, it is increasingly clear that help with problematic parenting practices should be provided early in the life of parent and infant, before the child has reached school age and become an entrenched contributor to a maladaptive cycle of interaction.

This critical gap in services for young families could be addressed by developing family support teams as collaborative services between psychiatry and obstetric and pediatric services. These teams would provide cross-disciplinary expertise in psychopharmacology, up-to-date developmental knowledge, and clinical skill in working with parents and infants. The availability of outreach to the home is also critical to engaging isolated and depressed young parents, particularly those with more than one young child.

The second major point of this chapter, namely that both depressed parents and disorganized or controlling infants and children may show large within-group variability, indicates that interventions around parenting have to be flexible and responsive to these wide individual differences in the maladaptive behaviors displayed. Negative and intrusive parent and child behaviors are relatively easy to identify, but recent research suggests that more helpless, fearful parental behavior is much harder to identify as problematic. In addition, the role-reversed behaviors of the caregiving child, which may look precociously advanced, may also be under-identified by current research and clinical assessments. Careful clinical description and research documentation of these relational patterns over time and over contexts is required for the design of effective interventions for parenting.

The work reviewed in this chapter adds to the body of previous work on parental depression in pointing to the early onset of disturbance among the infants of depressed parents. Given this early onset, parents need increased information and support for the parenting role in the early years. Currently, there are very few comprehensive attempts to provide medical, social service, or mental health support for parents of young children in the U.S. Simple screening procedures for depression among expectant parents and parents with young children constitute an easy-to-implement first-level intervention to identify depressed parents and provide further services.

Although relatively few clinical intervention studies have focussed specifically on improving early child outcomes among depressed parents in particular (although see Beardslee et al., 1997; Cicchetti, Rogosch, & Toth, 2000; Lyons-Ruth et al., 1990), an array of early intervention models for stressed low-income parents have now shown positive long-term effects on child and adolescent life outcomes and decreased aggression (Bryant & Ramey, 1987; Lyons-Ruth, Connell, Alpern, Lyubchik, & DiLallo, 2000; Olds et al., 1997; Schweinhart, Barnes, & Weikart, 1993). Thoughtful clinical models and well-designed controlled treatment trials are now needed to evaluate which service designs best meet the needs of depressed parents and their children in the first years of parenting.

SUMMARY

Studies to date have shown only a weak relationship between parental depression and disorganization of infant attachment strategies. This relation becomes somewhat stronger in studies of clinically diagnosed parents, particularly those with chronic interepisode dysthymia. Both recent representative survey data and a variety of smaller developmental studies have identified two different and statistically independent patterns of parent–child interaction among depressed parents. In one pattern, parents are more negative, intrusive, and role-reversing. We have termed this a *hostile, self-referential pattern*. In the other pattern, parents show reduced rates of positive, structuring behaviors, without elevated rates of negative interactions. We have termed this a *helpless, fearful pattern*. Furthermore, infants of hostile versus helpless parents display different forms of disorganized behavior, with infants of helpless, fearful parents displaying disorganized forms of secure approach behavior and infants of hostile, self-referential mothers displaying disorganized forms of insecure avoidant or ambivalent behavior.

In our own work, both the maternal helpless–fearful behaviors and the infant D-secure behaviors have been harder to identify. We suggest that these less negative-appearing behavioral organizations are likely to be especially frequent in depressed samples and may have been underidentified in previous research, as well as in previous clinical work. In addition, very recent work indicates that as parental behavior becomes more frightening or more withdrawing, gender differences appear in the infant's attachment behaviors, gender differences that are not seen in low-risk samples. Boys' disorganized behaviors more closely reflect the quality of the parent–infant interaction, as rated by observers. In contrast, girls appear more likely to inhibit conflict behavior and therefore are more likely to be classified as secure or avoidant, rather than disorganized, in the face of hostile or withdrawing parenting.

The literature indicates that parental depression may be better viewed as a correlate rather than a cause of problematic parent–child interactions. First, patterns of parent–child interaction are more strongly predicted by the type of parenting the parent experienced as a child rather than by the type of current psychiatric diagnosis. Second, problematic parent–child interactions do not remit when depressive episodes remit. Therefore, the most important clinical implication of this body of work is that the problematic parenting behaviors associated with parental depression, as well as with other parental diagnoses, require specific intervention strategies targeted toward those interaction patterns, in addition to the need for medication or individual psychotherapies aimed at relieving parental depressive symptoms.

REFERENCES

Ainsworth, M. S., Blehar, M. C., Waters, E., & Wall, S. (1978). *Patterns of attachment: A psychological study of the strange situation.* Potomac, MD: Erlbaum.

American Psychiatric Association. (1994). *Diagnostic and statistical manual of mental disorders* (4th ed.). Washington, DC: American Psychiatric Association.

Amsterdam, J., Maislin, G., Gold, P., & Winokur, A. (1989). The assessment of abnormalities in hormonal responsiveness at multiple levels of the hypothalamic-pituitary-adrenocortical axis in depressive illness. *Psychoneuroendocrinology, 14,* 43–63.

Beardslee, W., Wright, E., Salt, P., Gladstone, T., Versage, E., & Rothberg, P. (1997). Sustained change in parents receiving preventive interventions for families with depression: Evidence of change. *Development and Psychopathology, 9,* 109–130.

Belsky, J., Hertzog, C., & Rovine, M. (1986). Causal analyses of multiple determinants of parenting: Empirical and methodological advances. In M. Lamb, A. Brown, & B. Rogoff (Eds.), *Advances in developmental psychology* (Vol. 4, pp. 153–202). Hillsdale, NJ: Erlbaum.

Billings, A. G., & Moos, R. H. (1986). Children of parents with unipolar depression: A controlled 1-year follow up. *Journal of Abnormal Child Psychology, 14,* 149–166.

Boyce, T., Champoux, M., Suomi, S., & Gunnar, M. (1995). Salivary cortisol in nursery-reared rhesus monkeys: Reactivity to peer interactions and altered Circadian activity. *Developmental Psychobiology, 28,* 257–267.

Breslau, N., & Davis, G. (1986). Chronic stress and major depression. *Archives of General Psychiatry, 43*, 309–314.

Bryant, D. M., & Ramey, C. T. (1987). An analysis of the effectiveness of early intervention programs for environmentally at-risk children. In M. Guralnick (Ed.), *The effectiveness of early intervention for at-risk and handicapped children* (pp. 33–78). New York: Academic Press.

Cadoret, R., Winokur, G., Langbehn, D., Troughton, E., Yates, W., & Stewart, M. (1996). Depression spectrum disease: I. The role of gene–environment interaction. *American Journal of Psychiatry, 13*, 892–899.

Caspi, A., & Elder, G. (1988). Childhood precursors of the life course: Early personality and life disorganization. In E. M. Hetherington, R. Lerner, & M. Perlmutter (Eds.), *Child development in life-span perspective* (pp. 115–142). Hillsdale, NJ: Erlbaum.

Cicchetti, D., Rogosch, F., & Toth, S. (2000). The impact of parent–toddler psychotherapy for fostering cognitive development in offspring of depressed mothers. *Journal of Abnormal Child Psychology, 28*, 135–148.

Clarke, A. S. (1993). Social rearing effects on HPA axis activity over early development and in response to stress in young rhesus monkeys. *Developmental Psychobiology, 26*, 433–447.

Coplan, J., Andrews, M., Rosenblum, L., Owens, M., Friedman, S., Gorman, J., & Nemeroff, C. (1996). Persistent elevations of cerebrospinal fluid concentrations of corticotropin-releasing factor in adult nonhuman primates exposed to early-life stressors: Implications for the pathophysiology of mood and anxiety disorders. *Proceedings of the National Academy of Sciences, USA, 93*, 1619–1623.

Cox, M. J., Owen, M. T., Lewis, J. M., Riedel, C., Scalf-McIver, L., & Suster, A. (1985). Intergenerational influences on the parent–infant relationship in the transition to parenthood. *Journal of Family Issues, 6*, 543–564.

Cummings, M., & Cicchetti, D. (1990). Toward a transactional model of the relations between attachment and depression. In M. T. Greenberg, D. Cicchetti, & E. M. Cummings (Eds.), *Attachment in the preschool years: Theory, research, and intervention* (pp. 339–374). Chicago: University of Chicago Press.

DeMulder, E. K., & Radke-Yarrow, M. (1991). Attachment with affectively ill and well mothers: Concurrent behavioral correlates. *Development and Psychopathology, 3*, 227–242.

Downey, G., & Coyne, J. C. (1990). Children of depressed parents: An integrative review. *Psychological Bulletin, 108*, 50–76.

Dumas, J. E., Gibson, J. A., & Albin, J. B. (1989). Behavioral correlates of maternal depressive symptomatology in conduct-disorder children. *Journal of Consulting and Clinical Psychology, 57*, 516–521.

Eaton, W. W., & Kessler, L. G. (1981). Rates of symptoms of depression in a national sample. *American Journal of Epidemiology, 114*, 528–538.

Francis, D., Diorio, J., Liu, D., & Meaney, M. (1999). Nongenomic transmission across generations of maternal behavior and stress responses in the rat. *Science, 286*, 1155–1158.

Frankel, K., & Harmon, R. (1996). Depressed mothers: They don't always look as bad as they feel. *Journal of the American Academy of Child and Adolescent Psychiatry, 35,* 289–298.

Ge, X., Conger, R., Lorenz, F., Shanahan, M., & Elder, G. H. (1995). Mutual influences in parent and adolescent distress. *Developmental Psychology, 31,* 406–419.

Ge, X., Fan, J., & Wenk, E. (2000, March). *Trajectories of criminal offending of serious juvenile offenders.* Presented as part of the symposium Psychopathology Across Time: Studying Trajectories of Maladaptive Functioning From Adolescence Through Early Adulthood, Chicago, IL.

George, C., Kaplan, N., & Main, M. (1996). *Adult attachment interview.* Unpublished manuscript. University of California Berkeley.

Goodman, S., & Gotlib, I. (1999). Risk for psychopathology in the children of depressed mothers: A developmental model for understanding mechanisms of transmission. *Psychological Review, 106,* 458–490.

Gordon D., Burge, D., Hammen, C., Adrian, C., Jaenicke, C., & Hirohito, D. (1989). Observations of interactions of depressed women with their children. *American Journal of Psychology, 146,* 50–55.

Halfon, N., Schuster, M., & McLearn, K. (in press). *The health and social conditions of young children in American families.* Cambridge, England: Cambridge University Press.

Hammen, C., Burge, D., & Stansbury, K. (1990). Relationship of mother and child variables to child outcomes in a high risk sample: A causal modeling analysis. *Developmental Psychology, 26,* 24–30.

Hammen, C., Gordon, G., Burge, D., Jaenicke, C., & Hiroto, D. (1987). Maternal affective disorders, illness, and stress: Risk for children's psychopathology. *American Journal of Psychiatry, 144,* 736–741.

Hertsgaard, L., Gunnar, M., Erickson, M., & Nachmias, M. (1995). Adrenocortical response to the strange situation in infants with disorganized/disoriented attachment relationships. *Child Development, 66,* 1100–1106.

Jacobvitz, D., Hazen, N., & Riggs, S. (1997, April). *Disorganized mental processes in mothers, frightened/frightening caregiving, and disoriented/disorganized behavior in infancy.* Paper presented at the biennial meeting of the Society for Research in Child Development, Washington, DC.

Jansen, A., Nguyen, X., Karpitskiy, V., Mettenleiter, T., & Loewy, A. (1995). Central command neurons of the sympathetic nervous system: Basis of the fight-or-flight response. *Science, 270,* 644–646.

Kraemer, G. W. (1992). A psychobiological theory of attachment. *Behavioral Brain Science, 15,* 493–511.

Kraemer, G. W., & Clarke, A. S. (1996). Social attachment, brain function, and aggression. *Annals of the New York Academy of Sciences, 794,* 121–135.

Kremen, A. M., & Block, J. (2000, March). *Maladaptive pathways in adolescence.* Paper presented at the symposium "Psychopathology Across Time: Studying Trajectories of Maladaptive Functioning from Adolescence through Early Adulthood," Chicago, IL.

Ledingham, J. (1990). Recent developments in high risk research. In B. Lahey & A. Kazdin (Eds.), *Advances in clinical child psycholgy* (Vol. 13, pp. 91–137). New York: Plenum Press.

Lyons-Ruth, K. (1992). Maternal depressive symptoms, disorganized infant–mother attachment relationships and hostile–aggressive behavior in the preschool classroom: A prospective longitudinal view from infancy to age five. In D. Cicchetti & S. Toth (Eds.), *Rochester symposium on developmental psychopathology: Vol 4. A developmental approach to affective disorders* (pp. 131–171). Rochester, NY: University of Rochester Press.

Lyons-Ruth, K. (1995). Broadening our conceptual frameworks: Can we reintroduce relational strategies and implicit representational systems to the study of psychopathology? *Developmental Psychology, 31,* 432–436.

Lyons-Ruth, K. (1996). Attachment relationships among children with aggressive behavior problems: The role of disorganized early attachment patterns. *Journal of Consulting and Clinical Psychology, 64,* 64–73.

Lyons-Ruth, K., Alpern, L., & Repacholi, B. (1993). Disorganized infant attachment classification and maternal psychosocial problems as predictors of hostile–aggressive behavior in the preschool classroom. *Child Development, 64,* 572–585.

Lyons-Ruth, K., Bronfman, E., & Atwood, G. (1999). A relational diathesis model of hostile–helpless states of mind: Expressions in mother–infant interactions. In J. Solomon & C. George (Eds.), *Attachment disorganization* (pp. 33–70). New York: Guilford Press.

Lyons-Ruth, K., Bronfman, E., & Lyubchik, A. (2001). Frightening versus withdrawing maternal behaviors: Differential infant attachment responses are exacerbated by gender and risk status. Presented at the biennial meeting of the Society for Research in Child Development, as part of a symposium entitled "New Perspectives on Disorganized Attachment", E. Moss, Chair. Minneapolis, April, 2001.

Lyons-Ruth, K., Bronfman, E., & Parsons, E. (1999). Maternal disrupted affective communication, maternal frightened or frightening behavior, and disorganized infant attachment strategies. In J. Vondra & D. Barnett (Eds.), *Atypical patterns of infant attachment: Theory, research and current directions. Monographs of the Society for Research in Child Development, 64*(Serial No. 258), 67–96.

Lyons-Ruth, K., Connell, D., Alpern, L., Lyubchik, A., & DiLallo, J. (2000, July). *The impact of infant home-visiting services on behavior problems and social competence in kindergarten: A three-year follow-up.* Paper presented to the biennial meeting of the World Association for Infant Mental Health, Montreal, Canada.

Lyons-Ruth, K., Connell, D., Grunebaum, H., & Botein, S. (1990). Infants at social risk: Maternal depression and family support services as mediators of infant development and security of attachment. *Child Development, 61,* 85–98.

Lyons-Ruth, K., Easterbrooks, M. A., & Cibelli, C. D. (1997). Infant attachment strategies, infant mental lag, and maternal depressive symptoms: Predictors of internalizing and externalizing problems at age 7. *Developmental Psychology, 33*, 681–692.

Lyons-Ruth, K., & Jacobvitz, D. (1999). Attachment disorganization: Unresolved loss, relational violence, and lapses in behavioral and attentional strategies. In J. Cassidy & P. Shaver (Eds.), *Handbook of attachment: Theory, research, and clinical implications* (pp. 520–554). New York: Guilford Press.

Lyons-Ruth, K., Repacholi, B., McLeod, S., & Silva, E. (1991). Disorganized attach-ment behavior in infancy: Short-term stability, maternal and infant correlates, and risk-related subtypes. *Development and Psychopathology, 3*, 337–396.

Lyons-Ruth, K., Wolfe, R., & Lyubchik, A. (2000). Depression and the parenting of young children: Making the case for early preventive mental health services. *Harvard Review of Psychiatry, 8*, 148–153.

Lyons-Ruth, K., Wolfe, R., Lyubchik, A., & Steingard, R. (in press). Depressive symp-toms in parents of children under three: Sociodemographic predictors, current correlates, and associated parenting behaviors. In N. Halfon, M. Schuster, & K. McLearn (Eds.), *The health and social conditions of young children in American families*. Cambridge, England: Cambridge University Press.

Lyons-Ruth, K., Zoll, D., Connell, D., & Grunebaum, H. (1986). The depressed mother and her one-year-old infant: Environmental context, mother–infant interaction and attachment, and infant development. In E. Tronick & T. Field (Eds.), *Maternal depression and infant disturbance* (pp. 61–82). San Francisco: Jossey-Bass.

Main, M., & Hesse, E. (1990). Parents' unresolved traumatic experiences are related to infant disorganized attachment status: Is frightened or frightening parental behavior the linking mechanism? In M. T. Greenberg, D. Cicchetti, & E. M. Cummings (Eds.), *Attachment in the preschool years: Theory, research and inter-vention* (pp. 161–182). Chicago: University of Chicago Press.

Main, M., & Hesse, E. (1992). *Frightening/frightened, dissociated, or disorganized behav-ior on the part of the parent: A coding system for parent–infant interactions* (4th ed.). Unpublished manuscript, University of California, Berkley.

Main, M., Kaplan, H., & Cassidy, J. (1985). Security in infancy, childhood and adult-hood: A move to the level of representation. In I. Bretherton & E. Waters (Eds.), Growing points of attachment theory and research. *Monographs of the Society for Research in Child Development, 50*(1–2 Serial number 209), 66–104.

Main, M., & Solomon, J. (1990). Procedures for identifying infants as disorganized/ disoriented during the Ainsworth Strange Situation. In M. Greenberg, D. Cicchetti, & E. M. Cummings (Eds.), *Attachment in the preschool years: Theory, research and intervention* (pp. 121–160). Chicago: University of Chicago Press.

McLoyd, V. C. (1990). The impact of economic hardship on black families and chil-dren: Psychological distress, parenting, and socioemotional development. *Child Development, 61*, 311–346.

Mintz, J., Mintz, L., Arruda, M., & Hwang, S. (1992). Treatments of depression and the functional capacity to work. *Archives of General Psychiatry, 49*, 761–768.

Moss, E., Parent, S., Gosselin, C., Rousseau, D., & St. Laurent, D. (1996). Attachment and teacher-reported behavior problems during the preschool and the early school-age period. *Development and Psychopathology, 8,* 511–525.

Murray, L., Fiori-Cowley, A., Hooper, R., & Cooper, P. (1996). The impact of postnatal depression and associated adversity on early mother–infant interactions and later infant outcome. *Child Development, 67,* 2512–2526.

Murray, L., Woolgar, M., Briers, S., & Hipwell, A. (1999). The representation of family life of children of depressed and well mothers. *Social Development, 8,* 179–200.

Nemeroff, C. (1996). The corticotropin-releasing factor (CRF) hypothesis of depression: New findings and new directions. *Molecular Psychiatry, 1,* 336–342.

NICHD Early Child Care Research Network. (1997). The effects of infant child care on infant–mother attachment security: Results of the NICHD study of early child care. *Child Development, 68,* 860–879.

Olds, D., Eckenrode, J., Henderson, Jr., C., Kitzman, H., Powers, J., & Cole, R. (1997). Long-term effects of home visitation on maternal life course and child abuse and neglect: 15-year follow-up of a randomized trial. *Journal of the American Medical Association, 278,* 637–643.

Parsons, E. (1991). *Maternal behavior and disorganized attachment: Relational sequellae of traumatic experience.* Unpublished doctoral dissertation, Massachusetts School of Professional Psychology, Dedham, MA.

Radke-Yarrow, M. (1998). *Children of depressed mothers: From early childhood to maturity.* Cambridge, England: Cambridge University Press.

Radloff, L. (1977). The CES-D scale: A self-report depression scale for research in the general population. *Applied Psychological Measurement, 1,* 385–401.

Richters, J., & Pellegrini, D. (1989). Depressed mothers' judgements about their children: An examination of the depression-distortion hypothesis. *Child Development, 60,* 1068–1075.

Rogeness, G. A., & McClure, E. B. (1996). Development and neurotransmitter–environmental interactions. *Development and Psychopathology, 8,* 183–199.

Schuengel, C., Bakermans-Kranenburg, M., & van IJzendoorn, M. (1999). Frightening maternal behavior linking unresolved loss and disorganized infant attachment. *Journal of Consulting and Clinical Psychology, 67,* 54–63.

Schweinhart, L., Barnes, H., & Weikart, D. (1993). *Significant benefits: The High/Scope Perry Preschool Study through age 27.* Ypsilanti, MI: High/Scope Press.

Seifer, R., Sameroff, A. J., Dickstein, S., Keitner, G., Miller, I., Rasmussen, S., & Hayden, L. C. (1996). Parental psychopathology, multiple contextual risks, and one-year outcomes in children. *Journal of Clinical Child Psychology, 25,* 423–435.

Solomon, J., George, C., & De Jong, A. (1995). Children classified as controlling at age six: Evidence of disorganized representational strategies and aggression at home and at school. *Development and Psychopathology, 7,* 447–463.

Spangler, G., & Grossmann, K. E. (1993). Biobehavioral organization in securely and insecurely attached infants. *Child Development, 64,* 1439–1450.

Stevenson-Hinde, J., & Shouldice, A. (1995). Maternal interactions and self-reports related to attachment classification at 4.5 years. *Child Development, 66,* 583–596.

Teti, D. M. (1999). Conceptualizations of disorganization in the preschool years: An integration. In J. Solomon & C. George (Eds.), *Attachment disorganization* (pp. 213–242). New York: Guilford Press.

Teti, D. M., Gelfand, D. M., Messinger, D. S., & Isabella, R. (1995). Maternal depression and the quality of early attachment: An examination of infants, preschoolers, and their mothers. *Developmental Psychology, 34,* 361–376.

Turner, S. M., Beidel, D. C., & Costello, A. (1987). Psychopathology in the offspring of anxiety disorders patients. *Journal of Consulting and Clinical Psychology, 55,* 229–235.

van IJzendoorn, M. H. (1995). Adult attachment representations, paternal responsiveness, and infant attachment: A meta-analysis on the predictive validity of the Adult Attachment Interview. *Psychological Bulletin, 117,* 387–403.

van IJzendoorn, M. H., Goldberg, S., Kroonenberg, P. M., & Frenkel, O. J. (1992). The relative effects of maternal and child problems on the quality of attachment: A meta-analysis of attachment in clinical samples. *Child Development, 63,* 840–858.

van IJzendoorn, M. H., Schuengel, C., & Bakermans-Kranenburg, M. K. (1999). Disorganized attachment in early childhood: Meta-analysis of precursors, concomitants and sequelae. *Development and Psychopathology, 11,* 225–249.

Wartner, U. G., Grossman, K., Fremmer-Bombik, E., & Suess, G. (1994). Attachment patterns at age six in South Germany: Predictability from infancy and implications for preschool behavior. *Child Development, 65,* 1014–1027.

Weinberg, M. K., & Tronick, E. (1998). The impact of maternal psychiatric illness on infant development. *Journal of Clinical Psychiatry, 59,* 53–61.

Weinfield, N., Sroufe, L. A., Egeland, B., & Carlson, E. (1999). The nature of individual differences in infant–caregiver attachment. In J. Cassidy & P. Shaver (Eds.), *Handbook of attachment: Theory, research, and clinical implications* (pp. 68–88). New York: Guilford Press.

Weissman, M., & Paykel, E. (1974). *The depressed woman: A study of social relationships.* Chicago: University of Chicago Press.

Zahn-Waxler, C., & Kochanska, G. (1990). The origins of guilt. In R. Thompson (Ed.), *Nebraska Symposium on Motivation: Vol. 36. Socioemotional development* (pp. 183–258). Lincoln: University of Nebraska Press.

6

NEGATIVE COGNITIONS IN OFFSPRING OF DEPRESSED PARENTS: MECHANISMS OF RISK

JUDY GARBER AND NINA C. MARTIN

Depression is both phenomenologically and etiologically heterogeneous (Winokur, 1997). Multiple pathways can lead to the development of depression (e.g., Abramson, Metalsky, & Alloy, 1989; Akiskal & McKinney, 1975; Gotlib & Hammen, 1992), and offspring of depressed parents are likely to be at increased risk for psychopathology through multiple mechanisms (Goodman & Gotlib, 1999). It is likely that either multiple variables interact to increase the risk of psychopathology among offspring of depressed parents or that several, heterogeneous pathways produce similar outcomes (Cicchetti & Toth, 1998). As yet, however, neither the necessary nor the sufficient conditions have been identified that invariably produce psychopathology in all high-risk offspring.

We focus on one particular vulnerability factor for the development of depression in offspring of depressed parents: negative cognitions. We assert

Judy Garber was supported in part by National Institute of Mental Health (NIMH) Grant R01-MH57822-01A1 and William T. Grant Foundation Grant 95173096 and Nina Martin was supported in part by an NIMH training grant (T32-MH18921).

121

that such negative cognitions are part of a larger biopsychosocial causal model that likely involves other risk factors including genes, neurobiology, interpersonal relationships, and stressful life events (Garber & Flynn, 2001b; Goodman & Gotlib, 1999). Nevertheless, we hypothesize that negative cognitions increase individuals' risk for depression as well as other forms of psychopathology (Beck, 1967).

We begin by describing briefly the leading cognitive models of depression. Then, we summarize the empirical evidence that supports the contention that negative cognitions are indeed a risk factor for depression. Next, we examine the extent to which having a depressed parent increases the risk for the development of negative cognitions. That is, what is the evidence that offspring of depressed parents actually have depressive cognitions? Finally, we address the central question: If these offspring do show cognitive vulnerability, how does it develop? By what mechanisms does parental depression produce children's negative cognitions that then serve as a risk for depression?

COGNITIVE MODELS OF DEPRESSION

Beck (1967, 1976) asserted that depressed individuals' thinking is characterized by a negative cognitive triad: negative views of the self, the world, and the future. In addition, depressed individuals process information in a distorted manner, which serves to maintain this negative belief system. The content of depressed persons' cognitions is predominantly negative, self-derogating, and self-blaming; depressed individuals process new information through this negative cognitive filter, and they project their negative views into the future, leading to hopelessness (Kovacs & Beck, 1978).

The hopelessness theory of depression (Abramson et al., 1989), which is a revision of the reformulated helplessness model (Abramson, Seligman, & Teasdale, 1978), states that the proximal sufficient cause of the hopelessness subtype of depression is the expectation that highly desirable outcomes will not occur or that highly undesirable outcomes will occur and that the person is helpless to change these conditions. Such hopelessness is hypothesized to result from individuals making inferences that (a) the causes of negative events are global and stable, (b) the consequences of such events are negative, and (c) the events imply negative characteristics about the self.

Both cognitive theories (Abramson et al., 1989; Beck, 1976) are diathesis–stress models in which the negative cognitive style is the diathesis. That is, when faced with important negative life events, individuals who have the cognitive propensity to interpret the causes of these events in a particular way (i.e., global, stable, internal), to have a negative view of themselves, and to develop negative expectations of the future are more likely to become depressed than are individuals who do not have these cognitive tendencies. The combination of both negative life events and such a cognitive style is considered to be a sufficient cause of some depressions.

Thus, three types of cognitions are hypothesized to be important to the etiology of depression. Both models emphasize that a negative view of the self and negative expectations about the future are core parts of the cognitive vulnerability. In addition, the hopelessness theory posits that the tendency to make global, stable, and internal attributions regarding the causes of negative events is also a central feature.

EVIDENCE OF THE COGNITIVE VULNERABILITY TO DEPRESSION

Is there evidence of a cognitive vulnerability to depression? Do negative cognitions increase the likelihood that an individual will have a depressive episode? The empirical literature has shown that both depressed adults (Haaga, Dyck, & Ernst, 1991) and children (Garber & Hilsman, 1992; Gladstone & Kaslow, 1995) have a more depressive attributional style, negative expectations and hopelessness, cognitive distortions, and cognitive errors compared to nondepressed individuals.

Such covariation does not necessarily mean that cognitions are part of the causal chain that produces depression. Rather, these concurrent correlations indicate that cognitions could be a concomitant, cause, or consequence of the depressive syndrome (Barnett & Gotlib, 1988). Negative cognitions could be the result of the underlying depressive process and hold no particular causal status. Depressions that are caused by a biological process, such as Cushing's disease, have been found to be characterized by some of the same kinds of negative cognitions found in other depressions (Hollon, 1992). Thus, at least in some depressions, negative cognitions could be simply a symptom of the depressive disorder.

Alternatively, the experience of depression itself could lead to depressive cognitions; that is, negative cognitions could be a consequence of the depressive syndrome. Nolen-Hoeksema, Girgus, and Seligman (1992) reported that children who experienced higher levels of depressive symptoms developed more pessimistic explanatory styles than did their less depressed peers. Moreover, explanatory style became more pessimistic over time among children with higher levels of depressive symptoms, even after their depression declined. Nolen-Hoeksema et al. concluded that "a period of depression during childhood can lead to the development of a fixed and more pessimistic explanatory style, which remains with a child after his or her depression has begun to subside" (p. 418). In contrast, Lewinsohn and colleagues (Lewinsohn, Steinmetz, Larson, & Franklin, 1981; Rohde, Lewinsohn, & Seeley, 1994) have not found that depression permanently affected cognitive style in either adults or adolescents. Given the differences in the ages of the individuals in the Nolen-Hoeksema et al. and Lewinsohn studies, the "scarring" effect of depression on cognitive style may occur early in development. Indeed, Haines, Metalsky, Cardamone, and Joiner (1999) proposed that "perhaps an episode of depression has a stronger impact on attributional style when children are younger and their attributional style is still forming" (p. 84).

Cognitive theorists (Abramson et al., 1989; Beck, 1967) have suggested that one's cognitive style may make one vulnerable to and be a potential cause of depression. If this is so, then according to some researchers (e.g., Barnett & Gotlib, 1988) cognitive style should be a stable characteristic present both during and after depressive episodes. Just, Abramson, and Alloy (2001) have questioned this assertion. If negative cognitions are a stable characteristic of individuals who are susceptible to depression, then persons whose depressions have remitted should report a more negative cognitive style than individuals who have never been depressed, although perhaps not at the same level as those who are currently depressed.

Whereas some studies of adults have found that, compared with nondepressed controls, formerly depressed individuals continue to report more negative cognitions even after their depression has remitted (e.g., Eaves & Rush, 1984; Teasdale & Dent, 1987), most studies have found that the cognitions of remitted persons are not significantly different from nondepressed controls (Hamilton & Abramson, 1983; Lewinsohn et al., 1981; Persons & Miranda, 1992; Rohde, Lewinsohn, & Seeley, 1990). Similarly, the few studies of children and adolescents have not found cognitive differences between remitted and nondepressed individuals (Asarnow & Bates, 1988; McCauley, Mitchell, Burke, & Moss, 1988). Gotlib, Lewinsohn, Seeley, Rohde, and Redner (1993), however, did find that cognitions of remitted adolescents did not return to normal levels, although neither did their levels of depressive symptoms.

Taken together, these mixed findings have been used to argue against the idea that a stable cognitive style exists and makes one vulnerable to depression (Barnett & Gotlib, 1988; Segal & Dobson, 1992). Just et al. (2001), however, noted that these kinds of "remission" studies have several limitations: (a) treatment could have altered formerly depressed patients' cognitions, (b) the formerly depressed group might have been heterogeneous with regard to cognitive style, and (c) cognitive style might need to be activated to be assessed properly. The absence of stability of cognitive vulnerability does not necessarily mean, then, that it cannot be a risk factor for the development of depression.

Some longitudinal studies have found that cognitions predict depression (e.g., Cutrona, 1983; Metalsky, Joiner, Hardin, & Abramson, 1993), although others have not (e.g., Cochran & Hammen, 1985; Lewinsohn et al., 1981). Abramson et al. (1989) argued that results of these prospective studies have been mixed because some did not test a cognition–stress interaction theory. Whereas a cognitive-trait theory posits that all individuals who have the depressogenic cognitive predisposition should become depressed, the cognitive diathesis-stress model improves predictability by suggesting that cognitively vulnerable individuals become depressed only after they are faced with important negative life events.

Prospective studies have found support for the cognitive diathesis-stress model of depression in samples of both college students (Metalsky & Joiner, 1992; Metalsky et al., 1993) and children (Dixon & Ahrens, 1992; Hilsman & Garber, 1995; Nolen-Hoeksema et al., 1992; Panak & Garber, 1992; Robinson, Garber, & Hilsman, 1995). Garber and colleagues (Hilsman & Garber, 1995; Panak & Garber, 1992; Robinson et al., 1995) found in three short-term longitudinal studies using different stressors (grades, peer rejection, and school transition) and different time frames (e.g., a few days, several months) that cognitions (attributions, self-worth) measured before the stressors moderated the effect of the stressors on depressive symptoms in children. Thus, both cross-sectional and prospective studies involving children, adolescents, and adults have shown that a negative cognitive style may make one vulnerable to depressive symptoms and disorders. More studies needed to examine the stability of this cognitive vulnerability and test the cognitive diathesis-stress hypothesis with regard to diagnosed depressive disorders in addition to self-reported depressive symptoms.

DO OFFSPRING OF DEPRESSED PARENTS SHOW COGNITIVE VULNERABILITY?

Do offspring of depressed parents, who are known to be at increased risk for depression themselves (Downey & Coyne, 1990, Weissman et al., 1987), show the negative cognitive tendencies that are presumably a vulnerability factor for depression? Do these negative cognitions occur before these offspring ever experience a depressive episode? Such a finding would be consistent with the view that negative cognitions are not simply the result of depression. Furthermore, do those high-risk offspring who have negative cognitions then go on to develop depression? If so, the hypothesis that negative cognitions are a risk factor for the onset of depression would be supported.

Empirical Findings

Relatively few studies have examined the cognitions of offspring of depressed parents. Hirsch, Moos, and Reischl (1985) found that children of depressed parents reported lower self-esteem than offspring of nondepressed parents, although the depressed parents' children also had higher levels of depressive symptoms compared to controls. Jaenicke et al. (1987) found that offspring of unipolar mothers reported significantly more negative self-concepts, less positive self-schema, and a more depressogenic attributional style than children of medically ill and control mothers, but they did not control for children's current level of depression.

Similarly, Goodman, Adamson, Riniti, and Cole (1994) found that 8- to 10-year-old children of depressed mothers reported significantly lower perceived global self-worth than did children of well mothers, although here too they did not control for children's current level of depressive symptoms. Goodman et al. did find that children's self-esteem was not related to their lifetime history of depressive disorders. In a younger sample of 5- to 7-year-old children, however, Goodman, Brogan, Lynch, and Fielding (1993) reported no differences between offspring of depressed and nondepressed mothers with regard to self-perceived competence or locus of control. Perhaps the cognitive vulnerability to depression is either not well-developed or easily accessed among young children. Moreover, although some studies have found that offspring of depressed parents have more negative cognitions compared to controls, these findings too may be due to higher levels of depressive symptoms among the high-risk offspring. If so, then these negative cognitions may be a correlate of depression rather than a vulnerability factor that increases the risk of developing depression in the first place.

Garber and Robinson (1997) compared the cognitions of offspring of mothers with histories of nonbipolar mood disorders (high risk) to those of children of mothers without a history of psychiatric diagnoses (low risk). They found that the high-risk children, particularly those of mothers with a more chronic history of depression, had a significantly more negative cognitive style than did low-risk children. Moreover, even when controlling for children's current level of depressive symptoms, high- and low-risk children continued to differ with regard to their attributional style and perceived self-worth. Thus, children who were at risk for depression reported a more depressogenic cognitive style than their low-risk counterparts, regardless of their level of current depression.

Taylor and Ingram (1999) compared offspring of depressed and non-depressed mothers with regard to self-relevant information processing. Half of each group received a negative mood induction designed to prime their cognitive self-schema. The high-risk children in the induced negative mood state endorsed significantly fewer positive content words than all other groups and recalled a higher proportion of negative words than did high-risk children in the neutral prime condition; these findings held even when children's current level of depressive symptoms was controlled. Taylor and Ingram concluded that some dysfunctional cognitive self-structures might be dormant until activated by sad mood, particularly among high-risk offspring.

Taken together, these studies show that children of depressed parents have more negative cognitions, particularly about themselves and the causes of events, than offspring of nondepressed parents. A logical next question is whether the cognitive vulnerability actually predicts depression among offspring of depressed parents. Hammen (1988; Hammen, Adrian, & Hiroto, 1988) found in a sample of offspring of depressed mothers that even when controlling for current level of depressive symptoms, low self-esteem significantly predicted diagnoses of depression 6 months later. They also found that a less positive self-schema tended to predict subsequent depressive disorders. Attributional style, however, did not significantly predict depressive disorders 6 months later (Hammen et al., 1988), although a longer follow-up or a larger sample might yield a stronger effect for attributions. In addition, the Hammen sample included a wide age range (8 to 16 years old). Given the finding that the cognitive–stress interaction tends to be found among older rather than younger children (Nolen-Hoeksema et al., 1992; Turner & Cole, 1994), the inclusion of younger children in the Hammen study might have obscured the potential interaction effect. More studies are needed to examine moderators of the relation between negative cognitions and depression among high-risk offspring, including such factors as children's age and sex, the extent of stressful life events, and the severity and chronicity of parental depression.

Methodological Issues

Several important methodological issues should be considered in designing studies to examine the cognitions of offspring of depressed parents. The purpose of such studies is to explore whether individuals at risk for depression because they have a depressed parent show the negative cognitions that are hypothesized to be a vulnerability factor for depression. First, for these cognitions to be considered a risk factor, the offspring should be neither currently depressed nor have a history of depression. In three of the five studies that examined cognitions in high- and low-risk offspring, however, children's current levels of depressive symptoms were not controlled, so it was not possible to determine whether cognitions were simply part of high-risk offsprings' depression or were a vulnerability factor that preceded it. Moreover, none of these studies indicated whether the children had ever had an episode of a mood disorder, which could have subsequently altered their cognitive style (Nolen-Hoeksema et al., 1992).

A second important methodological issue concerns whether negative cognitions must be primed in order to be measured. Taylor and Ingram (1999) showed that affect priming made a difference in high-risk offspring's processing of self-referent information. In contrast, Garber and Robinson (1997) found differences between high- and low-risk children without using mood induction. It is possible, however, that completing these kinds of cognitive measures is a prime in and of itself. That is, asking multiple questions about one's beliefs about oneself, the future, and the causes of events could activate latent cognitive processes that are part of an associative web (Ingram, Miranda,

& Segal, 1998). On the other hand, some kinds of cognitions may require priming whereas others may not. More comprehensive studies are needed that compare high- and low-risk offspring both with and without a prime on various kinds of cognitive measures and that control for current level of depressive symptoms.

A third issue is the age of the children being studied. Children were 8 to 12 years old in the study by Taylor and Ingram (1999), and 5 to 7 years old in the study by Goodman et al. (1993). Goodman et al. did not find differences between high- and low-risk children's cognitions, and Taylor and Ingram found differences when children's cognitions were primed. In contrast, study participants in Hirsch et al. (1985) and in Garber and Robinson (1997) were adolescents. Thus, negative cognitions among young offspring of depressed parents either may not yet be present or may need to be primed in younger children.

Moreover, the issue of the heterogeneity of maternal depression should be considered in studies of high-risk offspring. Are negative cognitions characteristic of children of all depressed parents, or are particular features of parental depression associated with greater risk for these cognitions, such as the chronicity and severity of the parents' depressive episodes, comorbid psychopathology, and age of onset of the parents' depression? Garber and Robinson (1997) found that children of mothers with chronic depression were especially likely to manifest negative cognitions compared to offspring of mothers with less chronic depression histories. They speculated that this finding could have been due to both environmental and genetic factors. That is, children whose mothers had been depressed for longer periods of time would have had more exposure to the causal mechanisms that link maternal depression and child negative cognitions. In addition, chronic and recurrent maternal depression may reflect a greater genetic vulnerability to depression and its associated cognitive correlates.

A final, and perhaps most fundamental, question for the present discussion concerns the issue of specificity. To what extent are negative cognitions specific to offspring of depressed parents? Is there something in particular about having a depressed parent that increases children's likelihood of developing negative beliefs about themselves, the future, and the causes of events, or do offspring of parents with other kinds of psychopathology also develop such negative cognitive systems? Hammen and colleagues (Hammen, 1991a; Jaenicke et al., 1987) found that children of mothers with unipolar disorder experienced more negative cognitions about themselves than did offspring of both medically ill and well mothers; children of mothers with bipolar disorder showed a similar pattern as did the offspring of mothers with unipolar disorder, although not to as significant a degree. Further studies should contrast offspring of mothers with depression versus children of mothers with other kinds of both Axis I and II diagnoses with regard to cognitive style.

A MODEL OF THE RELATION BETWEEN PARENTAL DEPRESSION AND CHILD NEGATIVE COGNITIONS

Figure 6.1 shows a heuristic model of the relation between parental depression and children's negative cognitions. We propose that parental depression leads to negative cognitions through at least three nonmutually exclusive processes: modeling of parents' negative cognitions, dysfunctional parent–child relationships, and exposure to stressful life events. Although we discuss each of these processes separately, it is important to note that they are not independent. For example, depressed parents might have negative perceptions of their children, consistent with their own negative cognitive style, which then can influence how they interact with their children. Moreover, children likely learn about and imitate their parents' cognitions in the context of interactions with them. In addition, negative parent–child interactions themselves might be considered a stressful event. Indeed, Ostrander, Weinfurt, and Nay (1998) suggested that family nonsupportiveness was a stressor, and they found that it interacted with negative cognitions to predict depression. Thus, although each of the hypothesized mediators is discussed separately, they are likely to be interrelated.

In the remainder of the chapter we review evidence supporting each of the proposed mechanisms. Following the method for testing mediation outlined by Baron and Kenny (1986), we highlight the links between the various components of this model. We have already reviewed the association between (A), parental depression, and (C), negative cognitions in offspring. Next, we briefly review the links between parental depression (A) and each of the hypothesized mediators (B): modeling negative parental cognitions, dysfunctional parent–child interactions, and exposure to stressful life events. We then present the evidence supporting the link between the hypothesized mediators (B) and children's negative cognitions (C). Finally, we note other components of the model that we believe contribute to both the mediators and child cognitions independently of parental depression.

Modeling Negative Parental Cognitions

As described previously, evidence clearly indicates that currently depressed individuals experience more negative cognitions than nondepressed persons (Barnett & Gotlib, 1988; Haaga et al., 1991). Such negative beliefs extend to their perceptions of themselves as parents (Goodman, Sewell, Cooley, & Leavitt, 1993; Kochanska, Radke-Yarrow, Kuczynski, & Friedman, 1987) and may affect their perceptions of their children's behavior (Forehand, Lautenschlager, Faust, & Graziano, 1986). Thus, it is reasonable to assume that depressed parents have negative cognitions. The more critical question for the present discussion is whether these cognitions get transmitted to their children, and if so, how.

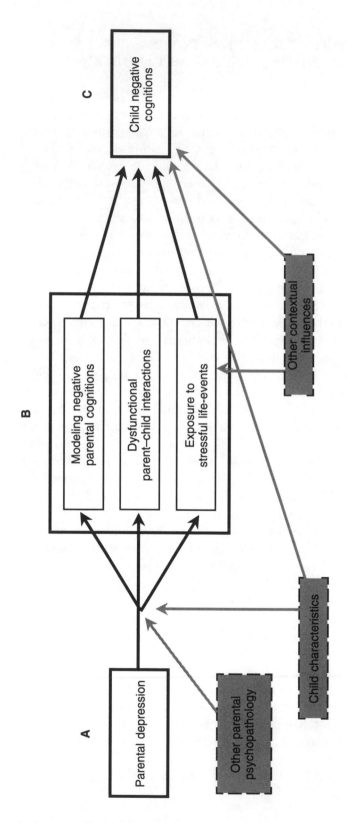

Figure 6.1. Model of the Relation Between Parental Depression and Child Negative Cognitions.

One simple mechanism that has been proposed (e.g., Garber & Flynn, in 2001b; Kovacs & Beck, 1978; Seligman & Peterson, 1986) is modeling. Depressed parents express negative beliefs about themselves, their world, and the people around them, and their children may simply copy what they hear. That is, children learn to think negatively by observing their parents' depressive verbalizations. Evidence of covariation between parents' and children's cognitions would be consistent with this modeling perspective and would support this particular link between B and C in Figure 6.1, although other factors such as shared genetic influences also could account for such covariation.

The results of studies explicitly testing covariation between parent's and children's cognitions have been mixed, possibly because different types of samples and measures have been used. Some researchers have found a significant mother–child correlation for attributions for negative events (Seligman and Peterson, 1986) and a significant mother–child covariation with regard to the negative cognitive triad (Stark, Schmidt, & Joiner, 1996). Others, however, have not found a significant relation between mothers and children on measures of either attributional style or perceived self-control (Kaslow, Rehm, Pollack, & Siegel, 1988) or dysfunctional attitudes and self-schema (Oliver & Berger, 1992).

In a sample of mothers with and without histories of depression, Garber and Flynn (2001a) found a significant association between mothers' and children's global self-worth, but not between either their hopelessness or their attributional style. However, they did find a significant correlation between mothers' and children's attributions regarding the same child-focused behaviors and events. These results were consistent with other studies that have reported a significant association between children's and parents' attributions about the children's behavior as opposed to an association between the children's attributions and their parents' general explanation of parental behavior (Fincham & Cain, 1986; Turk & Bry, 1992). Thus, one possible mechanism through which children learn attributions is observing their parents' explanations of things. Children may not simply copy what their parents say in general, but rather they might be more inclined to incorporate their parents' cognitions regarding particularly salient events such as their own behavior.

One factor that might affect parent–child covariation is the extent to which children are even aware of their parents' cognitions. How much do children actually attend to what their parents say, and how does this vary developmentally? Such awareness could be assessed by asking children to respond to cognitive measures in terms of how they think their parents would respond. The transmission process might be quite subtle, however, and children, particularly young ones, might not be cognizant of their parents' beliefs or, if they are aware, might be unable to articulate them.

Heterogeneity in children's awareness of their parents' cognitions probably is a function of other child characteristics such as age and personality.

How much children care about what their parents think and say also is likely affected by the quality of the parent–child relationship and children's developmental level. These factors might moderate parent–child covariation in cognitive style.

Another reason that studies have not consistently found covariation between parents' and children's cognitions is that cognitions might need activation by an immediate stressor or priming by a mood induction (Miranda, Persons, & Byers, 1990; Riskind & Rholes, 1984). Similarities between mothers' and children's cognitions might be more evident if measures were completed under such activating conditions. No study has yet examined parent–child covariation in primed and nonprimed conditions.

An important caveat about the interpretation of any parent–child correlation should be noted. Correlations between parents and children's cognitive styles do not necessarily indicate that they were the result of modeling and imitation, or that the direction of the relation is from parent to child. That is, parental cognitions could influence child cognitions or vice versa, or some shared third variable (e.g., genes, stressors) could contribute to the development of both parents' and children's cognitions. Thus, although some (e.g., Kaslow et al., 1988; Seligman & Peterson, 1986) have suggested that parent–child correlations are an indication of learning, this is only one of several possible mechanisms of cross-generational transmission.

The finding of a significant relation between parents' and children's cognitions about the child's behavior in particular rather than about their cognitive style in general (Garber & Flynn, 2001a; Turk & Bry, 1992) is at least more consistent with a learning perspective. That is, if the tendency to make internal, global, and stable attributions about negative events represented simply the transmission of a genetic predisposition, then such a tendency should be true with regard to either parent- or child-focused events. Thus, children likely acquire at least some of their cognitive style, particularly causal inferences, from observing their parents' explanations of their children's behaviors.

Dysfunctional Parent–Child Interactions

A second mechanism proposed to explain the link between parental depression and children's negative cognitions is nonsupportive and dysfunctional parent–child interactions. The basic premise is that depressed parents tend to engage in negative exchanges with their offspring; within these interactions parents communicate either directly through their words (e.g., criticism, derogating, blaming) or indirectly through their actions (e.g., ignoring, punishing) personal ascriptions about the child and negative attributions about the causes of events that then contribute to children developing negative beliefs about themselves and the world.

A growing empirical literature supports the first part of this hypothesis that relationships between depressed parents and their children are disrupted from infancy through late adolescence (Downey & Coyne, 1990; Goodman & Gotlib, 1999; Gotlib & Goodman, 1999; Hammen, 1991a). Young offspring of depressed caregivers have been found to have more insecure attachments compared to offspring of well mothers (DeMulder & Radke-Yarrow, 1991; Teti, Gelfand, Messinger, & Isabella, 1995). Furthermore, observations of depressed mothers interacting with their children reveal that these mothers are more negative (Garber, Braafladt, & Zeman, 1991; Lovejoy, 1991), more critical (Goodman et al., 1994; Hammen et al., 1988; Webster-Stratton & Hammond, 1988), less compromising (Kochanska, Kuczynski, Radke-Yarrow, & Welsh, 1987), more disengaged or intrusive (Cohn, Matias, Tronick, Connell, & Lyons-Ruth, 1986; Field, Healy, Goldstein, & Guthertz, 1990), less responsive and affectively involved (Cohn & Tronick, 1989; Goodman & Brumley, 1990), and use less productive communications than nondepressed mothers. In addition, negative reciprocal interaction patterns have been observed between depressed mothers and their children (Hammen, Burge, & Stansbury, 1990; Hops et al., 1987; Radke-Yarrow, 1998).

How do these negative interactions between depressed parents and their children contribute to the development of depressive cognitions in offspring? Bowlby (1980, 1988) emphasized that children's working models of themselves are influenced by the quality of the early parental relationship reflected in parents' words and actions. Children with caretakers who are consistently accessible and supportive will develop cognitive representations, or "working models," of the self and others as positive and trustworthy. In contrast, caretakers who are unresponsive or inconsistent will likely produce insecure attachments with their children leading to working models that include feelings of abandonment, self-criticism, and excessive dependency.

Beck and Young (1985) similarly suggested that a "child learns to construct reality through his or her early experiences with the environment, especially with significant others. Sometimes, these early experiences lead children to accept attitudes and beliefs that will later prove maladaptive" (p. 207). Parents who are critical and rejecting teach their children that they are unworthy.

Harter (1999) has suggested that caretakers' messages of approval and disapproval are incorporated into children's own sense of self-worth. Through an implicit process of internalization, children adopt the opinions and values of significant others. Caregivers who are nurturing and approving produce children with favorable self-images, whereas "socializing agents who are rejecting or punitive will produce children with very negative self-evaluations" (Harter, 1999; p. 167).

Thus, children who are exposed to parenting characterized by repeated criticism and rejection, lack of warmth, and intrusiveness tend to develop a highly self-critical and negative attitude toward themselves (Blatt & Homann,

1992; Garber & Flynn, 2001a; Ingram et al., 1998; McCranie & Bass, 1984). McCranie and Bass speculated that parental child-rearing practices involving rejection and inconsistent expressions of affection and control hinder the development of healthy self-esteem in children and thereby increase their vulnerability to depression. Ingram et al. (1998) similarly suggested that disruptions in the bonds between parents and children in the form of low warmth and affection lead to dysfunctional schemas about the self. Thus, through interactions with parents who are critical and rejecting in the absence of warmth and care, children internalize their parents' negative views into a self-schema of being unworthy of love or attention.

Dysfunctional parenting has been found to be associated with such child cognitions as low self-esteem (e.g., Johnson, Schulman, & Collins, 1991; Litovsky & Dusek, 1985; Parker, 1993), external locus of control (e.g., Levenson, 1973; Nowicki & Segal, 1974), dysfunctional attitudes (e.g., Randolph & Dykman, 1998; Whisman & Kwon, 1992; Whisman & McGarvey, 1995), self-criticism (e.g., Blatt, Wein, Chevron, & Quinlan, 1979; Brewin, Firth-Cozens, Furnham, & McManus, 1992; Frank, Poorman, & Van Egeren, 1997; Koestner, Zuroff, & Powers, 1991; McCranie & Bass, 1984; Whiffen & Sasseville, 1991), and enhanced attention to negative stimuli (Ingram & Ritter, 2000), although a few studies have not found a relation between perceptions of parenting and offsprings' cognitions (Oliver & Berger, 1992; Tiggemann, Winefield, Goldney, & Winefield, 1992). Most studies assessing the relation between offsprings' cognitions and parenting have been retrospective or cross-sectional, however. In one of the few longitudinal studies, Koestner et al. (1991) showed that restrictive and rejecting parenting measured earlier in childhood significantly predicted the development of self-criticism during adolescence. Thus, a significant link exists between perceptions of parenting and negative cognitions in offspring, although more longitudinal studies are needed. Studies also are needed that examine whether parents' actual behaviors as well as children's perceptions of their parents' behaviors predict child cognitions.

Studies of the parent–child relationship in families with a depressed parent have found some support for the association between parenting and negative child cognitions. Radke-Yarrow, Belmont, Nottelman, and Bottomly (1990) observed very young children's discourse with depressed and well mothers during a 35-minute period. Although depressed and well mothers did not differ in their rate of comments, depressed mothers were more negative, and mothers' negativity and child self-referent, unpleasant statements were significantly correlated. Radke-Yarrow et al. proposed that such parent communications may be an early precursor of the development of a negative self-concept in children.

Jaenicke et al. (1987) found a significant association between mothers' verbal criticism of their children and the children's tendency to make self-blaming attributions for negative events. Similarly, Goodman et al. (1994)

revealed a significant association between negative affective statements of depressed mothers and lower perceived self-worth in their children. Finally, in a short-term longitudinal study, Garber and Flynn (2001a) found that, controlling for prior levels of self-worth, parenting characterized by low levels of care and acceptance predicted low levels of global self-worth in young adolescents a year later. In addition, children's attributional style was predicted by maternal psychological control, which was characterized by guilt induction, shame, and withdrawal of love.

Thus, the parent–child relationship is likely to be an important context in which cognitive vulnerabilities to depression, such as low self-esteem and depressive attributional style, develop. In particular, child-rearing practices characterized by rejection, criticism, absence of warmth and affection, lack of autonomy, and manipulation of the love relationship are likely to result in self-denigrating and self-blaming attitudes, which then increase an individual's vulnerability to depression.

Exposure to Stressful Life Events

Stressful life events and depression are clearly related in both children and adults (Brown & Harris, 1978; Compas, Grant, & Ey, 1994). Negative life events have been found both to precede the onset of depression (e.g., Reinherz et al., 1989; Rueter, Scaramella, Wallace, & Conger, 1999) and to increase as the result of depression (Coyne, 1976; Hammen, 1991a). The relevant questions for the present discussion are whether offspring of depressed parents experience high levels of stress, and if so, how this stress contributes to their negative cognitions.

Children living with depressed parents are exposed to high levels of stress (Hammen et al., 1987; Hirsch et al., 1985). Hammen et al. reported that compared to families with medically ill or well mothers, families with unipolar depressed mothers had higher levels of negative life events, including marital discord, family conflict, and financial problems. Marriages of depressed individuals have been reported to be especially conflictual, tense, and hostile (e.g., Gotlib & Beach, 1995). The high levels of divorce, marital disruption, and negative spousal interactions observed in depressed patients and their spouses (Fadden, Bebbington, & Kuipers, 1987; Gotlib & Hammen, 1992) can be major stressors for children that adversely affect their development (Cummings & Davies, 1994; Grych & Fincham, 1990). Indeed, among offspring of depressed parents, those whose parents are divorced tend to have more behavioral problems than those whose parents have not divorced (Fendrich, Warner, & Weissman, 1990; Goodman et al., 1993). Such marital discord, with its associated hostility and anger, may be one mechanism through which maternal depression leads to negative cognitions and related psychopathology in children (Gotlib & Lee, 1990; Rutter & Quinton, 1984).

Thus, offspring of depressed parents are exposed to a variety of acute and chronic stressors that are, at least partially, the result of their parent's psychopathology (Hammen, 1991b). Moreover, offspring of depressed mothers in turn contribute to the occurrence of stressors. Adrian and Hammen (1993) found that, compared to children of nondepressed mothers, offspring of depressed mothers had higher levels of dependent life events, particularly interpersonal conflicts.

Not only are offspring of depressed mothers exposed to more stressors, but they also may be less competent to deal with them. Garber et al. (1991) reported that both depressed mothers and their children generated fewer and lower quality coping strategies than did nondepressed mothers and their children. This lack of adequate coping skills is likely to lead to a longer period of exposure to negative events and possibly the generation of even more stressors.

Parental depression appears to increase children's exposure to negative life events. Does such stress lead to the development of negative cognitions, and if so, by what processes? Exposure to the various normal disappointments, losses, and failures that occur over the typical course of development are certainly likely to affect a child's outlook on life. Experiences with chronically adverse life circumstances (e.g., abuse, poverty, parental discord) or major traumatic life events (e.g., parental death, rape) are particularly likely to affect children's sense of themselves, their world, and their future (Janoff-Bulman, 1992). When such events are uncontrollable and result in multiple and severe negative outcomes, children are likely to develop cognitions of universal helplessness and hopelessness (Abramson et al., 1989). Individuals who believe they are responsible for the negative events are more likely to develop a belief in personal helplessness and low self-esteem (Abramson et al., 1978).

Thus, negative life experiences can provide the foundation for the development of negative beliefs. Subsequent exposure to new negative life events can reactivate and reinforce these beliefs, particularly when the conditions resemble the circumstances under which they developed (Kovacs & Beck, 1978). Through generalization, the range of these beliefs may extend to stimulus conditions that are only marginally related to the original ones, and thus a negative cognitive style may emerge.

For example, early loss may create cognitions of abandonment and the belief that all losses are traumatic, uncontrollable, and irreversible (Beck, 1967; Brown & Harris, 1978). Loss of one's mother at an early age has realistic and significant implications for a child's future, and it sets the stage for later losses or major difficulties to be interpreted in global, stable, and internal terms (Abramson et al., 1989). Subsequent experiences with interpersonal disruptions such as rejection and conflict are likely to strengthen existing schemata about the fragility of interpersonal relationships and lead to hopelessness with respect to the social domain.

Rose and Abramson (1992) proposed a model of the development of cognitive vulnerability that emphasizes the role of negative life events. They suggested that when a negative event occurs, individuals are motivated to understand its causes, meaning, and consequences and to take action to deal with it. When the event is highly threatening or recurrent, individuals are especially motivated to engage in this epistemic activity. Through repetition of the negative event-specific cognitive process, a more general negative cognitive style is formed.

In a cross-sectional study, Rose, Abramson, Hodulik, Halberstadt, and Leff (1994) examined the links between certain developmental events, including early loss, parenting style, history of sexual abuse, and dysfunctional attitudes and attributional style in depressed adult inpatients. They found that, controlling for severity of depression, high levels of recalled negative parenting behaviors and history of sexual abuse were significantly associated with a more negative cognitive style, whereas early loss was not. They speculated that children develop depressogenic cognitive styles in response to early negative life events such as harsh and controlling parenting or abuse. Given the cross-sectional and retrospective nature of the data, however, the alternative explanation that individuals with a more depressive cognitive style have more negative recollections of their parents' behaviors cannot be ruled out.

Only a few studies have tested prospectively the relation between stressful life events and negative cognitions. In a 5-year longitudinal study, Nolen-Hoeksema et al. (1992) found that negative life events significantly predicted unfavorable changes in explanatory style over time, after controlling for children's level of depression at the time the life events were reported. In a short-term longitudinal study of young adolescents varying in risk for depression, Garber and Flynn (2001a) examined the relations among maternal depression history, stress, and children's negative cognitions. Negative life events significantly predicted depressive attributional style 1 year later, over and above maternal history of depression and prior attributions. In addition, Garber and Flynn reported that self-worth moderated the relation between life events and hopelessness a year later such that the association between life events and hopelessness was greater for children with low self-worth than for those with high self-worth. This study is especially relevant to the present discussion because it indicates that stressful life events may make a significant and unique contribution to the prediction of children's negative cognitions beyond the effect of maternal depression, supporting the hypothesized relations outlined in Figure 6.1.

Other factors may moderate whether a child develops a depressive cognitive style after exposure to stressful life events, such as the child's age at the time of the event, associated consequences of the event, amount of available social support, and the child's own coping resources. Children's age and level of cognitive development can affect their ability to process information about the causes, meaning, and consequences of the event. Brown and Harris (1978) found that depression was more common among women who had lost their mothers before age 11. Loss of one's mother at an early age may have significant global and stable implications for the future and may lead to cognitions of helplessness and abandonment.

In addition, the extent of the associated consequences of the negative event likely determines how much the child needs to process cognitively. For example, when the death of a parent is accompanied by losses of economic resources, home, friendships, and social status, a tremendous burden can be placed on a child's cognitive processing capacity. Furthermore, the availability of social support can influence children's understanding of life events not only by providing instrumental aid to the child but also by helping the child cognitively restructure the meaning of the event. Finally, children's coping responses can affect their interpretation of events. If they cope effectively, they may be less likely to see themselves as helpless and may remain more hopeful about their future. Longitudinal studies ought to examine the direct impact of negative life events on children's developing cognitive style as well as the possible moderating effects of these other factors. In addition, longitudinal studies should test the mediational model outlined in Figure 6.1—that is, to ascertain whether the relation between parental depression and child negative cognitions is at least in part the result of the stressful life events that arise from having a depressed parent.

Other Processes

In addition to the three processes outlined in Figure 6.1 that presumably mediate the relation between parental depression and children's negative cognitions, factors other than parental depression may influence both the mediators and the outcome of children's cognitive style. Parental depression is not a necessary condition for either the hypothesized mediators or the development of negative cognitions in children. Individuals may experience poor parent–child relationships or stressful life events or develop negative cognitions without ever having a depressed parent. Additionally, a common third variable, such as heredity, might account for the association between parental depression and child cognitions.

Other Parental Psychopathology

Other parental psychopathology besides depression could produce the same kinds of mediating processes outlined in Figure 6.1. Parent–child relationships in families where parents have substance use disorders or schizophrenia have been found to be characterized by serious dysfunction (e.g., conflict, hostility) and stressful life events (e.g., parental unemployment; Jacob, 1987). Offspring of parents with other disorders, such as substance abuse, have been found to report negative attributions and hopelessness (Perez-Bouchard, Johnson, & Ahrens, 1993).

Having a depressed parent may contribute uniquely to the development of negative cognitions in offspring. That is, something distinct about depressed parents produces vulnerability to negative cognitions in their offspring. Alternatively, parental depression may be associated with whatever mechanisms lead to negative cognitions, but these processes might also be produced by other kinds of parental psychopathology or other factors. Parental depression might be one distal cause of negative child cognitions, but the mechanisms that mediate this link could be produced by other factors as well. Although the research explicitly testing these alternative perspectives has not yet been conducted, we suggest that the latter view is probably more accurate. To address this specificity issue, studies are needed that explicitly compare offspring of parents diagnosed with different kinds of Axis I and II disorders regarding the hypothesized mediators and child cognitions.

Other Contextual Influences

Other contextual factors, including peers, teachers, and others within the child's social network, can contribute both directly and indirectly to the development of negative cognitions in children (Cole, 1991; Cole, Maxwell, & Martin, 1997; Harter, 1999). Peer support has been linked repeatedly with adolescent well-being (e.g., Epstein, 1983; Hartup, 1983). Frequent contact with a supportive friend is associated with higher levels of self-esteem (Hirsch, Engel-Levy, DuBois, & Hardesty, 1990), whereas peer rejection predicts the perception of low social competence (Panak & Garber, 1992), and victimization by peers is associated with lower self-esteem (Olweus, 1984). Chronic peer rejection or victimization may contribute to the development of heuristics for processing information that then influence children's interpretations of future life experiences (Crick & Dodge, 1994; Ingram, 1990). Thus, the quality of peer relationships can substantially affect children's developing sense of self and future, particularly regarding interpersonal interactions.

Feedback in the school environment also can contribute to children's developing cognitions of their competence, particularly about their academic performance (Cole, 1991). Dweck and colleagues (Dweck & Gilliard, 1975; Dweck & Licht, 1980; Dweck & Reppuci, 1973) have shown that the foundation for children's explanatory style for performance outcomes and their beliefs about their academic competence are laid during the early school years as a function of the direct feedback they receive from teachers. Based on such teacher input, boys learn to attribute their failures to lack of effort—an unstable and changeable cause, whereas girls learn that they lack ability—a stable attribute—and therefore tend to become helpless and give up (Dweck & Licht, 1980).

Other people within children's social networks, including siblings, grandparents, the nondepressed parent, coaches, and clergy, also can be important sources of information about the self and social relationships. These individuals can provide further input that confirms children's developing self-schema, and they can serve as important sources of social support that can buffer against some of the damaging messages received from the depressed parent (Robinson et al., 1995).

Finally, much of the research on parental depression has focused on mothers rather than fathers (e.g., Hammen, 1991a; Radke-Yarrow, 1998). The model outlined in Figure 6.1 regarding the impact of parental depression on children's cognitions likely holds for maternal as well as for paternal depression, although this contention has yet to be tested. Considerably less research has been conducted on the link between depressed fathers and children's cognitions. Future studies should explore how fathers' own cognitions and father–child interactions affect children's developing cognitive style.

Fathers also can either exacerbate or attenuate the effects of maternal depression (Goodman & Gotlib, 1999). Depressed mothers often marry men who themselves have psychopathology (Merikangas, 1984), which can add to the stress in the home. On the other hand, a high-functioning father who is caring and appropriately involved could buffer the negative effects of a rejecting and overcontrolling mother. Future studies should explore explicitly how complementary or conflicting parenting styles of mothers and fathers affect children's developing cognitive style (Phares & Compas, 1992).

Child Characteristics

A variety of child characteristics can moderate the proposed relations among parental depression, mediators, and children's cognitions, including children's age, sex, and IQ as well as their temperament and personality. With regard to age, for example, Harter (1999) has noted that normative changes in children's cognitive capacities affect the emergence of the self over time. Goodman and Gotlib (1999; Gotlib & Goodman, 1999) have suggested that parental depression is likely to affect how children negotiate various salient developmental tasks, such as the emergence of the self-system, depending on when in their development the parental depression occurs. More empirical work is needed to examine age differences in the development of children's cognitions.

With regard to sex differences, researchers have suggested that girls might be more likely to identify with and model the cognitions of their depressed mothers, whereas boys might be more likely to imitate their fathers (Hops, 1996; Peterson & Seligman, 1984). It may be that parent–daughter interactions differ from parent–son interactions both generally and with depressed parents in particular. Whether such differential interaction patterns for girls and boys exist and whether they lead to different cognitive outcomes should be the focus of future studies.

Finally, children's temperament may contribute to their transactions with parents, coping with stressors, and processing of information (Bell &

Harper, 1977; Kagan, 1994; Rutter, 1987). Children with more difficult temperaments might not only react more negatively to depressive parenting, but also exacerbate the parents' negative behaviors toward the child (Cutrona & Troutman, 1986). Thus, the effect of parental depression on children's developing cognitions may differ as a function of the temperamental characteristics of the child, in part, by affecting the parent–child relationship and children's responsivity to stress.

Genetic Influences

Another factor contributing to the link between parental depression and children's cognitions is heredity. Parents and children may share genes for depression, and negative cognitions may be the result of a common genetic vulnerability to depression (Blehar, Weissman, Gershon, & Hirschfeld, 1988). If the offspring manifest the negative cognitions before ever becoming depressed, however, then such a mechanism would be less tenable.

There also might be genes for depressive cognitions that cause both parents and children to experience negative thinking. Significant correlations between parents' and children's depression-related cognitions (e.g. Seligman & Peterson, 1986) are consistent with either a genetic or a social learning model. In a twin study, Schulman, Keith, and Seligman (1991) compared the intraclass correlations of 115 monozygotic (MZ) and 27 dizygotic (DZ) twins on the Attributional Style Questionnaire (Seligman, Abramson, Semmel, & von Baeyer, 1979) and found the correlations to be .48 for MZ twins and 0 for DZ twins. This finding is intriguing and should be replicated using more standard means of determining zygosity rather than the self-report method used by Schulman et al. (1991). Future twin studies also should include other measures of cognitive style, such as self-worth, hopelessness, and dysfunctional attitudes.

It also is possible that the depressive cognitive style is really a manifestation of neuroticism, which is presumably heritable (Eysenck & Eysenck, 1985). Watson and colleagues (Watson & Clark, 1984; Watson, Clark, & Harkness, 1994) have argued that self-report measures of depression, such as the Beck Depression Inventory (Beck, Ward, Mendelson, Mock, & Erbaugh, 1961), are really just measures of neuroticism. Dysfunctional cognitions and dysphoric affect may be components of a more general construct, neuroticism or negative emotionality itself (Watson et al., 1994). Studies consistently find correlations between self-report measures of depressive symptoms and measures of cognitive style (e.g., Barnett & Gotlib, 1988). This covariation could be the result if both depression and cognitions either reflect or result from a personality trait such as neuroticism. If depressogenic cognitive style is a manifestation of neuroticism and neuroticism is heritable, then by inference, depressogenic cognitions also could be genetic. Therefore, the relation between parental depression and children's negative cognitive style could be the result of shared genes for neuroticism that contribute to both.

IMPLICATIONS FOR CLINICIANS

Finally, if the factors described in the model shown in Figure 6.1 are indeed the mechanisms by which children develop negative cognitions, then what are the implications for prevention? Who and what should be the target of preventive interventions with offspring of depressed parents? Should efforts at prevention be focused directly on altering children's negative cognitions or on the factors that contribute to their development in the first place?

Prevention programs that aim to alter directly children's negative cognitions are beginning to show positive results in preventing depression (e.g., Clarke et al., 1995; Gillham, Reivich, Jaycox, & Seligman, 1995; Jaycox, Reivich, Gillham, & Seligman, 1994). More intervention studies are needed that target children who experience various kinds of risk factors, including being an offspring of a depressed parent, already having a negative cognitive style, having subthreshold levels of depression or anxiety, or being exposed to major negative life events (e.g., divorce, deaths, abuse).

Another strategy is to target the more distal causal mechanisms. Reducing the number of negative life events that children encounter would be a laudable goal, although not a very practical one. However, children can be taught ways of coping with stressors that can reduce their negative impact. Given that negative life events are a risk factor for both the development of a negative cognitive style and depression, some form of coping training should be implemented with high-risk individuals.

Finally, prevention programs should target families with dysfunctional patterns of parent–child interactions. Beardslee and colleagues (1992) have developed a psychoeducational preventive intervention with depressed parents and their children that teaches the family about the effects of living with a depressed parent, although it does not specifically alter the interaction patterns between depressed parents and their children. Prevention programs that help parents to be more positive and accepting of their children and less critical and emotionally controlling might increase the likelihood of children feeling confident and worthwhile and decrease the likelihood of their developing negative cognitive styles. Prevention studies that provide such parent training and explicitly examine its impact on children's developing cognitive styles should be conducted.

Intervention studies can provide a means of testing theory by providing an ethical and ecologically valid means of directly manipulating risk factors that are presumably part of the causal chain. Prevention programs with high-risk children and adolescents that target the presumed precursors of negative cognitions and associated depression, such as dysfunctional parent–child interactions and stressful life events, are important because they can have the pragmatic effect of reducing the likelihood of the occurrence of this widespread and often debilitating mental health problem. The model proposed in this chapter may provide a conceptual map on which to base such prevention efforts.

SUMMARY

We presented a model that explains how parental depression contributes to the development of negative cognitions about the self, future, and the causes of events. We proposed three nonmutually exclusive mechanisms through which such cognitions may develop in offspring of depressed parents: modeling of parents' negative cognitions, dysfunctional parent–child relationships, and exposure to stressful life events. The review of the literature indicated empirical support for the various connections in the model. Having a depressed parent clearly can have profound effects on children's developing sense of themselves and their world. It is important to keep in mind, however, that parental depression is only a marker of risk, like socioeconomic status and sex, and is not a causal explanation in and of itself. Rather, other processes that are associated with parental depression are responsible for the development of negative cognitions.

We also want to emphasize that parental depression is not a necessary cause of negative cognitions in children. That is, individuals can develop negative cognitions without ever having a depressed parent. To test this assertion, researchers should identify individuals who are exposed to the hypothesized mediators, such as dysfunctional parent–child relationships or high levels of stressful life events, and study them over time to see if they develop negative cognitions in the absence of a depressed parent. In addition, studies should assess adults with depressive disorders who did not, themselves, have depressed parents to see if they have negative cognitions and to determine whether they experienced any of the hypothesized mediating processes.

Moreover, parental depression is not a sufficient cause of negative cognitions. That is, having a depressed parent does not invariably lead to the development of negative cognitions. Other factors may moderate the link between parental depression and children's negative cognitions, including a supportive social network and various child characteristics.

Several important developmental questions also remain. Does the covariation between parents' and children's cognitive styles change with development? Do the factors associated with the development of a negative cognitive style (e.g., dysfunctional parenting, negative life events) change as a function of the child's age and level of cognitive maturity? In addition, more longitudinal studies are needed that examine whether negative cognitions mediate the link between parental and child depression.

REFERENCES

Abramson, L. Y., Metalsky, G. I., & Alloy, L. B. (1989). Hopelessness depression: A theory-based subtype of depression. *Psychological Review, 96,* 358–372.

Abramson, L. Y., Seligman, M. E. P., & Teasdale, J. (1978). Learned helplessness in humans: Critique and reformulation. *Journal of Abnormal Psychology, 87,* 49–74.

Adrian, C., & Hammen, C. (1993). Stress exposure and stress generation in children of depressed mothers. *Journal of Consulting and Clinical Psychology, 61,* 354–359.

Akiskal, H. S., & McKinney, W. T. (1975). Overview of recent research in depression: Integration of ten conceptual models into a comprehensive clinical framework. *Archives of General Psychiatry, 32,* 285–305.

Asarnow, J. R., & Bates, S. (1988). Depression in child psychiatric inpatients: Cognitive and attributional patterns. *Journal of Abnormal Child Psychology, 16,* 601–615.

Barnett, P. A., & Gotlib, I. H. (1988). Psychosocial functioning and depression: Distinguishing among antecedents, concomitants, and consequences. *Psychological Bulletin, 104,* 97–126.

Baron, R. M., & Kenny, D. A. (1986). The moderator–mediator variable distinction in social psychological research: Conceptual, strategic, and statistical considerations. *Journal of Personality and Social Psychology, 51,* 1173–1182.

Beardslee, W. R., Hoke, L., Wheelock, I., Rothberg, P. C., van de Velde, P., & Swatling, S. (1992). Initial findings on preventive intervention for families with parental affective disorders. *American Journal of Psychiatry, 149,* 1335–1340.

Beck, A. T. (1967). *Depression: Clinical, experiential, and theoretical aspects.* New York: Harper & Row.

Beck, A. T. (1976). *Cognitive therapy and the emotional disorders.* New York: International Universities Press.

Beck, A. T., Ward, C. H., Mendelson, M., Mock, J. E., & Erbaugh, J. K. (1961). An inventory for measuring depression. *Archives of General Psychiatry, 4,* 561–571.

Beck, A. T., & Young, J. E. (1985). Depression. In D. H. Barlow (Ed.), *Clinical handbook of psychological disorders: A step-by-step treatment manual* (pp. 206–244). New York: Guilford Press.

Bell, R. Q., & Harper, L. V. (1977). *Child effects on adults.* Hillsdale, NJ: Erlbaum.

Blatt, S. J., & Homann, E. (1992). Parent–child interaction in the etiology of dependent and self-critical depression. *Clinical Psychology Review, 12,* 47–91.

Blatt, S. J., Wein, S. J., Chevron, E., & Quinlan, D. M. (1979). Parental representations and depression in normal young adults. *Journal of Abnormal Psychology, 88,* 388–397.

Blehar, M. C., Weissman, M. M., Gershon, E. S., & Hirschfeld, R. M. (1988). Family and genetic studies of affective disorders. *Archives of General Psychiatry, 45,* 289–293.

Bowlby, J. (1980). *Attachment and loss: Vol. 3. Loss, sadness, and depression.* New York: Basic Books.

Bowlby, J. (1988). Developmental psychiatry comes of age. *American Journal of Psychiatry, 145,* 1–10.

Brewin, C. R., Firth-Cozens, J., Furnham, A., & McManus, C. (1992). Self-criticism in adulthood and recalled childhood experience. *Journal of Abnormal Psychology, 101,* 561–566.

Brown, G. W., & Harris, T. O. (1978). *Social origins of depression: A study of psychiatric disorder in women.* London: Tavistock.

Cicchetti, D., & Toth, S. L. (1998). The development of depression in children and adolescents. *American Psychologist, 53,* 221–241.

Clarke, G. N., Hawkins, W., Murphy, M., Sheeber, L. B., Lewinsohn, P. M., & Seeley, J. R. (1995). Targeted prevention of unipolar depressive disorder in an at-risk sample of high school adolescents: A randomized trial of a group cognitive intervention. *Journal of the Academy of Child and Adolescent Psychiatry, 34,* 312–321.

Cochran, S. D., & Hammen, C. L. (1985). Perceptions of stressful life events and depression: A test of attributional models. *Journal of Personality and Social Psychology, 48,* 1562–1571.

Cohn, J. F., Matias, R., Tronick, E. Z., Connell, D., & Lyons-Ruth, D. (1986). Face-to-face interactions of depressed mothers and their infants. In E. Z. Tronick & T. Field (Eds.), *Maternal depression and infant disturbance* (pp. 31–46). San Francisco: Jossey-Bass.

Cohn, J. F., & Tronick, E. (1989). Specificity of infants' response to mothers' affective behavior. *Journal of the American Academy of Child and Adolescent Psychiatry, 28,* 242–249.

Cole, D. A. (1991). Change in self-perceived competence as a function of peer and teacher evaluation. *Developmental Psychology, 27,* 682–688.

Cole, D. A., Maxwell, S. E., & Martin, J. M. (1997). Reflected self-appraisals: Strength and structure of the relation of teacher, peer, and parent ratings to children's self-perceived competencies. *Journal of Educational Psychology, 89,* 55–70.

Compas, B. E., Grant, K., & Ey, S. (1994). Psychosocial stress and child/adolescent depression: Can we be more specific? In W. M. Reynolds & H. F. Johnston (Eds.), *Handbook of depression in children and adolescents* (pp. 509–523). New York: Plenum Press.

Coyne, J. C. (1976). Toward an interactional description of depression. *Psychiatry, 39,* 28–40.

Crick, N. R., & Dodge, K. A. (1994). A review and reformulation of social information-processing mechanisms in children's social adjustment. *Psychological Bulletin, 115,* 74–101.

Cummings, E. M., & Davies, P. T. (1994). *Children and marital conflict: The impact of family dispute and resolution.* New York: Guilford Press.

Cutrona, C. E. (1983). Causal attributions and perinatal depression. *Journal of Abnormal Psychology, 92,* 161-172.

Cutrona, C. E., & Troutman, B. R. (1986). Social support, infant temperament, parenting self-efficacy: A mediational model of postpartum depression. *Child Development, 57,* 1507–1518.

DeMulder, E. K., & Radke-Yarrow, M. (1991). Attachment with affectively ill and well mothers: Concurrent behavioral correlates. *Development and Psychopathology, 3,* 227–242.

Dixon, J. F., & Ahrens, A. H. (1992). Stress and attributional style as predictors of self-reported depression in children. *Cognitive Therapy and Research, 16,* 623–634.

Downey, G., & Coyne, J. C. (1990). Children of depressed parents: An integrative review. *Psychological Bulletin, 108,* 50–76.

Dweck, C. S., & Gilliard, D. (1975). Expectancy statements as determinants of reactions to failure: Sex differences in persistence and expectancy change. *Journal of Personality and Social Psychology, 32,* 1077–1084.

Dweck, C. S., & Licht, B. (1980). Learned helplessness and intellectual achievement. In J. Garber & M. E. P. Seligman (Eds.), *Human helplessness: Theory and applications* (pp. 197–221). New York: Academic Press.

Dweck, C. S., & Reppuci, N. D. (1973). Learned helplessness and reinforcement responsibility in children. *Journal of Personality and Social Psychology, 25,* 109–116.

Eaves, G., & Rush, A. J. (1984). Cognitive patterns in symptomatic and remitted unipolar depression. *Journal of Abnormal Psychology, 93,* 31–40.

Epstein, J. L. (1983). The influence of friends on achievement and affective outcomes. In J. L. Epstein & N. Karweit (Eds.), *Friends in school: Patterns of selections and influence in secondary schools* (pp. 177–200). New York: Academic Press.

Eysenck, H. J., & Eysenck, M. W. (1985). *Personality and individual difference: A natural science approach.* New York: Plenum Press.

Fadden, G., Bebbington, P. E., & Kuipers, L. (1987). Caring and its burdens: A study of the spouses of depressed patients. *British Journal of Psychiatry, 151,* 660–667.

Fendrich, M., Warner, V., & Weissman, M. M. (1990). Family risk factors, parental depression, and psychopathology in offspring. *Developmental Psychology, 26,* 40–50.

Field, T., Healy, B., Goldstein, S., & Guthertz, M. (1990). Behavior state matching and synchrony in mother–infant interactions of nondepressed versus depressed dyads. *Developmental Psychology, 26,* 7–14.

Fincham, F. D., & Cain, K. M. (1986). Learned helplessness in humans: A developmental analysis. *Developmental Review, 6,* 310–333.

Forehand, R., Lautenschlager, G. J., Faust, J., & Graziano, W. G. (1986). Parent perceptions and parent–child interaction in clinic-referred children: A preliminary investigation of the effects of maternal depressive models. *Behavior Research and Therapy, 24,* 73–75.

Frank, S. J., Poorman, M. O., & Van Egeren, L. A. (1997). Perceived relationships with parents among adolescent inpatients with depressive preoccupations and depressed mood. *Journal of Clinical Child Psychology, 26,* 205–215.

Garber, J., Braafladt, N., & Zeman, J. (1991). The regulation of sad affect: An information processing perspective. In J. Garber & K. A. Dodge (Eds.), *The development of affect regulation and dysregulation* (pp. 208–240). New York: Cambridge University Press.

Garber, J. & Flynn, C. A. (2001a). Predictors of depressive cognitions in young adolescents. *Cognitive Therapy and Research, 25*, 353–376.

Garber, J., & Flynn, C. A. (2001b). Vulnerability to depression in childhood and adolescence. In R. Ingram & J. Price (Eds.), *Vulnerability to psychopathology: Risk across the lifespan* (pp. 175–225). New York: Guilford Press.

Garber, J., & Hilsman, R. (1992). Cognitions, stress, and depression in children and adolescents. *Child and Adolescent Psychiatric Clinics of North America, 1*, 129–167.

Garber, J., & Robinson, N. S. (1997). Cognitive vulnerability in children at risk for depression. *Cognitions and Emotions, 11*, 619–635.

Gillham, J., Reivich, K., Jaycox, L. H., & Seligman, M. E. P. (1995). Prevention of depressive symptoms in school children: Two year follow-up. *Psychological Science, 6*, 343–351.

Gladstone, T. R. G., & Kaslow, N. J. (1995). Depression and attributions in children and adolescents: A meta-analytic review. *Journal of Abnormal Child Psychology, 23*, 597–606.

Goodman, S. H., Adamson, L. B., Riniti, J., & Cole, S. (1994). Mothers' expressed attitudes: Associations with maternal depression and children's self-esteem and psychopathology. *Journal of the American Academy of Child and Adolescent Psychiatry, 33*, 1265–1274.

Goodman, S. H., Brogan, D., Lynch, M. E., & Fielding, B. (1993). Social and emotional competence in children of depressed mothers. *Child Development, 64*, 516–531.

Goodman, S. H., & Brumley, H. E. (1990). Schizophrenic and depressed mothers: Relational deficits in parenting. *Developmental Psychology, 26*, 31–39.

Goodman, S. H., & Gotlib, I. H. (1999). Risk for psychopathology in the children of depressed mothers: A developmental model for understanding mechanisms of transmission. *Psychological Review, 106*, 458–490.

Goodman, S. H., Sewell, D. R., Cooley, E. L., Leavitt, N. (1993). Assessing levels of adaptive functioning: The Role Functioning Scale. *Community Mental Health Journal, 29*, 119–131.

Gotlib, I. H., & Beach, S. R. H. (1995). A marital/family discord model of depression: Implications for therapeutic intervention. In N. S. Jacobson & A. S. Gurman (Eds.), *Clinical handbook of couple therapy* (pp. 411–436). New York: Guilford Press.

Gotlib, I. H., & Goodman, S. H. (1999). Children of parents with depression. In W. K. Silverman & T. H. Ollendick (Eds.), *Developmental issues in the clinical treatment of children and adolescents* (pp. 415–432). New York: Allyn & Bacon.

Gotlib, I. H., & Hammen, C. L. (1992). *Psychological aspects of depression: Toward a cognitive–interpersonal integration.* Chichester, England: Wiley.

Gotlib, I. H., & Lee, C. M. (1990). Children of depressed mothers: A review and directions for future research. In C. D. McCann & N. S. Endler (Eds.), *Depression: New directions in theory, research, and practice* (pp. 218–239). London: Royal College of Psychiatrists.

Gotlib, I. H., Lewinsohn, P. M., Seeley, J. R., Rohde, P., & Redner, J. E. (1993). Negative cognitions and attributional style in depressed adolescents: An examination of stability and specificity. *Journal of Abnormal Psychology, 102,* 607–615.

Grych, L. H., & Fincham, F. D. (1990). Marital conflict and children's adjustment: A cognitive–contextual framework. *Psychological Bulletin, 108,* 267–290.

Haaga, D., Dyck, M., & Ernst, D. (1991). Empirical status of cognitive theory of depression. *Psychological Bulletin, 110,* 215–236.

Haines, B. A., Metalsky, G. I., Cardamone, A. L., & Joiner, T. (1999). Interpersonal and cognitive pathways into the origins of attributional style: A developmental perspective. In T. Joiner & J. C. Coyne (Eds.), *The interactional nature of depression* (pp. 65–92). Washington, DC: American Psychological Association.

Hamilton, E. W., & Abramson, L. Y. (1983). Cognitive patterns and major depressive disorder: A longitudinal study in a hospital setting. *Journal of Abnormal Psychology, 92,* 173–184.

Hammen, C. L. (1988). Self cognitions, stressful events, and the prediction of depression in children of depressed mothers. *Journal of Abnormal Child Psychology, 16,* 347–360.

Hammen, C. L. (1991a). *Depression runs in families: The social context of risk and resilience in children of depressed mothers.* New York: Springer-Verlag.

Hammen, C. L. (1991b). The generation of stress in the course of unipolar depression. *Journal of Abnormal Psychology, 100,* 555–561.

Hammen, C. L., Adrian, C., & Hiroto, D. (1988). A longitudinal test of the attributional vulnerability model in children at risk for depression. *British Journal of Clinical Psychology, 27,* 37–46.

Hammen, C. L., Burge, D., & Stansbury, K. (1990). Relationship of mother and child variables to child outcomes in a high risk sample: A causal modeling analysis. *Developmental Psychology, 26,* 24–30.

Hammen, C., Gordon, D., Burge, D., Adrian, C., Jaenicke, C., & Hiroto, D. (1987). Maternal affective disorders, illness, and stress: Risk for children's psychopathology. *American Journal of Psychiatry, 144,* 736–741.

Harter, S. (1999). Causes, correlates, and the functional role of global self-worth: A life span perspective. In J. Kolligan & R. Sternberg (Eds.), *Perception of competence and incompetence across the life span* (pp. 67–98). New Haven, CT: Yale University Press.

Harter, S. (1999). *The construction of the self: A developmental perspective.* New York: Guilford Press.

Hartup, W. (1983). Peer relations. In P. Mussen (Ed.), *Handbook of child psychology: Vol. 4. Socialization, personality and social development* (4th ed., pp. 103–196). New York: Wiley.

Hilsman, R., & Garber, J. (1995). A test of the cognitive diathesis–stress model in children: Academic stressors, attributional style, perceived competence and control. *Journal of Personality and Social Psychology*, 69, 370–380.

Hirsch, B. J., Engel-Levy, A., DuBois, D. L., & Hardesty, P. H. (1990). The role of social environments in social support. In B. R. Sarason, I. G. Sarason, & G. R. Pierce (Eds.), *Social support: An interactional view* (pp. 367–393). New York: Wiley.

Hirsch, B. J., Moos, R. H., & Reischl, T. M. (1985). Psychosocial adjustment of adolescent children of a depressed, arthritic, or normal parent. *Journal of Abnormal Psychology*, 94, 154–164.

Hollon, S. D. (1992). Cognitive models of depression from a psychobiological perspective. *Psychological Inquiry*, 3, 250–253.

Hops, H. (1996). Intergenerational transmission of depressive symptoms: Gender and developmental considerations. In C. Mundt, M. J. Goldstein, K. Hahlweg, & P. Fiedler (Eds.), *Interpersonal factors in the origin and course of affective disorders* (pp. 113–129). London: Royal College of Psychiatrists.

Hops, H., Biglan, A., Sherman, L., Arthur, J., Friedman, L., & Osteen, V. (1987). Home observations of family interactions of depressed women. *Journal of Consulting and Clinical Psychology*, 55, 341–346.

Ingram, R. E. (1990). Self-focused attention in clinical disorders: Review and a conceptual model. *Psychological Bulletin*, 107, 156–176.

Ingram, R. E., Miranda, J., & Segal., Z. V. (1998). *Cognitive vulnerability to depression*. New York: Guilford Press.

Ingram, R. E., & Ritter, J. (2000). Vulnerability to depression: Cognitive reactivity and parental bonding in high-risk individuals. *Journal of Abnormal Psychology*, 109, 588–596.

Jacob, T. (1987). *Family interaction and psychopathology: Theories, methods, and findings*. New York: Plenum.

Jaenicke, C., Hammen, C., Zupan, B., Hiroto, D., Gordon, D., Adrian, C., & Burge, D. (1987). Cognitive vulnerability in children at risk for depression. *Journal of Abnormal Child Psychology*, 15, 559–572.

Janoff-Bulman, R. (1992). *Shattered assumptions: Towards a new psychology of trauma*. New York: Free Press.

Jaycox, L. H., Reivich, K., Gillham, J., & Seligman, M. E. P. (1994). Prevention of depressive symptoms in school children. *Behavior Research and Therapy*, 32, 801–816.

Johnson, B. M., Schulman, S., & Collins, W. A. (1991). Systematic patterns of parenting as reported by adolescents: Developmental differences and implications for psychosocial outcomes. *Journal of Adolescent Research*, 6, 235–252.

Just, N., Abramson, L. Y., & Alloy, L. B. (2001). Remitted depression studies as tests of the cognitive vulnerability hypothesis of depression onset: A critique and conceptual analysis. *Clinical Psychology Review*, 21, 63–83.

Kagan, J. (1994). On the nature of emotion. In N. Fox (Ed.), The development of emotion regulation: Biological and behavioral considerations. *Monographs of the Society for Research in Child Development, 59*(2–3), 7–24.

Kaslow, N. J., Rehm, L. P., Pollack, S. L., & Siegel, A. W. (1988). Attributional style and self-control behavior in depressed and nondepressed children and their parents. *Journal of Abnormal Child Psychology, 16*, 163–175.

Kochanska, G., Kuczynski, L., Radke-Yarrow, M., & Welsh, J. D. (1987). Resolutions of control episodes between well and affectively ill mothers and their young children. *Journal of Abnormal Child Psychology, 15*, 441–456.

Kochanska, G., Radke-Yarrow, M., Kuczynski, L., & Friedman, S. (1987). Normal and affectively ill mothers' beliefs about their children. *American Journal of Orthopsychiatry, 57*, 345–350.

Koestner, R., Zuroff, D. C., & Powers, T. A. (1991). Family origins of adolescent self-criticism and its continuity into adulthood. *Journal of Abnormal Psychology, 100*, 191–197.

Kovacs, M., & Beck, A. T. (1978). Maladaptive cognitive structures in depression. *American Journal of Psychiatry, 135*, 525–533.

Levenson, H. (1973). Perceived parental antecedents of internal, powerful others, and chance locus of control orientation. *Developmental Psychology, 9*, 260–265.

Lewinsohn, P. M., Steinmetz, J. L., Larson, D. W., & Franklin, J. (1981). Depression related cognitions: Antecedent or consequence? *Journal of Abnormal Psychology, 91*, 213–219.

Litovsky, V. G., & Dusek, J. B. (1985). Perceptions of child rearing and self-concept development during the early adolescent years. *Journal of Youth and Adolescence, 14*, 373–387.

Lovejoy, M. C. (1991). Maternal depression: Effects on social cognition and behavior in parent–child interactions. *Journal of Abnormal Child Psychology, 19*, 693–706.

McCauley, E., Mitchell, J. R., Burke, P., & Moss, S. (1988). Cognitive attributes of depression in children and adolescents. *Journal of Consulting and Clinical Psychology, 56*, 903–908.

McCranie, E. W., & Bass, J. D. (1984). Childhood family antecedents of dependency and self-criticism: Implications for depression. *Journal of Abnormal Psychology, 93*, 3–8.

Merikangas, K. R. (1984). Divorce and assortative mating among depressed patients. *American Journal of Psychiatry, 141*, 74–76.

Metalsky, G. I., & Joiner, T. E. (1992). Vulnerability to depressive symptomatology: A prospective test of the diathesis–stress and causal mediation components of the hopelessness theory of depression. *Journal of Personality and Social Psychology, 63*, 667–675.

Metalsky, G. I., Joiner, T. E., Hardin, T. S., & Abramson, L. Y. (1993). Depressive reactions to failure in a naturalistic setting: A test of the hopelessness and self-esteem theories of depression. *Journal of Abnormal Psychology, 102*, 101–109.

Miranda, J., Persons, J. B., & Byers, C. N. (1990). Endorsement of dysfunctional beliefs depends on current mood state. *Journal of Abnormal Psychology, 99*, 237–241.

Nolen-Hoeksema, S., Girgus, J., & Seligman, M. E. P. (1992). Predictors and consequences of childhood depressive symptoms: A 5-year longitudinal study. *Journal of Abnormal Psychology, 101*, 405–422.

Nowicki, S., & Segal, W. (1974). Perceived parental characteristics, locus of control orientation, and behavioral correlates of locus of control. *Developmental Psychology, 10*, 33–37.

Oliver, J. M., & Berger, L. S. (1992). Depression, parent–offspring relationships, and cognitive vulnerability. *Journal of Social Behavior and Personality, 7*, 415–429.

Olweus, D. (1984). Aggressors and their victims: Bullying at school. In N. Frude & H. Gault (Eds.), *Disruptive behaviors in schools* (pp. 57–76). New York: Wiley.

Ostrander, R., Weinfurt, K. P., & Nay, W. R. (1998). The role of age, family support, and negative cognitions in the prediction of depressive symptoms. *School Psychology Review, 27*, 121–137.

Panak, W., & Garber, J. (1992). Role of aggression, rejection, and attributions in the prediction of depression in children. *Development and Psychopathology, 4*, 145–165.

Parker, G. (1993). Parental rearing style: Examining for links with personality vulnerability factors for depression. *Social Psychiatry and Psychiatric Epidemiology, 28*, 97–100.

Perez-Bouchard, L., Johnson, J. L., & Ahrens, A. H. (1993). Attributional style in children of substance abusers. *American Journal of Drug and Alcohol Abuse, 19*, 475–489.

Persons, J. B., & Miranda, J. (1992). Cognitive theories of vulnerability to depression: Reconciling negative evidence. *Cognitive Therapy and Research, 16*, 485–502.

Peterson, C., & Seligman, M. E. P. (1984). Causal explanations as a risk factor for depression: Theory and evidence. *Psychological Review, 91*, 347–374.

Phares, V., & Compas, B. E. (1992). The role of fathers in child and adolescent psychopathology: Make room for Daddy. *Psychological Bulletin, 111*, 387–412.

Radke-Yarrow, M. (1998). *Children of depressed mothers.* Cambridge, England: Cambridge University Press.

Radke-Yarrow, M., Belmont, B., Nottelman, E., & Bottomly, L. (1990). Young children's self-conceptions: Origins in the natural discourse of depressed and normal mothers and their children. In D. Cicchetti & M. Beeghly (Eds.), *The self in transition: Infancy to childhood* (pp. 345–361). Chicago: University of Chicago Press.

Randolph, J. J., & Dykman, B. M. (1998). Perceptions of parenting and depression-proneness in the offspring: Dysfunctional attitudes as a mediating mechanism. *Cognitive Therapy and Research, 22*, 377–401.

Reinherz, H. Z., Stewart-Berghauer, G., Pakiz, B., Frost, A. K., Moeykens, B. A., & Holmes, W. M. (1989). The relationship of early risk and current mediators to depressive symptomatology in adolescence. *Journal of the American Academy of Child and Adolescent Psychiatry, 28,* 942–947.

Riskind, J. H., & Rholes, W. S. (1984). Cognitive accessibility and the capacity of cognitions to predict future depression: A theoretical note. *Cognitive Therapy and Research, 8,* 1–12.

Robinson, N. S., Garber, J., & Hilsman, R. (1995). Cognitions and stress: Direct and moderating effects on depressive versus externalizing symptoms during the junior high school transition. *Journal of Abnormal Psychology, 104,* 453–463.

Rohde, P., Lewinsohn, P. M., & Seeley, J. R. (1990). Are people changed by the experience of having an episode of depression? A further test of the scar hypothesis. *Journal of Abnormal Psychology, 99,* 264–271.

Rohde, P., Lewinsohn, P. M., & Seeley, J. R. (1994). Are adolescents changed by an episode of major depression? *Journal of the American Academy of Child and Adolescent Psychiatry, 33,* 1289–1298.

Rose, D. T., & Abramson, L. Y. (1992). Developmental predictors of depressive cognitive style: Research and theory. In D. Cicchetti & S. L. Toth (Eds.), *Rochester symposium on developmental psychopathology* (Vol. 4, pp. 323–349). Hillsdale, NJ: Erlbaum.

Rose, D. T., Abramson, L. Y., Hodulik, C. J., Halberstadt, L., & Leff, G. (1994). Heterogeneity of cognitive style among depressed inpatients. *Journal of Abnormal Psychology, 103,* 419–429.

Rueter, M. A., Scaramella, L., Wallace, L. E., & Conger, R. D. (1999). First onset of depressive or anxiety disorders predicted by the longitudinal course of internalizing symptoms and parent–adolescent disagreements. *Archives of General Psychiatry, 56,* 726–732.

Rutter, M. (1987). The role of cognitions in child development and disorder. *British Journal of Medical Psychology, 60,* 1–16.

Rutter, M., & Quinton, P. (1984). Parental psychiatric disorder: Effects on children. *Psychological Medicine, 14,* 853–880.

Schulman, P., Keith, D., & Seligman, M. E. P. (1991). Is optimism heritable? A study of twins. *Behavior Research and Therapy, 31,* 569–574.

Segal, Z. V., & Dobson, K. S. (1992). Cognitive models of depression: Report from a consensus development conference. *Psychological Inquiry, 3,* 214–224.

Seligman, M. E. P., Abramson, L. Y., Semmel, A., & von Baeyer, C. (1979). Depressive attributional style. *Journal of Abnormal Psychology, 88,* 242–247.

Seligman, M. E. P., & Peterson, C. (1986). A learned helplessness perspective on childhood depression: Theory and research. In M. Rutter, C. E. Izard, & P. B. Read (Eds.), *Depression in young people: Developmental and clinical perspectives* (pp. 223–249). New York: Guilford Press.

Stark, K. D., Schmidt, K. L., & Joiner, T. E. (1996). Cognitive triad: Relationship to depressive symptoms, parents' cognitive triad, and perceived parental messages. *Journal of Abnormal Child Psychology, 24,* 615–632.

Taylor, L., & Ingram, R. E. (1999). Cognitive reactivity and depressotypic information processing in children of depressed mothers. *Journal of Abnormal Psychology, 108*, 202–210.

Teasdale, J. D., & Dent, J. (1987). Cognitive vulnerability to depression: An investigation of two hypotheses. *British Journal of Clinical Psychology, 26*, 113–126.

Teti, D., Gelfand, D., Messinger, D., & Isabella, R. (1995). Maternal depression and the quality of early attachment: An examination of infants, preschoolers, and their mothers. *Developmental Psychology, 31*, 364–376.

Tiggemann, M., Winefield, H. R., Goldney, R. D., & Winefield, A. H. (1992). Attributional style and parental rearing as predictors of psychological distress. *Personality and Individual Differences, 13*, 835–841.

Turk, E., & Bry, B. H. (1992). Adolescents' and parents' explanatory styles and parents' causal explanations about their adolescents. *Cognitive Therapy and Research, 16*, 349–357.

Turner, J. E., & Cole, D. A. (1994). Developmental differences in cognitive diatheses for child depression. *Journal of Abnormal Child Psychology, 22*, 15–32.

Watson, D., & Clark, L. A. (1984). Negative affectivity: The disposition to experience aversive emotional states. *Psychological Bulletin, 96*, 465–490.

Watson, D., Clark, L. A., & Harkness, A. R. (1994). Structures of personality and their relevance to psychopathology. *Journal of Abnormal Psychology, 103*, 18–31.

Webster-Stratton, C., & Hammond, M. (1988). Maternal depression and its relationship to life stress, perceptions of child behavior problems, parenting behaviors, and child conduct problems. *Journal of Abnormal Child Psychology, 16*, 299–315.

Weissman, M. M., Gammon, G., John, K., Merikangas, K. R., Warner, V., Prusoff, B., & Sholomskas, D. (1987). Children of depressed parents: Increased psychopathology and early onset of major depression. *Archives of General Psychiatry, 44*, 847–853.

Whiffen, V. E., & Sasseville, T. M. (1991). Dependency, self-criticism, and recollections of parenting: Sex differences and the role of affect. *Journal of Social and Clinical Psychology, 10*, 121–133.

Whisman, M. A., & Kwon, P. (1992). Parental representations, cognitive distortions, and mild depression. *Cognitive Therapy and Research, 16*, 557–568.

Whisman, M. A., & McGarvey, A. L. (1995). Attachment, depressotypic cognitions, and dysphoria. *Cognitive Therapy and Research, 19*, 633–650.

Winokur, G. (1997). All roads lead to depression: Clinically homogeneous, etiologically heterogeneous. *Journal of Affective Disorders, 45*, 97–108.

7

PARENTAL DEPRESSION AND OFFSPRING DISORDERS: A DEVELOPMENTAL PERSPECTIVE

MARIAN RADKE-YARROW AND BONNIE KLIMES-DOUGAN

Parental influences on the behavior and development of offspring pose questions that are among the oldest and most intractable in the human sciences. Parental depression as an influence is a special case within this larger domain. The research questions and methods, as well as the level of research understanding, are similar in the diverse content areas of parent–offspring associations. Although some principles of transmission undoubtedly generalize across domains, it is likely, too, that biological and behavioral properties specific to a given parental condition, such as parental depression, introduce into these processes additional unique forces. Hence, consideration of both common and unique factors acting together is necessary for an understanding of depressed parent–offspring interdependencies.

With this perspective, the focus of this chapter is on the linkages between parental depression and offspring problems from a developmental perspective. Primary consideration is given to parental behavior, recognizing that the contributions of biological variables must be factored in for a full understanding of the processes underlying maladaptive social, emotional, and cognitive functioning in offspring of depressed parents. Indeed, genetic endowments of parent and child are implicit in many of the variables studied here. They may elicit different environments, or they may mediate responses to different environments (Lombroso, Pauls, & Leckman, 1995). Research has brought increasing awareness of the complexities in parent–offspring connections, emphasizing the multiple influences involved and the diversity of offspring outcomes. Less studied and little understood are how these many variables in parent and offspring act together to influence offspring development.

Since the 1980s, when parental depression and offspring disorders became a prominent focus in psychological and psychiatric research, descriptions of depressed parents and offspring problems have become a vast literature. Initially, determining the psychopathology in offspring in the presence of parental depression was the primary aim. Interests shifted gradually to identifying parental factors associated with increased risk of offspring disorders. Many factors have been considered, one variable at a time in cross-sectional studies. Questions regarding mechanisms involved in the associations and issues of diversity in mechanisms and outcomes have more recently come into focus (see reviews by Cummings & Davies, 1994; Downey & Coyne, 1990; Gelfand & Teti, 1990; and Goodman, 1992).

So many and varied factors have been identified sometimes, under some circumstances, for some problems, and for some offspring. This phase of research has been invaluable as a preexplanatory stage, but investigation must move past the demonstration of single risk factors and the enumeration of kinds of dysfunction in offspring of depressed parents. How do these factors interrelate? What combinations of factors are especially influential risk factors in the lives of these children? Are there protective combinations? What are the diverse imprints of parental depression on offspring? How do the risks presented by parental depression interact with the developmentally changing capacities and needs of the child? Because parental depression is a condition that may exist (intermittently or continuously) over the course of the child's development, it is necessary to consider its influences over time.

A shift in research questions and methods of inquiry is needed. Research is needed that has hardly been done, and perhaps we do not know how to do. We refer to research that in theory, design, method, and analysis incorporates the reality of multidetermined behavior and that forces consideration of multiple simultaneously and serially operating variables throughout the course of the individual's development.

A further modification in research is needed, namely, a more probing evaluation of offspring functioning. *Outcomes* in offspring disorders have become streamlined as *problems* present or absent, in diseaselike fashion. Yet, only if assessments take account of the form of the problem (which typically includes various comorbidities) and the developmental course of the problem can one hope to identify specific conditions and processes through which parental depression imparts its effects on the next generation.

In this chapter we attempt to take seriously the needed "shifts" in research. Our focus is not on all the associations and outcomes that have been reported. Rather, we explore research in which multiple, co-acting factors are considered in relation to offspring functioning. Development as a co-acting variable is a special focus: How does the child's stage of development affect depressed parent–offspring interdependencies? With an emphasis on developmental considerations, we focus first on the assessment of offspring, followed by examination of links between these offspring "outcomes" and variables in the behavior and environment of parental depression. We offer some thoughts regarding implications for intervention.

Our own longitudinal study (Radke-Yarrow, Martinez, Mayfield, & Ronsaville, 1998) provides examples of some of the issues addressed. In our study, 98 families were followed longitudinally. Inclusion was based primarily on the mother's diagnosis (major depression or bipolar disorder) or absence of a psychiatric diagnosis. In the depressed mother groups, fathers also frequently suffered from depression. Two siblings from each family were studied. In recruited families, the younger sibling was 2 to 3 years old, and the older sibling was 5 to 7 years old. Assessments were conducted every 3 to 5 years; the final visit, for which data are currently available, took place when the offspring were adolescents. In addition to diagnostic assessments, a broad range of other psychological variables were measured at each time period.

DEVELOPMENTAL FRAMEWORK

In research on offspring of depressed parents, a developmental focus has entered into theory more than into empirical studies. Whether or not investigators take development into account, the parent is always interacting with the child in the context of the child's age or developmental stage. The child presents himself or herself to the parent and responds to the parent in terms of developmentally dependent capacities, needs, and experiential history. Although developmental traits of children and developmental changes in them have been extensively elaborated in studies of normative child development, these traits have been given less attention in regard to how they interact with parenting and how they affect parents' influences, in the immediate circumstance and later in development.

Perhaps almost as predictable as children's developmental needs and changes, but without equal theoretical or research attention, are the developmental traits and developmental changes in the parents. Parents are confronted with changing parenting demands and satisfactions as well as their own life course issues. The introduction of a developmental perspective on both the parent and the child changes the conceptualization of parental depression as a risk factor to their offspring. Parent and child become reciprocal influences on each other, influences that evolve over time. This conceptualization changes research questions and calls for altering methods as appropriate to the questions posed.

In 1972, long before the burst of offspring studies in relation to parental depression, Weissman, Paykel, and Klerman presented a developmental model that should have been heeded by investigators. The model pointed out the relation of development-dependent variables in parent and child to the child's vulnerabilities at different ages. For each stage of development (infancy, childhood, adolescence), they identified salient parenting tasks, the depressed mother's impairment with respect to the tasks, and the likely locus of the child's problems in relation to the failed parenting. Unfortunately, the model did little to turn research to the issues of development. A quarter of a century later the specifics of the model appear inadequate, but the model addresses a key issue with which research must come to terms.

The "irrelevance" of development is dramatic in the early studies. The studies reviewed by Downey and Coyne (1990), covering more than a decade of research, show little evidence of interest in development. When investigators focused on children, the developmental context (with some notable exceptions, e.g., infant research) appears not to have been an important consideration in determining why a given parent variable was chosen for study of children of a given age, or why children of a given age were evaluated on a particular dysfunction. Development has been mistreated in other ways. Studies with two or more time-spaced assessments of offspring have typically relied on cross-sectional analyses, where group rates of disorder at each assessment are compared, individual progression is not followed through time, and individual variation is concealed.

DEVELOPMENTAL CONSIDERATIONS IN THE ASSESSMENT OF OFFSPRING PROBLEMS

Developmental considerations in how offspring problems are assessed and interpreted have been overlooked in two ways: (a) Age, or developmental stage, of the offspring is infrequently a planned, theory-based variable in studies of depressed parent–offspring associations, and (b) the developmental history of the child's problem is generally ignored, both in estimates of prevalence of disorders and in studies of parent–offspring associations.

Age as a Planned Variable

The various ways in which age of offspring enters into the design of studies reflect differences in theories regarding the etiology of offspring depression (more broadly, offspring psychopathology). They also reflect differences in investigators' sensitivities to the developmentally changing capacities and needs of the child as variables in parent–child transactions.

There are studies that have no age boundaries or very broad boundaries in the selection and analyses of offspring (e.g., 7 to 14 years, 8 to 16 years), but the age spans are too wide to be defined as one developmental stage. Often these studies include both prepubertal and postpubertal years. Still other studies focus on a single developmental period (e.g., infancy, preschool years, middle childhood, adolescence).

Studies without age boundaries suggest an underlying theory of an over-riding influence of genetic factors, expressed with little perturbation by maturation or the environment. Studies that include a broad but bounded age spread suggest no particular etiological theory, but they share the implicit assumption that the influences of parental depression do not vary significantly with age of offspring. A developmental orientation is implicit in studies of a single age period or stage.

One would not expect to find a great deal of age-specific information in this literature, and indeed that is the case. Systematic data on the prevalence and nature of offspring problems at successive periods covering the whole of childhood and adolescence are not available. It follows therefore that there is little information on how age of offspring and parental factors interact to increase risks to the offspring. Are processes of parental influence constant or changing in relation to developmental needs and capacities of the child?

Assessment of Developmental Pathways

Other developmental issues, in addition to noting the age of offspring are relevant in interpreting parent–offspring associations. A core issue pertains to the assessment of the child's problem in terms of developmental course. This is a matter of particular relevance in interpreting depressed parent–offspring problem associations. Is the child's problem a first-time problem, a problem with a long history, or a problem that was exhibited at some time earlier in the child's life? Because the majority of studies of offspring are cross-sectional, with measurements at single points in time, reported problems can have any one of these histories. Because the meaning of the child's current problem is dependent, in part, on the history of the problem, lacking this knowledge muddies interpretation of etiology and prognosis. A recurrent or persistent problem signals more serious difficulties than a temporary problem. Also, parental factors that initiate a problem are not necessarily the same factors that maintain or worsen the child's difficulties.

When developmental psychopathology acquired an identity and research momentum (e.g., Rutter & Garmezy, 1983; Sroufe & Rutter, 1984), it ushered in fresh concepts and a direction of inquiry in which these considerations are prominent. It has significantly reformulated traditional questions regarding depressed parent–offspring associations and continuity and discontinuity in offspring behavior. It now emphasizes the course of maladaptive development and the diversity of courses. Major research implications for assessments and treatment follow from these changes. Longitudinal data are essential, and individual development becomes the unit of study.

A focus on individual pathways of problem development accentuates diversity at many levels (Rutter, 1989). Children's ages at onset of problems differ. The progression of their problems varies. Diverse developmental pathways can lead to similar long-term outcomes, and similar early pathways can branch into diverse outcomes. These diversities are invisible in cross-sectional assessments of group averages in offspring problems. A view of offspring problems as a part of individual development, and as changing with development, brings a new set of issues to the questions of depressed parent influences.

Our purpose is to examine some of these issues. We use our own longitudinal study to illustrate. It has the advantage of providing data on the same children of depressed parents over the entire span of childhood (Radke-Yarrow et al., 1998; see earlier description). Pathway markers are at early childhood, middle childhood, early adolescence, and late adolescence. Problems of depression, anxiety, and externalizing–disruptive behavior are traced over time (see Table 7.1) for both the younger and older sibling cohort in this study. Because the individual child over time is the unit of analysis, a pathway approach provides dimensions of offspring problems not generally assessed; namely, developmental timing, the amount of developmental time that is damaged by problems, and patterns of problems.

The children represented in Table 7.1, offspring of depressed mothers (and often depressed fathers as well), show varied pathways of problems. For roughly half of the children in the risk groups, the pathway is indicative of early and persistent maladaptation as indicated by the evidence of continual problems of mood, anxiety, or disruption (row 1, column 1; row 6, columns 1 and 5. The younger offspring of bipolar mothers are the exception. Their problems typically begin in middle childhood, row 1, column 5.) Finding that, for a significant proportion of offspring, near-total development is characterized by problems is a major finding regarding the risk to offspring of depressed parents, and it has etiological and intervention implications. It suggests parental factors operating early and continuing as the child matures. It raises many questions: Does this pattern of persistence represent the same factors and processes operating overtime? Is there an increasing consolidation of maladaptive development? Do the risks and vulnerabilities at one stage predetermine the nature of further unfavorable development? This pattern directs attention, also, to child traits that may very early set in motion a style of interaction with the depressed parent that serves to maintain dysfunctional behavior.

Children with a pathway of continual problems are not a homogenous group, however. In continuing maladaptation, the exhibited problem behavior differs among children (columns 2, 3, 4, 6, 7, and 8) and may change with development. It is interesting to note that when the pathways of these chil-

Table 7.1
Developmental Pathways of Offspring Problems (in percentages)

Pathway of problems	Offspring of unipolar parents				Offspring of bipolar parents			
	Any	Dep	Ext	Anx	Any	Dep	Ext	Anx
Younger cohort–offspring studied from ages 2 1/2–15								
Continual	43	2	21	2	19	8	12	0
Recurrent	21	14	7	29	31	0	15	11
Only Early/Mid Childhood	24	43	24	45	23	19	4	35
First in Adolescence	2	2	7	0	8	15	15	0
Never a Problem	10	38	41	24	19	58	54	54
Older cohort–offspring studied from ages 5–19								
Continual	62	24	12	5	50	18	23	5
Recurrent	22	19	21	14	18	14	5	18
Only Early/Mid Childhood	7	19	24	28	9	14	4	18
First In Adolescence	7	14	14	31	18	27	18	23
Never a Problem	2	24	29	21	5	27	50	36

Note. In the younger cohort, number of offspring = 68; in the older cohort, number of offspring = 64. Any = mood, anxiety, or disruptive problems; Dep = problems with mood/depression; Ext = externalizing/disruptive problems; Anx = anxiety problems. From Table 7.2 in "Children of Depressed Mothers, From Early Childhood to Maturity" by M. Radke-Yarrow, P. Martinez, A. Mayfield, & D. Ronsaville, 1998, New York: Cambridge University Press. Copyright 1998 by Cambridge University Press. Adapted by permission.

dren are followed into late adolescence (the older siblings), depressive problems are continual or recurrent in 43% and 32% of children of unipolar and bipolar mothers, respectively. The chronicity presents a development-dependent change; by contrast the corresponding scores for the younger siblings are 16% and 8%. The few children showing such early depressive manifestations may be a particularly vulnerable group constitutionally or a group subjected to particular early parental–environmental conditions.

There are children with recurrent problems (rows 2 and 7), who, although manifesting repeated difficulties, have periods of healthy functioning. Do the onsets and remissions of their problems coincide with stressful or protective changes in their environments? Similar questions apply to children whose problems are concentrated at a single developmental stage (rows 3 and 8). Are problems triggered in periods of developmental transitions (e.g., from family to school and peers, from childhood to adolescence), when new developmental tasks make increased demands on the child and the depressed parent?

The developmental pathways described in the table are incomplete assessments. They leave out the *combinations* of troubled behaviors that the child may exhibit at a given time and the *sequences* in which problems evolve. Indeed, for these children, maladaptations expressed in multiple forms are more the rule than the exception. Internalizing and externalizing problems often appear together. Depressive and acting-out symptoms are more chronically manifested than anxiety. Anxiety problems tend to precede depressive problems. Clinically, it is possible to observe changes in the intensity of the child's problem, fluctuating symptoms, turning points in behavior, and successful functioning. Although it is difficult to make such discriminations in research, the heart of the problem of parent–offspring connections lies in gaining an understanding of the active interplay of parental factors and the child's ongoing behavior.

We have made the case here for developmental assessment of psychiatrically defined problems. This is not to ignore the importance of broader, more inclusive assessments of the child's cognitive functioning, health, and certainly day-to-day functioning in major developmentally expected social roles. There is scant evidence on the interrelations of these varied aspects of the child's adaptation over the course of development. A relevant bit of information comes from the children we have been describing. Roughly half of those with depressive disorders without externalizing difficulties have succeeded in school and with peers. This is not the case for depressed children whose pathways include externalizing problems.

A very few children have a developmental course without problems of clinical concern (rows 5 and 10). They may be the "resilient" or "invulnerable" children described in the literature as enjoying an absence of problems (e.g., Garmezy, 1985; Luthar & Zigler, 1991; Rutter, 1985). Indeed, a number of the children in our sample coming largely from bright and well-educated families exhibit competencies and talents that seem positively to influence their long-term trajectories. Similar to the pathways of vulnerable children, these children's successful adaptations are best illuminated by a developmental approach.

From this stock-taking of offspring assessment, we see many layers of evaluation, all of which have a bearing on the core question of interdependence with parental depression. The timing and evolution or progression of problems have major defining properties to be considered in investigating the origins of problems in offspring of depressed parents.

DEPRESSED PARENT–OFFSPRING INTERDEPENDENCIES

We turn now to the depressed parent as the source of the offspring problems. Research concerned with parents' behavioral risks has proceeded mainly along three lines: (a) characteristics of the parent's illness, indexing amount and severity of behavioral impairment, (b) conditions and relationships in families with a depressed parent, and (c) parenting behavior of the depressed parent. At each level, there are significant associations between parent variables and offspring functioning.

Parent Diagnostic Characteristics

Among the first parental variables to be studied are those that pertain to the diagnostic dimensions of parents' depression, such as age at onset of depression and depression severity and chronicity. Keller et al. (1986), for example, reported significant associations between rates of offspring problems and severity and chronicity of parent's depression, with greater severity and chronicity being linked to greater offspring impairment. Similar associations were found by Harder, Kokes, Fisher, and Strauss (1980); Hammen et al. (1987); and Radke-Yarrow et al. (1998). In the latter study, severity of mothers' depression is associated with a developmental pathway of recurrent disruptive problems over the course of childhood. In none of the studies are the associations impressive (e.g., in Keller et al., rank order correlations of .23 to .38; in Radke-Yarrow et al., [tau-b] – . 21 to – .28). Severity and chronicity do not convey the kinds of encounters that the parent has with the child, and, as ratings summarizing parental characteristics over time, they obscure possible critical developmental periods in which severity takes a heavy toll on the child. As for mechanisms, the findings equally invite genetic explanations and explanations in terms of a "dose" response (i.e., long exposure of the child to disordered parental behavior).

Along similar diagnostic lines, personality disorders of depressed parents (presumed to be long-term characteristics) have been investigated in relation to offspring problems (Cooper, Leach, Storer, & Tonge, 1977; Radke-Yarrow et al., 1998; Rutter & Quinton, 1984). They carry added risk for the offspring. Although this finding is only broadly descriptive, it directs attention to patterns of behavior as risks. Through further study of specific personality disorders, specific patterns of behavior are identified that interfere with developmental tasks and needs of the child. DeMulder, Tarullo, Klimes-Dougan, Free, and Radke-Yarrow (1995) reported that depressed mothers' with avoidant personality disorder exhibit parenting that is uninvolved or emotionally unavailable. This style of parenting is associated with a developmental course of externalizing behavior in the offspring. Dependent personality disorder (possibly expressed in overinvolvement with, and enmeshment of, the young child and later in role reversal behavior) is associated in later childhood with recurrent disruptive and oppositional problems. These are small links, but they move associations one step toward identifying what is undermined in the child. These hypothesized personality risks are reexamined when we look at specific observed parenting behavior in relation to offspring needs.

Family Environments of Children of Depressed Parents

One cannot for long view the depressed parents in isolation from their circumstances—the contexts of family conditions and relationships. The family is seen as a major locus of psychosocial risks to offspring of depressed parents.

There are difficulties in measuring the family environments associated with parental depression. They are the same difficulties that have long characterized studies of family effects on children: Multiple dimensions of family conditions and relationships, interrelated and often changing over time, do not readily lend themselves to assessment. Consequently, family environment often enters research in terms of broad descriptors of instrumental and affective dimensions, such as losses, marital discord, financial problems, and so on. This approach defines the family as a significant source of risk, but it reduces the environment to broad dimensions, obscures major differences within the categories, and ignores the specific involvements of the individual child.

The family environment as an influence on offspring of depressed parents has been measured mostly in terms of "stress," often with parental diagnosis and family stress treated as competitive factors in explaining offspring difficulties: Are offspring disorders accounted for by the parent's depression, or has a chaotic, painful, hostile family overwhelmed the child's adaptive capacities? Generally, we are dealing with "level' of stress. Clinical and research evidence leaves no doubt as to the prevalence and severity of stresses in families with a depressed parent (e.g., Brown & Harris, 1978; Emery, Weintraub, & Neale, 1982; Fendrich, Warner, & Weissman, 1990; see also Hammen, chapter 8, this volume). Should not stress be a strong predictor of offspring problems? Moreover, should not associations between family stress and offspring problems be informative as to how the negative outcomes in children are produced? Findings do not entirely match these expectations. The finding that extreme and persistent stress tends to erode healthy development is not surprising. However, there is an absence of specific consequences in offspring. This, too, is not surprising, given the heterogeneous conditions under the umbrella of stress. The chronic nature of family stress throughout the childhood years (Radke-Yarrow et al., 1998) almost precludes analyses in which the effects of special stressful events and conditions and of the timing of stress can be probed. Because depression involves interpersonal as much as personal impairments, family stress reflects parents' illness-related behavior and is inseparable from it. Interpretations of findings differ in the weight they assign to parental diagnosis and family stress as a cause for the disorders of offspring (e.g., Fendrich et al., 1990; Hammen et al., 1987). Reducing the diverse family turbulences to a quantitative score of judged level of stress has not delivered information on how the family variables lead to negative child outcomes or how individual offspring survive stressful family conditions.

What is missing in this genre of research is quite evident. By relying on overall ratings of the family unit, findings rest on an implicit assumption of the equal experience of stress by all family members. The individual child's experience of, and involvement in, particular stressful events and conditions are missed: (a) When, in development, does the child directly encounter the stressor? What are the interferences with specific developmental tasks? (b) How does a stressor indirectly affect the child as it affects the child's caregiver? (c) How do properties of the child affect his or her responses to stress and contribute to family stress?

The family environment is more than a general ambience of stress; it is a highly individual matter, as the following vignettes of three families illustrate. Marital discord is their common stressor, rated as a high level of stress. In family A, parents fight, threaten, denigrate each other, slam and throw objects in fits of anger. From their earliest years, the children are often in these battles and are denounced and yelled at. In family B, spousal harmony breaks down gradually. Discord is silence, absence, cold indifference, and disrespect between two depressed parents. The mother overinvests in her children as substitutes for her "lost" spouse. In family C, the mother suffers from bipolar illness. She exhibits outrageous behavior, bringing shame and ostracism to the family. Her husband is rejecting and hostile. He contributes nothing to the care of the children. The extreme plight of the family induces the church to intervene. It successfully provides help to the parents and children. For the children in these families, outcomes of marital discord include fear for their own safety, a negative self-image, an engulfing relationship with a depressed parent, and new supports from outside the family. Generalizing from these examples, stresses in the family should be investigated at two levels: (a) the ambience level, the contexts of anger, turmoil, unpredictability and so on, that are characteristic of family life; and (b) the specific stressful events and conditions that directly involve supports and relationships and particular qualities of the individual child.

From the evidence on family stress as contributor to offspring problems, it is clear that critical developmental and etiological questions are left for further research. One such issue is whether environmental stress precedes or precipitates offspring problems, or whether problems appear independent of stressful conditions but create stresses that, in turn, help to perpetuate problems. A number of intriguing observations and speculations relevant to these questions have come from neuroscientists: Drawing from work with affectively ill adults, Gold, Goodwin, and Chrousos (1988) pointed out that psychosocial stresses often precede the first affective episodes but that associations of stress and affective episodes become less evident as the disorder progresses. This distinction is very relevant to stress influences on the developing child, but it has yet to be investigated. Post (1992) and Post and Weiss (1998) advanced the hypothesis that early environmental stressors may affect brain development. Post speculated that the impact of stresses may be at the level of gene expression, that if such processes are verified, it would suggest "reconceptualization of the neurobiology of affective disorder as a sequentially evolving process, not a static one. This process highlights the potential roles of genetic dispositions, environmental (experiential) factors and developmental processes and their interaction in illness evolution" (pp. 1005–1007). These speculations reopen questions of the impact of early experiences on later development, now with neurobiological processes providing an additional dimension of inquiry.

Caregiver–Offspring Relationships

Embedded in the broader family environment are the depressed parent's contacts and relationships with the individual child. Within this narrowed focus, it is possible to examine family environment at the level of specific, interacting parental variables and to sight their probable functional significance for the developing child. Research on nondepressed parents, by its mapping of parental functions (e.g., as providers of security and nurturance, teachers, model managers and monitors of child behavior, interpreters, and so on), has provided guidelines for studies of depressed parents. Intuitively, depressive symptoms, in behavioral, cognitive, and vegetative characteristics, have a bearing on virtually all the functions of parenting.

At this point, it is important to digress, to recognize a marked cultural bias in psychological and psychiatric research on parental depression: The depressed parent who is studied, and about whom theories are formulated, is the mother. If parent-to-child transmission of psychopathology involves psychosocial family variables, and their interaction with genetic predispositions, lack of data on depressed fathers significantly limits understanding of transmission processes. Most conclusions about the behavioral–environmental risks of parental depression are based on depressed mothers. There is little evidence on how fathers' depressive symptoms translate into behavior and relationships in their families and with their children. As a result, we do not know much about the undermining influences of depressed fathers on their children and how they compare with the influences of depressed mothers.

Studies of depressed mothers have repeatedly found shortcomings in child management (e.g., Davenport, Zahn-Waxler, Adland, & Mayfield, 1984 [in this study fathers are also included]; Forehand, Lautenschlager, Faust, & Graziano, 1987; Kochanska, Kuczynski, Radke-Yarrow, & Welsh, 1987). Depressed mothers' attempts to regulate their children's behavior are described as minimal, inconsistent, and unrealistic—by inference, characteristics expressive of depressive symptoms of feelings of helplessness and absorption in self, with consequent inattentiveness to signals from the child. Depressed mothers' ineffective efforts to help their children, in the early years, to regulate their behavior are associated with a pathway of disruptive and depressive problems through childhood (Radke-Yarrow et al., 1998). The child's failure in accomplishing reasonable self-regulation in the preschool years has a demonstrated carry-over effect on succeeding developmental stages. Continuation of parents' illness supports an expectation of continuing problems in depressed parents' monitoring and regulating their children (Cox, Puckering, Pound, & Mills, 1987; Goodman & Brumley, 1990).

Depressive symptoms have consequences beyond their interference with the skills and responsibilities of parenting. Depressed mothers' emotional dysregulation and strong dependency needs create exceedingly complex and variable affective relationships with their children. Early disturbance in the attachment relationships is one example. Insecure attachment has high frequency with bipolar mothers (60%; DeMulder & Radke-Yarrow, 1991). Although frequencies of secure and insecure attachments with unipolar depressed mothers and well mothers do not differ significantly, (38% and 33%, respectively) some depressed mothers form excessively close and emotionally enmeshing relationships with their children (e.g., Anthony, 1971; Davenport et al., 1984; Radke-Yarrow et al., 1998). The infant and young child, especially, become the depressed mother's "possession" and comfort. This closeness may have the benefits of security at an early stage of development, but the risks of identifying with the highly symptomatic depressed mother, of assuming her depression-related qualities, and of having difficulties in developing a separateness from the mother eventually outweigh the benefits of this relationship. Such enmeshment in the very early years is associated with offspring disorders in later childhood when the mother's dependency needs and the children's autonomy needs are in strong conflict. The dependency enmeshment struggles are seen as a mechanism through which maternal depression is transmitted to offspring.

These studies also show an opposite to this affective intensity; namely, the negativity of depressed parents. Irritable, angry behavior is a common, pervasive, and chronic parental affect experienced by their children. Negativity is evident throughout childhood, shown even by "enmeshing" mothers, and exhibited by depressed fathers and mothers. In extreme cases, such parental negativity can take to the form of raw rejection of the children. As one depressed mother summed up her feelings, "they're nothing but trouble" and another unhesitantly declared about her 10-year-old daughter, "sometimes I feel I could kill her." This would seem a very probable avenue to negative self-concepts of offspring, such as those reported by Hammen (1991), Forehand et al. (1986), and others.

Depressed parents' pervasive negativity, not surprisingly, makes a difference in offspring development. Its heavy, chronic presence is predictive of disruptive–oppositional behavior disorders through the course of development (Radke-Yarrow et al., 1998). Not all of depressed parents' negativity is directed to the child: It enters into their interactions with other family members and other adults and their expressed outlook on life. We speculate that it is a contributor to the isolation from the outside world that depressed parents often directly or indirectly impose, thereby giving their children less access to normal families, extrafamilial social supports, and peers (Cummings & Davies, 1994; Davenport et al., 1984; Radke-Yarrow et al., 1998). For example, offspring of bipolar mothers hesitated to invite peers into their homes for fear of unpredictable unwelcoming behavior by the mother.

Like family stress, parental negativity is the background of day-to-day functioning in many of the families with a depressive parent. The early research of Cummings, Waxler, and Radke-Yarrow (1986) on the effects on young children of repeated exposure to anger in others is relevant to offspring of depressed parents. These authors studied the responses of toddlers to observed anger in the home. Anger elicited distress responses, which the authors summarized as often appearing inappropriately intense in relation to the exposure. These data remind us of the hypothesis of changing stress thresholds, possibly lowering thresholds and increasing susceptibility with repeated encounters (Gold et al., 1988; Post & Weiss, 1998).

These and other patterned behavioral and cognitive qualities in the syndrome of depression require further study that focuses on the kinds of concrete experiences that they create for children. Such close-range observations would seem to be the best hope for understanding how risk factors operate. This is the step most sorely lacking in research on the risks presented by parental depression. It is the evidence that should provide understanding of the role of the parent in the emergence, recurrence, and remission of offspring disorders.

Interpreting Coacting Variables

Parent's diagnosis, family stress, parent symptoms, and individual child qualities carve the sources of offspring disorders into separate entities. Their separateness is meaningful only as a first step in seeking answers regarding transmission processes. Theory, research, and intervention practices share the task of putting together these multiple contributors to offspring development. For research, the task is to use the wealth of information that now exists on the influences of single facets of parental depression to determine combinations of factors that interactively affect significant aspects of child behavior and development.

This is uncharted territory, and to explore it requires research for which there is no fully articulated model. What combinations of variables should be investigated? How are their coacting influences to be measured? Can principles become evident in the midst of so many contending elements? Combinations are not infinite. Theory and existing lines of research furnish guidelines. To illustrate the value and discovery in the approach, we offer three explorations of coacting variables.

In the first illustration, the combination of family stress and the severity of parent's illness results in additive and synergistic effects. Each risk alone, as reported earlier, is modestly associated with offspring problems. Cummings and Davies (1994) pointed out that parent's symptoms increase in the presence of family stress. In our study, when both of these risks are present, at a specific offspring developmental stage (adolescence), a very high rate (67%) of depressive problems appears. When neither of these risks is present, 26% of the adolescents are depressed. When only one of the risks is present, 43% have depressive problems. When family stress, highly symptomatic parent (mother) behavior, and a problematic child temperament ("difficult" or extremely inhibited) form the combination of risk factors, rates of internalizing problems in the children are again significantly elevated.

In the second illustration, the long-term implications of the child's problematic temperament were investigated, first as a single risk factor, then in combination (Radke-Yarrow et al., 1998). With well mothers and depressed mothers who are not highly symptomatic, the child's temperament characteristics are unrelated to offspring problems. On the other hand, a child with a problematic temperament, manifested in the early years, and paired with an irritable, angry, depressed mother, sets in motion a reciprocal process. Offspring problems begin early and are maintained or accelerate over time. Mother's theme of negativity also may increase over time.

In the third illustration, a supportive variable becomes a risk variable. It is this kind of influence of variables on each other that is brought out through the consideration of multiple variables in joint operation. In normal early parent–child relationships, closeness, warmth, and affection are supportive of a child's security and positive development. We have referred earlier to these variables in the context of severe depression. When exhibited by depressed mothers whose symptomatic themes are anger, anxiety, and dependency, closeness and affection can be excessive as well as mixed and alternating with irritability and anxiety (Radke-Yarrow et al., 1998). This combination of variables changes normally protective factors to risk factors. When closeness becomes inseparability, it lays the foundation for problems at later developmental stages when depressed mother's unchanging dependency needs come into conflict with the child's changing needs for independent identity, autonomy, and relationships beyond the mother.

In these illustrations, transition periods in offspring and parents' development are involved. In transitions, multiple parental risk factors converge with new and changing developmental task demands on offspring and parent. The functional significance of a given parent variable may be especially subject to change in the company of changing combinations of variables in these developmental periods. These examples are limited illustrations based on a single sample and on assessments in psychiatric categories. However, they do show the complexity of the question, What are the processes linking parental depression and offspring problems? They provide some insights into the consistent finding of an increased probability of problems, as well as into the lack of uniformity in the origins of these problems. By identifying and comparing patterns of interacting variables, mechanisms underlying parent–offspring associations become visible. The developmental stage of the offspring is always relevant in the pattern of variables, because it helps to define the domains in normal development that are being threatened by parental depression. Combinations of parent, family, and child factors can act additively to increase risk, but they can also contribute especially to the puzzles of transmission by virtue of the fact that the significance of a given condition depends on the context of other conditions in which it is operating.

IMPLICATIONS FOR CLINICIANS

Research has conclusively documented the multiplicity of risk factors that are brought together by the presence of parental depression. It follows that there are many considerations regarding strategies for prevention and intervention: We comment on the implications of findings in the preceding analyses.

1. Most, if not all, depression-related behavior is relevant to specific parenting roles and responsibilities. In therapy for the depressed parent, the specific implications of the illness for parenting skills and emotional and cognitive support to the child should be the essential focus. Individual parents exhibit varied impairments in parenting at different stages in their children's development. Hence, there is a need to focus on the particular parenting challenges of the individual parent.
2. For many of the children of depressed parents, problems are recurrent over the course of development. This finding suggests the need for early and continued monitoring of these problems. Because many chronically internalizing children perform adaptively (e.g., in school), their problems may go unnoticed unless there is special alertness.
3. Many of the depressed parent's and child's problematic behaviors are embedded in turbulent family relationships. The complex interdependence of problems in a family context signals the importance of intervention along multiple, coordinated lines.
4. The child is an active processor of his or her environment. A parent is a complicated figure for any child to "process." A child of a depressed parent must find meaning in the unpredictable and cyclical behavior of the parent, in the parent's behavior that is outside the "norms," and in the parent's insensitivities and negativity. How children "explain" the parent to themselves is likely to have a bearing on their abilities to cope with the stresses of parental depression. Therefore, cognitive support, as well as emotional support, would seem essential in interventions with children of depressed parents.

SUMMARY

We have not sought average qualities of depressed parents as a group, or their average influences on offspring, or modal offspring outcomes. Such objectives fade with the wealth of evidence on the diverse variables and processes involved. The reality of multiplicity and diversity is especially evident in research that takes a close look at depressed parent behavior and relationships with, and around, the child.

Many of the behavioral impairments of depressed parents involve dimensions common to parents regardless of the specific parents studied. Although the individual variables are not unique to depressed parents, their significance lies in the configurations and excesses that depression brings together, in ways that interfere with the child's normal developmental needs and tasks and enable and foster maladaptations. Many of these qualities operate early, are conditions throughout the growing years, and enter broadly into offspring functions. Some parent variables pose critical risks at particular developmental periods. Offspring at different ages have different capacities to deal with parents' impairments. On both accounts, vulnerabilities and coping abilities, children of depressed parents are changing "targets" in the course of development.

REFERENCES

Anthony, E. J. (1971). Folie à deux: A developmental failure in the process of separation–individuation. In J. B. McDevitt & C. F. Settlage (Eds.), *Separation–individuation: Essays in honor of Margaret Mahler* (pp. 253–273). New York: International Universities Press.

Brown, G. W., & Harris, T. (1978). *Social origins of depression: A study of psychiatric disorder in women.* London: Tavistock.

Cooper, S. F., Leach, C., Storer, D., & Tonge, W. L. (1977). The children of psychiatric patients. *British Journal of Psychiatry, 131,* 514–522.

Cox, A. D., Puckering, C., Pound, A., & Mills, M. (1987). The impact of maternal depression in young people. *Journal of Child Psychology and Psychiatry, 28,* 917–928.

Cummings, E. M., & Davies, P. (1994). Maternal depression and child development. *Journal of Child Psychology and Psychiatry, 35,* 73–112.

Cummings, E. M., Waxler, C., & Yarrow, M. (1986). Young children's responses to expressions of anger and affection by others in the family. *Child Development, 52,* 1274–1282.

Davenport, Y., Zahn-Waxler, C., Adland, M. L., & Mayfield, A. (1984). Early childrearing practices in families with a manic-depressive parent. *American Journal of Psychiatry, 141,* 230–235.

DeMulder, E., & Radke-Yarrow, M. (1991). Attachment with affectively ill and well mothers: Concurrent behavioral correlates. *Development and Psychopathology, 3,* 227–242.

DeMulder, E., Tarullo, L., Klimes-Dougan, B., Free, K., & Radke-Yarrow, M. (1995). Personality disorders of affectively ill mothers: Links to maternal behavior. *Journal of Personality Disorders, 2,* 199–212.

Downey, G., & Coyne, J. C. (1990). Children of depressed parents: An integrative review. *Psychological Bulletin, 108,* 50–76.

Emery, R. E., Weintraub, S., & Neale, J. (1982). Effects of marital discord on the school behavior of children of schizophrenic, affective disordered, and normal parents. *Journal of Abnormal Child Psychology, 16,* 215–225.

Fendrich, M., Warner, V., & Weissman, M. (1990). Family risk factors, parental depression, and psychopathology in offspring. *Developmental Psychology, 26,* 40–50.

Forehand, R., Lautenschlager, G. J., Faust, J., & Graziano, W. G. (1986). Parent perceptions and parent–child interactions in clinic-referred children: A preliminary investigation of the effects of maternal depressive moods. *Behavior Research and Therapy, 24,* 73–75.

Garmezy, N. (1985). Stress-resistant children: The search for protective factors. In J. E. Stevenson (Ed.), *Recent research in developmental psychopathology* (pp. 213–233). Oxford, England: Pergamon Press.

Gelfand, D., & Teti, D. (1990). The effects of maternal depression on children. *Clinical Psychology Review, 19,* 329–353.

Gold, P., Goodwin, F., & Chrousos, G. (1988). Clinical and biochemical manifestations of depression: Relation to the neurobiology of stress. *New England Journal of Medicine, 319,* 348–353.

Goodman, S. (1992). Understanding the effects of depressed mothers on their children. In E. F. Walker, R. H. Dworkin, & B. A. Cornblatt (Eds.), *Progress in experimental personality and psychopathology research Vol. 15* (pp. 47–109). New York: Springer.

Goodman, S., & Brumley, H. (1990). Schizophrenic and depressed mothers: Relational deficits in parenting. *Developmental Psychology, 26,* 31–39.

Hammen, C. (1991). *Depression runs in families: Children of depressed mothers.* New York: Springer-Verlag.

Hammen, C., Gordon, D., Burge, D., Adrian, C., Jaenicke, C., & Hiroto, D. (1987). Children of depressed mothers: Maternal strain and symptom predictors of dysfunction. *Journal of Abnormal Psychology, 96,* 190–198.

Harder, D., Kokes, B., Fisher, L., & Strauss, J. (1980). Child competence and psychiatric risk: IV. Relationships of parent diagnostic classifications and parent psychopathology severity to child functioning. *Journal of Nervous and Mental Disease, 168,* 343–347.

Keller, M. B., Beardslee, W. R., Dorer, D. J., Lavori, P. W., Samuelson, H., & Klerman, G. R. (1986). Impact of severity and chronicity of parental affective illness on adaptive functioning and psychopathology in children. *Archives of General Psychiatry, 43,* 930–937.

Kochanska, G., Kuczynski, L., Radke-Yarrow, M., & Welsh, J. D. (1987). Resolutions of control episodes between well and affectively ill mothers and their young child. *Journal of Abnormal Child Psychology, 15,* 441–456.

Lombroso, P., Pauls, D., & Leckman, J. (1995). Genetic mechanisms in childhood psychiatric disorders. In M. Hertzig & E. Farber (Eds.), *Annual progress in child psychiatry and child development* (pp. 171–205). New York: Brunner/Mazel.

Luthar, S. S., & Zigler, E. (1991). Vulnerability and competence: A review of the research on resilience in childhood. *American Journal of Orthopsychiatry, 61,* 6–22.

Post, R. (1992). Transduction of psychosocial stress into the neurobiology of recurrent affective disorder. *American Journal of Psychiatry, 149,* 999–1010.

Post, R., & Weiss, S. (1998). Sensitization and kindling phenomena in mood, anxiety, and obsessive–compulsive disorders: The role of serotonergic progression. *Biological Psychiatry, 44,* 193–206.

Radke-Yarrow, M., Martinez, P., Mayfield, A., & Ronsaville, D. (1998). *Children of depressed mothers: From early childhood to maturity.* New York: Cambridge University Press.

Rutter, M. (1985). Resilience in the face of adversity: Protective factors and resistance-psychiatric disorder. *British Journal of Psychiatry, 147,* 598–611.

Rutter, M. (1989). Pathways from childhood to adult life. *Journal of Child Psychology and Psychiatry, 30,* 23–51.

Rutter, M., & Garmezy, N. (1983). Developmental psychopathology. In E. M. Hetherington (Ed.), *Manual of child psychology: Vol. 4. Social and personality development* (pp. 775–911). New York: Wiley.

Rutter, M., & Quinton, D. (1984). Parental psychiatric disorder: Effects on children. *Psychological Medicine, 14,* 855–880.

Sroufe, L. A., & Rutter, M. (1984). The domain of developmental psychopathology. *Child Development, 55,* 17–29.

Weissman, M. M., Paykel, E. S., & Klerman, G. L. (1972). The depressed woman as a mother. *Social Psychiatry, 7,* 98–108.

8

CONTEXT OF STRESS IN FAMILIES OF CHILDREN WITH DEPRESSED PARENTS

CONSTANCE HAMMEN

Because depression is a common and impairing disorder, and one that is highly likely to afflict young women during childbearing years (Weissman & Olfson, 1995), there has been an extensive interest in the effects of parental depression from a wide range of perspectives. Increasingly, investigators have moved beyond primarily genetically based models of transmission (common in the early generation of offspring studies) to perspectives that emphasize "context" and call for "multifactorial" approaches (e.g., Cummings & Davies, 1994; Downey & Coyne, 1990; Goodman & Gotlib, 1999; Hammen, 1991a). Such terms imply that the environment in which children of depressed parents are raised may greatly affect their outcomes and experiences beyond, or in addition to, the effects of depression itself.

The environment is, indeed, a vital factor in the equation linking parental depression with child psychopathology and maladjustment. This chapter develops the perspective that children of depressed parents inherit not only biological predispositions to mood disorders but also "inherit" a family milieu that may be highly challenging and stressful. The context of stress for children of depressed parents includes not only the expression of parental symptoms, but also the ongoing or chronic stressful conditions that often accompany parental disorder such as financial, occupational, and marital difficulties. The depressed parent and child also experience elevated rates of episodic stressful life events. Furthermore, there is some evidence that depressed individuals—both adults and children—may contribute to the occurrence of episodic stressors, especially in the interpersonal realm. An even more challenging question is *how* stressful experiences affect the risk to children of depressed parents.

I begin with a review of the limited research on stressful experiences as a contributor to children's risk for disorder in families of depressed parents.

Following the review of data on stress exposure, I then consider possible processes by which such experiences may influence the development of disorders and psychosocial maladjustment. Many conceptual and empirical gaps in this topic area are noted and potential implications for prevention and treatment are discussed.

STRESS CONTEXT IN FAMILIES OF DEPRESSED PARENTS

Stress may be defined as an occurrence or an ongoing situation that has the potential to affect the individual's life in negative ways, and typically some activity or behavior on the part of the person is required to avoid, minimize, or counteract the negative consequences. Although an extended discussion of models of stress is beyond the scope of this chapter, most conceptualizations assume that the individual's reaction to stressors is mediated by the "meaning" of the stressors to the person's life, as defined by the context in which they occur (Brown & Harris, 1978) or by cognitive appraisal of the implications of such stressors to the self (e.g., Beck, 1967) and the resources available to cope with them (e.g., Lazarus & Folkman, 1984). Some of these ideas are revisited later in a discussion of the processes by which stress affects children of depressed parents.

Children of a depressed parent may be exposed to four different elements of the stress context. These include parental depression; ongoing or chronic stressful conditions that typically accompany depressive disorders (or indeed, all disorders) such as economic, relationship, and work problems; episodic life events of the parent that may affect the child; and the child's own episodic stressful life events. To the extent that the child may be impaired by psychological disorders, there is likely to be a fifth element, the child's own chronic stressful social, behavioral, and academic strains.

The following discussion explores the degree to which offspring studies have considered the role of stress in the lives of children of depressed parents.

Parental Depression as a Stressor

Aside from the ways in which depressive symptoms affect the quality of parenting—an issue addressed in other chapters—relatively little is known about children's[1] perceptions of their parents' symptoms. It is plausible to assume, however, that many of the symptoms displayed by a depressed parent might be distressing if witnessed by youngsters. Infants appear to react with distress to an unresponsive mother (e.g., Cohn, Matias, Tronick, Connell, & Lyons-Ruth, 1986; Field, 1984). Actual research data have rarely addressed the issue of children's responses to parental symptoms. It might be speculated, however, that young children might be afraid when their mother cries easily and upset by a parent who has too little energy or interest to play. Children might react to displays of symptoms, perhaps especially to those that mark changes in the parent's usual behavior, as problems to be solved and explained—perhaps even by making faulty causal attributions that blame themselves. Older children might be especially alarmed by a parent's expression of futility or worthlessness, portending hopelessness or even suicidality. Studies are needed that evaluate the direct impact of parents' symptoms of depression on children.

Children of all ages are likely to assume some of the burden of caretaking if the parent evidences helplessness, low energy, and loss of motivation. Some studies have shown that children's recognition of parents' severe depression may elicit caring behaviors and helpful caretaking on their part (e.g., Beardslee & Podorefsky, 1988; Radke-Yarrow, Zahn-Waxler, Richardson, & Susman, 1994). However, for many youngsters, the burden of dealing with the ill parent's symptoms may prove to be quite stressful, as it commonly is for adult family members (e.g., Coyne et al., 1987).

Whereas there have been numerous studies of the effects of depression on parents' cognitions and behaviors toward their children (e.g., reviewed in Cummings & Davies, 1994), the great majority of offspring studies have not characterized parental depression from the perspective of the children. It is acknowledged that the heterogeneous manifestations of the depression syndrome may have different effects on children, possibly varying with the developmental level of the child. However, almost no information exists on children's perceptions, with the exception of parental irritability.

Irritability, although not specific to depression or universally present in depression syndromes nor, may be one symptom with particularly adverse consequences. In the UCLA Family Stress Project, an offspring study comparing children of unipolar, bipolar, medically ill, and well women (Hammen, 1991a), children were asked to describe what their mothers were like when having problems. Irritability—far more frequently than other symptoms—was identified by children as the sign that something was different or wrong. In one of the few studies of the various expressions of depressed mothers' symptoms in interactions with their children, Radke-Yarrow (1998) reported clinicians' overall ratings of observations of mothers with their children at different follow-up

---

[1]Unless otherwise specified, the term *children* refers to both children and adolescents.

periods. She found that irritability was more frequently rated in mothers of older children compared with mothers of infants and toddlers; 43% of unipolar mothers were characterized as irritable overall. "Unavailability" or insensitivity to the child was rated in about one-third of the depressed mothers. Negativity and irritability tended to be stable over time, but also many of the women who had been initially "enmeshed" with their infants and toddlers became more irritable over time (Radke-Yarrow, 1998). Displays of irritability and anger by parents are usually upsetting and frightening to youngsters and often elicit feelings of anger from the children (e.g., reviewed in Cummings & Davies, 1994). It would be useful to have further studies of children's recognition of and reactions to specific symptoms or depressive patterns. It would be especially important to determine the extent to which certain behaviors or emotional displays are distressing to children.

Two studies specifically tested the effects of parental distress (symptoms of depression and emotional upset) as a stressor affecting family members such that they themselves react with symptoms. Ge, Conger, Lorenz, Shanahan, and Elder (1995) studied the mutual influences of emotional distress on mothers, fathers, and their adolescent children over three waves of follow-up. Their structural equation modeling analyses demonstrated significant reciprocal influences between parent and child symptoms over time even when prior symptoms were controlled. The results also indicated gender- and age-specific patterns, such that mother–son associations were strongest in early adolescence, whereas father–daughter associations were especially strong in middle adolescence. The authors pointed out that although the data clearly indicate reciprocal influences of emotional status, the results do not clarify whether the effects might also be accounted for by changes in interaction behavior between children and parents. Although there may be direct effects of parent–child interactions in families, such patterns do not exclude the operation of other mechanisms.

Hammen, Burge, and Adrian (1991) also tested the hypothesis that episodes of depression in mothers and children may serve as stressors influencing the timing of the other's depressive reactions. By carefully dating changes in mothers' and children's depressive episodes over a 2-year follow-up period, it was possible to determine whether there was temporal association between the episodes. Of 25 child diagnoses of depression during a defined period, only 6 were not temporally associated with maternal diagnoses. Overall, there was a statistically significant temporal association, and it was most pronounced in the unipolar depression group. Sometimes the mother's episode followed that of the child, and in other cases the reverse occurred (in one case the episodes were nearly simultaneous). The temporal associations are strongly suggestive of the impact of a family member's depression as a stressor influencing symptoms in other family members.

Taken together, these two studies are consistent with the thesis that depressive symptoms and syndromes are stressors eliciting depression in a significant other. However, much work remains to be done to evaluate the child's reaction to parental depression and to assess the impact of different symptom profiles on children of different ages.

Chronic Stress Associated With Parental Depression

Impaired functioning is by definition a necessary ingredient of psychiatric diagnosis. This truism obscures a profoundly important issue: Impaired functioning contributes to stressful circumstances that may in turn challenge the already symptomatic person's coping capacities and thereby perpetuate the disorder. This may be especially true for depressive disorders, because in our culture depression is rarely considered sufficient reason for people not carrying out their typical responsibilities. Additionally, preexisting dysfunctional characteristics often contribute both to developing depression and to adverse circumstances that may precipitate episode recurrences. Hence, for many people with recurrent depressive disorders, the depression and the preexisting vulnerabilities create a variety of chronic strains that provide a stressful family context in which the child is embedded. Thus, parents not only "have" depressive disorders, but they also likely experience marital difficulties, parenting problems, difficulties in their relationships with friends and extended family, occupational impairment and commensurate financial stresses, and often chronic health problems. All of these may directly or indirectly provide a stressful environment for their children.

In the following sections, several chronic stressors or adversities are discussed. However, family functioning, one of the most studied stressful context factors, is not addressed, because other chapters in this volume focus on parenting problems and their effects on children.

Chronic Stressors and Adverse Circumstances

The construct of stressful events and conditions has not been addressed directly by many offspring studies. However, several researchers have acknowledged the likely importance of such contextual factors. For example, many offspring researchers have at least implicitly acknowledged the potential role of social adversity by selecting depressed and control families from fairly similar social strata (e.g., Billings & Moos, 1985; Hammen, 1991a). Some have described socioeconomic status, which may be viewed in large part as a marker of exposure to chronic stressors in financial and occupational domains, demonstrating either no differences between proband groups or statistically controlling for it (e.g., Fendrich, Warner, & Weissman, 1990; Warner, Mufson, & Weissman, 1995).

In a further design consideration, several researchers have acknowledged at least implicitly that parental depressive disorders may represent a nonspecific stressful condition that affects children. To determine whether there is something additional or unique about exposure to parental depression beyond families dealing with significant stressful conditions, such studies have compared groups of depressed parents with physical illness control groups. For instance, in four studies unipolar depressed groups were compared with medically ill groups (Hammen, Burge, Burney, & Adrian, 1990; Hirsch, Moos, & Reischl, 1985; Klein, Clark, Dansky, & Margolis, 1988; Lee & Gotlib, 1989). All but Hirsch et al. found higher rates of diagnoses or maladjustment in offspring of depressed compared with medically ill parents.

Beyond design features and methodological controls for possible context factors, several investigations have explored the association between indicators of social adversity and children's outcomes in high-risk families. For instance, Billings and Moos (1985) assessed a variety of factors they called *stressors* consisting of negative events, medical conditions and physical symptoms, work stress, and quality of the physical home environment. Families with depressed parents scored higher than controls on most of the factors even when the depression had remitted. Moreover, at the 1-year follow-up, children's functioning was significantly correlated with the majority of such stressful conditions. Fergusson, Horwood, and Lynskey (1995) constructed an index of family social position based on a weighted sum of parental education levels, socioeconomic status, maternal age, ethnicity, and single- or two-parent family. The index was one of several factors that appeared to account for the association between mother and daughter depressive symptoms. Seifer et al. (1996) constructed a multiple-risk index as a composite of many contextual measures, including illness variables, life events, father absence, family size, minority status, mother education, family occupation, and home environment and family functioning variables. The multiple-risk index proved to be a stronger predictor of children's social competence and attachment outcomes than were measures of parent disorder—although the specific contributions of the various elements of the index were not evaluated. Boyle and Pickles (1997) constructed an index of economic disadvantage, counting the presence of each of the following elements: single-parent household, income below the poverty line, living in government-subsidized housing, and public assistance benefits. They found that controlling for economic disadvantage weakened but did not eliminate the association between maternal depression and children's emotional disorder in a community sample of 8–12-year-olds and their mothers.

Specific measures of chronic stress in major roles were used in the UCLA Family Stress Project (Hammen, 1991a). Interview-based ratings of ongoing conditions in quality of intimate relationships, work, finances, relationships with extended family, and health were compared across maternal groups. Table 8.1 presents mean chronic stress scores by group. The means indicate that women with recurrent unipolar depression were especially likely to have higher levels of ongoing stress than women in the other groups, with significant differences especially in occupational, financial, intimate relationship, and parent–child relationship stress. Hammen, Gordon, et al. (1987) com-

TABLE 8.1

Chronic Stress Exposure Across Role Domains by Group in the UCLA
Family Stress Project

| | Maternal Group | | | |
Variable	Unipolar	Bipolar	Medical	Normal
Marital/intimate	3.3	3.0	2.5	2.4
Job	3.3	2.9	2.5	2.3
Finances	3.1	2.8	2.5	2.4
Extended family	2.6	2.3	2.1	2.2
Parent–child	3.5	2.9	2.7	2.4
Health–self	2.4	2.4	3.1	2.0
Health–family	2.6	2.1	2.3	2.3

Note. Higher scores represent greater stress. From *Depression Runs in Families: The Social Context of Risk and Resilience in Children of Depressed Mothers,* by C. Hammen, 1991, New York: Springer-Verlag. Copyright 1991 by Springer-Verlag. Adapted with permission.

pared children's diagnostic ratings and psychosocial outcomes by group, controlling for maternal differences in chronic stress, and determined that children of unipolar women continued to display worse functioning on most outcomes even after controlling for differences in chronic stress exposure. Hammen, Adrian, et al. (1987) attempted to "dismantle" maternal diagnosis into three related components: an index of chronic stress, current depressive symptoms, and an index of severity and chronicity of depressive disorders and compared the relative contributions of these factors to children's outcomes 6 months after entry into the study. We found that chronic stress was a significant and unique predictor of many children's outcomes, beyond the effects related to current depression and past history of depression.

Recently, colleague Patricia Brennan and I attempted to replicate the findings of increased chronic stress in women with histories of depression, with a nonclinical community sample. Families from a sociodemographically homogeneous sample born during a 2-year period in a Brisbane, Australia hospital were recruited for a 15-year follow-up, with selection based on maternal self-reported depression at various earlier follow-ups. Using scores on the Structured Clinical Interview for *DSM IV* (SCID; First, Spitzer, Gibbon, & Williams, 1995) interviews to confirm maternal diagnostic status, we compared women with histories of major depressive episodes or dysthymic disorder to women who had never been diagnosed with depression on chronic stress variables. As shown in the upper section of Table 8.2, the depressed women had significantly greater chronic stress (composite score) compared with the never-depressed women. Although we have not yet analyzed the predictors of outcomes in the 15-year-old offspring, these data, along with the few studies reviewed, strongly suggest that clinical and community samples of children of depressed parents— experience elevated rates of stressful conditions.

TABLE 8.2
Stress Exposure in Children of Depressed and Nondepressed Mothers in
the Queensland, Australia, Study

Variable	Mothers with a history of depression ($n = 358$)		Mothers with no depression history ($n = 458$)		$t(814)$	p
	M	SD	M	SD		
Exposure to stress						
Mother chronic stress[a]	15.74	2.3	14.04	2.1	11.11	< .0001*
Mother total episodic stress	8.94	5.2	6.97	4.4	5.87	< .0001
Child chronic stress[b]	9.53	2.0	9.22	1.7	2.40[c]	< .017
Child total episodic stress	6.51	4.2	5.61	3.8	3.22	< .001
Generation of stress						
Mother number of interpersonal events	1.03	1.2	.66	.92	4.83	< .0001
Mother number of conflict events	.46	.79	.21	.47	5.59	< .0001
Child number of interpersonal events	1.64	1.6	1.46	1.4	1.65	< .05[†]
Child number of conflict events	.39	.77	.30	.55	2.04	< .04

[a]Maternal chronic stress is a composite of ratings of marital, work, financial, relations with own parents and siblings, and physical health. It excludes relations with the target child.
[b]Child chronic stress is a composite of close friend, social relations, dating relations, academic performance, and school behavior. Relationship with the mother is excluded.
[c]For child chronic stress, $t(813)$ was used.
* = two–tailed; [†] = one–tailed.

Marital Difficulties

A chronic stressor that has received considerable attention in the literature on offspring risk is parental marital status and marital quality. The general literature on depression indicates that divorce and marital conflict are common among depressed individuals (e.g., reviewed in Barnett & Gotlib, 1988; Gotlib & Beach, 1995). Rutter and Quinton (1984) showed that marital hostility mediates the association between parental psychopathology and children's maladjustment. In their review of studies of children of depressed parents, Downey and Coyne (1990) raised the question of whether the effects on children (especially externalizing difficulties) attributed to parental depression might actually be due to parental discord.

Several researchers have examined the contribution of marital discord to offspring outcome in high-risk families. Keller et al. (1986) found that marital discord was associated with greater impairment and disorder in children of depressed parents. Goodman, Brogan, Lynch, and Fielding (1993) tested a multiple risk factor model in 5–10-year-old children of depressed mothers. They found that parents' marital status and fathers' psychiatric condition explained most of the variance in measures of children's social and emotional competence. When the parents were divorced and when the father had a history of psychiatric diagnosis, maternal depression added little or no variance to the prediction of children's competence. Fendrich et al. (1990) examined diagnoses in 220 offspring with one or two depressed parents as a function of parental depression and other family risk factors. For all children, divorce was especially associated with conduct disorder, and poor marital adjustment was associated with presence of any disorder. Comparisons of the relative contribution of parental depression and family risk factors suggested that parental depression was a more important predictor of children's diagnoses. However, the investigators noted that their sample may not have been large enough to adequately test statistical interaction effects, given that few families with parental depression had low levels of risk factors such as marital discord. Fergusson et al. (1995) studied associations between maternal depression and adolescent depressive symptoms in a large birth cohort. They specifically examined the question of whether the apparent association between maternal and child depression (which was stronger for girls than for boys) would remain after taking into account adverse family factors, including marital conflict. They found that parental conflict—and other social context factors—accounted for most of the prediction of youth depression symptoms; maternal depression was only weakly associated with youth depression.

In view of these suggestive findings, it is surprising that many offspring researchers have not examined marital status or marital functioning as a predictor of children's outcomes. More work is certainly needed to explore not only whether effects of parental depression on children are largely mediated by marital conflict, but also the processes by which such effects occur. It is also important to evaluate the effects of age and gender of the children and whether children's particular symptoms are specific to marital discord (e.g., externalizing disorders).

Parental "Nonrandom Mating"

It has become increasingly apparent that depressed women have high rates of marriage to men with psychiatric disorders. Merikangas (1984) originally noted the existence of "assortative" mating, reflecting the high rates of couples concordant for depressive disorders (see also Merikangas, Weissman, Prusoff, & John, 1988). Relatively few studies have examined diagnosis patterns in parents with depression. However, these studies have noted increased rates of various disorders in husbands of depressed women, including substance abuse and antisocial personality disorder. For example, Goodman et al. (1993) determined from direct or mother-reported diagnoses that 55% of the mothers with unipolar major depression had husbands with a lifetime psychiatric diagnosis. Hammen (1991a) found that 64% of a treatment sample of women with recurrent unipolar disorder had been married to men with diagnosable disorders. In a clinic-referred sample of depressed children, Hammen, Rudolph, Weisz, Rao, and Burge (1999) reported a probability of

.74 that if the mother had a history of major depression, the father would also have a diagnosable disorder. Finally, in a community sample of Australian women with histories of depression, Hammen and Brennan (2000) conducted direct diagnostic interviews of both parents and found that 47% of women with histories of depression were married to men with diagnosable conditions (compared to 37% for nondepressed women). The rates of assortative mating were even higher based on Family History Research Diagnostic Criteria (Andreasen, Endicott, Spitzer, & Winokur, 1977) interviews of mothers' reports of their former husbands.

The existing studies of dual-parent diagnoses have clearly indicated increased risk of disorder for children (e.g., Warner et al., 1995; Weissman et al., 1984). Few studies have specifically examined combinations of father absence or presence and whether both parents had a diagnosis. It is likely that the presence of father disorder is directly stressful to the child if the father lives in the home, but the effects might vary depending on how much support he has provided for the child. The father's illness might also add stress if the combination of disorders in both parents portends marital discord or divorce. Conrad and Hammen (1993) found that for children with depressed mothers, having a healthy father present in the home was a protective factor, but that all other combinations of father presence with father illness status contributed to children's risk.

Overall, studies reviewed in this section suggest that ongoing strains are common in the lives of parents with recurrent unipolar depression. Although few studies have examined their impact directly, other investigations have acknowledged the role of such adversities through research designs and methodological and statistical controls for such factors. Nevertheless, there is little consistency in how such adversities are measured, and it is unclear whether such effects account for much of the apparent impact of parental depression on youngsters. Further studies of nonrandom mating should be undertaken to help shed more light on further sources of stressful conditions in the family. The possible mechanisms of chronic stress are addressed in later sections.

Parent Episodic Stressors

Research on children of depressed parents has only infrequently considered the possible impact of episodic, and usually more transitory, stressful life events on children's outcomes. This issue becomes significant to the extent that depressed parents may be more likely than nondepressed parents to experience stressors. For example, Hammen (1991b) examined stressful life events in a 1-year period for unipolar depressed women compared with bipolar, medically ill, and well women in the UCLA offspring study. Unipolar depressed women tended to have the highest total stress of all groups, but particularly for non-"fateful" events—events that were at least partially dependent on their own behaviors or characteristics. Such "dependent" events include the large content category of interpersonal events (e.g., ending a relationship) and its subcategory of conflict events (e.g., argument with mother-in-law). These types of events were especially likely to be high among women with unipolar depression, even though most of the events had not occurred while the women were actually in a depressed state. Thus, it appeared that there was something about the women's lives and behaviors—not solely the depressed mood—that contributed to the highly stressful lives to which they, and their children, were exposed.

The lower half of Table 8.2 presents similar data from the previously described Hammen and Brennan community sample of women with and without histories of major depressive disorder or dysthymic disorder. As Table 8.2 indicates, depressed women showed significantly more total episodic stress in the previous year than did nondepressed women. As in the Hammen (1991b) study, the depressed women showed significantly more frequent interpersonal life events, and more of those with a conflict theme. These two studies (also see Daley et al., 1998) demonstrate the phenomenon we have termed *stress generation* in which individuals with depression histories have high rates of stressful life events to which they have contributed—a pattern that appears to reflect enduring features of the person's life and characteristics rather than effects related specifically to depressed mood. Such tendencies have been shown to increase the likelihood of further depression in those already at risk (e.g., Daley et al., 1997; Davila, Hammen, Burge, Paley, & Daley, 1995).

Although Hammen (1991b) did not evaluate the contribution of mothers' stressful life events to children's outcomes, a study of depression in adolescent girls by Goodyer, Cooper, Vize, and Ashby (1993) did address this association. Similar to Hammen and colleagues, they found that mothers with histories of depression, or any psychopathology (chiefly anxiety disorders), reported higher rates of stressful events than mothers with no diagnoses. Moreover, both maternal depression and stressful life events in the previous year significantly predicted the presence of major depression in the daughters.

In the Christchurch, New Zealand study of adolescent outcomes, Fergusson et al. (1995) found that family stressful life events helped to account for the association between maternal depressive symptoms and daughters' subsequent depressive symptoms. Similarly, Billings and Moos's (1985) 1-year follow-up of children of depressed parents found that children's emotional and health problem scores were modestly but significantly correlated with parents' negative life events in the previous year. Seifer et al. (1996) included parents' stressful events in their Multiple Risk Index, and the latter was more associated with young children's social competence and attachment status than was maternal psychopathology.

Although few in number, the offspring studies that included measures of parent stressful life events found that the stressors contributed to, or helped to mediate, the impact of maternal depression on children's outcomes. Moreover, the results are consistent with research by McGuffin, Katz, and Bebbington (1988) on genetic factors in depression suggesting that the tendency to experience stressful life events itself runs in families. This tendency contributes to a stressful environment that exposes the members to increased risk of depressive reactions in response to personally meaningful negative life events. Although data suggest that parental depression occurs in the context of stressful life events, as we note below, little information exists about the mechanisms of such risk factors for children. Furthermore, there is great need to examine developmental issues in stress exposure and stress processes. For example, we know little about whether parents' stressors directly affect children at different ages or have their effects indirectly through their influence on parent–child interactions. These and related issues are explored further in later sections.

Children's Chronic and Episodic Stress

Almost no research on offspring of depressed parents has specifically evaluated children's own stressful circumstances and life events. In addition to exposure to a stressful environment stemming from the parents' lives and environment, children may be at risk for elevated rates of their own life events. To evaluate this possibility, researchers with the UCLA offspring project developed interview procedures for assessing chronic and episodic life events for children, modeled on those we had developed for adults. Both mothers and their children were interviewed, and the stress data were compiled from both sources. As reported by Adrian and Hammen (1993), children of unipolar mothers had significantly higher levels of chronic and episodic stress over a 3-year period than all other groups. Interestingly, the children—similar to unipolar depressed mothers—had significantly higher levels of stressors that were at least partly dependent on their behaviors or characteristics. Children of unipolar depressed mothers had significantly more peer conflict events than did the children of well or medically ill mothers (but did not differ in this respect from children of bipolar mothers).

Table 8.2 presents more recent data from the 15-year-old Australian community sample of children of depressed and nondepressed women. The offspring of depressed women not only were exposed to higher levels of their mothers' chronic and episodic stress, but also experienced significantly higher levels of their own chronic and episodic stress. Furthermore, like their depressed mothers, offspring in the high-risk group had significantly more frequent interpersonal and conflict events in the past year than did offspring of nondepressed women, thus replicating the "stress generation" pattern previously described for depressed women (e.g., Hammen, 1991b) and their offspring (Adrian & Hammen, 1993). The sections below emphasize the significance of possible developmental and gender issues in stress exposure and stress generation.

MECHANISMS LINKING PARENTAL DEPRESSION, STRESS, AND CHILDREN'S OUTCOMES

Although the research on the context of stress in families of a depressed parent is not large, it does paint a consistent picture: Children in such families are exposed to higher levels of chronic and episodic stress than are children in families with nondepressed parents. There is sufficient uniformity in the findings to proceed to the next level of analysis, namely, examination of the mechanisms by which stress affects the association between parental depression and children's outcomes. Unfortunately, the research on the topic is quite sparse, and the following sections are largely speculative, offering several scenarios that may explain possible processes in the stress–outcome association in high-risk families.

Stress as a Precipitant of Children's Symptoms

Stress is commonly viewed as a moderator of outcomes in classic diathesis–stress models. In this view, children experience increased levels of depression and other symptoms as a reaction to stress. Stress is an especially important moderator in this perspective, because children of depressed parents are exposed to comparatively high levels of chronic and episodic stress. The diathesis would consist of any of a number of possibilities—genetic, neurobiological, cognitive, attachment insecurity, or other risk factors, such that high levels of stress precipitate symptoms in the presence of some vulnerability. At high levels of stress, possibly even relatively mild vulnerabilities would be sufficient to trigger depression. Correspondingly, variations in the outcomes experienced by children of depressed parents might be accounted for, in part, by different levels of exposure to stressors; some children of depressed parents may have underlying diatheses for depressive reactions but might not experience high levels of symptoms if their exposure to stress is limited.

A growing empirical foundation supports the link between chronic and episodic stress and depressive episodes and symptoms in children and adolescents (e.g., reviewed in Compas, Grant, & Ey, 1994). In offspring studies, however, such tests have been infrequent (e.g., Fergusson et al., 1995; Goodyer et al., 1993). In two related offspring studies, children's own stressors moderated the association between dysfunctional cognitions and depressive outcomes. In the longitudinal UCLA high-risk study, Hammen (1988) found that children and adolescents who had negative cognitions about themselves were more likely to develop depressive reactions following higher levels of stressful life events. Hammen and Goodman-Brown (1990) found that the youngsters in the UCLA high-risk study who were especially sociotropic (highly valuing social relationships) were especially likely to develop depression following stressors with interpersonal content. They appeared to have a specific vulnerability, such that matching the content of stressors with the domain to which they attributed particular significance produced depression. However, the elevation of nonmatching events (outside the domain of vulnerability) did not precipitate depression.

In addition to the need for further research specifically evaluating the role of stress as a moderator between maternal depression and children's depressive symptoms, other issues must be addressed. One question is whether stress provokes other symptoms besides depression. Comparatively more data have been collected regarding the stress–depression relationship than other disorders, but pathways to specific disorders should be investigated. Another question is the role of chronic stress in relation to depressive symptoms: Is there a functional relationship between chronic stress and depressive symptoms, and does chronic stress modify the processes linking episodic life events and depression?

Another critically important issue is whether there are developmental differences, such that stressors affect younger and older children in different ways, and does the content of stressors that provoke symptoms differ for children of different ages? A related issue is possible developmental differences in children's reactions to their own stressors and those affecting other members of the family. For instance, it may be that younger children are less directly affected by the ill parent's own stressors (and more affected if at all by the parent's own reactions to their stressors). In contrast, older children and adolescents may be more directly affected by others' stressors as well as their own because of their greater capacity for empathy and greater expectations that they will play a role in helping the parent to deal with the stressor or its consequences. Children of all ages and both genders are hypothesized to react with depressive symptoms to events that are construed as losses to their sense of worth and competence, but the specific sources of self-views and the capacity to interpret events to be personally meaningful are likely to vary developmentally and by gender. Moreover, important developmental differences may exist in the relative roles of parental depression and familial stress on children's outcomes.

Stress Affects the Parent–Child Relationship

A further possible mechanism of the stress–outcome relationship in children of depressed parents may be more indirect, with parental behavior mediating the association between family stress and children's outcomes. Although this model would not account for the effects of the child's own stressful circumstances and events on symptoms and functional outcomes, it may nonetheless characterize the consequences of maternal stress on the child.

The model would hold that in addition to the effects of the mother's symptoms on her parenting behaviors as discussed elsewhere in this volume, stressful conditions and events might also affect her interactions with the child. Stressors—both chronic and episodic—might distract the mother so that she is inattentive or inconsistent with the child or perhaps less available altogether. Stress might make a mother tense, worried, and potentially irritable and impatient, so that interactions with children might be marked by criticism and irritation. Thus, both availability and quality of parenting might be affected, potentially predicting symptoms in the child—with the symptoms possibly reflecting the duration of the stressor and the characteristics of the parent–child interactions.

Burge and Hammen (1991) attempted to tease apart the differential effects of parenting related to maternal depressive symptoms and maternal chronic stress in the UCLA high-risk study. Two summary dimensions of maternal interaction style, positivity (positive and confirmatory remarks minus negative and disconfirmatory comments toward the child) and task productivity (task focused and problem-solving comments minus off-task remarks), were derived from observations of brief mother–child interactions during which the two discussed a topic on which they commonly disagreed (such as chores or allowance). Maternal depression level (as measured by the Beck Depression Inventory [BDI] score; Beck et al., 1961) and a maternal chronic stress composite score (excluding mother–child relationship quality) were each entered last while controlling for the other variables in a series of hierarchical multiple regression analyses to predict parenting interactions. Positivity of the quality of maternal communication was significantly predicted by the combination of depression and chronic stress ($R = .46$). However, whereas chronic stress was a significant incremental predictor above and beyond depression, the BDI score did not make an independent contribution beyond that of chronic stress. With respect to task productivity, however, the reverse was true: Depression level was the major incremental predictor, but chronic stress did not add significantly beyond the effect of BDI score. Thus, it appeared that ongoing stressful conditions diminished the positive quality of the interactions, whereas depression was a much stronger determinant than stress on inability to stay focused on the task with the child. It should be noted that these analyses applied to all women in the study. Bipolar, medically ill, and well women as well as those with unipolar depression could also have high levels of stress and temporary elevations in depressed mood that affected their interactions with their children.

Harnish, Dodge, and Valente (1995) attempted to test a mediating role of maternal interaction quality on first graders' externalizing behaviors (teacher rated) as a function of maternal depressive symptoms. They also included socioeconomic status (SES) in their model; although it is not a direct measure of chronic stress, low SES is nonetheless a marker of stressful economic conditions. Results of structural equation modeling indicated that interaction quality mediated the association between SES and child externalizing problems, suggesting that stressful economic conditions may erode the quality of mother–child interaction, which in turn, affects children's symptoms. Moreover, the effects of maternal depressive symptoms on children's externalizing problems were partially mediated by mother–child interaction quality even after controlling for socioeconomic status. Taken together, the results are generally consistent with the idea that maternal depression and stressful conditions may both affect maternal quality of interaction with the child, which in turn predicts child symptoms (see also Hammen, Burge, & Stansbury, 1990).

More research on the impact of stress on the quality of parental behavior among depressed parents clearly is needed. Examination of the role of specific episodic stressors is also desirable, although it is likely that chronic, ongoing stressful conditions would result in the most enduring parent–child interaction difficulties with long-term consequences for children.

Furthermore, parental stress is likely to disrupt availability and consistency of parenting. One study that addressed the issue indirectly evaluated the impact of children's stressors on depression as a function of maternal symptoms during a 1-year follow-up of the UCLA high-risk families (Hammen et al., 1991). Analyses indicated a significant interaction of maternal symptoms and child life event stress. Specifically, regardless of high or low levels of stressors, children whose mothers were not significantly symptomatic during the year did not become depressed. In contrast, children with high levels of stress who also had highly symptomatic mothers tended to develop depressive reactions. The results were interpreted as consistent with the important role that mothers play to help buffer the ill effects of their children's stressors. When the mothers suffered from symptoms, they may not have been emotionally or even physically available to help their children cope with their own stressors. Thus, these children were at greater risk for the development of depressive symptoms. This interpretation is speculative, however, and research is needed to directly evaluate maternal assistance in helping children in high-risk families to cope with stressful events.

Modeling Poor Cognitive and Behavioral Coping With Stress

Exposure to stress in families with depressed parents may also affect the children through dysfunctional coping skills. One version of the stress model might propose that children are exposed to extraordinarily high levels of stress so that normal coping skills are insufficient. An alternative view is that exposure to depressed parents yields inadequate coping skills in children, whereas children of well parents with normal skills would be able to adapt or cope more effectively in the face of stress. Parental depression may expose and model for the child poor coping responses to life demands. While depressed, the parent may exhibit poor emotion regulation, depressotypic cognitive style, and faulty interpersonal problem-solving skills. Moreover, the parent may suffer from enduring personal characteristics that create vulnerability to depression (such as dysfunctional cognitions and impaired problem solving). Thus, even when not in a depressive episode, the parent may continue to model dysfunctional skills.

It might be further speculated that children who experience psychological distress and maladjustment early in life have further impediments to learning useful and constructive coping skills. Those children whose peer interactions and school performance are affected may not accomplish important developmental tasks necessary for effective problem solving and interpersonal negotiation. A vicious cycle ensues, which a depressed and stressed parent may be especially ill equipped to help the child overcome.

Although it would be fruitful to investigate children's skills in coping with stress in high-risk families, little research with this focus exists. Indirect evidence from offspring cognition and emotion regulation is reviewed elsewhere in this volume (see Ashman & Dawson, chapter 3, this volume; and Garber & Martin, chapter 6, this volume). However, one example of suggestive research in this topic is a study by Garber, Braafladt, and Zeman (1991), who found that children of depressed mothers (and the mothers themselves) generated fewer and poorer quality coping responses compared to nondepressed mothers and their children. There is also a relatively small body of research on protective and resilience factors in high-risk children that seems consistent with the importance of good coping skills and problem-solving capabilities. For instance, Beardslee, Schultz, and Selman (1987) found that good interpersonal negotiation skills predicted resilience in children of depressed parents. Other investigators have noted the importance of higher intelligence in predicting better outcomes for high-risk children (e.g., Radke-Yarrow & Sherman, 1990).

A fuller discussion of possible individual skills and competencies that moderate the impact of parental depression, or mediate the challenges of dysfunctional parenting, is beyond the scope of this chapter. However, research that specifically addresses competencies for interpreting, preventing, or dealing with stressful life events of various kinds would be a fruitful target in understanding children's outcomes in high-risk families exposed to high stress levels.

Stress Sensitization

Parental depression and stress may also be linked to children's outcomes through neurobiological events that occur when children are exposed to severe stress and adversity. It is possible that early exposure, in particular, alters the brain of the developing child in ways that directly increase the chances of maladjustment generally or depression specifically. Alternatively, the neurobiological consequences of adversity may sensitize the child to later stressors, so that psychological disorders are more likely to occur in the presence of relatively mild stress. Some evidence of the consequences of early stress exposure is beginning to emerge from studies of human infants (e.g., Gunnar, 1998; Heim, Ehlert, Hanker, & Hellhammer, 1998). These topics are covered elsewhere in this volume and therefore are not discussed further here.

Interpersonal Processes and Stress

The relatively high levels of chronic and episodic stress in depressed parents and their children, as well as particular patterns of the interpersonal content of such adversities, suggest yet another process of intergenerational transmission. It may be that children acquire from their parents and their family milieu a set of dysfunctional interpersonal skills and cognitions. Subsequently, the interpersonal difficulties contribute to the generation of stressful life events and conditions, triggering depressive or other dysfunctional reactions. In this view, therefore, both parental depression and stress occurrence mediate an association between parental "relational pathology" (e.g., Lyons-Ruth, 1995) and children's problematic outcomes.

An emerging interpersonal perspective on adult depression has increasingly focused on the difficulties observed among many depressed individuals in their marital and family relationships (e.g., Gotlib & Hammen, 1992; Joiner & Coyne, 1999). These difficulties are believed to reflect enduring cognitive representations about the self and others, as well as behavioral patterns that indicate maladaptive social problem solving, such as dependency and reassurance seeking. The phenomenology of depressive syndromes may heighten problematic interpersonal strategies. However, the underlying cognitive–behavioral schemas may have arisen in the earliest parent–child attachment relationships and subsequently have been elaborated and reinforced in conflictual and unrewarding intimate social relationships. In this view, stressful life events and ongoing conditions, such as the quality of the marital and parenting relationships, occur in part because of the characteristic cognitions and behaviors of the vulnerable individual and the failure to resolve or prevent adverse events. The interpersonal perspective, therefore, may subsume several of the other proposed mechanisms noted: the direct effects of stress on parent and child depression, parental stress further eroding effective interpersonal behaviors. These may result in children's acquisition of poor cognitive and interpersonal skills through observation and direct experiences.

No studies of depressed parents have directly examined elements of an interpersonal risk model of transmission of depression. However, offspring studies have certainly extensively documented parents' difficulties in parent–child interactions and marital relationships, as previously discussed. Evidence of stress generation among offspring of depressed women (as in Adrian & Hammen, 1993; see also Table 8.2) is consistent with this approach. Recently, Hammen and Brennan (2001) compared social functioning of two groups of depressed adolescents, those who were offspring of depressed women and those whose mothers were never depressed. The depressed groups were both impaired on many measures of social functioning compared with nondepressed youth, but those who were offspring of depressed women were significantly more interpersonally impaired (but not more academically dysfunctional), consistent with an interpersonal perspective on intergenerational transmission. Depressed adolescents of depressed mothers had more negative cognitions on various measures of their views of their competence in relationships and more evidence of social impairments and interpersonal life events.

Considerably more research is needed to investigate the role of stressful events and circumstances in the processes of transmission of risk for depression and other dysfunction among children of depressed parents. As noted, little is known about whether increased stress is unique to depressed families, or if it occurs in other high-risk families as well. Although chronic stress seems inherent in the impairments of most ongoing or intermittent psychological disorders, there is reason to expect uniquely high levels of interpersonal events among those with recurrent depression. Less research has been conducted on stress processes in children and adolescents. Although it is likely that the parameters of the stress–depression relationship are similar to those of adults, there are doubtless developmental and gender-specific associations to be studied. For instance, Rudolph and Hammen (1999) found higher levels of interpersonal life events among adolescents compared with children, and girls were more likely than boys to develop depressive symptoms associated with negative social events. Further studies of children's use of resources in coping with stressors are needed, including the role of both parents, peers, and personal skills and competencies.

IMPLICATIONS FOR CLINICIANS

Virtually all of the contributors to this volume are likely to recommend that adult depression be viewed as a family matter. When an adult is depressed, it is likely to signal that the spouse and children are involved, either as contributors to the current distress or as unwitting targets of the consequences of the mood disorder and its underlying causes. Thus, to break the cycle of intergenerational transmission of depression, it is often necessary to treat the entire family, or at least to evaluate the children's own mental health and functioning, and to educate the affected parents about the potential effects of their disorders on their children. At the simplest level, information to families and guidance in helping them to recognize depression as an illness may be useful. In some families such interventions would be important and perhaps sufficient, whereas other families might require much more intensive treatment.

Truly preventive interventions, initiated before children experience ill effects, are much more difficult to implement. It might simply be difficult to find families in which parental depression has not begun to have effects even at children's early ages or to develop preventive interventions for very young children. Preventive interventions targeted at older children (e.g., Beardslee, Wright, Salt, & Drezner, 1997) show promise and may stimulate further studies comparing outcomes of younger and older children with different types of interventions.

Beyond general recommendations for treatment and prevention with families, a stress perspective suggests more specific ideas. It seems obvious to call for psychotherapy as an adjunct to psychopharmacological interventions, with a focus not only on evaluating and trying to resolve ongoing and episodic stressors, but also to assess potential patterns of stress generation. Recurring problems of marital or parent–child difficulties indicate that dysfunctional cognitions and behaviors may be contributing to their occurrence and maintenance. Therapy requires a focus on both current resolution of these thoughts and behaviors as well as learning future prevention skills. Parents might also be taught more effective skills, specifically in helping their children to resolve their own stressors or to prevent the escalation of circumstances into major events. Problem-solving techniques both for parents and their children might be helpful, although clearly those stressors that are embedded in the functioning of the family may require ongoing family interventions.

At the level of policy, a simple although far-reaching suggestion would be to alter practice guidelines to include psychoeducational guidance about the possible consequences to families with parental depression. Both primary care and specialized mental health sector professionals should be urged to recognize the scope and significance of the problem of intergenerational transmission of depression. Such education may have a dual benefit: With education and possible intervention, such transmission is not inevitable. Active treatment of the parent's problems in their full context would be a powerful intervention to prevent depression in children that might also reduce the risk of depression recurrence in the parent.

SUMMARY

At least four different kinds of stressful conditions affect children of depressed parents: expressions of parental symptoms; chronic stressful conditions that commonly accompany adult depression, including marital discord; parental episodic stressors; and children's own stressful life events. In each of these areas, offspring of depressed parents are likely to be challenged by levels of stress that exceed their coping capabilities. We speculated that their abilities to deal effectively with such threats may be compromised by the acquisition—in part through modeling—of maladaptive cognitive and behavioral coping skills and by dysfunctional interpersonal schemas and problem-solving. Moreover, stressful conditions likely erode parents' abilities to interact positively and constructively in consistent ways with their children and undermine their availability and supportiveness when the children face their own stressors. Despite promising leads from research on these speculations, however, considerably more research is needed to help specify the sources, clarify the reactions, and illuminate the mechanisms of stress processes in the intergenerational transmission of depression.

REFERENCES

Adrian, C., & Hammen, C. (1993). Stress exposure and stress generation in children of depressed mothers. *Journal of Consulting and Clinical Psychology, 61*, 354–359.

Andreasen, N., Endicott, J., Spitzer, R., & Winokur, G. (1977). The family history method using diagnostic criteria. *Archives of General Psychiatry, 34*, 1229–1235.

Barnett, P. A., & Gotlib, I. H. (1988). Psychosocial functioning and depression: Distinguishing among antecedents, concomitants, and consequences. *Psychological Bulletin, 104*, 97–126.

Beardslee, W. R., & Podorefsky, D. (1988). Resilient adolescents whose parents have serious affective and other psychiatric disorders: Importance of self-understanding and relationships. *American Journal of Psychiatry, 145*, 63–69.

Beardslee, W. R., Schultz, L. H., & Selman, R. L. (1987). Level of social–cognitive development, adaptive functioning, and *DSM–III* diagnoses in adolescent offspring of parents with affective disorders: Implication of the development of the capacity for mutuality. *Developmental Psychology, 23*, 807–815.

Beardslee, W. R., Wright, E. J., Salt, P., & Drezner, K. (1997). Examination of children's responses to two preventive intervention strategies over time. *Journal of the American Academy of Child and Adolescent Psychiatry, 36*, 196–204.

Beck, A. T. (1967). *Depression: Clinical, experimental, and theoretical aspects.* New York: Harper & Row.

Beck, A. T., Ward, C. H., Mendelsohn, M., Mock, J., & Erbaugh, J. (1961). An inventory for measuring depression. *Archives of General Psychiatry, 4*, 561–571.

Billings, A. G., & Moos, R. H. (1985). Children of parents with unipolar depression: A controlled 1-year follow-up. *Journal of Abnormal Child Psychology, 14*, 149–166.

Boyle, M., & Pickles, A. (1997). Influence of maternal depressive symptoms on ratings of childhood behavior. *Journal of Abnormal Child Psychology, 25*, 399–412.

Brown, G. W., & Harris, T. (1978). *Social origins of depression.* London: Free Press.

Burge, D., & Hammen, C. (1991). Maternal communication: Predictors of outcome at follow-up in a sample of children at high and low risk for depression. *Journal of Abnormal Psychology, 100*, 174–180.

Cohn, J. F., Matias, R., Tronick, E., Connell, D., & Lyons-Ruth, K. (1986). Face-to-face interactions of depressed mothers and their infants. In E. Tronick & T. Field (Eds.), *Maternal depression and infant disturbance* (New Directions for Child Development, No. 34, pp. 31–46). San Francisco: Jossey-Bass.

Compas, B., Grant, K., & Ey, S. (1994). Psychosocial stress and child/adolescent depression: Can we be more specific? In W. M. Reynolds & H. F. Johnston (Eds.), *Handbook of depression in children and adolescents* (pp. 509–523). New York: Plenum Press.

Conrad, M., & Hammen, C. (1993). Protective and resilience factors in high and low risk children: A comparison of children of unipolar, bipolar, medically ill and normal mothers. *Development and Psychopathology, 5,* 593–607.

Coyne, J. C., Kessler, R. C., Tal, M., Turnbull, J., Wortman, C. B., Greden, J. F. (1987). Living with a depressed person. *Journal of Consulting and Clinical Psychology, 55,* 347–352.

Cummings, E. M., & Davies, P. T. (1994). Maternal depression and child development. *Journal of Child Psychology and Psychiatry, 35,* 73–112.

Daley, S., Hammen, C., Burge, D., Davila, J., Paley, B., Lindberg, N., & Herzberg, D. (1997). Predictors of the generation of episodic stress: A longitudinal study of late adolescent women. *Journal of Abnormal Psychology, 106,* 251–259.

Daley, S., Hammen, C., Davila, J., & Burge, D. (1998). Axis II symptomatology, depressions, and life stress during the transition from adolescence to adulthood. *Journal of Consulting and Clinical Psychology, 66,* 595–603.

Davila, J., Hammen, C., Burge, D., Paley, B., & Daley, S. (1995). Poor interpersonal problem-solving as a mechanism of stress generation in depression among adolescent women. *Journal of Abnormal Psychology, 104,* 592–600.

Downey, G., & Coyne, J. C. (1990). Children of depressed parents: An integrative review. *Psychological Bulletin, 108,* 50–76.

Fendrich, M., Warner, V., & Weissman, M. M. (1990). Family risk factors, parental depression, and psychopathology in offspring. *Developmental Psychology, 26,* 40–50.

Fergusson, D., Horwood, L. J., & Lynskey, M. (1995). Maternal depressive symptoms and depressive symptoms in adolescents. *Journal of Child Psychology and Psychiatry, 36,* 1161–1178.

Field, T. (1984). Early interactions between infants and their postpartum depressed mothers. *Infant Behavior and Development, 7,* 517–522.

First, M. B., Spitzer, R. L., Gibbon, M., & Williams, J. B. W. (1995). *Structured Clinical Interview for DSM-IV Axis I Disorders.* Washington, DC: American Psychiatric Press.

Garber, J., Braafladt, N., & Zeman, J. (1991). The regulation of sad affect: An information-processing perspective. In J. Garber & K. Dodge (Eds.), *The development of affect regulation and dysregulation* (pp. 208–240). New York: Cambridge University Press.

Ge, X., Conger, R., Lorenz, F., Shanahan, M., & Elder, G. (1995). Mutual influences in parent and adolescent psychological distress. *Developmental Psychology, 31,* 406–419.

Goodman, S., Brogan, D., Lynch, M. E., & Fielding, B. (1993). Social and emotional competence in children of depressed mothers. *Child Development, 64,* 516–531.

Goodman, S., & Gotlib, I. (1999). Risk for psychopathology in the children of depressed mothers: A developmental model for understanding mechanisms of transmission. *Psychological Bulletin, 106,* 458–490.

Goodyer, I., Cooper, J. P., Vize, C., & Ashby, L. (1993). Depression in 11–16-year-old girls: The role of past parental psychopathology and exposure to recent life events. *Journal of Child Psychology and Psychiatry, 34,* 1103–1115.

Gotlib, I., & Beach, S. (1995). A marital/family discord model of depression: Implications for therapeutic intervention. In N. S. Jacobson & A. S. Gurman (Eds.), *Clinical handbook of couple therapy* (pp. 411–436). New York: Guilford Press.

Gotlib, I., & Hammen, C. (1992). *Psychological aspects of depression: Toward a cognitive–interpersonal integration.* Chichester, England: Wiley.

Gunnar, M. R. (1998). Quality of early care and buffering of neuroendocrine stress reactions: Potential effects on the developing human brain. *Preventive Medicine, 27,* 208–211.

Hammen, C. (1988). Self cognitions, stressful events, and the prediction of depression in children of depressed mothers. *Journal of Abnormal Child Psychology, 16,* 347–360.

Hammen, C. (1991a). *Depression runs in families: The social context of risk and resilience in children of depressed mothers.* New York: Springer-Verlag.

Hammen, C. (1991b). The generation of stress in the course of unipolar depression. *Journal of Abnormal Psychology, 100,* 555–561.

Hammen, C., Adrian, C., Gordon, D., Burge, D., Jaenicke, C., & Hiroto, D. (1987). Children of depressed mothers: Maternal strain and symptom predictors of dysfunction. *Journal of Abnormal Psychology, 96,* 190–198.

Hammen, C., & Brennan, P. A. (2000). *Interpersonal dysfunction in depressed mothers.* Unpublished manuscript.

Hammen, C., & Brennan, P. A. (2001). Depressed adolescents of depressed and nondepressed mothers: Tests of an interpersonal impairment hypothesis. *Journal of Consulting and Clinical Psychology, 69,* 284–294.

Hammen, C., Burge, D., & Adrian, C. (1991). Timing of mother and child depression in a longitudinal study of children at risk. *Journal of Consulting and Clinical Psychology, 59,* 341–345.

Hammen, C., Burge, D., Burney, E., & Adrian, C. (1990). Longitudinal study of diagnoses in children of women with unipolar and bipolar affective disorder. *Archives of General Psychiatry, 47,* 1112–1117.

Hammen, C., Burge, D., & Stansbury, K. (1990). Relationship of mother and child variables to child outcomes in a high risk sample: A causal modeling analysis. *Developmental Psychology, 26,* 24–30.

Hammen, C., & Goodman-Brown, T. (1990). Self–schemas and vulnerability to specific life stress in children at risk for depression. *Cognitive Therapy and Research, 14,* 215–227.

Hammen, C., Gordon, D., Burge, D., Adrian, C., Jaenicke, C., & Hiroto, D. (1987). Maternal affective disorders, illness, and stress: Risk for children's psychopathology. *American Journal of Psychiatry, 144,* 736–741.

Hammen, C., Rudolph, K., Weisz, J., Rao, U., & Burge, D. (1999). The context of depression in clinic-referred youth: Neglected areas in treatment. *Journal of the American Academy of Child and Adolescent Psychiatry, 38,* 64–71.

Harnish, J., Dodge, K., & Valente, E. (1995). Mother–child interaction quality as a partial mediator of the roles of maternal depressive symptomatology and socioeconomic status in the development of child behavior problems. *Child Development, 66,* 739–753.

Heim, C., Ehlert, U., Hanker, J. P., & Hellhammer, D. H. (1998). Abuse-related post-traumatic stress disorder and alterations of the hypothalamic-pituitary-adrenal axis in women with chronic pelvic pain. *Psychosomatic Medicine, 60,* 309–318.

Hirsch, B. J., Moos, R. H., & Reischl, T. M. (1985). Psychosocial adjustment of adolescent children of a depressed, arthritic, or normal parent. *Journal of Abnormal Psychology, 94,* 154–164.

Joiner, T., & Coyne, J. (Eds.). (1999). *The interactional nature of depression: Advances in interpersonal approaches.* Washington, DC: American Psychological Association.

Keller, M. B., Beardslee, W. R., Dorer, D. J., Lavori, P. W., Samuelson, H., & Klerman, G. R. (1986). Impact of severity and chronicity of parental affective illness on adaptive functioning and psychopathology in children. *Archives of General Psychiatry, 43,* 930–937.

Klein, D. N., Clark, D. C., Dansky, L., & Margolis, E. T. (1988). Dysthymia in the offspring of parents with primary unipolar affective disorder. *Journal of Abnormal Psychology, 97,* 265–274.

Lazarus, R. S., & Folkman, S. (1984). *Stress, appraisal, and coping.* New York: Springer.

Lee, C. M., & Gotlib, I. H. (1989). Clinical status and emotional adjustment of children of depressed mothers. *American Journal of Psychiatry, 146,* 478–483.

Lyons-Ruth, K. (1995). Broadening our conceptual frameworks: Can we reintroduce relational strategies and implicit representations systems to the study of psychopathology? *Developmental Psychology, 31,* 432–436.

McGuffin, P., Katz, R., & Bebbington, P. (1988). The Camberwell Collaborative Depression Study: III. Depression and adversity in the relatives of depressed probands. *British Journal of Psychiatry, 152,* 775–782.

Merikangas, K. R. (1984). Divorce and assortative mating among depressed patients. *American Journal of Psychiatry, 141,* 74–76.

Merikangas, K. R., Weissman, M. M., Prusoff, B. A., & John, K. (1988). Assortative mating and affective disorders: Psychopathology in offspring. *Psychiatry, 51,* 48–57.

Radke-Yarrow, M. (1998). *Children of depressed mothers: From early childhood to maturity.* New York: Cambridge University Press.

Radke-Yarrow, M., & Sherman, T. (1990). Hard growing: Children who survive. In J. Rolf, A. Masten, D. Cicchetti, K. Nuechterlein, & S. Weintraub (Eds.), *Risk and protective factors in the development of psychopathology* (pp. 97–119). Cambridge, England: Cambridge University Press.

Radke-Yarrow, M., Zahn-Waxler, M., Richardson, D., & Susman, A. (1994). Caring behavior in children of clinically depressed and well mothers. *Child Development, 65*, 1405–1414.

Rudolph, K., & Hammen, C. (1999). Age and gender as determinants of stress exposure, generation, and reactivity in youngsters: A transactional perspective. *Child Development, 70*, 660–677.

Rutter, M., & Quinton, P. (1984). Parental psychiatric disorder: Effects on children. *Psychological Medicine, 14*, 853–880.

Seifer, R., Sameroff, A., Dickstein, S., Keitner, G., Miller, I., Rasmussen, S., & Hayden, L. (1996). Parental psychopathology, multiple contextual risks, and one-year outcomes in children. *Journal of Clinical Child Psychology, 25*, 423–435.

Warner, V., Mufson, L., & Weissman, M. M. (1995). Offspring at high and low risk for depression and anxiety: Mechanisms of psychiatric disorder. *Journal of the American Academy of Child and Adolescent Psychiatry, 34*, 786–797.

Weissman, M. M., & Olfson, M. (1995). Depression in women: Implications for health care research. *Science, 269*, 799–801.

Weissman, M., Prusoff, B., Gammon, G., Merikangas, K., Leckman, J., & Kidd, K. (1984). Psychopathology in the children (ages 6–18) of depressed and normal parents. *Journal of the American Academy of Child and Adolescent Psychiatry, 23*, 78–84.

II

Moderators of Risk

9

FAMILY CONTEXT: FATHERS AND OTHER SUPPORTS

VICKY PHARES, AMY M. DUHIG, AND M. MONICA WATKINS

Although there is a wealth of information regarding the children of mothers who are depressed, there is far less information about the children of fathers who are depressed (Kaslow, Deering, & Racusin, 1994). Possible reasons for this lack of research on depressed fathers include the greater prevalence of major depression in women than in men, the possibility that fathers are more difficult than mothers to recruit into research, the greater research attention to maternal as opposed to paternal parenting processes, and theory-based research that centers on an unquestioned sexist assumption of the central role of mothers and the lack of importance of fathers to the development of their children (Phares, 1992, 1996). Be this as it may, the knowledge base about children of depressed fathers is growing. This chapter reviews the research that has been conducted on children of depressed fathers. Other important family members such as grandparents and siblings are also discussed with a focus on the ramifications of the family context in relation to parental depression.

Preparation of this chapter was supported in part by National Institute of Mental Health Grant R29 49601-05.

CHILDREN OF DEPRESSED FATHERS

Research on depressed fathers seems scant only when compared to the number of studies of children of depressed mothers. In fact, a number of studies have focused on children of depressed fathers, and these studies have allowed some tentative conclusions about the context of paternal versus maternal depression.

We identified 19 studies that explored paternal depression in relation to children's and adolescents' functioning. Significant correlations between paternal depression and child emotional and behavioral problems were found in 14 of these studies (representing 11 different samples; Atkinson & Rickel, 1984; Beardslee, Schultz, & Selman, 1987; Billings & Moos, 1983, 1985; Carro, Grant, Gotlib, & Compas, 1993; el-Guebaly, Offord, Sullivan, & Lynch, 1978; Forehand & Smith, 1986; Harjan, 1992; Jacob & Johnson, 1997; Jacob & Leonard, 1986; Klein, Clark, Dansky, & Margolis, 1988; Marchand & Hock, 1998; Orvaschel, Walsh-Allis, & Ye, 1988; Thomas & Forehand, 1991). In the remaining 5 studies (representing 3 different samples), no significant correlations were found between paternal depression and child emotional and behavioral problems (Keller et al., 1986; Klein, Depue, & Slater, 1985; Radke-Yarrow, Cummings, Kuczynski, & Chapman, 1985; Radke-Yarrow, Nottelmann, Martinez, Fox, & Belmont, 1992; Zahn-Waxler, Cummings, McKnew, & Radke-Yarrow, 1984).

A number of specific findings are notable from this research. Jacob, Krahn, and Leonard (1991) found that children experience difficulties if their parents are depressed. Depression in parents is associated with problems of adjustment and diagnosable disorders in their children (Beardslee, Bemporad, Keller, & Klerman, 1983; Downey & Coyne, 1990). Children of depressed parents show a higher rate of internalizing and externalizing problems when compared to children of nondepressed parents (Lee & Gotlib, 1991a; Phares, 1996; Phares & Compas, 1992). There is generally a high rate of impairment among children of parents with an affective disorder (Beardslee, Versage, & Gladstone, 1998). Kaslow and colleagues (1994) also noted that increased paternal depressive mood was associated with decreased cognitive performance in sons and with increased cognitive performance in daughters. These patterns have been found across all developmental levels, including infancy and toddlerhood (Carro et al., 1993), childhood (Orvaschel et al., 1988), and adolescence (Jacob & Johnson, 1997).

Studies have consistently found that parents who are depressed tend to view their children as having more problems than parents who are not depressed. Parents who are depressed have also described their families as less expressive and cohesive and as more conflictual than do parents who are not depressed (Lee & Gotlib, 1991b). Although fathers' and mothers' reports of child and family functioning are influenced by their own psychological symptoms (Phares, Compas, & Howell, 1989), there is clear evidence that children and adolescents of depressed parents have more difficulties than children of nondepressed parents. Thus, parental depression in both fathers and mothers appears to influence children's emotional and behavioral functioning in a number of ways.

Comparable findings have been identified in relation to children's lower levels of competence when exposed to paternal psychopathology. Adolescents who have depressed fathers and depressed mothers showed lower levels of competence (such as social competence and academic competence) than adolescents who have nondepressed parents (Phares, Blum, & Williams, 1997). It is interesting that this pattern of results varied according to the informant for the adolescent's competence. Specifically, adolescents with depressed fathers showed lower levels of competence according to fathers and teachers, whereas adolescents with depressed mothers showed lower levels of competence according to fathers, mothers, teachers, and the adolescents themselves (Phares et al., 1997). This study highlights the complexity of findings depending on which informants are included.

Given the wealth of information about children of depressed mothers, it is noteworthy that the differences between the effects of maternal and paternal depression are relatively few. When the functioning of children of depressed mothers is compared with the functioning of children of depressed fathers, few differences emerge (Beardslee et al., 1987; Billings & Moos, 1983, 1985; Harjan, 1992; Jacob & Johnson, 1997; Marchand & Hock, 1998; Orvaschel et al., 1988). Children of depressed mothers and children of depressed fathers appear to have comparable risk for developing emotional and behavioral problems.

Overall, paternal depression appears to be a risk factor for the development of higher levels of emotional and behavioral problems and lower levels of competence in children and adolescents (Jacob & Johnson, 1997; Phares, 1996; Phares & Compas, 1993). Fathers, as well as mothers, have been shown to play a significant role in the development of child and adolescent psychopathology (Phares & Compas, 1992).

Because of the important ramifications of both paternal and maternal depression, it is worthwhile to explore the theoretical models that would help explain these findings. Other theoretical models (such as genetic influences, neurobiological models, cognitive models, and interpersonal mechanisms) are discussed throughout this book, so this section focuses on family functioning and family context in relation to paternal as well as maternal depression.

MECHANISMS RELATED TO FAMILY FUNCTIONING AND FAMILY CONTEXT: FAMILY SYSTEMS THEORIES

Family functioning and family context are important in understanding paternal and maternal depression and subsequent child or adolescent functioning. Family systems models of depression indicate that the depression of one parent has an impact on the relationships in which that parent is involved directly. Family relationships and children themselves can also influence parental depression (Becvar & Becvar, 1993). This is to say that the presence of a depressed parent or a depressed family member can have a tremendous influence on the parenting and agreeableness of all family members and vice versa (Jacob & Johnson, 1997). Family systems theories are designed to direct attention away from the individual and toward relationships and relationship issues in which individuals are involved. There is an emphasis on reciprocity and shared responsibility (Becvar & Becvar, 1993; Nichols, 1996).

Family systems have subsystems that are important for family functioning and should be considered in research and in clinical interventions. These subsystems are the marital (or co-parenting) subsystem, the parent–child dyad, and the sibling subsystem (Erel & Burman, 1995; Nichols, 1996). Each subsystem interacts with and influences the other subsystems (Erel & Burman, 1995).

Although family systems theories are not pragmatic (Becvar & Becvar, 1993), the concepts of reciprocity and the interconnections between subsystems within families are important additions to understanding paternal and maternal depression. Reciprocity in family systems theories highlight the bi-directional influences between depressed parents and their children, rather than just focusing on paternal and maternal influences on children. Several examples underscore this bi-directionality and the reciprocity of effects. In a sample of depressed fathers, depressed mothers, and nondepressed parents, fathers and mothers showed comparable levels of positivity toward their children, but children showed significantly more positivity toward their father than their mother (Jacob & Johnson, 1997). The same study found somewhat different patterns of congeniality. Specifically, mothers showed higher rates of congeniality toward children than did fathers, and children in turn showed higher rates of congeniality toward their mothers than their fathers (Jacob & Johnson, 1997).

The reciprocal connection between children's behavior and parents' emotional well-being is probably best illustrated by a series of laboratory-based studies that explored the effects of interacting with a child who exhibited externalizing behaviors (i.e., attention-deficit/hyperactivity disorder, conduct disorder, and oppositional defiant disorder). In this series of studies with an experimental design, Lang and Pelham and colleagues (e.g., Lang, Pelham, Atkeson, & Murphy, 1999; Pelham & Lang, 1993; Pelham et al., 1997) randomly assigned parents to interact with a child confederate who exhibited either externalizing behavior or nonclinical behavior. The parent's mood was measured before and after interacting with the child. Both fathers and mothers reported significantly greater distressed mood (such as higher levels of depression) after interacting with children exhibiting externalizing behavior problems than fathers and mothers who interacted with children exhibiting nonclinical behavior. In addition, fathers and mothers felt more parental role inadequacy after interacting with child confederates who showed externalizing behavior problems. These studies suggest that disturbed behavior in children may affect paternal and maternal depression. Thus, the reciprocity of behavior between children and parents must be taken into account when studying children of depressed fathers and depressed mothers.

Interparental conflict (i.e., conflict within the parental subsystem) is discussed later in this chapter and throughout this book. One example of the impact of subsystems within the family is illustrated by the connection between marital satisfaction and family functioning. In a sample of families with a depressed father, Kaslow, Warner, John, and Brown (1992) found that higher levels of marital satisfaction were associated with more family cohesiveness. Thus, both reciprocity within families and acknowledgment of subsystems within families are important concepts that are highlighted within family systems theories.

Regardless of whether it is the mother or the father who is depressed, family systems theories suggest that child functioning might be influenced through maladaptive functioning in the co-parenting dyad, the parent–child dyad, or the sibling dyads. Evidence suggests that the family context and the family environment can serve as moderating factors between paternal depression and child adjustment.

FAMILY CONTEXT AND FAMILY ENVIRONMENT AS MODERATING FACTORS IN RELATION TO PATERNAL DEPRESSION

A number of factors moderate the connections between paternal depression and child functioning. Family context and family environment can moderate the connections between paternal depression and child functioning. Parental behaviors such as criticism, hostility, and rejection in the context of parental depression can exacerbate the maladjustment of children of depressed parents (Kaslow et al., 1994). Parental depression appears to alter the parent–child relationship through parental behavior (such as harsher communication, decreased positive interactions, restrictive behaviors, and punishing behaviors), which then puts the child at greater risk for the development of emotional and behavioral problems (Jacob & Johnson, 1997; Marchand & Hock, 1998).

Likewise, family disruption or a change in family constellation may be especially difficult for children in families with a depressed parent, given the sometimes tenuous attachment to their distressed parents (Kaslow et al., 1994). Conversely, a stable family constellation in which the child still lives with a nondisordered father (even if there is a depressed mother) was associated with lower rates of child psychopathology (Hammen, 1991).

With regard to specific factors of the family environment, a number of studies have found that families with a depressed parent are less cohesive, less adaptable, show less care, and are more overprotective than families in which neither parent is psychologically disturbed (Fendrich, Warner, & Weissman, 1990; Kaslow et al., 1992). Given that these characteristics of the family environment are associated with child emotional and behavioral problems even without a depressed parent (Dadds, 1995), it is likely that they would constitute an even greater risk for the children when they have a depressed parent.

Age of the child at the time of onset of parental depression seems to be related to the severity of the effects of parental depression. Young children who experience longer periods of parental depression are more likely to experience maladaptive outcomes than children who are older or who experience briefer periods of parental depression (reviewed in Goodman & Gotlib, 1999). Other individual characteristics of the child (such as child temperament, gender, intellectual functioning, and social–cognitive skills) may moderate the impact of parental depression. In particular, there is evidence that children with a difficult temperament, children with lower intellectual functioning, children with limited social–cognitive skills, and girls as a group appear to be at greater risk for the maladaptive effects of parental depression than are children with an easy temperament, children with average or above average intellectual functioning, children with adequate social–cognitive skills, and boys as a group (reviewed in Goodman & Gotlib, 1999).

There may also be interaction effects between parental gender and child gender. Investigation in this area has been limited, largely because of the dearth of research on depressed fathers. However, some evidence suggests that adolescents' perceptions of their depressed parents differ across child and parent gender. Specifically, adolescent daughters of fathers with psychopathology showed greater internalizing emotional and behavioral problems such as depression and anxiety, whereas adolescent sons of mothers with psychopathology showed greater externalizing emotional and behavioral problems such as lower acceptance and higher negative affect (Bosco, Renk, Dinger, Epstein, & Phares, 1997). Although this research is preliminary, the findings highlight the importance of exploring gender in parents and children as possible moderating factors regarding parental psychopathology.

Overall, many factors within the family appear to moderate the impact of parental depression. In addition to the factors already discussed in this section, other factors such as having two parents rather than only one depressed parent, experiencing high levels of interparental conflict, being exposed to high levels of negative emotions, and experiencing low levels of parental emotional availability are all linked to greater risk for the development of emotional and behavioral problems. Specifically, assortative mating, interparental conflict, and emotional availability have been identified as moderating factors in relation to paternal depression.

Assortative Mating, Increased Risk for Psychopathology in Offspring, and Transgenerational Issues

Assortative mating has been described as the tendency for a psychologically distressed person to have children with another psychologically distressed person. This phenomenon has been well documented for psychiatric disorders as a whole, and more specifically for alcohol abuse, anxiety disorders, and depression (Hammen, Rudolph, Weisz, Rao, & Burge, 1999; McLeod, 1993; Merikangas & Spiker, 1982; Merikangas, Weissman, Prusoff, & John, 1988). Assortative mating appears to put the offspring at an increased risk for the development of psychopathology. This increased risk is due not only to genetic influences but also to environmental influences that result when one or both parents are psychologically distressed. Regarding increased environmental risk, depression in one spouse is likely to arouse stress in the other (Coyne, 1976), so that children of a parent with depression are at higher risk for poor parenting from both of their primary caregivers. Another implication of assortative mating is marital distress. Marital discord has been shown to be a significant contributor to children's maladjustment generally and is hypothesized to be a mechanism of transmission of negative outcomes in children of depressed parents (e.g., Downey & Coyne, 1990).

The risk for the development of psychopathology appears to be even greater when both parents, rather than just one of them, have a disorder. For example, Merikangas et al. (1988) found that when neither parent had a psychiatric diagnosis, one-third of their children had a psychiatric diagnosis. The number of diagnosed children increased to more than one-half when one parent was diagnosed with a disorder, and when both parents had a psychiatric diagnosis, approximately three-fourths of the children met criteria for a disorder. In a more recent study, Dierker, Merikangas, and Szatmari (1999) found that patterns of psychopathology among offspring were similar for mothers and fathers. Spouse concordance for psychopathology was greater among parents with substance abuse problems than among those with anxiety disorders, and there was a direct relationship between the number of affected parents and the magnitude of psychopathology in children, particularly with respect to the anxiety disorders. Additionally, rates of conduct disorders were elevated only among offspring of dually affected parents, irrespective of the specific parental disorders. These findings underscore the importance of the contribution of both mothers and fathers, particularly those with concordance for psychiatric disorders, to the development of psychopathology in offspring. Parental depression was not examined in this study.

The results are mixed when we consider the increased risk for psychopathology in children based on the number of parents with depressive disorders. In one study, the presence of a depressed father did not increase the likelihood of a child's insecure attachment with a depressed mother, but the researchers did not assess emotional and behavioral problems (Radke-Yarrow et al., 1985). When emotional and behavioral problems were examined in a follow-up study, the presence of a depressed father did not increase the likelihood of child psychopathology (Radke-Yarrow et al., 1992). The picture is somewhat more complex when considering depressed fathers who reside in the home versus outside of the home. As summarized in Hammen (1991), Hammen and colleagues found that children were more likely to meet diagnostic criteria for a variety of disorders when fathers were absent from the home, regardless of whether there was parental psychopathology. Children also displayed increased levels of diagnoses when fathers were disordered, regardless of whether the father lived in the home. Paternal disorder and paternal absence, however, did not have an additive effect resulting in increased child psychopathology. When children lived with a nondisordered father (irrespective of the presence or absence of psychopathology in the mother), they had lower rates of psychopathology than other groups of children (i.e., those who lived with a disordered father, those who did not live with a disordered father, or those whose nondisordered father was absent). One problem with this study, however, was that the sample size was too small to test for the effects of specific paternal disorder. In a more recent study, paternal depressive symptoms in a nonclinical community sample stood out as a significant predictor of child internalizing behaviors even when maternal depressive symptoms were controlled statistically (Marchand & Hock, 1998). Moreover, paternal symptoms were found to be related to maternal restrictive and punishing behaviors. Thus, the experience of depressive symptoms in fathers may also relate to internalizing behaviors in children indirectly by influencing mothers' caregiving behavior (Marchand & Hock, 1998).

Studies examining parents and offspring that include three generations are rarely found in the literature. What can be gleaned from the limited number of studies is that transgenerational patterns of psychopathology do exist (Kovacs, Devlin, Pollack, Richards, & Mukerji, 1997; Orvaschel, 1990; Warner, Weissman, Mufson, & Wickramaratne, 1999). The study by Warner and colleagues found a relatively strong link between grandparents', parents', and grandchildren's psychopathology. Specifically, they found that both grandparents' and parents' depression was associated with anxiety in their grandchildren and children, respectively. Having grandparents and parents with a positive history of depression resulted in increased levels of anxiety. Moreover, almost half of the grandchildren in families in which both the parents and grandparents were depressed had some form of psychopathology and showed severe impairment. One surprising finding of the study was that grandparent depression had a stronger effect on the risk for anxiety in grandchildren than did parental depression. Taken together, these findings suggest that psychopathology in parents and grandparents plays a role in childhood dysfunction.

Interparental Conflict and Paternal Depression

Another way in which the family influences child or adolescent functioning is through interparental conflict. Researchers commonly characterize the family as having three subsystems. These subsystems are the marital (or co-parental), parent–child, and sibling subsystems. Each of these subsystems influences and are influenced by the other subsystems. Some researchers regard the marital relationship as the core of family solidarity and as the key determinant of the quality of family life (Erel & Burman, 1995). A number of researchers have reported a significant correlation between parents' reports of marital satisfaction and the observed positive attention toward children (Erel & Burman, 1995; Lee & Gotlib, 1991b). Conversely, interparental conflict has been found consistently to be associated with increased emotional and behavioral problems in children and adolescents (Bosco et al., 1997; Cummings & Davies, 1994; Epstein, Renk, Smith, Bosco, & Phares, 1998).

It has been hypothesized that marital disharmony leads to child behavior problems because it affects the quality of the parent–child subsystem adversely (Erel & Burman, 1995). The stress of interparental conflict can lead parents to become more inconsistent and ineffective in their parenting behavior, which can increase the rate of child misbehaviors. Interparental conflict can also reduce the responsivity of parents to their child's emotional needs and signals. This reduced responsivity diminishes the quality of the emotional relationships or attachments between parents and children and increases the rate of various types of childhood problems (Cummings & Davies, 1994). Cummings and Davies noted that children from homes with a great deal of conflict are at particular risk for externalizing disorders, internalizing problems, dysfunctional social skills, dysfunctional relationships, discordant parent–child relationships, and diminished academic achievement. Gottman (1998) noted that interparental conflict is also associated with health problems in children.

Jacob and colleagues (1991) noted that difficulties in the parent–child relationship are likely due to distress, including interparental conflict. Interestingly, the particular type of distress is irrelevant in their opinion. (The connections between interparental conflict, paternal depression, and child and adolescent functioning are discussed in more detail elsewhere in this book.)

Expression of Emotion and Emotional Availability Within the Family

The problems that children and adolescents experience when their parent is depressed or experiencing interparental conflict could be linked to the expression of emotion or emotional availability within the family. Lee and Gotlib (1991b) proposed that family disruption (interparental conflict or parental psychopathology) influence the type of relationship that parents have with their children. Parents become less emotionally available to their children when there is family disruption because they become more self-focused and are less able to provide warm and consistent parenting to their children.

Emotional availability could be described as a parent's supportive presence and acceptance of emotional expression in a child (Biringen & Robinson, 1991). A study by Frankel and Harmon (1996) factor analyzed maternal emotional availability with the following variables: warm–kind tone of voice; positive affect; quality of verbalizations; contingent responsivity to child positive behavior; structures and mediates environment; reads cues and responds sensitively; connectedness; mirroring; flexibility; consistency; and enjoyment–pleasure. They found no difference between depressed and nondepressed women on ratings of emotional availability to their children. According to Kaslow and colleagues (1994), *expression of emotion* refers to family members' reports of the emotional aspects of their communication patterns. Critical attitudes, hostile attitudes, and extreme emotional overinvolvement are the key aspects of expression of emotion that have been examined for their association with psychiatric disorders in family members. *Affective style* refers to how the emotional atmosphere of a family is manifested behaviorally. Negative affective styles in mothers are associated with the coping style of a child (Kaslow et al., 1994).

Few researchers or clinicians question the proposition that a lack of parental emotional support and parental stimulation have negative effects on children. Schakel (1987) noted that affective and social deprivation, parents' detachment or indifference, and parents' inability to understand and meet the emotional needs of their children can create relationships that can harm the psychological welfare of children. Kaslow and colleagues (1994) reported that children of depressed mothers who show elevated levels of expression of negative emotions are at a higher risk for mood disorders and other problems than are children whose depressed mothers are less critical and less over-involved.

Emotions are of special significance in families who are dealing with affective illness. It is notable that parental anger appears to serve as a mediator between paternal and maternal depression and children's and adolescents' emotional and behavioral problems (Renk, Phares, & Epps, 1999). Radke-Yarrow and Zahn-Waxler (1990) also noted that compared to nondepressed mothers, depressed mothers are more hostile, less affectionate or less consistent in affection, less communicative, less skillful in management of children, more likely to avoid punishment and discipline, more negative in attributional styles, more critical of the child, and more negative, unresponsive, and inconsistent in parent–infant interactions. Children of these depressed parents are more likely to have their distress go unattended or to have them dealt with in terms of the parents' needs (Radke-Yarrow & Zahn-

Waxler, 1990). Such problems in parenting are associated with family disorganization, enmeshment, and over-dependency between family members, marital conflict, and poor family problem-solving strategies (Cummings & Davies, 1994).

A measure of parental emotional availability, called the Lum Emotional Availability of Parents (LEAP) Scale, has been developed and validated recently (Lum & Phares, 1999). The measure can be completed by children aged 9 and older regarding the emotional availability of their father and mother. Emotional availability is represented by items such as "My father/mother is willing to talk about my troubles," and "My father/mother asks questions in a caring manner." Based on a study of nonclinical and clinically referred children and adolescents, lower levels of paternal and maternal emotional availability were predictive of higher rates of emotional and behavioral problems for children and adolescents. Lower levels of parental emotional availability were significant in predicting emotional and behavioral problems even after controlling for paternal and maternal behavior, such as affection and control. Emotional availability of parents and expression of emotion in families are critical components that influence children's and adolescents' emotional and behavioral functioning (Lee & Gotlib, 1991b). Unfortunately, emotional availability has not been studied extensively in samples of depressed fathers.

SIBLINGS IN RELATION TO CHILD AND PARENTAL DEPRESSION

In addition to the parent–child relationship, it is important to consider sibling relationships in the context of parental depression. In a recent study, Hammen et al. (1999) found that approximately 40% of children with depression also had a sibling with a psychiatric diagnosis or legal problem. Another line of research addressing substance abusing parents suggests that children with opiate addicted parents aggregate at a high level for both depressive and anxiety disorders when the parents also have a lifetime history of depressive disorders (Rende & Weissman, 1999). This pattern was not true for addicted parents without a history of depression or in children whose parents have a history of alcohol abuse (Rende & Weissman, 1999). These findings are consistent for children of depressed parents without addictions as well (Rende, Wickramaratne, Warner, & Weissman, 1995). Thus, it appears that children who are depressed tend to have siblings who also have psychiatric disorders.

Given the connection between parental depression and child depression, the sibling relationships of children who are depressed are noteworthy. There is some indication that depressed children have impaired sibling relationships (Puig-Antich et al., 1993). These relationships may be characterized as receiving less support from their siblings (Daniels & Moos, 1990), having antagonistic relationships with their siblings (Puig-Antich et al., 1993), and perceiving increased stress as a result of their relationship with their siblings (Daniels & Moos, 1990). These types of relationships could complicate treatment of the depressed child and perhaps exacerbate problematic emotional and behavioral problems of each of the siblings (Hammen et al., 1999).

On the other hand, well-functioning children could serve as a protective factor against the development of psychopathology for their siblings. For example, sibling relationships predict lower depressive symptoms in children with only one parent in the home (Huntley & Phelps, 1990), indicating that in the absence of a parent, the sibling relationship may be especially important as a buffer against depressive symptoms. Furthermore, siblings, particularly younger siblings, in close but nonenmeshed relationships have identified their sibling relationships as important sources of emotional and instrumental support during times of stress and family transitions (Dunn, 1996; Jenkins, 1992). These supportive sibling relationships may help decrease risk for psychopathology by playing a protective role.

In another line of inquiry, researchers have examined the contributions of parental negative affectivity (e.g., depression and hostility) to variations in the quality of sibling relationships. Relative to nondepressed parents, depressed parents have been found to be less involved with and less affectionate toward their children, to feel more guilt and resentment, and to experience more general difficulty in managing and communicating with their children (Rutter, 1990a). These higher levels of parental negative affectivity have been found to be related to higher levels of negativity and lower levels of positivity within sibling relationships (Brody, Stoneman, & McCoy, 1994). The effects of interacting with a depressed or hostile parent may disrupt the children's capacities to regulate their emotions and behavior (Fabes & Eisenberg, 1992), resulting in less supportive and more conflicted sibling interactions. The effects of parental negative affectivity on sibling relationships have been proposed to be mediated by their effect on parent–child relationships (Brody, 1998). The literature is relatively consistent in demonstrating that the effects of parental psychological adjustment on sibling relationships are mediated by the extent to which disruptions in these areas lead to hostile parenting. If parenting is not hostile, marital distress and parental depression have no significant effect on sibling relationship quality (Brody et al., 1994). Overall, relationships with siblings and other factors can serve to buffer the effects of parental depression.

PROTECTIVE FACTORS WITHIN THE FAMILY

In recent years, there has been an increased emphasis on studying risk and protective factors for psychosocial adjustment of children and adolescents (e.g., see Haggerty, Sherrod, Garmezy, & Rutter, 1994). Several areas of risk and protective factors have received a considerable amount of attention, including factors internal to the child (e.g., gender, intellectual functioning, temperament), factors outside of the family (e.g., involvement in activities outside the home, peers), and factors within the family (e.g., siblings, grandparents, the presence of a well-functioning parent when the other has a psychological disorder). A review of the factors within the child and outside of the family are beyond the scope of this chapter; here we focus on factors within the family that help to buffer the potential effects of parental depression. Unfortunately, few studies have been conducted to determine which factors are associated with better outcomes for children with depressed parents. It is also important to remember that the effect of any one risk factor alone, such as parental depression, is relatively small (e.g., Reid & Crisafulli, 1990). Other problems usually are evidenced in families with a depressed parent (e.g., marital conflict, conflictual relationships between parent and child), which are also risk factors for problematic child functioning. It appears that the cumulative effects of multiple family stressors are most problematic for children and adolescents (Forehand, Biggar, & Kotchick, 1998).

On the positive side, several family protective factors appear to promote resilience in children under adversity. Among those factors that are receiving research attention are having a close relationship with a caring parent figure, authoritative parenting styles (i.e., warmth, structure, high expectations), socioeconomic advantages, connections to extended supportive family networks, secure attachment relations, and interparental harmony (Cicchetti, Rogosch, & Toth, 1997; Masten & Coatsworth, 1998; Voydanoff & Donnelly, 1999). For example, a close relationship with a competent parent is related to enhanced outcomes among children who are exposed to marital discord (Rutter, 1990b), which is often associated with parental depression. Parental competence, such as providing emotional support and stability, has also been found to be related to resiliency. Garmezy (1989) found that children whose parents are more competent tend to be protected from the adverse effects of their environment. More specifically, some evidence suggests that when one parent is depressed, the other parent often attempts to compensate for the depressed parent. For instance, in families with a depressed mother, fathers have been found to be more caring for their children than fathers with nondepressed wives (Hops et al., 1987). In another study, nondepressed fathers had more positive interactions with their infants than did their depressed wives, and fathers attempted to compensate for their wives by being more positive in their interactions with their children (Hossain et al., 1994). These effects may not be entirely beneficial, however, as the depressed mother's feelings of inadequacy and incompetence may be perpetuated and may result in more difficulties in the mother–child relationship (Teichman & Teichman, 1990). Several studies have also found that having a healthy father in the home is associated with lower rates of disorder among children of depressed mothers (Conrad & Hammen, 1989; Goodman, Brogan, Lynch, & Fielding, 1993), but this pattern was not found in a study of postpartum depression (Carro et al., 1993).

Other protective factors have been identified that appear to increase parental well-being, which can then influence the parent–child relationship. Marital happiness was found to be associated with parental well-being, which in turn was associated with nurturing and supportive parenting behavior (Voydanoff & Donnelly, 1998).

Several mechanisms by which fathers either exacerbate or attenuate the effects of maternal depression on children have been proposed (Goodman & Gotlib, 1999). Goodman and Gotlib proposed that fathers with depression or another disorder increase the risk of psychopathology in their children through genetic and environmental factors. Conversely, well fathers could provide a positive role model for their children, have an increased role in caregiving for their children, and offer support to the depressed mother, which may result in better parenting.

Grandparents and other extended family members can also provide support that may be absent in the home (Grizenko & Pawliuk, 1994; Werner, 1993). It appears that having at least one person in a child's life who offers unconditional acceptance promotes self-esteem and self-efficacy in the child (Werner, 1993). If the parents are not able to provide a positive climate of warmth, affection, emotional support, and clear-cut and reasonable structure and limits (which is a family structure in which children do well), other family members can serve this function (Werner, 1993).

Cicchetti and colleagues (1997) highlighted the need to consider protective factors within the developmental trajectory of children's lives. That is, protective factors can be omnipresent and enduring in children's lives (e.g., a strong and stable parent–child relationship that exists from infancy to adulthood), or they can serve as transient buffers in children's lives (e.g., a relationship with a stable role model that occurs for a brief, but meaningful, period of time). Thus, protective factors within families with a depressed parent should be considered in relation to the developmental pathways of children's lives. It appears that a greater number of protective factors is associated with better outcomes in children and adolescents (Sameroff, Seifer, & Bartko, 1997). Clearly, then, it is important that prevention and treatment programs identify and enhance protective factors in the lives of children of depressed fathers.

IMPLICATIONS FOR CLINICIANS

The risk and protective factors that are highlighted throughout this chapter point to a number of preventive interventions (e.g., Beardslee, 1998). Because these preventive interventions are covered in Gladstone & Beardslee's chapter (chapter 12, this volume), we provide here only a brief discussion of the clinical implications of working with children of depressed fathers and mothers. In general, whenever a father or mother is treated for a psychological problem, the therapist should consider the possibility that the children might need therapeutic intervention. Preventive interventions and clinical interventions could be conducted in a number of ways. Preventive interventions might take a psychoeducational approach, for example, by informing depressed parents about the potential impact of their functioning on their children and helping children learn ways to cope with their parents' depression (Beardslee, 1998). Conversely, a more traditional treatment strategy could be adopted, for example, by involving depressed children of depressed fathers in empirically supported treatments (Kaslow & Thompson, 1998). Preventive interventions as well as more traditional treatment strategies, such as self-control interventions or skills training interventions, have been found to be effective in decreasing children's emotional and behavioral problems and increasing their adaptive functioning (Beardslee, 1998; Kaslow & Thompson, 1998). Both psychoeducational and traditional approaches would probably involve depressed fathers in the assessment and treatment of their children to some extent.

Regarding assessment, evidence from a meta-analysis suggests that fathers and mothers show moderate correspondence in rating their children's internalizing emotional and behavioral problems and show high levels of correspondence in rating their children's externalizing emotional and behavior problems and total emotional and behavioral problems (Duhig, Renk, Epstein, & Phares, 2000). Furthermore, fathers and mothers tend to report their children's emotional and behavioral problems at similar levels and tend not to show significant differences in the rates of emotional and behavioral problems that they report. Thus, fathers' ratings can be considered comparable to mothers' ratings in clinical assessments of children and adolescents.

Regarding therapy, the difficulty of getting men, and especially men who are fathers, into psychological treatment has received considerable attention in the literature (Carr, 1998; Hecker, 1991). Fathers are rarely included in treatment for child or family difficulties (Lazar, Sagi, & Fraser, 1991; Smith, Williams, & Phares, 2000). The majority of children in clinical settings, however, have at least some type of contact with their fathers (Phares & Lum, 1997). Although the lack of inclusion of fathers in treatment is often due to reluctance on the part of fathers, there is also evidence that clinicians' personal and professional characteristics may be related to engaging fathers in treatment. In a study of social workers and psychologists working within child protective agencies and public schools, male therapists were significantly more likely to include fathers in treatment than were female therapists (Lazar et al., 1991). Differences may also stem from professional orientation: Psychologists with a family systems orientation were more likely to include fathers in treatment than were psychologists with other theoretical orientations (Smith et al., 2000).

Another possible reason for the difficulty in including fathers in treatment is that therapists often neglect clinical issues that are of importance to fathers, such as the difficulty of balancing work and family duties and the struggle of being a noncustodial father (Dickstein et al., 1991). These issues are important for therapists to consider, regardless of whether the father is depressed. Overall, fathers, and especially depressed fathers, should be included in psychological assessments and interventions that are meant to help mothers, children, and the family (Carr, 1998; Hecker, 1991).

SUMMARY

Although depression in fathers is not as prevalent as depression in mothers, it is imperative that paternal depression continue to be explored in the context of child and family functioning. Given the transactional nature of depression within families (Goodman & Gotlib, 1999; Kaslow et al., 1994), it is important to include fathers in studies of depression within the family. Even when fathers are "absent" from children's lives, their brief contact with them or the children's memory of them can still have psychological ramifications for the children (Phares & Renk, 1998). Including fathers in research and clinical work with paternal and maternal depression should help to elucidate the mechanisms through which emotional and behavioral problems in children develop.

REFERENCES

Atkinson, A. K., & Rickel, A. U. (1984). Postpartum depression in primiparous parents. *Journal of Abnormal Psychology, 93*, 115–119.

Beardslee, W. R. (1998). Prevention and the clinical encounter. *American Journal of Orthopsychiatry, 68*, 521–533.

Beardslee, W. R., Bemporad, J., Keller, M. B., & Klerman, G. L. (1983). Children of parents with a major affective disorder: A review. *American Journal of Psychiatry, 140*, 825–832.

Beardslee, W. R., Schultz, L. H., & Selman, R. L. (1987). Level of social–cognitive development, adaptive functioning, and DSM-III diagnoses in adolescent offspring of parents with affective disorders: Implications of the development of the capacity for mutuality. *Developmental Psychology, 23*, 807–815.

Beardslee, W. R., Versage, E. M., & Gladstone, T. R. G. (1998). Children of affectively ill parents: A review of the past 10 years. *Journal of the American Academy of Child and Adolescent Psychiatry, 37*, 1134–1141.

Becvar, D. S., & Becvar, R. J. (1993). *Family therapy: A systemic integration.* Boston: Allyn & Bacon.

Billings, A. G., & Moos, R. H. (1983). Comparisons of children of depressed and nondepressed parents: A social–environmental perspective. *Journal of Abnormal Child Psychology, 11*, 463–486.

Billings, A. G., & Moos, R. H. (1985). Children of parents with unipolar depression: A controlled 1-year follow-up. *Journal of Abnormal Child Psychology*, *14*, 149–166.

Biringen, Z., & Robinson, J. (1991). Emotional availability in mother–child interactions: A reconceptualization for research. *American Journal of Orthopsychiatry*, *61*, 258–271.

Bosco, G. L., Renk, K., Dinger, T. M., Epstein, M. K., & Phares, V. (1997, August). *Parental psychopathology and adolescents' perceptions of parents.* Poster presented at the Annual Convention of the American Psychological Association, Chicago, Illinois.

Brody, G. H. (1998). Sibling relationship quality: Its causes and consequences. *Annual Review of Psychology*, *49*, 1–24.

Brody, G. H., Stoneman, Z., & McCoy, J. K. (1994). Contributions of family relationships and child temperaments to longitudinal variation in sibling relationship quality and sibling relationship styles. *Journal of Family Psychology*, *8*, 274–286.

Carr, A. (1998). The inclusion of fathers in family therapy: A research based perspective. *Contemporary Family Therapy*, *20*, 371–383.

Carro, M. G., Grant, K. E., Gotlib, I. H., & Compas, B. E. (1993). Postpartum depression and child development: An investigation of mothers and fathers as sources of risk and resilience. *Development and Psychopathology*, *5*, 567–579.

Cicchetti, D., Rogosch, F. A., & Toth, S. L. (1997). Ontogenesis, depressotypic organization, and the depressive spectrum. In S. S. Luthar, J. A. Burack, D. Cicchetti, & J. R. Weisz (Eds.), *Developmental psychopathology: Perspectives on adjustment, risk, and disorder* (pp. 273–313). New York: Cambridge University Press.

Conrad, M., & Hammen, C. (1989). Role of maternal depression in perceptions of child maladjustment. *Journal of Consulting and Clinical Psychology*, *57*, 663–667.

Coyne, J. C. (1976). Toward an interactional description of depression. *Psychiatry*, *39*, 28–40.

Cummings, E. M., & Davies, P. (1994). *Children and marital conflict: The impact of family dispute and resolution.* New York: Guilford Press.

Dadds, M. R. (1995). *Families, children, and the development of dysfunction.* Thousand Oaks, CA: Sage Publications.

Daniels, D., & Moos, R. H. (1990). Assessing life stressors and social resources among adolescents: Applications to depressed youth. *Journal of Adolescent Research*, *5*, 268–289.

Dickstein, L. J., Stein, T. S., Pleck, J. H., Myers, M. F., Lewis, R. A., Duncan, S. F., & Brod, H. (1991). Men's changing social roles in the 1990's: Emerging issues in the psychiatric treatment of men. *Hospital and Community Psychiatry*, *42*, 701–705.

Dierker, L. C., Merikangas, K. R., & Szatmari, P. (1999). Influence of parental concordance for psychiatric disorders on psychopathology in offspring. *Journal of the American Academy of Child and Adolescent Psychiatry*, *38*, 280–288.

Downey, G., & Coyne, J. C. (1990). Children of depressed children: An integrative review. *Psychological Bulletin, 108,* 50–76.

Duhig, A. M., Renk, K., Epstein, M. K., & Phares, V. (2000). Interparental agreement on internalizing, externalizing, and total behavior problems: A meta-analysis. *Clinical Psychology: Science and Practice, 7,* 435–453.

Dunn, J. (1996). Brothers and sisters in middle childhood and early adolescence: Continuity and change in individual differences. In G. H. Brody (Ed.), *Sibling relationships: Their causes and consequences* (pp. 31–46). Norwood, NJ: Ablex.

el-Guebaly, N., Offord, D. R., Sullivan, K. T., & Lynch, G. W. (1978). Psychosocial adjustment of the offspring of psychiatric inpatients: The effect of alcoholic, depressive and schizophrenic parentage. *Canadian Psychiatric Association Journal, 23,* 281–289.

Epstein, M. K., Renk, K., Smith, A. M., Bosco, G. L., & Phares, V. (1998, August). *Interparental conflict and child adjustment: Convergent and discriminant validity.* Poster presented at the Annual Convention of the American Psychological Association, San Francisco, California.

Erel, O., & Burman, B. (1995). Interrelatedness of marital relations and parent–child relations: A meta-analytic review. *Psychological Bulletin, 118,* 108–132.

Fabes, R. A., & Eisenberg, N. (1992). Young children's coping with interpersonal anger. *Child Development, 63,* 116–128.

Fendrich, M., Warner, V., & Weissman, M. M. (1990). Family risk factors, parental depression, and psychopathology in offspring. *Developmental Psychology, 26,* 40–50.

Forehand, R., Biggar, H., & Kotchick, B. A. (1998). Cumulative risk across family stressors: Short- and long-term effects for adolescents. *Journal of Abnormal Child Psychology, 26,* 119–128.

Forehand, R., & Smith, K. A. (1986). Who depresses whom? A look at the relationship of adolescent mood to maternal and paternal mood. *Child Study Journal, 16,* 19–23.

Frankel, K. A., & Harmon, R. J. (1996). Depressed mothers: They don't always look as bad as they feel. *Journal of the American Academy of Child and Adolescent Psychiatry, 35,* 289–298.

Garmezy, N. (1989). The role of competence in the study of children and adolescents under stress. In B. H. Schneider & G. Attili (Eds.), *Social competence in developmental perspective* (pp. 25–39). Norwell, MA: Kluwer.

Goodman, S. H., Brogan, D., Lynch, M. E., & Fielding, B. (1993). Social and emotional competence in children of depressed mothers. *Child Development, 64,* 516–531.

Goodman, S. H., & Gotlib, I. H. (1999). Risk for psychopathology in the children of depressed mothers: A developmental model for understanding mechanisms of transmission. *Psychological Review, 106,* 458–490.

Gottman, J. M. (1998). Psychology and the study of marital processes. *Annual Review of Psychology, 49,* 169–197.

Grizenko, N., & Pawliuk, N. (1994). Risk and protective factors for disruptive behavior disorders in children. *American Journal of Orthopsychiatry, 64*, 534–544.

Haggerty, R. J., Sherrod, L. R., Garmezy, N., & Rutter, M. (1994). *Stress coping and development: Risk and resilience in children.* Cambridge, England: Cambridge University Press.

Hammen, C. (1991). *Depression runs in families: The social context of risk and resilience in children of depressed mothers.* New York: Springer-Verlag.

Hammen, C., Rudolph, K., Weisz, J., Rao, U., & Burge, D. (1999). The context of depression in clinic-referred youth: Neglected areas in treatment. *Journal of the American Academy of Child and Adolescent Psychiatry, 38*, 64–71.

Harjan, A. (1992). Children of parents with affective disorders: The role of an ill mother or an ill father. *European Journal of Psychiatry, 6*, 74–87.

Hecker, L. L. (1991). Where is Dad? 21 ways to involve fathers in family therapy. *Journal of Family Psychotherapy, 2*, 31–45.

Hops, H., Biglan, A., Sherman, L., Arthur, J., Friedman, L., & Osteen, V. (1987). Home observations of family interactions of depressed women. *Journal of Consulting and Clinical Psychology, 55*, 341–346.

Hossain, Z., Field, T., Gonzalez, J., Malphurs, J., Valle, C., & Pickens, J. (1994). Infants of depressed mothers interact better with their nondepressed fathers. *Infant Mental Health Journal, 15*, 348–357.

Huntley, D. K., & Phelps, R. E. (1990). Depression and social contacts of children from one-parent families. *Journal of Community Psychology, 18*, 66–72.

Jacob, T., & Johnson, S. L. (1997). Parent–child interaction among depressed fathers and mothers: Impact on child functioning. *Journal of Family Psychology, 11*, 391–409.

Jacob, T., Krahn, G. L., & Leonard, K. (1991). Parent–child interactions in families with alcoholic fathers. *Journal of Consulting and Clinical Psychology, 53*, 176–181.

Jacob, T., & Leonard, K. (1986). Psychosocial functioning in children of alcoholic fathers, depressed fathers and control fathers. *Journal of Studies on Alcohol, 47*, 373–380.

Jenkins, J. (1992). Sibling relationships in disharmonious homes: Potential difficulties and protective effects. In F. Boer & J. Dunn (Eds.), *Children's sibling relationships: Developmental and clinical issues* (pp. 125–138). Hillsdale, NJ: Erlbaum.

Kaslow, N. J., Deering, C. G., & Racusin, G. R. (1994). Depressed children and their families. *Clinical Psychology Review, 14*, 39–59.

Kaslow, N. J., & Thompson, M. P. (1998). Applying the criteria for empirically supported treatments to studies of psychosocial interventions for child and adolescent depression. *Journal of Clinical Child Psychology, 27*, 146–155.

Kaslow, N. J., Warner, V., John, K., & Brown, R. (1992). Intrainformant agreement and family functioning in depressed and nondepressed parents and their children. *The American Journal of Family Therapy, 20*, 204–217.

Keller, M. B., Beardslee, W. R., Dorer, D. J., Lavori, P. W., Samuelson, H., & Klerman, G. R. (1986). Impact of severity on chronicity of parental affective illness and adaptive functioning and psychopathology in children. *Archives of General Psychiatry, 43,* 930–937.

Klein, D. N., Clark, D. C., Dansky, L., & Margolis, E. T. (1988). Dysthymia in the offspring of parents with primary unipolar affective disorder. *Journal of Abnormal Psychology, 97,* 265–274.

Klein, D. N., Depue, R. A., & Slater, J. F. (1985). Cyclothymia in the adolescent offspring of parents with bipolar affective disorder. *Journal of Abnormal Psychology, 94,* 115–127.

Kovacs, M., Devlin, J. B., Pollack, M., Richards, C., & Mukerji, P. (1997). A controlled family history study of childhood-onset depressive disorder. *Archives of General Psychiatry, 54,* 613–623.

Lang, A. R., Pelham, W. E., Atkeson, B. M., & Murphy, D. A. (1999). Effects of alcohol intoxication on parenting behavior in interactions with child confederates exhibiting normal or deviant behaviors. *Journal of Abnormal Child Psychology, 27,* 177–189.

Lazar, A., Sagi, A., & Fraser, M. W. (1991). Involving fathers in social services. *Children and Youth Services Review, 13,* 287–300.

Lee, C. M., & Gotlib, I. H. (1991a). Adjustment of children of depressed mothers: A 10-month follow-up. *Journal of Abnormal Psychology, 100,* 473–477.

Lee, C. M., & Gotlib, I. H. (1991b). Family disruption, parental availability and child adjustment. In R. J. Prinz (Ed.), *Advances in behavioral assessment of children and families* (pp. 171–199). Bristol, PA: Jessica Kingsley Publisher Ltd.

Lum, J. J., & Phares, V. (1999, August). *Assessing emotional availability of parents: Child, adolescent, and parent perceptions.* Poster presented at the Annual Convention of the American Psychological Association, Boston, Massachusetts.

Marchand, J. F., & Hock, E. (1998). The relation of problem behaviors in preschool children to depressive symptoms in mothers and fathers. *The Journal of Genetic Psychology, 159,* 353–366.

Masten, A. S., & Coatsworth, J. D. (1998). The development of competence in favorable and unfavorable environments: Lessons from research on successful children. *American Psychologist, 53,* 205–220.

McLeod, J. D. (1993). Spouse concordance for depressive disorders in a community sample. *Journal of Affective Disorders, 15,* 43–52.

Merikangas, K., & Spiker, D. (1982). Assortative mating among inpatients with primary affective disorder. *Psychological Medicine, 12,* 753–764.

Merikangas, K., Weissman, M., Prusoff, B. A., & John, K. (1988). Assortative mating and affective disorders: Psychopathology in offspring. *Psychiatry, 51,* 48–57.

Nichols, W. C. (1996). *Treating people in families: An integrative framework.* New York: Guilford Press.

Orvaschel, H. (1990). Early onset psychiatric disorder in high risk children and increased familial morbidity. *Journal of the American Academy of Child and Adolescent Psychiatry, 29,* 184–188.

Orvaschel, H., Walsh-Allis, G., & Ye, W. (1988). Psychopathology in children of parents with recurrent depression. *Journal of Abnormal Child Psychology, 16,* 17–28.

Pelham, W. E., & Lang, A. R. (1993). Parental alcohol consumption and deviant child behavior: Laboratory studies of reciprocal effects. *Clinical Psychology Review, 13,* 763–784.

Pelham, W. E., Lang, A. R., Atkeson, B. M., Murphy, D. A., Gnagy, E. M., Greiner, A. R., Vodde-Hamilton, M., & Greenslade, K. E. (1997). Effects of deviant child behavior on parental distress and alcohol consumption in laboratory interactions. *Journal of Abnormal Child Psychology, 25,* 413–424.

Phares, V. (1992). Where's Poppa? The relative lack of attention to the role of fathers in child and adolescent psychopathology. *American Psychologist, 47,* 656–664.

Phares, V. (1996). *Fathers and developmental psychopathology.* New York: Wiley.

Phares, V., Blum, A. B., & Williams, T. Y. (1997, June). *Child and adolescent competence and self-esteem: The relation with parental psychopathology.* Poster presented at the Eighth Scientific Meeting of the International Society for Research in Child and Adolescent Psychopathology, Paris, France.

Phares, V., & Compas, B. (1992). The role of fathers in child and adolescent psychopathology: Make room for daddy. *Psychological Bulletin, 111,* 387–412.

Phares, V., & Compas, B. (1993). Fathers and developmental psychopathology. *Current Directions in Psychological Science, 2,* 162–165.

Phares, V., Compas, B. E., & Howell, D. C. (1989). Perspectives on child behavior problems: Comparisons of children's self-reports with parent and teacher reports. *Psychological Assessment: A Journal of Consulting and Clinical Psychology, 1,* 68–71.

Phares, V., & Lum, J. J. (1997). Clinically referred children and adolescents: Fathers, family constellations, and other demographic factors. *Journal of Clinical Child Psychology, 26,* 216–223.

Phares, V., & Renk, K. (1998). Perceptions of parents: A measure of adolescents' feelings about their parents. *Journal of Marriage and the Family, 60,* 646–659.

Puig-Antich, J., Kaufman, J., Ryan, N. D., Williamson, D., Dahl, R. E., Lukens, E., Todak, G., Ambrosini, P., Rabinovich, H., & Nelson, B. (1993). The psychosocial functioning and family environment of depressed adolescents. *Journal of the American Academy of Child and Adolescent Psychiatry, 32,* 244–253.

Radke-Yarrow, M., Cummings, E. M., Kuczynski, L., & Chapman, M. (1985). Patterns of attachment in two- and three-year-olds in normal families and families with parental depression. *Child Development, 56,* 884–893.

Radke-Yarrow, M., Nottelmann, E., Martinez, P., Fox, M. B., & Belmont, B. (1992). Young children of affectively ill parents: A longitudinal study of psychosocial development. *Journal of the American Academy of Child and Adolescent Psychiatry, 31,* 68–77.

Radke-Yarrow, M., & Zahn-Waxler, C. (1990). Research on affectively ill parents: Some considerations for theory and research on normal development. *Development and Psychopathology, 2,* 349–366.

Reid, W. J., & Crisafulli, A. (1990). Marital discord and child behavior problems: A meta-analysis. *Journal of Abnormal Child Psychology, 18,* 105–117.

Rende, R., & Weissman, M. M. (1999). Sibling aggregation for psychopathology in offspring of opiate addicts: Effects of parental comorbidity. *Journal of Clinical Child Psychology, 28,* 342–348.

Rende, R., Wickramaratne, P., Warner, V., & Weissman, M. M. (1995). Sibling resemblance for psychiatric disorders in offspring at high and low risk for depression. *Journal of Child Psychology and Psychiatry, 36,* 1353–1363.

Renk, K., Phares, V., & Epps, J. (1999). The relationship between parental anger and behavior problems in children and adolescents. *Journal of Family Psychology, 13,* 209–227.

Rutter, M. (1990a). Commentary: Some focus and process considerations regarding effects of depression on children. *Developmental Psychology, 26,* 60–67.

Rutter, M. (1990b). Psychosocial resilience and protective mechanisms. In J. Rolf, A. S. Masten, D. Cicchetti, K. H. Nuechterlein, & S. Weintraub (Eds.), *Risk and protective factors in the development of psychopathology* (pp. 181–214). New York: Cambridge University Press.

Sameroff, A. J., Seifer, R., & Bartko, W. T. (1997). Environmental perspectives on adaptation during childhood and adolescence. In S. S. Luthar, J. A. Burack, D. Cicchetti, & J. R. Weisz (Eds.), *Developmental psychopathology: Perspectives on adjustment, risk, and disorder* (pp. 507–526). New York: Cambridge University Press.

Schakel, J. A. (1987). Emotional neglect and stimulus deprivation. In M. R. Brassard, R. Germain, & S. N. Hart (Eds.), *Psychological maltreatment of children and youth* (pp. 100–109). New York: Pergammon Press.

Smith, A. M., Williams, R., & Phares, V. (2000, August). *Parental involvement in treatment: A survey of clinicians.* Poster presented at the Annual Convention of the American Psychological Association, Washington, DC.

Teichman, Y., & Teichman, M. (1990). Interpersonal view of depression. *Journal of Family Psychology, 3,* 349–367.

Thomas, A. M., & Forehand, R. (1991). The relationship between paternal depressive mood and early adolescent functioning. *Journal of Family Psychology, 4,* 260–271.

Voydanoff, P., & Donnelly, B. W. (1998). Parents' risk and protective factors as prediction of parental well-being and behavior. *Journal of Marriage and the Family, 60,* 344–355.

Voydanoff, P., & Donnelly, B. W. (1999). Risk and protective factors for psychological adjustment and grades among adolescents. *Journal of Family Issues, 20,* 328–349.

Warner, V., Weissman, M. M., Mufson, L., & Wickramaratne, P. J. (1999). Grandparents, parents, and grandchildren at high risk for depression: A three-generation study. *Journal of the American Academy of Child and Adolescent Psychiatry, 38*, 289–296.

Werner, E. E. (1993). Risk, resilience, and recovery: Perspectives from the Kauai Longitudinal Study. *Development and Psychopathology, 5*, 503–515.

Zahn-Waxler, C., Cummings, E. M., McKnew, D. H., & Radke-Yarrow, M. (1984). Altruism, aggression, and social interactions in young children with a manic–depressive parent. *Child Development, 55*, 112–122.

10

CHILDREN COPING WITH PARENTAL DEPRESSION: PROCESSES OF ADAPTATION TO FAMILY STRESS

BRUCE E. COMPAS, ADELA M. LANGROCK, GARY KELLER,
MARY JANE MERCHANT, AND MARY ELLEN COPELAND

Depression is both the consequence of stressful events and a significant source of psychosocial stress for depressed individuals and their families. Considerable evidence now shows that depressive symptoms, as well as the onset and recurrence of depressive disorders, are associated with exposure to stressful life events and chronic strains in the environment (e.g., Hammen, Burge, Burney, & Adrian, 1990; Lewinsohn, Allen, Seeley, & Gotlib, 1999). It has also been established that depression contributes to the occurrence of stressful events and chronic strains, primarily in the context of the disrupted and stressful interpersonal relationships of depressed individuals (e.g., Hammen, Davila, Brown, Ellicott, & Gitlin, 1992). As such, depression is associated with significant interpersonal demands and challenges for depressed individuals and for those who live with them.

Nowhere is the relationship between stress and depression more evident than in families in which a mother or father suffers from depression.

Preparation of this chapter was supported by a grant from the Garfield Foundation of Kaiser Permanente Health Care.

Parental depression is a source of significant stress for children, and familial stress constitutes a significant risk for the development of psychopathology in these children (Hammen, 1997). This kind of stress is particularly pernicious for children of depressed parents. Because stress is an important mediator of the impact of parental depression on children's adjustment, it is axiomatic that the ways children respond to and cope with this kind of stress are also potentially important mediators of children's adjustment. It follows that it will be important to understand how children try to cope with family stress related to parental depression.

Despite the importance of understanding children's coping with parental depression, only a few studies of this issue have appeared in the literature (Klimes-Dougan & Bolger, 1998; Radke-Yarrow, 1998; Radke-Yarrow & Brown, 1993). As Hammen (1997) observed: "It must be emphasized that there are very few data on the topic of coping among children of depressed parents, and virtually no studies in which offspring have been asked what they did to try to deal with parental disturbance or related stressors" (p. 149). To address this gap, we present initial findings from an ongoing program of research on the ways that children cope with parental depression. Drawing on the reports of both parents and children, our findings suggest that certain types of involuntary stress responses and specific volitional coping responses mediate the impact of parental depression on child adjustment. We highlight the implications of these findings for interventions to help families cope with parental depression.

PARENTAL DEPRESSION AS A RISK FACTOR FOR CHILD PSYCHOPATHOLOGY

The first generation of research on parental depression established the significance of emotional and behavioral problems of children of depressed parents. Research by Beardslee, Cummings, Gotlib, Hammen, Weissman, and others provided compelling evidence that children who are raised by a parent, typically their mother, who suffers from a depressive disorder are at risk for depression themselves (e.g., Beardslee et al., 1988; Cummings & Davies, 1994; Hammen, 1991; Lee & Gotlib, 1991; Weissman et al., 1987). Furthermore, the problems manifested by children of depressed parents are not limited to depression; these children are also at risk for other internalizing problems (e.g., anxiety, somatic symptoms) and for externalizing disorders, including aggression, conduct problems, and oppositional behavior problems (Anderson & Hammen, 1993). Although less compelling, evidence also suggests that depression in fathers as well as in mothers is associated with maladjustment in children (Jacob & Johnson, 1997; Phares & Compas, 1992). This first wave of research was essential in calling attention to parental depression as a major, but previously neglected, risk factor for child psychopathology.

As evidence of the significant risks associated with growing up with a parent who is depressed has accumulated, researchers have turned increased attention to possible mediators and moderators of the relationship between parental depression and children's emotional and behavioral problems. Goodman and Gotlib (1999) have provided a conceptual framework that can serve as a guide for research on the mechanisms of risk associated with parental depression. Important factors include genetic transmission of vulnerability to depression; innate dysfunctional neuroregulatory mechanisms; exposure to parents' negative cognitions, affect, and behavior; and child vulnerabilities, including skill deficits or maladaptive styles or behavioral tendencies. The mediator that has received the most attention, and for which evidence is currently the strongest, involves stress processes within the family.

STRESS AS A MEDIATOR OF PARENTAL DEPRESSION AND CHILD PSYCHOPATHOLOGY

Hammen's seminal research on stress and parental depression is summarized in chapter 8 of this volume. Several aspects of this research have particularly important implications for the potential role of coping processes (Hammen, 1992). The symptoms of depression manifested by a parent lead to disruptions in parenting and in parent–child interactions that are stressful for children. Depressed parents are more likely than nondepressed parents to display irritability or anger in interactions with their children, to worry and be overly intrusive in their children's activities, and to withdraw and be unresponsive to their children (e.g., Gelfand & Teti, 1990; Malphurs et al., 1996). Parental depression is also strongly associated with marital conflict and discord, contributing to another source of stress in children's home environments (Cummings & Davies, 1992; Fendrich, Warner, & Weissman, 1990). Taken together, these interactions suggest that parental depression is associated with a pattern of parenting that is negative, inconsistent, unpredictable, and unsupportive. Furthermore, stressors associated with parental depression are a consequence of the parent's depressive symptoms or disorder, and as such they are likely to be beyond the control of children in these families.

In addition to these significant stressors within the family, children of depressed parents are exposed to stressors outside of the family. Anderson and Hammen (1993) have shown that children of depressed parents are significantly more likely than other children to experience stressful events such as peer conflict and academic failures that are at least in part a result of their own behavior and characteristics. An increased level of conflict with peers is a salient example of stress that is at least in part dependent on characteristics of the child and therefore potentially under the child's control. Thus, it is important to understand how children cope with stress that emanates from their parents' depression as well as stress from outside the family that may be at least in part the result of child characteristics.

COPING AS A MEDIATOR OF STRESS PROCESSES

The identification of stress as a mediator of parental depression and child psychopathology leads to a series of questions regarding the ways that children in these families may respond to and cope with stress. First, what are the specific types of stress within and outside the family that threaten and challenge the well being of children of depressed parents? Second, how do children cope with these stressors? Third, do children's coping responses mediate the relationship between stress and children's adjustment in families of depressed parents? Before addressing these questions, we briefly consider several broader issues in the conceptualization and nature of the ways that children cope with and respond to stress.

Defining Coping and Stress Responses

Our research is guided by a conceptual framework in which *coping* is defined as "conscious volitional effort to regulate emotion, thought, behavior, physiology, and the environment in response to stressful events or circumstances" (Compas, Connor-Smith, Saltzman, Thomsen, & Wadsworth, 2001; p. 89). Regulation involves a broad array of responses, including efforts to initiate, terminate or delay, modify or change, reorient, or modulate the amount or intensity of a thought, emotion, behavior, or physiological reaction. These regulatory processes both draw on and are constrained by the biological, cognitive, social, and emotional development of the individual (Compas, 1998).

Within this model, coping and other stress responses are distinguished along two broad dimensions—voluntary versus involuntary responses, and engagement versus disengagement (Compas, Connor-Smith, Osowiecki, & Welch, 1997; Compas et al., 2001). Voluntary responses (or coping) are within conscious awareness and are experienced as under the individual's volitional control. Involuntary stress responses are experienced as automatic and not under personal control, and they can occur within or outside of conscious awareness. The distinction between controlled or volitional responses and automatic or involuntary responses is supported by a wide range of empirical evidence, including research on associative conditioning and learning (Shiffrin, 1997; Shiffrin & Schneider, 1977); research on cognitive processes in emotions and emotional disorders (Gotlib & Neubauer, 2000; Mathews & MacLeod, 1994; McNally, 1995); research distinguishing temperamental characteristics from intentional behavior and cognitive processes (Rothbart, 1991);

and research on social cognition (e.g., Bargh, 1997; Mischel, 1997). For example, threatening cues in the environment, which are experienced as stressful and therefore may initiate coping behavior, are processed on both an automatic, uncontrolled level as well as a controlled, strategic level (Mathews & MacLeod, 1994). Researchers have recently begun to examine these two levels of processing in children (e.g., Daleiden & Vasey, 1997; Vasey, El-Hag, & Daleiden, 1996). Both voluntary and involuntary stress responses can be further distinguished as engaging with a stressor or one's responses to the stressor, or disengaging from the stressor or one's responses. The origins of the engagement–disengagement dimension can be found in the concept of the fight (engagement) or flight (disengagement) response (e.g., Cannon, 1933, 1934; Gray, 1991) and in the contrast between approach and avoidance responses (Krohne, 1996).

Coping responses are further distinguished by the orientation of the individual to either enhance a sense of personal control over the environment and one's reactions (*primary control coping*), to adapt to the environment (*secondary control coping*), or to *disengage* from the environment (e.g., Rudolph, Dennig, & Weisz, 1995). *Primary control coping* refers to coping attempts that are directed toward influencing objective events or conditions or directly regulating one's emotions, such as problem solving or regulated emotional expression. Whether directed at the source of stress or one's emotional response, primary control coping responses involve taking direct action to change the situation or the self, including directly changing one's emotions. *Secondary control coping* involves efforts to fit with or adapt to the environment and includes responses such as acceptance and cognitive restructuring. The primary–secondary control distinction has been used to describe both the nature of coping responses themselves, as well as the goals underlying the responses (Rudolph et al., 1995). Disengagement coping may reflect the relinquishment of efforts to achieve either primary or secondary control.

Empirical support for this model has come from several recent studies of adolescents coping with a range of stressors. Connor-Smith, Compas, Wadsworth, Thomsen, and Saltzman (2000) used confirmatory factor analyses to test the model and found support for the broad distinction between volitional coping and involuntary responses to stress. Volitional coping responses were further distinguished into three factors consistent with the model described above: *primary control coping* (problem solving, emotional expression, emotional modulation), *secondary control coping* (cognitive restructuring, positive thinking, acceptance, distraction), and *disengagement coping* (wishful thinking, denial). Involuntary stress responses formed two factors, *involuntary engagement* (intrusive thoughts, rumination, emotional arousal, physiological arousal, impulsive action) and *involuntary disengagement* (avoidance, escape, emotional numbing, cognitive interference).

Additional support has come from studies of adolescents coping with interpersonal stress (Connor-Smith & Compas, in press), economic strain and family conflict (Wadsworth & Compas, 2000), recurrent pain (Thomsen, Compas, Colletti, Stanger, Boyer, & Konik, 2000), and a sample of Navajo youth coping with peer stressors (Reichman, Wadsworth, Benson, & Compas, 2000). Ayers, Sandler, West, and Roosa (1996) reported similar findings and identified four factors in children's coping responses: active coping (cognitive decision making, direct problem solving, seeking understanding, positive cognitive restructuring), social support (emotion focused support, problem focused support), distraction (distracting action, physical release of energy), and avoidance (cognitive avoidance, avoidant action). Similarly, Walker, Smith, Garber, and Van Slyke (1997) identified three factors that they used to develop a measure of coping with pediatric pain—active coping (e.g., problem solving, social support), passive coping (e.g., self-isolation, disengagement), and accommodative coping (e.g., acceptance, distract/ ignore). These studies generally converge on three aspects of coping that parallel the distinction between primary control coping (or active coping), secondary control coping (or distraction or accommodative coping), and disengagement coping (or avoidance or passive coping).

Vermont Raising Healthy Children Project

We now turn our attention to how children cope with parental depression. We have been involved in the development and evaluation of a family-focused preventive intervention (Raising Healthy Children) for children of depressed parents (see Keller, Copeland, Compas, Langrock, & Merchant, 2000, for a description of the intervention and its implementation). This project offered an opportunity to study the types of stressors that face children of depressed parents and the ways that children cope with these stressors. Only three previous studies have examined how children cope with parental depression, and their findings have been inconclusive. Radke-Yarrow (1998; Radke-Yarrow & Brown, 1993) reported on the general coping efforts of children dealing with parental depression. Analyses comparing coping strategies with later behavioral adjustment revealed no significant differences in the general coping efforts for subsequently resilient and troubled youths. Comparing children of depressed and well mothers, Klimes-Dougan and Bolger (1998) also reported no significant differences in children's general coping styles. However, these studies may have been limited by problems with the methods used to assess children's coping. The authors focused their analyses on two scales from a measure of children's coping that are labeled *internalizing* (e.g., crying about a problem) and *externalizing* (e.g., ventilating one's anger about a problem) coping (Causey & Dubow, 1992). Both of these scales are somewhat confounded with symptoms of emotional and behavioral problems, and neither represents the regulation or modulation of cognition, emotion, or behavior. As a consequence, it is not surprising that these studies did not identify coping responses to parental depression that may have been adaptive. In our ongoing research, we have examined the dimensions of primary control coping, secondary control coping, and disengagement coping, providing a more detailed sampling of children's self-regulation.

We describe the participants in the present study, the types of stressors they have reported, the ways the children have attempted to cope with these stressors, and the role of coping as a mediator of the association between stress and children's adjustment. Throughout this research we have obtained reports of stress, coping, and adjustment from parents and their adolescent children, allowing for comparisons across these two important sources of information (see Compas, Langrock, Keller, & Merchant, 2000, and Langrock, Compas, Keller, Merchant, & Copeland, 2000a, 2000b, for detailed reports of these findings).

Sample Characteristics

Participants in this study included 59 adults (51 mothers, 8 fathers) who met criteria for major depression or dysthymia and 94 children from these families (M = 2.3 children per family) between the ages of 7 and 18 years (M = 11.5) evenly divided between boys and girls. Parents were in their mid to late 40s (fathers M = 48.9 years, mothers M = 42.6 years) and were primarily Caucasian and of middle socioeconomic status. Sixty-four percent of the depressed parents were married, 29% were either divorced or separated, and 7% were single.

The families participating in this study were part of a longitudinal project evaluating an intervention to help families cope with parental depression (Keller et al., 2000) and were recruited primarily through direct member mailings to Vermont Kaiser Permanente Family Health Care members, newspaper advertisements, and physician referral. Families were considered eligible for this study if at least one parent met diagnostic criteria for major depressive disorder (MDD) or dysthymia either currently or within the lifetime of their child and if the index parent lived with and parented at least one child between the ages of 7 and 18 years. Interviews were conducted with identified parents to assess criteria of the fourth edition of the *Diagnostic and Statistical Manual of Mental Disorders* (*DSM–IV*; American Psychiatric Association, 1994) for major depression and dysthymia using the *DSM–IV* Checklist Interview (adapted from the third revised Diagnostic and Statistical Manual of Mental Disorders [*DSM–III–R*] Checklist; American Psychiatric Association, 1987; Hudziak et al., 1993). All of the identified parents met the criteria for MDD (96%), dysthymia (2%), or both (2%). At the time of the initial assessment, 39% of the parents met criteria for a current depressive episode and 61% met criteria for lifetime depressive disorder. For parents diagnosed with lifetime depressive disorder, 80% experienced a depressive episode within the past 2 years (range = 1.5 months to 3 years). The mean for parents' self-reports of current levels of depressive symptoms on the

Beck Depression Inventory–II (BDI-II; Beck, Streer, Ball, & Ranieri, 1996) was 19.6 (SD = 10.5). Although inclusion in the study was not dependent on current (i.e., during the past 2 weeks) levels of depressive symptoms, 32% of the identified parents reported moderate depressive symptoms (scores of 20 to 28), and 19% reported severe levels of current depressive symptoms (scores of 29 or greater).

Parents reported that their children exhibited moderate to high levels of anxiety–depression symptoms (mean T score of 60, which is one standard deviation above the normative mean) and moderately elevated levels of aggression (mean T score of 58) on the Child Behavior Checklist (CBCL; Achenbach, 1991). Compared to the normative data for the CBCL, the percentages of children scoring above the clinical cut-off (i.e., the 98th percentile) were 15% for anxious and depressed symptoms and 12% for aggressive symptoms. Adolescents (ages 11–18 years old; n = 55) reported moderate to significant symptoms of anxiety–depression (mean T score of 57) and aggressive behavior problems (mean T score of 57) on the Youth Self-Report (YSR; Achenbach, 1991). Based on the normative data for the YSR, 9% of the adolescents exceeded the clinical cut-off for anxiety–depression symptoms and 9% exceeded the cut-off for aggressive behavior problems. Thus, consistent with previous research on rates of psychopathology for children of depressed parents, the rate of internalizing and externalizing problems was approximately 6 to 7 times higher than in a normative population (according to parents' reports) and 4 to 5 times higher than the expected rate (according to adolescents' self-reports; Achenbach, 1991). Parents' ratings of their children's anxiety–depression symptoms and aggression behaviors on the CBCL did not differ for parents above or below the cut-off for moderate to severe depressive symptoms on the BDI-II, $t(91) = -.48, p > .10$, for anxiety–depression and $t(93) = -.62, p > .10$, for aggression. This is consistent with previous research, which has found that current levels of parents' depressive symptoms were not associated with inflated reports of their children's problems (Richters, 1992).

Sources of Stress Associated With Parental Depression

The first question of interest focused on stress processes within these families that might be associated with a parent's depression. Although previous research has clearly established that stressors within the family are associated with parental depression, the exact nature of these stressors has not been well documented. Hammen (1997) proposed that parental depression may manifest itself in different subtypes, the most salient being dysphoric withdrawal (a parent who is tearful, slow, withdrawn, quiet) and hostility (a parent who is irritable, restless, complaining, demanding). Gelfand and Teti (1990) described these two subtypes as follows: "a depressed mother whose caregiving is manifested by anger, rejection, and harsh, capricious discipline might have a different impact on a child's self-esteem and behavior than one

[who] is characteristically apathetic, self-absorbed, tearful, and irresolute as a disciplinarian" (p. 342). However, we are not aware of any studies that have measured specific stressors related to parental withdrawal as opposed to parental intrusiveness. In addition, there is extensive evidence that parental depression is also associated with elevated levels of marital conflict, which may represent another important source of stress for children in these families (Cummings & Davies, 1992).

We examined the types of stress associated with parental depression by presenting parents and their adolescent children with a list of 11 stressors that reflect parental withdrawal, parental intrusiveness, and marital conflict, three areas of parenting behavior previous research has shown to be affected by parental depression (Downey & Coyne, 1990; Gelfand & Teti, 1990; Malphurs et al., 1996). Examples of items from the parents' report form (parallel items were presented to adolescents) are presented in Exhibit 10.1. Several findings in the reports were striking (Langrock et al., 2000a, 2000b). All of the children and adolescents in these families were faced with stressors related to both parental withdrawal and parental intrusiveness, and most children and adolescents were faced with parental conflict. Mean levels of stressors reported by both parents and adolescents indicated that the adolescents were exposed to moderate levels of parental withdrawal, intrusiveness, and marital conflict in the past 6 months. Parental withdrawal stressors and parental intrusiveness stressors were significantly correlated in both parents' reports ($r = .42$, $p < .01$) and adolescents' reports ($r = .43$, $p < .01$). Parents' reports of withdrawal and marital conflict, but not their reports of intrusiveness, were significantly correlated with their current depressive symptoms on the BDI-II, indicating that parental withdrawal and marital conflict may increase with the level of depressive symptoms. The validity of the reports of the occurrence of these stressors is supported by the significant correlations between parents' and adolescents' reports of intrusiveness ($r = .53$, $p < .01$), marital conflict ($r = .46$, $p < .01$), and parental withdrawal ($r = .26$, $p < .05$). Adolescents rated these stressors as moderately stressful when they occurred, suggesting that these types of interactions constitute sources of chronic, low-level stress within the home. Furthermore, adolescents reported that they had relatively little control over these stressors, with a mean score of 2.19 (very little control) on a 5-point scale ($1 = $ *no control* and $5 = $ *a great deal control*). Thus, these stressors reflect chronic, uncontrollable stress in the family environments of children of depressed parents.

Consistent with previous research, the level of stress associated with both parental withdrawal and parental intrusiveness was associated with higher symptoms of both anxiety–depression and aggressive behavior for the children (Langrock et al., 2000a, 2000b). Significant correlations were found both for parents' reports of stress and their children's emotional and behavioral problems on the CBCL (correlations ranged from .22 to .32, $p < .05$) and adolescents' reports of stress and their own emotional and behavioral

EXHIBIT 10.1
Parental Withdrawal, Parental Intrusiveness, and Family Conflict Stressors
(Parent Report Form)

Parental Withdrawal
  My child wishes that I would spend more time with her.
  My child thinks I don't listen or pay attention to things happening in her life.
  My child sees me crying a lot or acting sad.
  My child thinks that I don't want to do things as a family.
Parental Intrusiveness
  My child thinks I am too upset, tense, grouchy, angry, and easily frustrated.
  My child thinks I worry about bad things happening to him.
  When my child asks me for something, she is unsure how I will react.
  Sometimes, I make my child feel responsible for the way I feel.
Marital Conflict
  My child hears her parents arguing about things.
  My child thinks her parents have a hard time getting along.
  Her father and I have a hard time talking to each other.

problems as reported on the YSR (correlations ranged from .28 to .56, $p <$ .05). However, it is noteworthy that marital conflict stressors were not correlated with symptoms of anxiety–depression or aggression in either parents' or adolescents' reports.

These findings present a closer look at the type and level of stressors that children and adolescents in this sample experienced as a result of their parent's depression. Others have hypothesized that children of depressed parents might be exposed to either parental withdrawal or parental intrusiveness, perhaps as a consequence of different subtypes in the manifestation of a parent's depression (Gelfand & Teti, 1990; Hammen, 1997). All of the children in our sample had parents who were withdrawn and unavailable as well as intrusive and irritable in their interactions with their children. Although the data do not allow for analyses of how these parenting behaviors occurred over time, they suggest a pattern in which depressed parents vacillate between withdrawing from their children and engaging with them in a hostile and irritable manner. This pattern is likely to undermine children's feelings of security and closeness within the family, provide little in the way of warmth and support, undermine children's feelings of their own worth, and provide inconsistent structure and discipline. Stressors related to parental withdrawal were correlated with the parents' current depressive symptoms, suggesting that withdrawal and unavailability may increase during a depressive episode. It is noteworthy that levels of parental conflict in these families were relatively low and were not significantly correlated with parental withdrawal and parental intrusiveness. In light of previous research showing the impact of parental conflict and discord on the adjustment of children of depressed parents (Cummings & Davies, 1992; Fendrich et al., 1990), it appears that our measure of marital conflict did not adequately capture the types of conflict and discord that are most salient in families of depressed parents.

Children's Coping With Family Stressors

Having considered the specific types of stressors that confront children of depressed parents, we can now examine the ways that children respond to and cope with these stressors. We have assessed adolescents' self-reports and parents' reports of child and adolescent coping and involuntary stress responses with the parental depression version of the Responses to Stress Questionnaire (RSQ; Connor-Smith et al., 2000). Both the adolescent self-report and parent report versions of the RSQ contain 60 items that ask respondents to report how they (or their child) responded during the past 6 months to the any of the 11 stressors related to parental depression that they endorsed. As described above, confirmatory factor analyses of the RSQ have identified five primary factors: primary control coping, secondary control coping, disengagement coping, involuntary engagement, and involuntary disengagement (Connor-Smith et al., 2000). Involuntary responses, as contrasted with coping (voluntary) responses, are experienced or perceived as not within the child's control. Examples of items from the parent report version are presented in Exhibit 10.2.

Comparisons between the five types of coping and stress responses in parents' reports revealed significant differences in their relative use, with involuntary engagement responses (e.g., rumination, emotional arousal, physiological arousal) reported most frequently, primary control coping (e.g., problem solving, emotional regulation) and involuntary disengagement (e.g., emotional numbing, escape) least frequently, and secondary control coping (e.g., acceptance, positive thinking) and disengagement coping (e.g., avoidance, denial) falling in the middle. Similar analyses of adolescents' reports on the RSQ indicated that involuntary engagement and secondary control coping were reported most frequently, primary control coping and involuntary disengagement were reported least frequently, with disengagement coping falling in the middle. These data indicate that children and adolescents used all three types of coping to try to manage stress associated with their parents' depression, and they displayed involuntary responses that were characterized as both engaging with and disengaging from stress. The relatively high levels of rumination and arousal (involuntary engagement) suggest that these children and adolescents were relatively ineffective in regulating their cognitive, emotional, and physiological responses to the stressors associated with parental depression.

An important question in examining parent and adolescent reports of adolescents' coping involves the degree of correspondence across the reports of these two informants (Langrock et al., 2000a). Cross-informant correlations provide an important source of criterion validity in the measurement of children's coping (Compas et al., 2001). It is noteworthy that correlations between parent and adolescent reports were positive and greater than .30 in magnitude for all five factors on the RSQ (rs ranged from .34 for involuntary

EXHIBIT 10.2
Coping and Involuntary Stress Responses: Scales and Sample Items
(Parent Report Form)

Primary Control Coping
  Problem solving (e.g., she tries to think of different ways to change the problem)
  Emotional expression (e.g., she lets someone or something know how she feels)
  Emotional modulation (e.g., she does something to calm herself down)
Secondary Control Coping
  Positive thinking (e.g., he tells himself that everything will be all right)
  Cognitive restructuring (e.g., he tells himself that things could be worse)
  Acceptance (e.g., he just takes things as they are, he goes with the flow)
  Distraction (e.g., he imagines something really fun or exciting happening in his
    life).
Disengagement Coping
  Avoidance (e.g., she tries not to think about it, to forget all about it)
  Denial (e.g., she tries to believe it never happened)
  Wishful thinking (e.g., she deals with the problem by wishing it would just go
    away)
Involuntary Engagement
  Rumination (e.g., he can't stop thinking about how he is feeling)
  Intrusive thoughts (e.g., thoughts just pop into his head)
  Emotional arousal (e.g., he get upset by things that don't usually bother him)
  Physiological arousal (e.g., he feels it in his body)
  Impulsive action (e.g., sometimes he acts without thinking)
Involuntary Disengagement
  Emotional numbing (e.g., she doesn't feel anything at all, it's like she has no
    emotions)
  Cognitive interference (e.g., her mind goes blank, she can't think at all)
  Inaction (e.g., she just freezes, she can't do anything)
  Escape (e.g., she just has to get away).

disengagement to .52 for primary control coping; all $ps < .05$). Thus, even though parental reports of their children's coping were obtained from parents with a history of past or current depression, their reports showed moderate correspondence with those of their children. Moreover, correspondence between parent and child reports for measures of relatively unobservable coping responses (e.g., cognitive restructuring) were equal in magnitude to more directly observable behaviors (e.g., emotional expression). As a point of comparison, these correlations compared quite favorably with the correlations of parent reports on the CBCL and adolescent reports on the YSR of anxiety–depression symptoms ($r = .35, p < .01$) and aggressive behavior problems ($r = .33, p < .02$). The degree of correspondence between informants for measures of coping and psychopathology is consistent with Richters (1992) conclusion that parental depression was not associated with elevated reports of child behavior problems.

Associations Among Family Stressors and Coping

The findings that we have reported thus far indicate that children and adolescents in families of depressed parents are exposed to a variety of stressors and that they respond with a range of coping strategies and involuntary stress responses. We now examine the association between the amount of stress that children and adolescents faced and the ways that they coped with and responded to stress (Langrock et al., 2000a, 2000b). Previous research on the relationship between stress and coping responses has suggested that increased exposure to stress disrupts more complex forms of cognitive functioning, interferes with more complex forms of coping such as primary and secondary control coping, and is associated with an increase in disengagement coping responses (Matthews & Wells, 1997). That is, as stressor load increases, the demands made on the individual interfere with cognitive functioning. The results of correlation analyses of both parental reports and adolescent reports in this sample are consistent with this pattern: Children and adolescents who were exposed to high levels of parental stressors, compared with children exposed to low parental stress, were lower in their use of primary and secondary control coping and were higher in the use of disengagement coping. Furthermore, exposure to more stress was related to higher levels of involuntary engagement and disengagement stress responses. Specifically, in parents' reports, stressors related to both parental withdrawal and intrusiveness were inversely related to primary and secondary control engagement (correlations ranged from −.28 to −.43, $p < .05$) and positively correlated with disengagement coping ($rs = .26$ and .31, $p < .05$). Similarly, in adolescents' reports parental withdrawal and intrusiveness stressors were correlated with less secondary control coping ($rs = −.37$ and −.52, $ps < .01$, respectively) and more involuntary engagement and involuntary disengagement responses ($rs = .26–.57$, $p < .05$). Thus, children exposed to higher levels of stress used fewer potentially adaptive coping strategies and reported more maladaptive stress responses.

These data present a disconcerting picture of stress and coping processes for children of depressed parents. As stress levels in these families increase, it may become increasingly important for children to be able to increase their efforts to regulate their thoughts, emotions, and behavior. However, it appears that as stress increases in these families the opposite pattern occurs—under higher stress, children and adolescents are less able to engage in self-regulatory responses that could help them to adjust to family stress. The ineffectualness of self-regulatory responses is further reflected in the heightened levels of involuntary engagement and disengagement responses under increased stress. Thus, children of depressed parents may be doubly at risk as a consequence of exposure to stress and the disruption of adaptive self-regulatory responses. The cross-sectional nature of this study, however, prohibits any inferences about the causal direction of the relationship between stress exposure and coping. That is, stress may have disrupted effective coping, but it is equally plausible that ineffective coping responses may have resulted in increased stress.

Family Stressors, Coping, and Symptoms of Anxiety–Depression and Aggression

We next turn to two questions that represent the litmus test in all analyses of coping: Is coping related to symptoms of psychopathology, and does coping mediate the relationship between stress and symptoms? We can draw on the broader literature on children and adolescents coping with stress to formulate hypotheses regarding these associations. In general, prior studies indicate that primary and secondary control coping are associated with lower levels of emotional and behavioral problems, whereas disengagement coping is associated with more problems (Compas et al., 2001). However, because adolescents in our study rated stressors related to parental depression as relatively uncontrollable, it is possible that efforts to adapt to the stressors through secondary control coping responses would be the most effective. That is, previous research has shown that secondary control coping is more effective in uncontrollable situations, whereas active, primary control coping is more adaptive in controllable situations (e.g., Compas, Malcarne, & Fondacaro, 1988; Osowiecki & Compas, 1998, 1999).

Our findings from both parents' reports and adolescents' reports of coping and emotional and behavioral problems were consistent with this overall pattern. In correlation analyses, secondary control coping was related to lower symptoms of anxiety–depression and fewer aggressive behavior problems (rs ranged from $-.37$ to $-.56$, $p < .05$). However, primary control coping was related only to fewer aggressive symptoms and only in parents' reports ($r = -.23$, $p < .05$); disengagement coping was not significantly correlated with either type of symptoms in either parents' or adolescents' reports. Furthermore, higher symptoms of anxiety–depression and aggression were associated with higher levels of involuntary engagement stress responses ($rs = .40$ to $.48$, $p < .01$). This finding is consistent with previous research that has shown that engagement responses such as rumination, intrusive thoughts, and emotional and physiological arousal are related to increased symptoms of depression and anxiety (e.g., Nolen-Hoeksema, Larson, & Grayson, 1999).

These findings provide the first data that we are aware of on the relationship between coping and symptoms in children of depressed parents. However, they are potentially confounded because in each set of analyses reports of coping and symptoms were obtained from a single informant (either parents or adolescents). A more stringent test of the association between coping and symptoms involves the examination of cross-informant correlations, that is, the association between parents' reports of their children's coping and adolescents' reports of their symptoms, and adolescents' reports of their coping with parents' reports of their children's symptoms. These analyses are not subject to the problems of shared method variance when either parents or adolescents provide reports of both coping and symptoms. The results of the cross-informant analyses from this sample provide more evidence for the association of coping and adjustment in children of depressed parents (Langrock et al., 2000a). In analyses of adolescents' reports of their coping on the RSQ with parent reports of emotional and behavioral problems on the CBCL (n = 55), secondary control was significantly correlated with fewer anxiety–depression symptoms (r = –.32, p < .05); disengagement coping was positively correlated with aggression (r = .30, p < .05); involuntary engagement was correlated with more anxiety–depression symptoms (r = .29, p < .05); involuntary disengagement was correlated with more aggression (r = .28, p < .05); and primary control coping was not related to either anxiety–depression symptoms or aggressive behavior. Analyses of parents' reports of their children's coping with adolescents' reports on the YSR (n = 53) revealed that secondary control coping was significantly correlated with fewer anxiety–depression symptoms (r = –.42, p < .01); involuntary engagement was significantly correlated with more anxiety–depression symptoms (r = .32, p < .05); and primary control coping, disengagement coping, and involuntary disengagement responses were not correlated with either type of symptoms.

Although associations between coping and reports of child psychopathology were stronger within informant, cross-informant associations were significant and validate Richters's (1992) conclusion that parents who are depressed can rate their children's behavior independently of their own symptoms. Thus, consistent with the analyses within parent and adolescent reports, the cross-informant correlations underscore the significant relationship between the use of secondary control coping strategies (acceptance, distraction, positive thinking, cognitive restructuring) and lower symptoms of anxiety–depression and involuntary engagement responses (e.g., rumination, intrusive thoughts, emotional and physiological arousal) and higher anxiety–depression symptoms.

A further test of the role of coping with parental depression involves examination of coping as a mediator of the association between stress and symptoms; that is, whether coping accounts for the association between family stress and children's symptoms (Langrock et al., 2000b). Correlation analyses indicated that secondary control coping could be tested as a mediator of parental withdrawal stressors and parental intrusiveness stressors for both symptoms of anxiety–depression, and aggression, and involuntary engagement stress responses could be tested as a mediator of parental withdrawal stressors and symptoms of anxiety–depression, and aggression (Baron & Kenny, 1986). Because there were no significant correlations between marital conflict stressors and parent's ratings of their children's symptoms, we could not test coping as a mediator of marital conflict.

Both secondary control coping and involuntary engagement responses mediated the effects of parental withdrawal stressors on parent's ratings of children's symptoms of anxiety–depression, and aggression (Langrock et al., 2000b). That is, when secondary control coping and involuntary engagement responses were included in the regression analyses, secondary control coping and involuntary engagement stress responses were significant predictors of anxiety–depression symptoms and aggression, and the association between parental withdrawal stressors and symptoms was no longer significant. In addition, secondary control coping responses mediated the association between parental intrusiveness stressors and both anxiety–depression and aggressive symptoms. These findings indicate that coping and involuntary stress responses are important pathways through which the stress associated with parental depression affects children and adolescents. Furthermore, although mediating effects were significant for both symptoms of anxiety–depression and aggression, the proportion of variance accounted for in the mediation models predicting symptoms of anxiety–depression was greater (R^2 ranged from .22 to .23 for anxiety–depression and from .13 to .15 for aggression), suggesting that these responses play a greater role in symptoms of anxiety–depression than aggression.

These findings are summarized in Figure 10.1. The pathways from parental withdrawal stressors are negative to secondary control coping and positive to involuntary engagement responses. Similarly, the path from parental intrusiveness stressors is negative to secondary control coping. These pathways represent the associations between stress and increased involuntary engagement and decreased secondary control coping. The paths from secondary control coping to anxiety–depression and aggressive symptoms are negative, whereas the paths from involuntary engagement responses to both types of symptoms are positive. Finally, the paths from parental withdrawal and parental intrusiveness stressor to symptoms are represented by dotted lines, because these paths were mediated (statistically accounted for) by coping and stress responses.

To summarize these findings: Compared to children who are exposed to low levels of parental stress, children who are exposed to higher rates of parental withdrawal and parental intrusiveness stressors are less likely to use secondary control coping to adapt to and regulate their responses to these stressors. Thus, these children are affected not only by their exposure to these stressors, but also by their inability to use coping responses that may be the most adaptive. Furthermore, children exposed to high levels of these stressors are more likely than children exposed to low levels of stress to respond with high levels of emotional and physiological arousal, intrusive thoughts, and rumination, all of which are associated with higher levels of anxiety–depression and aggression symptoms.

Coping with Nonfamily Stressors: Peer Stress and Symptoms of Anxiety–Depression and Aggression

A final question involves the ways that children of depressed parents are affected by and cope with stress that does not involve their interactions with their depressed parent. Hammen and colleagues found that stressors involving peers were to a certain extent dependent on the characteristics of

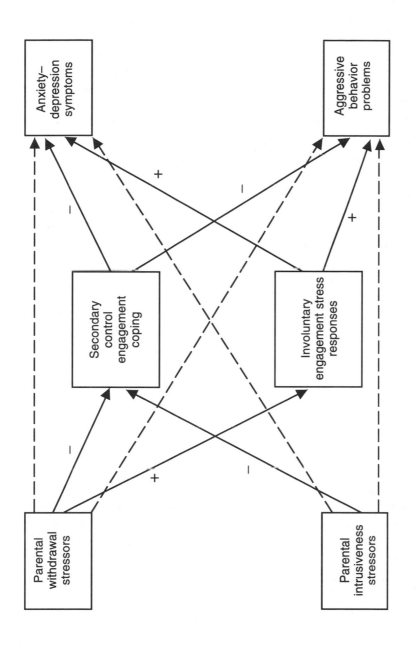

Figure 10.1. Summary of Path Analyses of Coping and Involuntary Responses as Mediators of Stress, Anxiety–Depression Symptoms, and Aggression

children of depressed parents; that is, these children interacted with their broader environment in ways that added more stress to their lives (Adrian & Hammen, 1993). To examine the ways that children of depressed parents coped with nonfamily stress, we (Compas et al., 2000) had adolescents in the present sample complete a second version of the RSQ that asked how they coped with stressors involving their peers. Children of depressed parents rated peer stressors as more under their control (M = 2.71) than stressors involving their depressed parent (M = 2.19). However, they did not report using more primary control coping (e.g., problem solving) in association with higher perceptions of control over these stressors. Their reports of the ways that they responded to and coped with peer stressors were moderately to highly correlated with their reports of their coping with family stress (rs ranged from .25, p < .05, for involuntary disengagement responses, to .78, p < .01, for secondary control coping). These correlations reflect a substantial degree of consistency in the ways that they coped with stress within and outside the family. Furthermore, adolescents' reports of their coping with and responses to peer stressors were significantly related to their self-reports of symptoms on the YSR. Primary control coping and secondary control coping were correlated with lower symptoms of anxiety–depression and aggression (rs ranged from −.21 to −.49), whereas disengagement coping was not correlated with symptoms. Involuntary engagement and disengagement responses were correlated with more anxiety–depression symptoms and aggression (rs ranged from .15 to .53). These findings indicate that the poor self-regulation skills of children of depressed parents may compromise their coping with stress outside as well as within their family environments.

IMPLICATIONS FOR CLINICIANS

These findings have important implications for the development of intervention programs for children of depressed parents. Programs designed to teach children more effective ways to deal with their own involuntary stress responses and uncontrollable stressors have the potential to reduce the likelihood of children of depressed parents developing psychopathology. Specifically, these results suggest that one effective avenue for intervention is to teach children of depressed parents that they are not responsible for and cannot control the stressors associated with their parents' depression (see Beardslee et al., 1997, for similar findings). Therefore, interventions can teach children the secondary control coping skills to accept their parents' depression, cognitively reframe these problems, maintain a positive mental attitude, and distract themselves through pleasant activities. At the same time, it appears to be essential to reduce the stressor load for children within these families, because their ability to use secondary control coping is diminished as family stress increases. Therefore, interventions must directly address the parenting styles of depressed parents while helping children to cope with family stress.

SUMMARY

Children who grow up in a household in which one or both parents suffer from depression are at enormous risk for a range of problems in their emotional and behavioral development. A high priority is the identification of processes that place these children at risk and the factors that can protect children from these risks in order to develop and deliver interventions to ameliorate and prevent problems. Previous research has shown that stress processes within families of depressed parents are an important source of risk for children (Hammen, 1997). Findings presented here from our ongoing research provide further information on the nature of stress processes within families of depressed parents. These findings indicate that volitional coping responses and involuntary stress responses are important sources of risk and of protection from risk. Specifically, the use of secondary control coping strategies, including acceptance, distraction, positive thinking, and cognitive restructuring, are associated with reduced symptoms of both internalizing and externalizing disorders. In contrast, stress responses that occur at a more automatic level and involve increased engagement with the sources of stress and responses to stress (e.g., ruminating about the stress and one's emotions, high levels of emotional and physiological reactivity to stress) are associated with higher levels of internalizing and externalizing symptoms. It is of even greater concern that as levels of stress increase within families of depressed parents, children are less likely to use secondary control engagement responses and are more likely to exhibit responses of involuntary engagement. Thus, children are doubly exposed to the risk of stress and ineffective attempts at self-regulation.

The take-home messages of these findings are clear. First, children of depressed parents are exposed to significant stress associated with both parental withdrawal and parental intrusiveness. It is striking that most children in this sample were exposed to stressors associated with both types of problematic parenting. This suggests that children of depressed parents, at least in the present sample, are exposed to a family environment in which the depressed parent vacillates between being unavailable to the child as a consequence of her or his own depression and being intrusive in the child's life in a worried and hostile manner. The picture of the home environment for these children is one of unpredictability and high levels of negative affect. Although parental conflict has been shown to be an important characteristic of families of depressed parents (Cummings & Davies, 1992), it was a less salient stressor in the current sample, perhaps as a result of limitations in our measure of conflict.

Second, increased exposure to these stressors is associated with decreased use of potentially adaptive coping responses, particularly with decreased secondary control coping, and increased levels of involuntary engagement stress responses. As the load from stressors increases, it appears that children's adaptive capacities become constrained and restricted. They appear less able to generate coping strategies that involve more complex forms of cognitive coping, including accepting the stressors with their parents, trying to distract themselves with alternative thoughts or activities, and reframing or thinking about the stressful situations in a more positive manner. Conversely, children in these families appear to have been less able to control problematic involuntary stress responses as the stressor load increased. As stressors increased, children responded with more ruminative and intrusive negative thoughts, both of which have been shown to be associated with increased symptoms of anxiety and depression in previous research (Nolen-Hoeksema et al., 1999). Under heightened stress, children in this sample also responded with increased emotional and physiological reactivity, reflecting further deterioration in their ability to self-regulate their behavior and emotions.

Third, levels of stress, coping responses, and involuntary stress responses were all significantly related to children's symptoms of anxiety–depression and aggression. A consistent pattern was found in which secondary control coping responses were associated with lower symptoms of anxiety–depression and aggression, whereas primary control coping strategies were not related to symptoms. Thus, it appears particularly effective for children of depressed parents to cope by adapting to rather than trying to change the stressors that occur within the family. This is consistent with their perceptions that these stressors are relatively uncontrollable and less controllable than stressors that they encounter in their peer relationships. Previous research has suggested that primary control coping is more adaptive in response to controllable stressors, whereas secondary control coping may be more adaptive with uncontrollable stress (Compas et al., 1988; Osowiecki & Compas, 1998, 1999). The current findings are consistent with this pattern. In addition to identifying the positive features of secondary control coping, these findings indicate that involuntary responses of rumination and stress reactivity were, as expected, associated with higher levels of symptoms and behavior problems. Poor self-regulation of thoughts, emotions, behaviors, and physiological responses to stress were associated with significantly poorer adjustment in these children. Secondary control coping and involuntary engagement responses were negatively correlated in both adolescents' reports (–.74) and parents' reports (–.72), indicating that poor self-regulation in the present sample was characterized by not accepting and adapting to stressors associated with parental depression in these families.

Fourth, the present findings provide the first evidence that we are aware of that coping and involuntary stress responses mediate the relationship between family stress and children's symptoms. In addition to replicating the association between stress and symptoms in children of depressed parents, the present data indicate that this association is accounted for by the inability to use secondary control coping responses and by heightened levels of involuntary engagement responses. As stress within families of depressed parents increases, it contributes to a breakdown in adaptive coping and an increase in stress reactivity and rumination. These responses are then linked to increases in both internalizing and externalizing symptoms for children of depressed parents.

Although the findings that we have summarized here suggest that coping is an important factor to consider in the adjustment of children of depressed parents, this research was limited by several factors that should be addressed in subsequent research. First, the findings are based on data collected at a single point in time and as a consequence are subject to the usual caveats that limit cross-sectional research. Most important, the direction of the relationships among family stressors, children's coping, and children's symptoms cannot be discerned. We have tested models in which we hypothesize that stressors initiate coping and involuntary responses, which in turn lead to symptoms of anxiety–depression and aggression. It is equally plausible, however, that children in these families who display the highest symptoms are less able to cope effectively and also contribute to stressful interactions with their parents. Prospective research is needed to disentangle the direction of these associations. Second, although reports were obtained from both parents and their adolescent children, all of these analyses are nonetheless based on questionnaire data. Researchers should use methods of observing the ways that children of depressed parents respond to stress under controlled conditions and direct observations of coping in the context of interactions between depressed parents and their children. The promising nature of the cross-sectional findings from this research suggest that it would be worthwhile to invest in more extensive and costly research designs to better understand the coping of children of depressed parents. Third, the present sample was not sufficiently large to examine age-related differences in the types of stress that confront children and adolescents in families of depressed parents, nor in their coping and stress responses. Future research is needed to examine possible developmental differences in the ways that children and adolescents cope with parental depression.

REFERENCES

Achenbach, T. M. (1991). *Integrative guide for the 1991 CBCL/4-18, YSR, and TRF profiles*. Burlington: University of Vermont, Department of Psychiatry.

Adrian, C., & Hammen, C. (1993). Stress exposure and stress generation in children of depressed mothers. *Journal of Consulting and Clinical Psychology, 61*, 354–359.

American Psychiatric Association. (1987). *Diagnostic and statistical manual of mental disorders* (3rd ed., rev.). Washington, DC: Author.

American Psychiatric Association. (1994). *Diagnostic and statistical manual of mental disorders* (4th ed.). Washington, DC: Author.

Anderson, C. A., & Hammen, C. (1993). Psychosocial outcomes of children of unipolar depressed, bipolar, medically ill, and normal women: A longitudinal study. *Journal of Consulting and Clinical Psychology, 61,* 448–454.

Ayers, T. S., Sandler, I. N., West, S. G., & Roosa, M. W. (1996). A dispositional and situational assessment of children's coping: Testing alternative models of children's coping. *Journal of Personality, 64,* 923–958.

Bargh, J. A. (1997). The automaticity of everyday life. In R. S. Wyer (Ed.), *The automaticity of everyday life: Vol. 10. Advances in social cognition* (pp. 1–61). Mahwah, NJ: Erlbaum.

Baron, R. M., & Kenny, D. A. (1986). The moderator–mediator variable distinction in social psychological research: Conceptual, strategic, and statistical considerations. *Journal of Personality and Social Psychology, 51,* 1173–1182.

Beardslee, W. R., Keller, M., Lavori, P., Klerman, G., Dorer, D., & Samuelson, H. (1988). Psychiatric disorder in adolescent offspring of parents with affective disorders in a non-referred sample. *Journal of Affective Disorders, 15,* 313–322.

Beardslee, W. R., Salt, P., Versage, E., Gladstone, T., Wright, E., & Rothberg, P. (1997). Sustained change in parents receiving preventive interventions for families with depression. *American Journal of Psychiatry, 154,* 510–515.

Beck, A. T., Streer, R. A., Ball, R., & Ranieri, W. F. (1996). Comparison of Beck Depression Inventories—IA and II in psychiatric outpatients. *Journal of Personality Assessment, 67,* 588–597.

Cannon, W. (1933). *The wisdom of the body.* New York: Norton.

Cannon, W. (1934). The significance of emotional level. *Scientific Monthly, 38,* 101–110.

Causey, D., & Dubow, E. (1992). Development of a self-report coping measure for elementary school children. *Journal of Clinical Child Psychology, 21,* 47–59.

Compas, B. E. (1998). An agenda for coping research and theory: Basic and applied developmental issues. *International Journal of Behavioral Development, 22,* 231–237.

Compas, B. E., Connor, J. K., Osowiecki, D. M., & Welch, A. (1997). Effortful and involuntary responses to stress: Implications for coping and chronic stress. In B. H. Gottlieb (Ed.), *Coping with chronic stress* (pp. 105–130). New York: Plenum Press.

Compas, B. E., Connor-Smith, J. K., Saltzman, H., Thomsen, A. H., & Wadsworth, M. E. (2001). Coping with stress during childhood and adolescence: Progress, problems, and potential in theory and research. *Psychological Bulletin, 127,* 87–127.

Compas, B. E., Langrock, A. M., Keller, G., & Merchant, M. J. (2000). *Cross-situational consistency and variability in coping responses of children of depressed parents.* Manuscript submitted for publication.

Compas, B. E., Malcarne, V. L., & Fondacaro, K. M. (1988). Coping with stressful events in older children and young adolescents. *Journal of Consulting and Clinical Psychology, 56,* 405–411.

Connor-Smith, J. K., & Compas, B. E. (in press). Vulnerability to social stress: Coping as a mediator or moderator of sociotropy and symptoms of anxiety and depression. *Cognitive Therapy and Research.*

Connor-Smith, J. K., Compas, B. E., Wadsworth, M. E., Thomsen, A. H., & Saltzman, H. (2000). Responses to stress in adolescence: Measurement of coping and involuntary stress responses. *Journal of Consulting and Clinical Psychology, 68,* 976–992.

Cummings, E. M., & Davies, P. (1992). Parental depression, family functioning, and child adjustment: Risk factors, processes, and pathways. In D. Cicchetti & S. Toth (Eds.), *Rochester symposium on developmental psychology: Vol. 4. A developmental approach to the affective disorders* (pp. 283–322). Rochester, NY: University of Rochester Press.

Cummings, E. M., & Davies, P. (1994). Maternal depression and child development. *Journal of Child Psychology and Psychiatry, 35,* 73–112.

Dalcidcn, E. L., & Vasey, M. W. (1997). An information-processing perspective on childhood anxiety. *Clinical Psychology Review, 17,* 407–429.

Downey, G., & Coyne, J. C. (1990). Children of depressed parents: An integrative review. *Psychological Bulletin, 108,* 50–76.

Fendrich, M., Warner, V., & Weissman, M. M. (1990). Family risk factors, parental depression, and psychopathology in offspring. *Developmental Psychology, 26,* 40–50.

Gelfand, D., & Teti, D. (1990). The effects of maternal depression on children. *Clinical Psychology Review, 10,* 329–353.

Goodman, S. H., & Gotlib, I. H. (1999). Risk for psychopathology in the children of depressed mothers: A developmental model for understanding mechanisms of transmission. *Psychological Review, 106,* 458–490.

Gotlib, I. H., & Neubauer, D. L. (2000). Information-processing approaches to the study of cognitive biases in depression. In S. L. Johnson, A. M. Hayes, T. M. Field, N. Schneiderman, & P. M. McCabe (Eds.), *Stress, coping, and depression* (pp. 117–143). Mahwah, NJ: Erlbaum.

Gray, J. A. (1991). The neuropsychology of temperament. In J. Strelau & A. Angleitner (Eds.), *Explorations in temperament: International perspectives on theory and measurement* (pp. 105–128). New York: Plenum Press.

Hammen, C. (1991). *Depression runs in families: The social context of risk and resilience in children of depressed mothers.* New York: Springer-Verlag.

Hammen, C. (1992). The family-environmental context of depression: A perspective on children's risk. In D. Cicchetti & S. Toth (Eds.), *Rochester symposium on developmental psychology: Vol. 4. A developmental approach to the affective disorders* (pp. 251–281). Rochester, NY: University of Rochester Press.

Hammen, C. (1997). Children of depressed parents: The stress context. In S. Wolchik & I. N. Sandler (Eds.), *Handbook of children's coping: Linking theory and intervention* (Issues in Clinical Child Psychology, pp. 131–157). New York: Plenum Press.

Hammen, C., Burge, D., Burney, E., & Adrian, C. (1990). Longitudinal study of diagnoses in children of women with unipolar and bipolar affective disorder. *Archives of General Psychiatry, 47,* 1112–1117.

Hammen, C., Davila, J., Brown, G., Ellicott, A., & Gitlin, M. (1992). Psychiatric history and stress: Predictors of severity of unipolar depression. *Journal of Abnormal Psychology, 101,* 45–52.

Hudziak, J. J., Helzer, J. E., & Wetzel, M. W. (1993). The use of the *DSM–III–R* Checklist for initial diagnostic assessments. *Comprehensive Psychiatry, 34,* 375–383.

Jacob, T., & Johnson, S. L. (1997). Parent–child interaction among depressed fathers and mothers: Impact on child functioning. *Journal of Family Psychology, 11,* 391–409.

Keller, G., Copeland, M. E., Comaps, B. E., Langrock, A. M., & Merchant, M. J. (2000). *Raising healthy children: Prevention of adverse effects of parental depression.* Unpublished manuscript.

Klimes-Dougan, B., & Bolger, A. K. (1998). Coping with maternal depressed affect and depression: Adolescent children of depressed and well mothers. *Journal of Youth and Adolescence, 27,* 1–15.

Krohne, H. W. (1996). Individual differences in coping. In M. Zeidner & N. S. Endler (Eds.), *Handbook of coping: Theory, research, and application* (pp. 381–409). New York: Wiley.

Langrock, A. M., Compas, B. E., Keller, G., Merchant, M. J., & Copeland, M. E. (2000a). *Coping with the stress of parental depression: Comparison of adolescents' and parents' reports of children's coping and emotional/behavioral problems.* Manuscript submitted for publication.

Langrock, A. M., Compas, B. E., Keller, G., Merchant, M. J., & Copeland, M. E. (2000b). *Coping with the stress of parental depression: Parents' reports of children's coping and emotional/behavioral problems.* Manuscript submitted for publication.

Lee, C., & Gotlib, I. H. (1991). Adjustment of children of depressed mothers: A ten-month follow-up. *Journal of Abnormal Psychology, 100,* 473–477.

Lewinsohn, P. M., Allen, N. B., Seeley, J. R., & Gotlib, I. H. (1999). First onset versus recurrence of depression: Differential processes of psychosocial risk. *Journal of Abnormal Psychology, 108,* 483–489.

Malphurs, J. E., Field, T., Larraine, C., Pickens, J., & Pelaez-Nogueras, M. (1996). Altering withdrawn and intrusive interaction behaviors of depressed mothers. *Infant Mental Health Journal, 17,* 152–160.

Mathews, A., & MacLeod, C. (1994). Cognitive approaches to emotion and emotional disorders. *Annual Review of Psychology, 45,* 25–50.

Matthews, G., & Wells, A. (1997). Attentional processes, dysfunctional coping, and clinical intervention. In M. Zeidner & N. S. Endler (Eds.), *Handbook of coping: Theory, research, and applications* (pp. 573–601). New York: Wiley.

McNally, R. J. (1995). Automaticity and the anxiety disorders. *Behavior Research and Therapy, 33,* 747–754.

Mischel, W. (1997). Was the cognitive revolution just a detour on the road to behaviorism? On the need to reconcile situational control and personal control. In R. J. Wyer (Ed.), *The automaticity of everyday life: Advances in social cognition* (Vol. 10, pp. 181–186). Mahwah, NJ: Erlbaum.

Nolen-Hoeksema, S., Larson, J., & Grayson, C. (1999). Explaining the gender differences in depressive symptoms. *Journal of Personality and Social Psychology, 77,* 1061–1072.

Osowiecki, D. M., & Compas, B. E. (1998). Psychological adjustment to cancer: Control beliefs and coping in adult cancer patients. *Cognitive Therapy and Research, 22,* 483–499.

Osowiecki, D. M., & Compas, B. E. (1999). Coping and perceived control in adjustment to breast cancer. *Cognitive Therapy and Research, 23,* 169–180.

Phares, V., & Compas, B. E. (1992). The role of fathers in child and adolescent psychopathology: Make room for daddy. *Psychological Bulletin, 111,* 387–412.

Radke-Yarrow, M. (1998). *Children of depressed mothers.* New York: Cambridge University Press.

Radke-Yarrow, M., & Brown, E. (1993). Resilience and vulnerability in children of multiple risk families. *Development and Psychopathology, 5,* 581–592.

Reichman, T., Wadsworth, M., Benson, M., & Compas, B. E. (2000). *Coping with stress in adolescence: A comparison of Native American and Euro-American youth.* Manuscript submitted for publication.

Richters, J. E. (1992). Depressed mothers as informants about their children: A critical review of the evidence for distortion. *Psychological Bulletin, 112,* 485–499.

Rothbart, M. K. (1991). Temperament: A developmental framework. In J. Strelau & A. Angleitner (Eds.), *Explorations in temperament: International perspectives on theory and measurement* (pp. 61–74). New York: Plenum Press.

Rudolph, K. D., Dennig, M. D., & Weisz, J. R. (1995). Determinants and consequences of children's coping in the medical setting: Conceptualization, review, and critique. *Psychological Bulletin, 118,* 328–357.

Shiffrin, R. M. (1997). Attention, automatism, and consciousness. In J. D. Cohen & J. W. Schooler (Eds.), *Scientific approaches to consciousness* (pp. 49–64). Mahwah, NJ: Erlbaum.

Shiffrin, R. M., & Schneider, W. (1977). Controlled and automatic human information processing: II. Perceptual learning, automatic attending, and a general theory. *Psychological Review, 84,* 127–190.

Thomsen, A. H., Compas, B. E., Colletti, R. B., Stanger, C., Boyer, M. A., & Konik, B. (2000). Parent reports of coping and stress responses in children with current abdominal pain. *Journal of Pediatric Psychology.*

Vasey, M. W., El-Hag, N., & Daleiden, E. L. (1996). Anxiety and the processing of emotionally threatening stimuli: Distinctive patterns of selective attention among high- and low-test-anxious children. *Child Development, 67,* 1173–1185.

Wadsworth, M. E., & Compas, B. E. (2000). *Coping with family conflict and economic strain: The adolescent perspective.* Manuscript submitted for publication.

Walker, L. S., Smith, C. A., Garber, J., & Van Slyke, D. A. (1997). Development and validation of the Pain Response Inventory for Children. *Psychological Assessment, 9,* 392–405.

Weissman, M. M., Gammon, G. D., John, K., Merikangas, K. R., Warner, V., Prusoff, B. A., & Sholomskas, D. (1987). Children of depressed parents: Increased psychopathology and early onset of major depression. *Archives of General Psychiatry, 44,* 847–853.

11

GENDER-SPECIFIC VULNERABILITY TO DEPRESSION IN CHILDREN OF DEPRESSED MOTHERS

LISA SHEEBER, BETSY DAVIS, AND HYMAN HOPS

We begin this chapter with the oft repeated mantra, "more research is needed." We open with what would normally be the end to a chapter as a means of conveying the current status of the literature relative to why girls may be at particular risk for depressive symptoms and disorders as a function of maternal depression. Hops (1992) reviewed the clinical and developmental literature, and he proposed that the rates and type of psychopathology in children of depressed women may vary as a function of child age and gender. In particular, he and others (e.g., Cummings & Davies, 1994) have suggested that the greatest risk posed by maternal depression may be to preadolescent boys and adolescent girls, with the former demonstrating increased incidence of behavioral disorders and the latter demonstrating increased incidence of depressive disorders. As we discuss below, there is modest empirical support for the assertion that adolescent daughters of depressed women are at particular risk for depressive disorders and symptoms. However, the evidence that boys of depressed mothers are differentially vulnerable to behavioral disturbances is very limited (Cummings & Davies, 1994; Harnish, Dodge, & Valente, 1995). We have thus chosen to focus primarily on the risk for depression posed to daughters of depressed women, while continuing to examine socialization practices and other relevant constructs by gender.

Hops (1992) suggested that girls' differential vulnerability may derive from socialization experiences that shape their behavioral repertoires to emphasize stereotypical female behaviors often associated with depression. Our review of the literature for this chapter revealed that although Hops's prior writings on this topic (1992, 1995) have been cited by others, new data either to support or disconfirm the hypothesis are scarce. Consequently, we emphasize the need for continued research in this area.

We begin the chapter by presenting an overview of Hops's model of the socialization of depressive behavior in girls. This is followed by a section describing the particular vulnerability experienced by adolescent girls. We then discuss the socialization mechanisms within Hops's model in more detail, reviewing relevant research and highlighting areas where the data remain equivocal. We conclude the chapter with a brief discussion of the clinical implications and some suggestions for future research.

MODEL OVERVIEW

Following a review of the clinical and developmental literature, Hops (1992, 1995, 1996; Hops, Sherman, & Biglan, 1990) posited two paths by which parents may inadvertently increase their daughters' risk for depressive symptoms and disorder. First, familial socialization processes may normalize and encourage girls' expression of depressive-like behaviors. Depressive-like behaviors, such as sadness or self-derogation, are normal at low levels, but may be symptomatic of depressive disorders when occurring excessively and in the context of other depressive symptoms. Second, differential parental reinforcement of gender-typic behaviors may lead girls to display less instrumental and more relationship-focused behaviors, both of which are related to theoretically derived and empirically supported risk factors for depression. These gender-typic behavioral patterns, learned in early childhood and reinforced over time, are hypothesized to hamper girls' ability to meet the normative challenges of adolescence, thus contributing to the increased prevalence of depressive symptoms at this developmental stage. In this way, the model is similar to that presented by Nolen-Hoeksema (1994), who suggested that pre-existing gender differences in risk factors for depression translate to greater depressive symptoms when girls are faced with the stresses of adolescence. Finally, maternal depression may add to, or interact with, gender-socialized vulnerabilities to increase girls' risk for depression by: a) exposing them to a serious and chronic stressor; b) providing them with a model of depressive, cognitive, and interpersonal functioning; and c) eliciting caretaking behavior for them.

GIRLS' GREATER VULNERABILITY TO DEPRESSION

Adolescent girls experience greater rates of depressive symptoms and disorder than do younger girls or boys of any age. In this section, we examine reasons why adolescence may be a period of particular vulnerability for girls. We also review the evidence that, amongst children of depressed women, daughters are at greater risk for depression than are sons.

Adolescence as a Period of Developmental Risk for Depression

It is by now well-established that in adolescence, as in adulthood (Nolen-Hoeksema, 1987), female individuals are twice as likely as male individuals to experience unipolar depressive disorders (Kashani et al., 1987; Lewinsohn, Hops, Roberts, Seeley, & Andrews, 1993; Nolen-Hoeksema & Girgus, 1994; Velez, Johnson, & Cohen, 1989). This imbalance, not evident in prepubertal children, is reflective of the gradual increase in girls' rates of depression that begins in early adolescence and peaks in mid-adolescence (Hankin et al., 1998), at least among Caucasian adolescents (Hayward, Gotlib, Schraedley, & Litt, 1999).

Adolescent girls' increased risk for depressive symptoms and disorder has been attributed, in part, to the multiple challenges they face in this developmental period. In summarizing the literature about the emerging gender differences in depression, Nolen-Hoeksema (1998; Nolen-Hoeksema & Girgus, 1994) has noted the important role of biological changes in adolescence. For example, Caucasian girls report significant concerns about their appearance in relation to the development of secondary sex characteristics, whereas their male counterparts do not experience pubertal changes in physical appearance as distressing. Adolescent girls also face an increased probability of sexual abuse, contributing to concerns about personal safety not as frequently experienced by adolescent boys (Nolen-Hoeksema & Girgus, 1994). Furthermore, it appears that the transition from elementary school into the more complex social and academic milieu of the middle school poses unique challenges for female adolescents. The transition into middle school coincides with the pubertal changes noted above for a large number of adolescent girls, but not necessarily for adolescent boys who mature later. Evidence suggests that the interaction of biological and school change accounts for both lower self-esteem (Simmons & Blyth, 1987) and higher levels of depressed mood (Petersen, Sarigiani, & Kennedy, 1991).

The family environment may also be more challenging for girls than boys during adolescence. Mothers and their adolescent daughters express higher levels of hostility and conflict than other parent–adolescent dyads (Hill, Holmbeck, Marlow, Green, & Lynch, 1985; Steinberg, 1987, 1988). Furthermore, girls spend equal amounts of time with their parents and peers, whereas boys spend significantly more time with peers (Montemayor, 1983). The greater proximity to the family may leave girls more vulnerable when family relations are strained. All of these challenges suggest that adolescence may be a particularly difficult time for girls, with the difficulties relating to, and perhaps contributing to, an increased vulnerability for depressive functioning.

Risk for Depression in Adolescent Daughters of Depressed Women

Few researchers of maternal depression in clinical samples have examined whether the risk for psychopathology among offspring varies as a function of child gender (see Goodman & Gotlib, 1999; Gotlib & Goodman, 1999). Perhaps because of the relatively small sample sizes typical of studies with clinically diagnosed participants, most research has examined rates of diagnosis without distinguishing between types of psychopathology or examining gender as a moderator. Evidence of gender-differentiated risk has, therefore, been derived primarily from studies of children's observed affective behavior in clinical samples and self-reported symptoms in community samples. In an examination of young children of depressed and nondepressed mothers, Radke-Yarrow, Nottelmann, Belmont, and Welsh (1993) reported significant synchrony in bouts of negative affect between depressed mothers and their daughters but not between mothers and sons. In a study of children and adolescents of depressed and well mothers, Hops and colleagues (1990) found that older adolescent girls in families of depressed mothers displayed more dysphoric and less happy affect.

In several community samples, maternal depressive symptoms have been found to be significantly associated with depressive symptoms in adolescent girls but not in adolescent boys (Davies & Windle, 1997; Thomas & Forehand, 1991). For example, Fergusson, Horwood, and Lynskey (1995) reported a significant prospective correlation between maternal depressive symptoms and subsequent depressive symptoms in adolescent girls but not boys. Similar findings have emerged in Hops's (1992, 1996) own research on the covariation of depressive symptoms between parents and adolescents over a 4-year period (Hops, 1992, 1996). In this project, all combinations of same- and opposite-sex parent–child dyads were examined. Consistent correlations were observed only between mother and daughter reports. One-year lagged analyses indicated that maternal depressive symptoms were predictive of daughters' subsequent symptoms, but the reverse was not true. Divergent results have emerged from one large community-based study. Ge, Conger, Lorenz, Shanahan, and Elder (1995) reported significant cross-sex concordance between parental and child distressed behavior.

SOCIALIZATION MECHANISMS TO EXPLAIN GENDER DIFFERENCES

In this section, we examine more closely the risk factors associated with gender socialization. In particular, we review the evidence for Hops's hypothesis that familial socialization processes may increase girls' risk for depression by reinforcing both depressive-like behaviors (e.g., sadness or self-derogation) and gender-typic behavioral styles (i.e., relationship-orientation and low instrumentality).

Socialization of Depressive-like Behaviors

Higher levels of depressive symptoms reported by girls may be conceptualized as stereotypic female behaviors (e.g., being more emotional or self-deprecating) that are intensified under stressful circumstances (Hops, 1995; Kavanagh & Hops, 1994). There is some evidence that girls may be differentially socialized to display depressive behaviors. In a recent review on parental socialization of emotion, Eisenberg, Cumberland, and Spinrad (1998) reported that although parents do not typically report reacting differently to girls' and boys' emotional displays, observational data suggest that there are indeed differences, "albeit perhaps less than one might expect" (p. 254). A series of studies indicated that parents put more pressure on boys to control their emotions and "unnecessary" crying. Block (1983) reported that parents were quicker to respond to crying in girls than in boys. Moreover, evidence suggests that mothers of young children are more likely to discuss sadness with girls and anger with boys, and as a result girls may learn that sadness is a more acceptable emotion than anger (Eisenberg et al., 1998; Fivush, 1998). Parents' meta-messages about the acceptability of emotional expressions are apparently clear to children in that boys expect their parents to disapprove of their expression of sadness more so than do girls (Fuchs & Thelen, 1988).

Parents' reactions to children's negative emotions may also provide them with gender-differentiated strategies for regulating negative affect. Some evidence (admittedly limited) suggests that compared to girls, boys may be more often encouraged to use distraction and problem-solving (Eisenberg et al., 1998). In fact, one study indicated that school-age children expected fathers to respond to boys' emotional expressions with problem-solving and mothers to respond to girls by focusing on feelings (Dino, Barnett, & Howard, 1984). Similarly, in a review of the origins of ruminative coping styles, Nolen-Hoeksema (1998) indicated that failure to teach girls active strategies for coping with negative affect contributes to girls' greater use of ruminative style of responding to depressed moods. Furthermore, she suggested that to the extent girls are told they are naturally emotional, they may have lower expectations that their behavior can influence their affective experiences.

These data suggest that parents' early gender-differentiated responses to children's emotional behaviors has an effect on children's ability and motivation to regulate emotion, but large gaps remain in the literature. In particular, the largely cross-sectional studies do not provide evidence that parents' behaviors are predictors and not consequences of children's sex-typed behaviors. For example, if girls display more sadness and boys more anger, it would be reasonable to hypothesize that parents' tendency to discuss sadness with girls and anger with boys emerged consequent to the children's behavioral propensities. Similarly, the tendency of parents to be more emotion-focused in response to young girls and problem-focused in response to young boys may reflect girls' earlier verbal and emotional development (Keenan & Shaw, 1997). That is, parents may speak more with girls than boys about emotion states because girls appear more able to process the information. It is important to keep in mind that the research discussed here focuses on parents' responses to children's normative emotional expressions. Although we consider it reasonable to construe depressive symptoms as being at one end of a continuum of normative affective expression, the connection between early socialization of depressive-like behaviors and subsequent depressive functioning is, at this point, speculative. Further research, with an emphasis on longitudinal designs, is needed to better establish this connection.

Socialization of Risk Factors for Depression

As noted above, the acceptance and encouragement of depressive-like behaviors in girls may set the stage for elevated levels of depressive symptoms. However, familial processes may also increase girls' risk for depression in subtler ways. In this section, we review the literature related to socialization processes that may render girls vulnerable by both engendering depressogenic cognitive and interpersonal styles and failing to provide them with effective behavioral repertoires for responding to the demands of adolescence and adulthood (Hops, 1996; Nolen-Hoeksema, 1994; Ruble & Martin, 1998). As regards to depressogenic socialization processes, particular attention has been directed toward the socialization of girls to be more relationship-oriented and less instrumental than boys (Compas, Ey, & Grant, 1993; Peterson, 1991; Powers & Welsh, 1999). Below we discuss evidence that parental socialization processes vary as a function of child gender. Then we examine in more detail evidence regarding adolescent gender differences in these domains and their potential associations with depressive functioning. Although we deal with the evidence for relationship orientation and instrumentality separately, we consider it likely that the two operate in tandem to increase girls' vulnerability to depression.

Gender-Differentiated Socialization

As noted above, it has been proposed that parents socialize girls to be more relationship-oriented and less instrumental than boys. Huston (1983) reported that girls receive more encouragement for dependency and affectionate behavior. They are also reported to receive more support for nurturant play (Ruble, Greulich, Pomerantz, & Gochberg, 1993). Block (1983) reported that in Baby X studies in which infants are "assigned" a gender (i.e., the same baby is referred to as a boy and a girl in interactions with different partici-pants), adults provided more reinforcement for nurturant play when the baby was said to be a girl; such evidence is compelling in that Baby X studies control for gender differences in children's actual behavior. On a related note, evidence suggests that mothers encourage girls more than boys to have concern for others, share, and behave prosocially (see Keenan & Shaw, 1997, for a review). Moreover, they may be less attentive to girls' assertive behav-ior (Kerig, Cowan, & Cowan, 1993).

Parents may also impede the development of girls' sense of mastery by limiting their activities and freedom. In a 1983 review of the literature, Block reported that mothers were more likely to give unnecessary assistance to girls than to boys and were more likely to reward frustration with physical com-fort. Huston (1983) similarly concluded that girls are given more help in achievement situations. Block also reported that in teaching tasks, fathers set lower standards and paid less attention to the cognitive elements of the tasks with girls than with boys, focusing instead on joking, playing, and pro-tecting. Furthermore, it has been reported that boys were given a greater variety of toys and more freedom to explore, hence providing them with greater opportunity to manipulate and receive feedback from their physical environment and to develop leadership abilities (Block, 1983; Ruble et al., 1993; Ruble & Martin, 1998).

Some evidence suggests that gender-differentiated parenting behaviors continue into adolescence. Adolescent girls are allowed less independence and freedom of activity (Block, 1978; Simmons & Blyth, 1987). Similarly, parents of adolescent girls underestimate their daughters' competencies in traditionally male areas (Eccles, Jacobs, & Harold, 1990) and report lesser achievement-oriented aspirations for them than do parents of boys (Simmons & Blyth, 1987). In fact, it has been suggested that differences in parental expectations (Nolen-Hoeksema & Girgus, 1994) and pressure to conform to sex-role prescribed activities and behavioral styles may increase with adoles-cence (Hill & Lynch, 1983).

The evidence reviewed thus far lends support to the hypothesis that gender-differentiated socialization patterns may contribute to girls' greater vulnerability to depression. However, it is important to note that the major-ity of studies from which the above evidence is drawn were conducted in the 1970s and early 1980s and that socialization patterns may have shifted since this research was published. Moreover, in a recent meta-analysis of research dating back to the 1950s, Lytton and Romney (1991) concluded that despite the modest evidence of parental encouragement for sex-typed activities, the evidence did not support overall differences in parental restrictiveness or encouragement of either achievement or dependency differed as a function of child gender. Hence, the evidence for the shaping of differential activities for girls and boys appears to be stronger than that for other areas of gender socialization.

Relationship Orientation

It has been widely reported that girls are more relationship oriented than are boys (Nolen-Hoeksema & Girgus, 1994; Wong & Cszikmihalyi, 1991). Relationship orientation has been broadly construed to include many related variables that, although not necessarily problematic, may nonetheless render girls more prone to depression. First, it has been suggested that girls are socialized to be more dependent on others for support and self-esteem (Hops et al., 1990; Maccoby, 1990) such that they are likely to experience distress in the face of relationship strain or disruption (Leadbeater, Blatt, & Quinlan, 1995). For example, Leadbeater and colleagues reported that girls' reports of interpersonal vulnerability were more closely tied to depressive symptoms than were boys' reports. It has also been suggested that this dependency may make the adolescent-appropriate transitions from the family environment into more complex social milieus more challenging for girls than for boys (Hops, 1996; Powers & Welsh, 1999). Evidence that social support (Avison & McAlpine, 1992; Schraedley, Gotlib, & Hayward, 1999) and social stress (Moran & Eckenrode, 1991) are more strongly related to depression in girls than in boys is consistent with this hypothesis in that it suggests that the quality of girls' social relationships may be more closely tied to their well-being. However, the gender difference in the importance of social support is not always found (e.g., Moran & Eckenrode, 1991). Moreover, in their review of evidence regarding gender differences in adolescent depression, Nolen-Hoeksema and Girgus (1994) make a compelling argument that the literature does not support the hypothesis that girls are more dependent on others.

It has also been proposed that girls' socialization experiences predispose them to be more nurturing than boys (e.g., Zahn-Waxler, Cole, & Barrett, 1991). The developmental literature reveals that sex differences in nurturant behavior are observed early in life (Radke-Yarrow, Zahn-Waxler, Richardson, & Susman, 1994; Zahn-Waxler & Smith, 1992). Thus, it has been argued that young girls may develop an overgeneralized sense of responsibility for the well-being of others (Zahn-Waxler & Robinson, 1995). Furthermore, in adults it is well-documented that women take more responsibility for the nurturing and caretaking of those in their social networks, exposing themselves to a broader range of stressors and the incumbent risk for depression (McGrath, Keita, Strickland, & Russo, 1990). Taken together, this pattern of results suggests that similar relationship burdens may pose a risk for the emotional well-being of girls in adolescence when their social worlds begin to broaden. However, we are unaware of research specifically addressing the relation between adolescent caretaking behaviors and depression.

Third, it has been proposed that girls are raised to be more concerned with the feelings and perspectives of others (Hops, 1996; Keenan & Shaw, 1997; Maccoby, 1990) and that this concern may render them less effective in asserting their own positions and influencing their social environments. The interaction style of girls in groups is focused on cooperation and maintenance of positive relationships between group members, whereas boys are more focused on competition and dominance; these differences have been shown to exist throughout the life span (Nolen-Hoeksema & Girgus, 1994). These interactional differences result in girls finding it difficult to influence boys; the reverse is not true (Serbin, Sprafkin, Elman, & Doyle, 1984). Such difficulties may render social interactions less reinforcing and contribute to feelings of learned helplessness, both of which are obvious risk factors for depression. It has been suggested that differences in the interactional styles of girls and boys may become particularly problematic in adolescence when the sex-segregated peer groups of childhood begin to give way to more mixed-sex social and occupational activities (Maccoby, 1990; Nolen-Hoeksema, 1994). However, the hypothesis that these gender-differentiated interactional styles so hamper girls' social functioning in adolescence that they contribute to the greater incidence of depression remains to be tested.

Instrumentality

It has been proposed that gender-typic socialization processes do not promote the development of instrumental and problem-solving skills in girls and thus result in narrower behavioral repertoires for addressing the challenges of adolescence (e.g., Allgood-Merten, Lewinsohn, & Hops, 1990). Furthermore, girls' socialization experiences may also result in their having lower perceptions of self-efficacy (Ruble et al., 1993). Thus, girls may have the combined disadvantage of inadequate skills and depressive cognitions derived from both failure experiences and the inadvertent messages of socialization agents. Perhaps the strongest evidence in support of the instrumentality hypothesis comes from Nolen-Hoeksema's work demonstrating the positive correlation between ruminative coping and depression. She contrasted ruminative responses to distressed affect, which are both more passive in nature and more characteristic of female individuals, with the more assertive, instrumental styles of coping displayed by male individuals (Nolen-Hoeksema, 1998). Additional evidence for the instrumentality hypothesis comes from two large-scale epidemiological studies of depression indicating that girls' lower levels of instrumentality (Allgood-Merten et al., 1990) and higher levels of female sex-role identification (Wichstrom, 1999) account, at least in part, for observed gender differences in depression. Similarly, Nolen-Hoeksema and Girgus (1994) reported that adolescent girls' engagement in stereotypical feminine-type activities (e.g., cooking and sewing) was associated with greater depressive symptoms. Although these data support the instrumentality hypothesis, these studies are based solely on adolescents' self-reports. Whether girls actually demonstrate deficits in instrumental behavior and whether such deficits are related to gender differences in depression cannot be determined from the available data.

There is also modest evidence that girls have lower evaluations of their own efficacy and that such evaluations are related to depressive symptoms (Avison & McAlpine, 1992; Ohannessian, Lerner, Lerner, & von Eye, 1999). In a recent review, Ruble et al. (1993) reported that preadolescents girls, in comparison to boys, report lower expectations for success, more maladaptive attributions for success and failure, and poorer self-esteem. Although gender differences did not emerge in all of the studies reviewed by Ruble and colleagues, the direction of effects was consistent when gender differences were observed. However, it is important to remain cognizant of the likelihood that disturbances in perceived self-competence may be consequences rather than causes of depressive symptoms. Two recent longitudinal studies by Cole and colleagues (Cole, Martin, Peeke, Seroczynski, & Fier, 1999; Cole, Martin, Peeke, Seroczynski, & Hoffman, 1998) suggest that children's underestimates of their own competence emerge as a function of depressive symptoms and that controlling for depression eliminates the observed gender differences.

INCREASED RISK POSED BY MATERNAL DEPRESSION

The socialization-based model presented here is not specific to daughters of depressed women, but rather is relevant to understanding adolescents girls' vulnerability to depression in general. Given the high incidence of depression in girls with depressed mothers, however, it is important to explicate the manner in which maternal depression functions to place them at greater risk. It is likely that maternal depression operates, in part, as a nonspecific stressor, increasing the risks that already exist for girls as a function of gender-typic behavioral styles and the normative challenges of adolescence. Weissman et al.'s (1987) finding that having a depressed parent accelerates the onset of depressive disorders in children is notable in this regard. We expect that the vulnerability factors engendered by girls' socialization experiences would function similarly in response to other stressors. This is consistent with evidence that girls respond to stressors such as marital discord (Cummings, Davies, & Simpson, 1994) and economic hardship (Conger, Conger, Matthews, & Elder, 1999) with internalizing symptoms.

Furthermore, the intergenerational transmission of depression appears to be mediated by familial processes that are associated with, but not unique to, maternal depression. That is, maternal depression is associated with disruptions in marital and parenting relationships that operate as the more direct links to adverse child outcomes (Rutter & Quinton, 1984). As an extreme example of this, Andrews, Brown, and Creasey (1990) reported that the transmission of psychopathology from mothers to daughters was explained, at least in part, by the increased risk of abuse of the daughters at the hands of the mothers' domestic partners. Furthermore, maternal parenting behavior has been shown to be a major mechanism by which maternal depression exerts its influence on child outcomes (Billings & Moos, 1983; Schwartz, Dorer, Beardslee, Lavori, & Keller, 1990; Whitbeck et al., 1992). Numerous studies have demonstrated that compared to nondepressed mothers, depressed mothers display aversive parenting behaviors characterized by fewer positive and more negative behaviors (e.g., Hammen et al., 1987; Radke-Yarrow, 1990), the use of physical punishment (Ghodsian, Zajicek, & Wolkind, 1984), and lower levels of affectionate responding (Reid & Morrison, 1983).

Although the impairments in parenting associated with maternal depression are not specific to interactions between mothers and daughters, girls may nonetheless be at greater risk than boys. First, as noted earlier, girls' relationships with their mothers during adolescence are more conflictual (Steinberg, 1987, 1988), and as a result daughters of depressed mothers may be exposed to greater levels of aversive interactions than sons. Second, if (as described earlier) girls are allowed lesser autonomy and have been socialized to be more relationship and family oriented, they may be more sensitive to disturbances in parent–child relationships. This finding has been noted in a number of studies of adolescent depression (e.g., Avison & McAlpine, 1992; Rubin et al., 1992; Slavin & Rainer, 1990). It should be noted, however, that not all studies demonstrate this differential sensitivity. In fact, in a recent multimethod study we (Sheeber, Hops, Alpert, Davis, & Andrews, 1997) found that the relations between depressive symptoms and both family conflict and support did not differ across gender in a community sample of adolescents. Understanding the circumstances in which girls are more vulnerable to family processes is an important direction for ongoing research; it is unclear at this point whether differential socialization processes are operative.

Maternal depression contributes more specific risks, however. First, depressed women provide a model for depressive interpersonal behaviors; this model may prove to be especially salient to their same-sex offspring. Microsocial observations of family interactions have demonstrated that women's depressive behaviors are reinforced by the behavior of other family members. In particular, it appears that women's depressive behavior is negatively reinforced by reduced aggressiveness on the part of both their spouses (Biglan et al., 1985; Hops et al., 1987) and their children (Dumas & Gibson, 1990). Thus, not only do children observe depressive behavior, but they also learn that it is effective in influencing the social environment. More recently, we have found that parents of adolescents with elevated depressive symptoms are more likely than parents of nondepressed adolescents to reinforce depressive behavior, with mothers increasing facilitative behavior and fathers decreasing aggressive behavior contingent on adolescent displays of depressive behavior (Sheeber, Hops, Andrews, Alpert, & Davis, 1998). Powers and Welsh (1999) have reported indirect evidence that girls' submissive behavior (which is associated with increasing depression over time) may be reinforced by reductions in maternal assertiveness. Although neither of these studies allows us to draw any conclusions as to whether reinforcing responses to adolescent depressive behaviors are more or less likely in the context of maternal depression, they suggest that should children adopt depressive patterns of behavior, they may find them to be effective.

Depressed women may also impart to their children their own deficits in problem-solving and coping with distressed affect and hence increase the children's susceptibility to depression (Compas et al., 1988; Kashani, Burbach, & Rosenberg, 1988). Garber, Braafladt, and Zeman (1991) found that compared to nondepressed mothers, depressed mothers responded to children's negative affect with more directive, less supportive, and less problem-solving behavior. In the same study, both depressed mothers and their children generated fewer and poorer strategies for responding to negative affect and had lower expectations that their strategies would be effective. Similarly, Nolen-Hoeksema, Wolfson, Mumme, and Guskin (1995) found that children of depressed mothers demonstrate more passive, helpless responses to frustration than do children of nondepressed mothers, especially when the mothers demonstrate ruminative styles of depression. Furthermore, there is preliminary evidence that children and adolescents use conflict resolution strategies similar to those of their parents (Hamilton, Hammen, Minasian, & Jones, 1993; Kashani et al., 1988). Depressed mothers' inability to provide models of effective coping or to help their children to resolve difficult situations and emotional states may thus compound the risks inherent in socialization experiences for the daughters of depressed mothers. An important step for future research in this area is to examine whether children's styles of coping with problem situations and the experience of negative affect contribute to the transmission of depressive symptoms from mothers to their children.

Depressive behavior clearly elicits caretaking and a sense of responsibility in those who are exposed to it (Biglan, Rothlind, Hops, & Sherman, 1989; Hokanson, Loewenstein, Hedeen, & Howes, 1986; Stephens, Hokanson, & Welker, 1987). As a function of socialization processes that lead girls to be more nurturing, this burden falls differentially on girls and women. In general, it has been hypothesized that caretaking and support responsibilities take a toll on women and increase their risk for depression (McGrath, Keita, Strickland, & Russo, 1990). Leadbeater et al. (1995) reported that girls demonstrate greater reactivity than boys to stressful events occurring to others. Gore, Aseltine, and Colten (1993) reported that adolescent girls who were more involved with their mothers' problems reported higher levels of depressive symptoms than those who were less involved. It is likely that such challenges are amplified for female children of depressed mothers in that they do not have the skills to effectively nurture their mothers or relieve their distress. Zahn-Waxler et al. (1991) noted that given exposure to extreme, chronic distress of others, empathic feelings may develop into responsibility and guilt, both of which may serve as a an additional vulnerability factor for the development of depressive disorder. Longitudinal studies that directly address this potential mechanism for the intergenerational transmission of depression are needed.

IMPLICATIONS FOR CLINICIANS

The findings in the preceding sections identify a number of potential targets for behavior change that could prove effective for reducing risk of depressive disorder in the offspring of depressed women. Given our focus on family processes as the mechanism by which risk of disorder is transmitted across generations, we think in terms of interventions that influence the parenting behavior of depressed women and their partners so as to reduce their offsprings' exposure to stressful circumstances and improve their ability to regulate dysphoric affect and cope with the stressors that do occur. For example, young children of both sexes may benefit from direct teaching of active responses to alter negative affective states and interpersonal problem situations, a set of skills that boys may be learning to a greater extent than girls. Moreover, it may be important to help parents to recognize and discontinue the inadvertent reinforcement of children's depressive behavior, which may be more common in parents of girls, and replace them with contingencies that reinforce adaptive social and problem-solving behaviors. Mothers may also benefit from learning strategies to reduce their emotional reliance on their children. More generally, behavioral interventions to reduce family conflict, particularly between mothers and daughters, and to increase prosocial interactions would be beneficial.

SUMMARY AND FUTURE DIRECTIONS

The evidence that the nature and extent of risk for psychopathology posed to children of depressed mothers varies as a function of child gender and age is modest, owing in large part to the dearth of studies with samples of clinically diagnosed women. At present, there is very little evidence that the prepubertal sons of depressed women are at differential risk for conduct problems. On the other hand, available evidence does suggest that adolescent daughters of depressed women are at elevated risk for depressive and symptoms disorders. This conclusion is based on findings from several lines of research, including (a) observed covariation in depressive symptoms between mothers and adolescent daughters in community samples (Hops, 1995, 1996); (b) daughters' greater overall negative affect and greater synchrony in mother–daughter negative affect in the offspring of women with unipolar depressive disorder (Hops et al., 1990; Radke-Yarrow et al., 1993); and (c) greater rates of depressive disorder in both male and female children of clinically depressed women (Downey & Coyne, 1990). Given that similar relations between maternal depression and adverse child outcomes have been observed in community and clinical samples (e.g., Hammen, Burge, Burney, & Adrian, 1990; Hops, 1992, 1996), and given our own research bias toward conceptualizing depression as a class of behaviors that range in frequency and intensity from low levels of distress and impairment to more problematic clinical levels (Davis, Sheeber, Hops, & Tildesley, 2000; Hops, 1992, 1995, 1996), we anticipate that similar findings regarding girls' differential vulnerability to depressive functioning would emerge in samples of clinically diagnosed women.

However, it is also possible that the more extreme levels of symptoms and the associated impairment in familial functioning would render offspring of both sexes increasingly vulnerable. Thus, we think that the first step for continued research is to establish whether the risk for psychopathology posed to offspring of clinically depressed mothers varies as a function of child gender. Although the smaller sample sizes characteristic of clinical research pose a clear obstacle to the examination of moderating variables in general, and gender in particular, we think that research in this area is clearly warranted because of the prevalence of depression in women, the demonstrated risk posed to their children, and the above described preliminary evidence regarding differential gender effects. Certainly, the dramatic increase in depressive symptoms with the onset of adolescence, especially for girls, suggests that developmental stage is an important moderator that must be considered in future studies. Moreover, such research may set the stage for more accurate and effective targeting of preventive interventions for children of depressed women. That said, however, the current evidentiary base does not seem to justify targeting preventive interventions for children of depressed women differentially as a function of child gender.

As regards the role of gender-typic socialization processes, the research to date does more to suggest the potential usefulness of continued research than to support firm conclusions. The work reviewed is largely consistent with the hypothesis that differences between the early socialization experiences of boys and girls result in gender differences in instrumentality and relationship orientation. In particular, it appears that there are gender-typic differences in parents' responses to children's emotional displays as well as in the activities which parents encourage in their young children. The extent of gender differences in other areas of socialization, however, is unclear. It appears, moreover, that girls are more nurturing and less instrumental than boys and that they have a more communal, less competitive approach to communication. The data regarding girls' greater dependency and lesser sense of self-efficacy are more equivocal. Finally, preliminary evidence supports the hypotheses that daughters of depressed mothers may be at additional risk as a function of greater familial and parent–child discord, a maternal model of depressive behavior, family processes that reward depressive behavior, and deficits in maternal ability to nurture the development of effective problem-solving and coping strategies.

It is important to note, however, that the model we present here has not been examined directly. Rather, findings from a range of studies covering developmental, social, and clinical domains have been pulled together to develop and support a potential explanation for girls' apparently greater risk. Thus, a great deal of research is still needed before firm conclusions can be drawn regarding the role of gender-differentiated socialization processes in offspring's risk for depression. Support for the socialization model begins with the evidence that parents' gender-differentiated responses to their children, beginning early in life and continuing through adolescence, socialize girls to be more relationship oriented and less instrumental than boys, as well as more inclined toward the expression of depressive behavior and affect.

In considering this evidence, a number of caveats should be noted. First, as the literature is correlational and largely cross-sectional, we cannot rule out the possibility that parents' sex-differentiated behavior toward their children emerge, at least in part, as a function of gender differences in children's behavioral and developmental repertoires. Of course, even if true, this would not negate the likelihood that parents' behavioral responses contribute to their children's ongoing development of gender-typical behavioral styles. However, longitudinal studies that control for the children's initial behavioral styles would provide stronger evidence of parental socialization. Second, much of the literature on the encouragement of gender-stereotyped behavior is dated, raising the specter of shifting cohort effects, especially given that the last three decades have seen a remarkable shift in gender equality and opportunities for women to demonstrate competence in areas previously denied them. Identifying cohort differences in the proposed mediators of depression may weaken the hypothesized link in the model given that more recent studies continue to demonstrate significantly higher levels of depressive symptoms in adolescent girls compared to boys (e.g., Jacobson & Crockett, 2000). Socialization processes may have changed, but we still must account for girls' greater vulnerability.

The model that we have presented further posits that girls' low instrumentality, relationship orientation, and comfort with expression of distressed affect are proximal variables accounting for girls' greater vulnerability to depression in adolescence. As described earlier, however, the research examining the association between many of these variables and adolescent depression is relatively sparse (with some notable exceptions, such as research on ruminative coping). Hence, important areas of further study are to examine these associations and to assess whether they account for observed gender differences in observed symptoms.

Future investigations directed at addressing the two key mediational relations proposed here are needed. First, there is very little research using longitudinal data to examine (a) whether differential socialization practices are associated with depressive symptoms in adolescence, (b) whether these associations are mediated by gender-stereotyped behavior as hypothesized, and (c) whether they mediate the relations between maternal and adolescent symptoms. Studies of the meditational relations are more difficult because they require following a child's development beginning at a very early age to witness the presence or absence of gender-specific socialization practices and continuing with follow-up assessments into adolescence when depressive symptoms dramatically increase.

REFERENCES

Allgood-Merten, B., Lewinsohn, P., & Hops, H. (1990). Sex differences and adolescent depression. *Journal of Abnormal Psychology, 99*, 55-63.

Andrews, B., Brown, G. W., & Creasey, L. (1990). Intergenerational links between psychiatric disorder in mothers and daughters: The role of parenting experiences. *Journal of Child Psychology and Psychiatry, 31*, 1115–1129.

Avison, W. R., & McAlpine, D. D. (1992, June). Gender differences in symptoms of depression among adolescents. *Journal of Health and Social Behavior, 33*, 77–96.

Biglan, A., Hops, H., Sherman, L., Friedman, L. S., Arthur, J., & Osteen, V. (1985). Problem-solving interactions of depressed women and their husbands. *Behavior Therapy, 16*, 431–451.

Biglan, A., Rothlind, J., Hops, H., & Sherman, L. (1989). Impact of distressed and aggressive behavior. *Journal of Abnormal Psychology, 98*, 218–228.

Billings, A. G., & Moos, R. H. (1983). Comparisons of children of depressed and nondepressed parents: A social–environmental perspective. *Journal of Abnormal Child Psychology, 11*, 463–486.

Block, J. H. (1978). Another look at sex differentiation in the socialization behaviors of mothers and fathers. In J. Sherman & F. Denmark (Eds.), *Psychology of women: Future directions of research* (pp. 29–87). New York: Psychological Dimensions.

Block, J. H. (1983). Differential premises arising from differential socialization of the sexes: Some conjunctures. *Child Development, 54*, 1335–1354.

Cole, D. A., Martin, J. M., Peeke, L. A., Seroczynski, A. D., & Fier, J. (1999). Children's over- and underestimation of academic competence: A longitudinal study of gender differences, depression, and anxiety. *Child Development, 70*, 459–473.

Cole, D. A., Martin, J. M., Peeke, L. G., Seroczynski, A. D., & Hoffman, K. (1998). Are cognitive errors of underestimation predictive or reflective of depressive symptoms in children: A longitudinal study. *Journal of Abnormal Psychology, 107*, 481–496.

Compas, B. E., Ey, S., & Grant, K. E. (1993). Taxonomy, assessment, and diagnosis of depression during adolescence. *Psychological Bulletin, 114*, 323–344.

Compas, B. E., Malcarne, V. L., & Fondacaro, K. M. (1988). Coping with stressful events in older children and young adolescents. *Journal of Consulting and Clinical Psychology, 56,* 405–411.

Conger, R. D., Conger, K. J., Matthews, L. S., & Elder, G. H., Jr. (1999). Pathways of economic influence on adolescent adjustment. *American Journal of Community Psychology, 27,* 519–541.

Cummings, E. M., & Davies, P. T. (1994). *Children and marital conflict: The impact of family dispute and resolution.* New York: Guilford Press.

Cummings, E. M., Davies, P. T., & Simpson, K. S. (1994). Marital conflict, gender, and children's appraisals and coping efficacy as mediators of child adjustment. *Journal of Family Psychology, 8,* 141–149.

Davies, P. T., & Windle, M. (1997). Gender-specific pathways between maternal depressive symptoms, family discord, and adolescent adjustment. *Developmental Psychology, 33,* 657–668.

Davis, B., Sheeber, L. B, Hops, H., & Tildesley, E. (2000). Child responses to parent depressive interactions in conflict situations: Implications for child depression. *Journal of Abnormal Child Psychology, 28,* 451–465.

Dino, G. A., Barnett, M. A., & Howard, J. A. (1984). Children's expectations of sex differences in parents' responses to sons and daughters encountering interpersonal problems. *Sex Roles, 11,* 709–717.

Downey, G., & Coyne, J. C. (1990). Children of depressed parents: An integrative review. *Psychological Bulletin, 108,* 50–76.

Dumas, J. E., & Gibson, J. A. (1990). Behavioral correlates of maternal depressive symptomatology in conduct-disorder children: II. Systemic effects involving fathers and siblings. *Journal of Consulting and Clinical Psychology, 58,* 877–881.

Eccles, J. S., Jacobs, J. E., & Harold, R. D. (1990). Gender role stereotypes, expectancy effects, and parents' socialization of gender differences. *Journal of Social Issues, 46*(2), 183–201.

Eisenberg, N., Cumberland, A., & Spinrad, T. L. (1998). Parental socialization of emotion. *Psychological Inquiry, 9*(4), 241–273.

Fergusson, D. M., Horwood, L. J., & Lynskey, M. T. (1995). Maternal depressive symptoms and depressive symptoms in adolescents. *Journal of Child Psychology and Psychiatry, 36,* 1161–1178.

Fivush, R. (1998). Methodological challenges in the study of emotional socialization. *Psychological Inquiry, 9,* 281–283.

Fuchs, D., & Thelen, M. H. (1988). Children's expected interpersonal consequences of communicating their affective state and reported likelihood of expression. *Child Development, 59,* 1314–1322.

Garber, J., Braafladt, N., & Zeman, J. (1991). The regulation of sad affect: An information-processing perspective. In J. Garber & K. A. Dodge (Eds.), *The development of emotional regulation and dysregulation* (pp. 208–242). Cambridge, England: Cambridge University Press.

Ge, X., Conger, R. D., Lorenz, F. O., Shanahan, M., & Elder, G. H. (1995). Mutual influences in parent and adolescent psychological distress. *Developmental Psychology, 31*, 406–419.

Ghodsian, M., Zajicek, E., & Wolkind, S. (1984). A longitudinal study of maternal depression and child behaviour problems. *Journal of Child Psychology and Psychiatry and Allied Disciplines, 25*, 91–109.

Goodman, S. H., & Gotlib, I. H. (1999). Risk for psychopathology in the children of depressed mothers: A developmental model for understanding mechanisms of transmission. *Psychological Review, 106*, 458–490.

Gore, S., Aseltine, R. H., Jr., & Colten, M. E. (1993). Gender, social-relational involvement, and depression. *Journal of Research on Adolescence, 3*, 101–125.

Gotlib, I. H., & Goodman, S. H. (1999). Children of parents with depression. In W. K. Silverman & T. H. Ollendick (Eds.), *Developmental issues in the clinical treatment of children* (pp. 415–432). Boston: Allyn & Bacon.

Hamilton, E. B., Hammen, C., Minasian, G., & Jones, M. (1993). Communication styles of children of mothers with affective disorders, chronic medical illness, and normal controls: A contextual perspective. *Journal of Abnormal Child Psychology, 21*(1), 51–63.

Hammen, C., Burge, D., Burney, E., & Adrian, C. (1990). Longitudinal study of diagnoses in children of women with unipolar and bipolar affective disorder. *Archives of General Psychiatry, 47*, 1112–1117.

Hammen, C., Gordon, D., Burge, D., Adrian, C., Jaenicke, C., & Hiroto, D. (1987). Communication patterns of mothers with affective disorders and their relationship to children's status and social functioning. In K. Hahlweg & M. J. Goldstein (Eds.), *Understanding major mental disorder: The contribution of family interaction research* (pp. 103–119). New York: Family Process Press.

Hankin, B., Abramson, L., Moffitt, T., Silva, P., McGee, R., & Angell, K. (1998). Development of depression from preadolescence to young adulthood: Emerging gender differences in a 10-year longitudinal sample. *Journal of Abnormal Psychology, 107*, 128–140.

Harnish, J., Dodge, K., & Valente, E. (1995). Mother–child interaction quality as a partial mediator of the roles of maternal depressive symptomatology and socioeconomic status in the development of child behavior problems. *Child Development, 66*, 739–753.

Hayward, C., Gotlib, I. H., Schraedley, M. A., & Litt, I. F. (1999). Ethnic differences in the association between pubertal status and symptoms of depression in adolescent girls. *Journal of Adolescent Health, 25*, 143–149.

Hill, J. P., Holmbeck, G. N., Marlow, L., Green, T. M., & Lynch, M. E. (1985). Menarcheal status and parent–child relations in families of seventh-grade girls [Special Issue: Time of maturation and psychosocial functioning in adolescence: II]. *Journal of Youth and Adolescence, 14*, 301–316.

Hill, J. P., & Lynch, M. E. (1983). The intensification of gender-related role expectations during early adolescence. In J. Brooks-Gunn & A. Petersen (Eds.), *Girls at puberty: Biological and psychosocial perspectives* (pp. 201–208). New York: Plenum Press.

Hokanson, J. E., Loewenstein, D. A., Hedeen, C., & Howes, M. J. (1986). Dysphoric college students and roommates: A study of social behaviors over a three-month period. *Personality and Social Psychology Bulletin, 12*(3), 311–324.

Hops, H. (1992). Parental depression and child behaviour problems: Implications for behavioural family intervention. *Behaviour Change, 9*(3), 126–138.

Hops, H. (1995). *Gender-related differences in depressive and aggressive behavior: Effects of familial social contingencies.* Unpublished manuscript.

Hops, H. (1996). Intergenerational transmission of depressive symptoms: Gender and developmental considerations. In C. Mundt, M. J. Goldstein, K. Hahlweg, & P. Fiedler (Eds.), *Interpersonal factors in the origin and course of affective disorders* (pp. 113–128). London: Gaskell/Royal College of Psychiatrists.

Hops, H., Biglan, A., Sherman, L., Arthur, J., Friedman, L., & Osteen, V. (1987). Home observations of family interactions of depressed women. *Journal of Consulting and Clinical Psychology, 55*, 341–346.

Hops, H., Sherman, L., & Biglan, A. (1990). Maternal depression, marital discord, and children's behavior: A developmental perspective. In G. R. Patterson (Ed.), *Depression and aggression in family interaction* (pp. 185–208). Hillsdale, NJ: Erlbaum.

Huston, A. C. (1983). Sex-typing. In P. H. Mussen (Ed.), *Handbook of child psychology* (pp. 387–467). New York: Wiley.

Jacobson, J. C., & Crockett, L. J. (2000). Parental monitoring and adolescent adjustment: An ecological perspective. *Journal of Research on Adolescence, 10*(1), 65–97.

Kashani, J. H., Beck, N. C., Hoeper, E. W., Fallahi, C., Corcoran, C. M., McAllister, J. A., Rosenberg, T. K., & Reid, J. C. (1987). Psychiatric disorders in a community sample of adolescents. *American Journal of Psychiatry, 144*, 584–589.

Kashani, J. H., Burbach, D. J., & Rosenberg, T. K. (1988). Perception of family conflict resolution and depressive symptomatology in adolescents. *Journal of the American Academy of Child and Adolescent Psychiatry, 27*, 42–48.

Kavanagh, K., & Hops, H. (1994). Good girls? Bad boys? Gender and development as contexts for diagnosis and treatment. In T. H. Ollendick & R. J. Prinz (Eds.), *Advances in clinical child psychology* (pp. 45–79). New York: Plenum Press.

Keenan, K., & Shaw, D. (1997). Developmental and social influences on young girls' early problem behavior. *Psychological Bulletin, 121*, 95–113.

Kerig, P. K., Cowan, P. A., & Cowan, C. P. (1993). Marital quality and gender differences in parent–child interaction. *Developmental Psychology, 29*, 931–939.

Leadbeater, B. J., Blatt, S. J., & Quinlan, D. M. (1995). Gender-linked vulnerabilities to depressive symptoms, stress, and problem behaviors in adolescents. *Journal of Research on Adolescence, 5*(1), 1–29.

Lewinsohn, P. M., Hops, H., Roberts, R. E., Seeley, J. R., & Andrews, J. A. (1993). Adolescent psychopathology: I. Prevalence and incidence of depression and other *DSM–III–R* disorders in high school students. *Journal of Abnormal Psychology, 102*, 133–144.

Lytton, H., & Romney, D. M. (1991). Parents' differential socialization of boys and girls: A meta-analysis. *Psychological Bulletin, 109,* 267–296.

Maccoby, E. E. (1990). Gender and relationships: A developmental account. *American Psychologist, 45,* 513–520.

McGrath, E., Keita, G. P., Strickland, B. R., & Russo, N. F. (1990). *Women and depression: Risk factors and treatment issues.* Washington, DC: American Psychological Association.

Montemayor, R. (1983). Parents and adolescents in conflict: All of the families some of the time and some families most of the time. *Journal of Early Adolescence, 3,* 83–103.

Moran, P. B., & Eckenrode, J. (1991). Gender differences in the costs and benefits of peer relationships during adolescence. *Journal of Adolescent Research, 6,* 396–409.

Nolen-Hoeksema, S. (1987). Sex differences in unipolar depression: Evidence and theory. *Psychological Bulletin, 101,* 259–282.

Nolen-Hoeksema, S. (1994). An interactive model for the emergence of gender differences in depression in adolescence. *Journal of Research on Adolescence, 4,* 519–534.

Nolen-Hoeksema, S. (1998). Ruminative coping with depression. In J. Heckhausen & C. S. Dweck (Eds.), *Motivation and self-regulation across the life span* (pp. 237–256). New York: Cambridge University Press.

Nolen-Hoeksema, S., & Girgus, J. (1994). The emergence of gender differences in depression during adolescence. *Psychological Bulletin, 115,* 424–443.

Nolen-Hoeksema, S., Wolfson, A., Mumme, D., & Guskin, K. (1995). Helplessness in children of depressed and nondepressed mothers. *Developmental Psychology, 31,* 377–387.

Ohannessian, C. M., Lerner, R. M., Lerner, J. V., & von Eye, A. (1999). Does self-competence predict gender differences in adolescent depression and anxiety? *Journal of Adolescence, 22,* 397–411.

Petersen, A. C., Sarigiani, P. A., & Kennedy, R. E. (1991). Adolescent depression: Why more girls? *Journal of Youth and Adolescence, 20,* 247–271.

Peterson, C. (1991). The meaning and measurement of explanatory style. *Psychological Inquiry, 2,* 1–10.

Powers, S. I., & Welsh, D. P. (1999). Mother–daughter interactions and adolescent girls' depression. In M. J. Cox & J. Brooks-Gunn (Eds.), *Conflict and cohesion in families: Causes and consequences* (pp. 243–281). Mahwah, NJ: Erlbaum.

Radke-Yarrow, M. (1990). Family environments of depressed and well parents and their children: Issues of research methods. In G. R. Patterson (Ed.), *Depression and aggression in family interaction* (pp. 169–184). Hillsdale, NJ: Erlbaum.

Radke-Yarrow, M., Nottelmann, E., Belmont, B., & Welsh, J. D. (1993). Affective interactions of depressed and nondepressed mothers and their children. *Journal of Abnormal Child Psychology, 21,* 683–695.

Radke-Yarrow, M., Zahn-Waxler, C. Richardson, D., & Susman, A. (1994). Caring behavior in children of clinically depressed and well mothers. *Child Development, 65,* 1405–1414.

Reid, W. H., & Morrison, H. L. (1983). Risk factors in children of depressed parents. In H. L. Morrison (Ed.), *Children of depressed parents* (pp. 33–46). New York: Grune & Stratton.

Rubin, C., Rubenstein, J. L., Stechler, G., Heeren, T., Halton, A., Housman, D., & Kasten, L. (1992). Depressive affect in "normal" adolescents: Relationship to life stress, family, friends. *American Journal of Orthopsychiatry, 62,* 430–441.

Ruble, D. N., Greulich, F., Pomerantz, E. M., & Gochberg, B. (1993). The role of gender-related processes in the development of sex differences in self-evaluation and depression. *Journal of Affective Disorders, 29,* 97–128.

Ruble, D. N., & Martin, C. L. (1998). Gender development. In N. Eisenberg (Ed.), *Social, emotional, and personality development* (pp. 933–1016). New York: Wiley.

Rutter, M., & Quinton, D. (1984). Parental psychiatric disorder: Effects on children. *Psychological Medicine, 14,* 853–880.

Schraedley, M. A., Gotlib, I. H., & Hayward, C. (1999). Gender differences in correlates of depressive symptoms in adolescents. *Journal of Adolescent Health, 25,* 98–108.

Schwartz, C. E., Dorer, D. J., Beardslee, W. R., Lavori, P. W., & Keller, M. B. (1990). Maternal expressed emotion and parental affective disorder: Risk for childhood depressive disorder, substance abuse, or conduct disorder. *Journal of Psychiatric Research, 24*(3), 231–250.

Serbin, L. A., Sprafkin, C., Elman, M., & Doyle, A. (1984). The early development of sex differentiated patterns of social influence. *Canadian Journal of Social Science, 14,* 350–363.

Sheeber, L., Hops, H., Alpert, A., Davis, B., & Andrews, J. (1997). Family support and conflict: Prospective relations to adolescent depression. *Journal of Abnormal Child Psychology, 25,* 333–344.

Sheeber, L., Hops, H., Andrews, J. A., Alpert, A., & Davis, B. (1998). Interactional processes in families with depressed and nondepressed adolescents: Reinforcement of depressive behavior. *Behaviour Research and Therapy, 36,* 417–427.

Simmons, R. G., & Blyth, D. A. (1987). *Moving into adolescence. The impact of pubertal change and school context.* New York: Aldine de Gruyter.

Slavin, L. A., & Rainer, K. L. (1990). Gender differences in emotional support and depressive symptoms among adolescents: A prospective analysis. *American Journal of Community Psychology, 18,* 407–421.

Steinberg, L. (1987). Recent research on the family at adolescence: The extent and nature of sex differences. *Journal of Youth and Adolescence, 16,* 191–197.

Steinberg, L. (1988). Reciprocal relation between parent–child distance and pubertal maturation. *Developmental Psychology, 24,* 122–128.

Stephens, R. S., Hokanson, J. E., & Welker, R. (1987). Responses to depressed interpersonal behavior: Mixed reactions in a helping role. *Journal of Personality and Social Psychology, 52,* 1274–1282.

Thomas, A. M., & Forehand, R. (1991). A response to Levant: There is little disagreement but a need for more research. *Journal of Family Psychology, 4,* 276–277.

Velez, C. N., Johnson, J., & Cohen, P. (1989). A longitudinal analysis of selected risk factors for childhood psychopathology. *Journal of the American Academy of Child and Adolescent Psychiatry, 28,* 861–864.

Weissman, M. M., Gammon, G., John, K., Merikangas, K. R., Warner, V., Prusoff, B. A., & Sholomskas, D. (1987). Children of depressed parents: Increased psychopathology and early onset of major depression. *Archives of General Psychiatry, 44,* 847–853.

Whitbeck, L. B., Hoyt, D. R., Simons, R. L., Conger, R. D., Elder, G. H., Lorenz, F. O., & Huck, S. (1992). Intergenerational continuity of parental rejection and depressed affect. *Journal of Personality and Social Psychology, 63,* 1036–1045.

Wichstrom, R. (1999). The emergence of gender differences in depressed mood during adolescence: The role of intensified gender socialization. *Developmental Psychology, 33,* 232–245.

Wong, M. M., & Czikszentmihalyi, M. (1991). Affiliation motivation and daily experience: Some issues on gender differences. *Journal of Personality and Social Psychology, 60,* 154–164.

Zahn-Waxler, C., Cole, P. M., & Barrett, K. C. (1991). Guilt and empathy: Sex differences and implications for the development of depression. In J. Garber & K. A. Dodge (Eds.), *The development of emotion regulation and dysregulation* (pp. 243–272). Cambridge, England: Cambridge University Press.

Zahn-Waxler, C., & Robinson, J. (1995). Empathy and guilt: Early origins of feelings of responsibility. In J. P. Tangney & K. W. Fischer (Eds.), *Self-conscious emotions: The psychology of shame, guilt, embarrassment, and pride* (pp. 143–173). New York: Guilford Press.

Zahn-Waxler, C., & Smith, K. D. (1992). The development of prosocial behavior. In V. B. Van Hasselt & M. Hersen (Eds.), *Handbook of social development: A lifespan perspective* (pp. 229–256). New York: Plenum Press.

III

Intervention, Integration, and Recommendations

12

TREATMENT, INTERVENTION, AND PREVENTION WITH CHILDREN OF DEPRESSED PARENTS: A DEVELOPMENTAL PERSPECTIVE

TRACY R. G. GLADSTONE AND WILLIAM R. BEARDSLEE

Research in the past three decades has established unequivocally an association between parental depression and poor outcome in children (Beardslee, Versage, & Gladstone, 1998; Downey & Coyne, 1990). Numerous studies have reported that relative to children with well parents, children from homes with affectively ill parents (i.e., parents with depressive illness or bipolar disorder) have higher rates of psychiatric disorders (e.g., Radke-Yarrow & Klimes-Dougan, chapter 7, this volume; Radke-Yarrow, Nottelmann, Martinez, Fox, & Belmont, 1992). In addition, children of affectively ill parents are at risk for a number of internalizing (e.g., Rubin, Both, Zahn-Waxler, Cummings, & Wilkinson, 1991) and externalizing (e.g., Harnish, Dodge, & Valente, 1995) problems relative to children whose parents are not ill, including general difficulties in functioning (Forehand & McCombs, 1988), more concerns about guilt (Zahn-Waxler, Kochanska, Krupnick, & McKnew, 1990), interpersonal difficulties (Rubin et al., 1991), and attachment difficulties (Teti, Gelfand, Messinger, & Isabella, 1995).

In recent years, research groups have focused on understanding the nature of the relation between parental depression and child functioning. Etiological studies have focused on genetic (e.g., Kendler, Neale, Kessler, Heath, & Eaves, 1993; Silberg & Rutter, chapter 2, this volume) and psychosocial (e.g., Rutter, 1990) explanations for the intergenerational transmission of psychopathology. Longitudinal studies have revealed that the disadvantages associated with growing up in a home with an affectively ill parent persist over time, even after parental depression subsides (Radke-Yarrow & Klimes-Dougan, chapter 7, this volume; Zahn-Waxler et al., 1988). Mediators and moderators of the relation between parental depression and child outcome have been explored in depth (e.g., Hammen, 1991, chapter 8, this volume). Finally, the impact of parental depression on children has been explored developmentally, revealing that the effects of parental depression, and particularly maternal depression, are different for children at each developmental stage (Goodman, 1992).

Children of affectively ill parents clearly represent a population at high risk for future depression and other forms of psychopathology. To date, however, this population has been neglected by researchers who focus mainly on treating, intervening in, and preventing disorders. We are aware of only a handful of research groups who have targeted this population in the development of intervention protocols. Here we review this research critically. Because parental depression affects children differentially at each developmental stage and the salient developmental issues shift throughout childhood and adolescence, we review this literature from a developmental perspective. That is, we identify some salient developmental issues for infants, toddlers, and adolescents, and we review the relevant research on treatment and intervention for children of depressed parents during these developmental stages, with a focus on ways in which the literature addresses these key issues. Because we are not aware of any literature on treatment or intervention with children of depressed parents during middle childhood, we omit this developmental stage in our review. Ultimately, we argue that a preventive approach is required to address the unique vulnerabilities of children with depressed parents.

Throughout this chapter, our discussion of the impact of parental depression on children generally refers to depressed mothers. As noted by Goodman (1992), most research on the intergenerational transmission of affective illness has focused on the relationship between depressed mothers and their children. When study results refer to both mothers and fathers, we note this in our review. In addition, a range of definitions has been used to refer to depressive symptoms in parents. Specifically, some researchers label mothers as *depressed* if they endorse a standard number of symptoms on a self-report measure of depressive symptoms (e.g., Pelaez-Nogueras, Field, Cigales, Gonzalez, & Clasky, 1994); others define depression or other affective illness through structured diagnostic interviews (e.g., Beardslee et al., 1993). These diagnostic distinctions are clarified throughout this review.

INFANCY (BIRTH TO 12 MONTHS)

Overall, research on the developmental tasks of infancy relevant to the functioning of children with depressed parents falls into two distinct clusters. Specifically, infants have (a) internal goals, including a need to maintain homeostasis, feelings of security, and positive emotions, and (b) goals involving engagement in the social environment (Tronick, 1989). Cicchetti, Ganiban, and Barnett (1991) defined the first of these areas as homeostatic regulation, which they argue is primary in the first 3 months of life. The second area, involving the regulation of emotion and attention, is primary in months 4 through 9. Cicchetti et al. hypothesized that children who do not negotiate these developmental tasks during infancy are at risk for emotional dysregulation, which in turn places them at risk for a number of negative outcomes, including disruptions in cognitive, emotional, and social development.

A brief review of the literature on infant homeostatic and emotional regulation reveals that healthy infants are alert, active, and socially aware from the first days of life. In developing the Neonatal Behavioral Assessment Scale (NBAS), Brazelton (1973) demonstrated that neonates and very young infants respond to auditory and visual stimuli, respond to stress, show an ability to disregard distraction, and have motor skills and reflexive behaviors. Moreover, Murray and Cooper (1997) observed "a remarkable sensitivity in infants to the quality of their interpersonal environment from the first days of life" (p. 111). Research indicates that infants engage in reciprocal communication with their primary caregivers in the first months of life and that infants' communication experiences influence their own and their caregivers' emotional experiences (Tronick, 1989). Specifically, when infants are able to achieve their goals of homeostatic and emotional regulation, they experience positive emotions; when their efforts to achieve their goals are thwarted, particularly by insensitive or inconsistent maternal response, negative affective responses ensue.

Recent efforts to connect maternal depression and infant homeostatic and emotional regulation have revealed striking results. In the area of homeostatic regulation, research indicates that, relative to very young infants of nondepressed mothers, infants of depressed mothers evidence more sleep problems and crying (Cutrona & Troutman, 1986; Field, 1992, chapter 4, this volume). They have been described as more tense, less content, more fussy, and less physically active than infants of well mothers (e.g., Whiffen & Gotlib, 1989). In addition, Field and her colleagues (Field, 1997, chapter 4, this volume; Field, Fox, Pickens, & Nawrocki, 1995; Field, Pickens, Fox, Nawrocki, & Gonzalez, 1995) examined more physiological measures of homeostatic regulation and found that infants of depressed mothers, relative to infants of nondepressed mothers, had lower vagal tone (i.e., heart rate variability, which is associated with emotional reactivity and expressivity) at 6 months, less developed motor tone, lower activity levels, poorer orientation skills, and, at 3 months, were found to have right frontal EEG asymmetry, a pattern of brain electrical activity similar to that seen in chronically depressed adults.

A consistent relation between maternal depression and child outcome also has emerged in the area of emotional regulation. In fact, depressed mothers have been observed to be more distracted and preoccupied in their interactions with their infants and have themselves exhibited more dysregulated affect in their interactions with their babies, relative to mothers who are not depressed (Campbell, Cohn, Flanagan, Popper, & Meyers, 1992; Field, 1992, chapter 4, this volume). Murray and colleagues studied the speech patterns of depressed and nondepressed mothers in interactions with their infants and found that depressed mothers were more self-focused and less focused on their infants' actions (Murray, Kempton, Woolgar, & Hooper, 1993). Field and her colleagues found that depressed mothers and their 3-month-old infants, relative to nondepressed mother–infant dyads, were less likely to match behavior states (i.e., exhibit harmonious interactions), and matching behavior states were more likely to be negative and less likely to be positive than the matching behavior states of nondepressed mother–infant dyads (Field, Healy, Goldstein, & Guthertz, 1990; Field, chapter 4, this volume). Tronick (1989) suggested that, because depressed mothers' interactions with their infants are often poorly timed and intrusive, and because these mothers often display negative affect toward their infants, infants are unable to achieve the goals of interaction. Ultimately, with repeated negative interaction experiences, infants develop representations of themselves as ineffective.

Taken together, the research outlined above suggests several areas of focus for treatment and intervention efforts. Specifically, treatment and intervention programs are needed to address the deficits in homeostatic and emotional regulation frequently observed in infants with affectively ill parents. To date, we are aware of only two research groups that have studied directly the treatment of this group of infants. The research of Field and her colleagues addresses both homeostatic and emotional regulation, and Murray's Cambridge studies focus on emotional regulation in infants of depressed mothers. This research is reviewed in subsequent sections.

An Intervention Targeting Homeostatic Regulation

Based on studies of massage therapy benefits for high-risk preterm infants, Field and her colleagues (Field, chapter 4, this volume; Field et al., 1996) explored the effects of massage versus a rocking control in 1- to 3-month-old infants born to depressed adolescent mothers. They hypothesized that, relative to infants in a control group, massaged infants would exhibit greater daily weight gain, more organized sleep behaviors, more positive affect, and less physiological distress 6 weeks later. Mothers of these infants were single parents, were categorized as low socioeconomic status, and were on public assistance. Sixty-five percent were African American, and 35% were Hispanic. They were classified as depressed on the basis of a diagnosis of dysthymia on a structured diagnostic interview and their scores on a self-report measure of depressive symptoms. Infants who were assigned randomly to the massage therapy group were provided two 15-minute massages each week over a 6-week interval. Infants were massaged by a researcher trained on the procedure (see Field et al., 1996, for a description of the massage protocol). Infants who were assigned to the rocking control group were held in a cradled position by the researcher and rocked in a rocking chair for two 15-minute periods per week over the same 6-week interval.

Infants were observed during and immediately after the first and last massage–rocking sessions, and their behaviors were recorded using a time-sampling unit method. Among other things, infants' sleep–wake behavior, body movements, head turning, facial expressions (i.e., grimaces, smiles), startles, and clenched fists were noted. In addition, saliva samples were obtained immediately before and after the massage–rocking sessions and were assessed for indications of stress. Infants' nursery school teachers maintained records of daytime formula intake and rated the infants' temperaments on a standardized questionnaire. Mothers kept records of infants' nighttime bottle feedings. Finally, urine samples were collected on the first and last days of the study and were assessed for hormones indicating degree of stress.

Results indicated that infants who were assigned to the massage group were more alert and active during the massage, and they cried less and evidenced less physiological stress during the massage, relative to infants in the rocking group while they were being rocked. During the rocking session, infants were more likely to sleep than were infants in the midst of massage; however, following the sessions, massage group infants were more likely to sleep than were rocking group infants. In addition, infants in the massage group evidenced more change over the 6-week course of the study than did rocking group infants, as seen in a modest weight gain, improvements on emotionality, sociability, and soothability dimensions of temperament, and physiological indications of lowered stress. Such changes were not seen in infants assigned to the rocking group. This research suggests that a short-term, cost-effective intervention program targeting infants of depressed mothers in their first months of life may possibly counteract some of the risk associated with maternal postpartum depression and may ultimately assist infants in physiological self-regulation.

Interventions Targeting Emotional Regulation

In a series of studies, Field and her colleagues evaluated several different treatment and intervention programs that targeted the relation between maternal depression and emotional regulation in infants (see also Field, chapter 4, this volume). In all of these studies, participants consisted of a sample of young, low-income (e.g., on public assistance), ethnically diverse (i.e., African American, Hispanic, Caucasian) mothers and their newborn infants. Generally, mothers were classified as depressed on the basis of their scores on a self-report measure of depressive symptoms. Overall, infants were healthy and full-term.

Hart, Field, and Nearing (1998) addressed emotional regulation in their investigation of a short-term intervention with newborn infants and their depressed mothers. Based on findings that Brazelton-based interventions have a small positive effect on parenting quality, these researchers hypothesized that depressed mothers who saw the NBAS administered (Brazelton, 1973; Brazelton & Nugent, 1995) and then were instructed to administer a similar instrument to their infants (i.e., the Mother's Assessment of the Behavior of her Infant [MABI]; Field, Dempsey, Hallock, & Schuman, 1978) would see improvements in their infants 1 month later.

Mothers randomly assigned to the experimental group watched an examiner administer the NBAS to their infant and heard explanations of the infant's behaviors, strengths, and preferences; they then readministered the MABI to their infants at home weekly for 1 month. Mothers in the control group did not watch as the NBAS was administered to their infants. They were instructed to complete weekly assessments of their baby's developmental milestones and of their own parenting attitudes for 1 month. Mothers were contacted by phone throughout the month to ensure compliance.

When the NBAS was readministered to all of the infants 1 month later, by an examiner who was unaware of the infant's group status, interesting findings emerged. As hypothesized, no group differences in NBAS ratings were reported at delivery, but 1 month later infants in the experimental group were rated as more skilled on social interaction and state organization than were infants in the control group. Moreover, mothers of infants in the experimental group noted improvements in their infants' social, motor, and state organization skills. This research suggests that assisting mothers in recognizing and appreciating their infants' capabilities, and encouraging them to interact regularly with their infants rather than just attending to their physical needs, may ultimately eliminate some of the risk factors associated with maternal depression.

In the second of these studies (Pelaez-Nogueras et al., 1994), a group of 3-month-old infants were seated in an infant seat and made to participate in a 3-minute interaction with their mother and with their nursery provider. The order of these interactions was randomized. Mothers were instructed to play with their infants; nursery providers were told to interact with the infants as they would at the nursery. Interactions were recorded and analyzed using a standardized rating scale. Infants and mothers–providers were assessed for a variety of behaviors, including physical activity, facial expression, vocalizations, head orientation, and gaze behavior. Results indicated that, overall, the nursery providers received higher ratings, as did the infants when they were interacting with the nursery providers. These researchers concluded that infants' low activity levels and negative affect were specific to their interactions with their depressed mothers. That infants exhibited healthier behavior when with nondepressed familiar adults suggests that exposure to alternative nondepressed caregivers may actually encourage resilience in infants of depressed mothers. This is consistent with the findings of Beardslee and Podorefsky (1988), who reported that resilience during adolescence was associated with positive relationships with adults outside of the home.

In a third study, Malphurs et al. (1996) explored the effects of interaction coaching on the behaviors of depressed mothers and their infants. Interaction coaching is a technique designed to enhance maternal sensitivity and responsivity to the interaction cues of infants. Specifically, interaction coaching involves instruction by an examiner at two intervals: the first occurs before any interaction begins, and the second while the mother is interacting with her child (delivered through an earpiece speaker). These authors described two types of coaching, imitation (e.g., "imitate everything your baby does") and attention (e.g., "do whatever you can to keep your baby's attention"). Malphurs and colleagues also described two interaction patterns commonly seen in depressed mothers: withdrawn (i.e., passive, understimulating) or overly intrusive (i.e., overstimulating).

In this study, infants were between the ages of 3 and 6 months. At the start of the study, based on behavioral observations garnered from casual mother–infant interactions prior to coaching sessions, mothers were categorized as withdrawn or intrusive. All mothers were then assigned randomly, regardless of their interaction style, to either an imitation coaching or an attention coaching session. Following a single, 2-minute coaching session, mother–infant dyads were observed for a 2-minute spontaneous play interaction to determine whether mothers persisted in following the coaching instructions. All interactions were videotaped and coded based on standardized rating scales. It was hypothesized that imitation coaching for intrusive mothers and attention coaching for withdrawn mothers would result in significant improvement in infant behavioral ratings.

Results indicated that, when mothers were coached in a manner that complemented their interaction style (i.e., intrusive mothers coached in imitation condition, withdrawn mothers coached in attention condition), their interaction behaviors were improved. That is, among other findings, intrusive mothers during imitation coaching exhibited less intrusive affect, less intrusive physical activity, more contingent responsivity, and better total scores. Likewise, and relative to their precoaching behaviors, withdrawn mothers exhibited better gaze behavior, increased facial expressions, increased game playing, increased contingent responsivity, and better total scores during attention coaching. Results also indicated that the benefits of attention coaching with withdrawn mothers were sustained during a 2-minute spontaneous play interaction (postphase), whereas intrusive mothers' behavior generally returned to baseline immediately when coaching was terminated. These results suggest that teaching mothers to interact positively with their infants, and targeting the teaching approach to the interactive style of the particular mother, may ultimately assist infants in engaging in their social environment.

Finally, Pelaez-Nogueras, Field, Hossain, and Pickens (1996) investigated the effects of depressed mothers' touching on infants' affect and attention in an attempt to verify suggestions in the literature that touch therapy may enhance the growth and development of premature infants. They hypothesized that depressed mothers, who are more often in negative mood states and are less responsive to their infants than are well mothers (see Field, 1992), could use a touching intervention to compensate for the potentially harmful effects of their depression on their infants' mood and behavior.

In this study, mothers were assigned randomly to an experimental or a control group. Groups were further divided based on participants' classification as depressed or nondepressed based on responses to a self-report measure of depressive symptoms. Infants participated in this study when they were 3 months old. Participants in the experimental group were instructed to interact with their infants while the infants were seated in a car seat for four consecutive 90-second periods: normal interaction; still-face interaction without touching (i.e., neutral expression, no smiling or speaking); still-face interaction with touching (i.e., stroking and rubbing rhythmically the infants' arms, legs and feet in a specified manner); and normal interaction. Participants in the control group were instructed to interact normally with their infants for all four periods of the study. Mothers adopting the still-face posture were monitored by a research assistant to ensure compliance. Interactions were videotaped and coded continuously for both infant and mother behavior by two independent raters who did not know the hypotheses of the study or the mothers' depression status.

The results indicated that, as predicted, infants of depressed mothers responded positively to the touch intervention and showed more positive affect (smiling, vocalizations) and less negative affect (grimaces, crying) than did the infants of nondepressed mothers. Although infants of depressed and nondepressed mothers were similarly distressed by the still-face, no-touch period, infants of depressed mothers were soothed by the touch procedure, whereas infants of nondepressed mothers maintained their distressed posture. Pelaez-Nogueras and colleagues argued that the still-face procedure likely mimicked the behavior of depressed mothers toward their infants. They therefore suggested that encouraging depressed mothers to actively touch their infants may partially counteract the negative effects of unresponsive parenting.

Conclusions

Several issues deserve mention in this review of the treatment and intervention literature for infants of depressed mothers. First, although infant behavior and development are the key outcome variables of concern in this presentation, the majority of the studies reviewed above focus on interventions with depressed mothers, or on the mother–infant dyad, rather than on the infant. Support for this approach comes from several areas. Research by Cooper and Murray (1997) suggested that addressing maternal depressive symptoms alone may not affect the mother–infant relationship but that a focus on mother–infant interaction may optimize child outcome. Field (1992) argued that the behavioral repertoire of the infant is too limited for direct intervention, thus necessitating a focus on the mother–infant relationship to access infant outcome (see also Field, chapter 4, this volume). Cicchetti (1987) argued that the study of psychopathology in infancy requires a focus on the relational system of parent–child–environment rather than on the infant alone.

Second, all of the studies reviewed in this section use a sample of postpartum depressed mothers. However, research on postpartum and more chronic forms of depression suggests the possibility that the effects of postpartum depression on infant behavior and development are not representative of the effects of more chronic maternal depression on offspring. In fact, depression occurs in 25–30% of new mothers during the first 3 months after delivery (O'Hara, Neunaber, & Zekoski, 1984), but only 30% of the mothers who experience postpartum depression remain depressed 6 months following delivery (Campbell, Cohn, & Meyers, 1995). Research also indicates that, when depression remits by 6 months, there are no lasting effects of maternal depression on infant behavior, emotional competence, or cognitive development (Campbell et al., 1995; Field, 1992, chapter 4, this volume). It is thus possible that there are qualitative differences between postpartum depression and more chronic major depressive disorders (see Campbell et al., 1992) and that only the latter category of maternal disorder is associated with long-term risk in children. Further research is indicated to compare the effects of postpartum versus more chronic maternal depression on infants.

On a related point, the research outlined above was conducted with a sample of low-income adolescent single mothers who were classified as depressed on the basis of their responses on self-report measures of depressive symptoms. Thus, it is not clear that the findings reported here are applicable to the larger population of depressed women (i.e., Caucasian women, middle class women, and so on) or that they are specific to clinical depression (i.e., the negative behavioral and interactional effects may be associated with the mothers' low socioeconomic status rather than with their status as dysphoric). In fact, research indicates that multiple risk factors in low-income depressed samples may confound the effects of depression on child outcome (Downey & Coyne, 1990). As an example, Murray and colleagues found that the communication styles of infants and nondepressed mothers who were experiencing difficult circumstances mimicked the communication patterns observed in depressed mothers and their infants (Murray, Fiori-Cowley,

Hooper, & Cooper, 1996). Thus, further research exploring treatment and intervention for more representative samples of depressed mothers and their infants is indicated.

TODDLERHOOD (12 TO 36 MONTHS)

The developmental tasks of toddlerhood relevant to the functioning of children with depressed parents cluster into the areas of attachment–autonomy and development of social–emotional competence. According to Bowlby (1969, 1973, 1980), a primary task of the early years of life is the formation of an attachment relationship with a primary caregiver. Bowlby asserted that separation from the primary caregiver is inherently anxiety provoking for young children. However, through repeated positive interactions with the primary caregiver, toddlers form secure internal working models of this relationship, which enable them to tolerate brief separations. Moreover, as toddlers gain independence and begin to explore their environment, they are able to use this secure relationship as a base for the development of healthy relationships throughout life. Lieberman (1992) wrote of the securely attached toddler as one who has developed a "goal-directed partnership" with the primary caregiver, so that the parent is able to understand the child's strivings for independence and to adjust his or her rules to facilitate the child's growth, while the child is able to internalize the parent's emotional support and behavioral standards. Lieberman further characterized children's aggression and oppositional behaviors as normative during the toddler years as they struggle to develop an autonomous sense of themselves. However, Bowlby (1969, 1973, 1980) maintained that children with parents who are unavailable, either physically or psychologically, may develop an insecure primary attachment that may ultimately impede the child's social and emotional growth.

The second area involves socioemotional development that occurs in the 2nd and 3rd years of life. Cicchetti and Sroufe (1978) referred to the period of time from 12 to 36 months as a time of emotional acquisition and differentiation. Zahn-Waxler and Radke-Yarrow (1982) discussed the development of prosocial (i.e., helping behaviors, cooperation) and hostile–aggressive behaviors in young children from 12 to 18 months of age. Zahn-Waxler and colleagues (Zahn-Waxler, Radke-Yarrow, Wagner, & Chapman, 1992) asserted that, from ages 12 to 24 months, children evidence the early stages of moral development, during which their tendency for self-concern shifts to empathic concern for others, and they respond to stress in others with helping and cooperation. Cicchetti and Schneider-Rosen (1986) discussed the period of time from 18 to 36 months as a time of self-other differentiation, self-assertion, and self-awareness. Goodman (1992) hypothesized that the advances in socioemotional development that occur in this period provide a foundation for healthy peer relationships during middle childhood.

The relation between maternal depression and attachment–autonomy behaviors has been established with some consistency. Specifically, research suggests that attachment relationships between depressed mothers and toddlers are more insecure, relative to nondepressed mother–toddler dyads (Teti et al., 1995). Likewise, Ciccheti, Rogosch, and Toth (1998) reported fewer secure and more insecure toddlers in their group of depressed mother–toddler dyads, relative to their control group of nondepressed mother–toddler dyads, and this association is not explained by contextual risk (i.e., stressful life events, marital stress, limited social supports). Radke-Yarrow, Cummings, Kuczynski, and Chapman (1985) reported that 79% of 2- to 3-year-old children of affectively ill parents are observed to be insecurely attached to their caregivers, versus only 24% of toddlers of parents who have never been psychiatrically ill. Despite the consistency of these findings, it is important to remember that not all children of depressed parents are insecurely attached (DeMulder & Radke-Yarrow, 1991) and that insecure attachments may be corrected and thus may be an important target for intervention (see also Radke-Yarrow & Klimes-Dougan, chapter 7, this volume). Several researchers have hypothesized that the link between maternal depression and insecure attachment during toddlerhood may reflect the greater difficulty for depressed mothers, relative to well mothers, in tolerating their child's oppositional and aggressive behavior and in accepting their child's independence strivings as age-appropriate rather than as a personal rejection (see Cicchetti, Toth, & Rogosch, 2000; Lieberman, 1992; Zahn-Waxler, Iannotti, Cummings, & Denham, 1990).

Likewise, efforts to connect maternal depression and socioemotional competence have revealed that toddlers with depressed caregivers exhibit deficits in socioemotional development. Relative to toddlers of healthy mothers, toddlers of depressed mothers have been found to exhibit more atypical, dysregulated aggression (i.e., hostility to an unknown adult) and are reportedly more at risk for externalizing problems at age 5 (Zahn-Waxler, Iannotti, et al., 1990). In addition, relative to toddlers with non-ill parents, toddlers with mothers or fathers diagnosed with bipolar disorder were found to act more aggressively toward peers following separation from their parents, to exhibit less altruism toward peers, and to be more visibly upset during others' fights (Zahn-Waxler, McKnew, Cummings, Davenport, & Radke-Yarrow, 1984). Moreover, Zahn-Waxler, Kochanska, et al. (1990) reported that, relative to well mothers who fostered empathy in their toddlers, depressed mothers were more likely to foster feelings of guilt in their children by overemphasizing their toddler's causal role in events. These depressed mothers were found to be more inconsistent in their parenting, to exhibit more negative tone in their interactions with their toddlers, and to adopt a more overprotective stance in managing their toddler's aggressive behaviors.

Taken together, the research outlined above suggests several areas of focus for treatment and intervention efforts. Specifically, treatment and intervention programs designed to target toddlers of depressed mothers are needed to address the formation and maintenance of secure attachments and to encourage the development of prosocial behaviors and social competence during early toddlerhood, in order to encourage healthy peer relationships in middle childhood. To date, we are aware of only one research group that has studied directly the treatment of toddlers of depressed mothers (Cicchetti, Toth, & Rogosch, 2000), and these researchers have focused on attachment issues as primary during this developmental stage. This research is reviewed in the next section.

An Intervention Targeting Attachment

The study reviewed in this section was designed to explore the utility of applying toddler–parent psychotherapy (TPP; Lieberman, 1992) as a preventive intervention for families with maternal depressive disorder. TPP uses joint mother–toddler sessions and concepts drawn from attachment theory to alter the relationship between the mother and the child. Specifically, the therapist observes mother–child interactions and assists the mother in understanding her own attachment history, including ways in which her relationship with her own mother is reflected in her relational patterns with her toddler. The therapist aims to develop a positive, stable relationship with the mother that can serve as a working model of the secure relationship she may have been missing from childhood. The hope is that mothers use this therapeutic relationship as a guide in encouraging healthy attachment relationships with their own children. Drawing on research connecting attachment insecurity to maternal depression, Cicchetti et al. hypothesized that depressed mother–toddler dyads who participated in TPP would evidence more secure attachment relationships at the conclusion of the intervention than would depressed mother–toddler dyads in the control group. It was further expected that the percentage of secure attachments in the group of depressed mother–toddler dyads participating in the intervention would mimic findings for a nondepressed control group.

Participants in the study reported here included 108 mothers (mean age = 32 years) who were primarily Caucasian (95%), married (80 to 85% in the depressed groups), and categorized in the two highest socioeconomic status levels (74%). Mothers who were classified as depressed ($n = 63$) met diagnostic criteria for major depressive disorder at some point since the birth of their toddler, although only 13% were depressed in the postpartum period exclusively. Nondepressed mothers ($n = 45$) were recruited from the vicinity of the depressed mothers and were screened for present or past psychopathology; only women with no history of disorder were included as nondepressed controls. At baseline, toddlers were on average 20 months of age.

Depressed mothers were assigned randomly to the treatment (TPP; $n = 27$) or a no-treatment control ($n = 36$) group. Baseline assessments were conducted on all participants and included, among other items, a diagnostic interview, completion of self-report measures, a demographic interview, and training and completion of a measure of attachment security. Dyads in the TPP group participated in an average of 46 therapy sessions over an average of 59 weeks; depressed and nondepressed controls merely participated in the assessment sessions at baseline and at the conclusion of treatment. The diagnostic interview was readministered at the conclusion of treatment (when the child turned 3 years old), as was the demographics interview, the attachment measure, and a self-report measure of depressive symptoms.

The results indicated that, at baseline, more toddlers of depressed mothers were classified as insecurely attached than were toddlers in the nondepressed control group. At follow-up, as predicted, fewer toddlers with depressed mothers who were assigned to the TPP group were classified by their mothers as insecurely attached (26%), relative to toddlers with depressed mothers assigned to the control group (47%). Moreover, as hypothesized, the frequency of toddlers classified as insecurely attached in the depressed TPP group was statistically comparable to the frequency of toddlers classified as insecurely attached in the nondepressed control group. Cicchetti and his colleagues suggested that these results support an understanding of attachment security as malleable, an idea consistent with findings from Egeland and Sroufe (1981). Moreover, they asserted that these results support the effectiveness of an attachment theory model of intervention in protecting children of depressed mothers from a host of social and emotional difficulties.

Conclusions

This review of treatment and intervention literature for toddlers of depressed mothers highlights avenues for future research. First, further research is needed to explore the treatment of attachment issues in toddlers of depressed mothers. Although the work of Cicchetti and his colleagues (2000) supports the use of TPP in protecting children from the potentially harmful affects of maternal depression, the use of a no-intervention control group precludes us from concluding that TPP, versus nonspecific therapeutic effects, accounts for the changes observed. The inclusion of a second treatment group would address this apparent shortcoming. A potential alternative treatment–intervention approach may be derived from the work of Zahn-Waxler, Iannotti, and their colleagues (1990). These researchers found that certain parenting characteristics (e.g., anticipating and responding to the child's needs, communicating an understanding of the child's perspective, providing direct guidance during the child's peer interactions) of depressed mothers reduced risk for their children of future externalizing problems, some of which are associated with attachment insecurity. Perhaps this work can serve as a foundation for further study on the effectiveness of training depressed mothers to manage the normative independence strivings of their toddlers.

Second, research is needed to examine treatment and intervention approaches to address the development of prosocial behaviors in toddlers of depressed mothers. Hammen (1992; chapter 8, this volume) has noted that, whereas correlations between maternal depression and child outcome remain strong, it is the nature of the caregiving provided by depressed mothers, more than the depression itself, that influences the quality of attachment between toddlers and their mothers. As noted by Zahn-Waxler, Iannotti, et al. (1990), not all depressed mothers show deficits in child-rearing practices. An important direction for future research may involve the identification of factors that enable depressed mothers to succeed in developing secure attachments with their children and in assisting their children in the development of social competence. The identification of these factors may inform and direct treatment and intervention efforts with depressed mothers and may encourage resilient outcomes in their children.

ADOLESCENCE (10 TO 18 YEARS)

In his discussion of the prevention and treatment of adolescent mental health issues, Kazdin (1993) asserted that, in the field of developmental psychopathology, researchers have attended to issues of childhood more often than they have to development within the adolescent years. Defined broadly as the period of time from the onset of puberty to the departure from the family of origin (Kazdin, 1993), adolescence is a time when risks for dysfunction increase (see Rutter, 1986) and when individuals are particularly vulnerable to the onset of significant psychiatric disorders (e.g., psychosis, major affective illness; see Kazdin, 1990). Research has indicated that family relationships change during adolescence (Steinberg, 1981) and that the frequency of negative family interactions increase during this developmental period (Jacob, 1974). Hence, a careful exploration of the relation between adolescent development and parental depression is indicated.

Two developmental tasks of adolescence are relevant to the functioning of children with depressed parents: advancements in self-understanding and the development of the communication skills essential for the formation of meaningful interpersonal relationships. In a review of the development of self-understanding, Damon and Hart (1982) noted that, during adolescence, children's self-perceptions shift from the physical to the psychological. That is, prior to age 8, children reportedly define themselves in terms of what they look like or what they are able to do. Beginning in early adolescence, children distinguish between mind and body, and they begin to understand that they are different from others because they have unique thoughts and feelings. Later during adolescence, individuals begin to integrate different thoughts about themselves into an internally consistent self-system, resulting in an increase in self-awareness and self-consciousness.

The work of Sullivan informs a second major developmental task of adolescence. Sullivan (1953) wrote of early adolescence as the time during which children develop the capacity for significant relationships with peers (*chumships*). It is assumed that, by establishing an intimate, collaborative relationship during adolescence, youngsters establish a foundation for successful personal relationships throughout life. Selman (1980) argued that, during adolescence, youngsters advance in their understanding of friendship. Beardslee, Schultz, and Selman (1987) wrote of adolescence as a critical period for developing the capacity for expressing mutuality in relationships.

Recent efforts to connect maternal depression and adolescent development in self-understanding have revealed that adolescents whose mothers are depressed have lower self-concepts than adolescents whose mothers are not depressed (Hirsch, Moos, & Reischl, 1985). Jaenicke and colleagues (1987) reported that adolescents whose mothers are depressed are more likely than adolescents with non-depressed mothers to blame themselves for negative outcomes. This research suggests the possibility that depressed mothers' negative attributional styles are transmitted to their offspring during adolescence, a finding supported by Seligman et al. (1984). Moreover, Jaenicke and colleagues (1987) found a significant relation between adolescents' negative self-cognitions and negative interactions with their mothers. Given the increased incidence of conflict between parents and children in families with parental affective illness (see Prince & Jacobson, 1995), it follows that adolescents in these families exhibit more negative self-views. In fact, Jaenicke and colleagues (1987) also reported that adolescents with depressed mothers were less likely than adolescents of well mothers to recall positive self-descriptive adjectives, a finding that supports this hypothesis. Regarding the connection between parental affective illness and adolescent social functioning, Selman, Beardslee, Schultz, Krupa, and Podorefsky (1986) reported a small but significant negative relation between the duration of parental affective illness and adolescents' developmental level of interpersonal negotiation strategies.

To our knowledge, only two research groups have studied directly the treatment or prevention of dysfunction in adolescents of depressed parents (Beardslee et al., 1993; Clarke et al., 2000). Beardslee and colleagues have developed their intervention program to address the key factor of self-understanding during adolescence, whereas Clarke and colleagues have focused more on the growth of interpersonal strategies during adolescence. This research is reviewed in the next section.

A Family-Based Intervention Program

Beardslee and colleagues (1993) have focused their work on families with parental affective disorder, with the goal of preventing the onset of the disorder in nonsymptomatic early adolescents aged 8 to 15 years. Based on earlier investigations of risk and resiliency in adolescents whose parents are affectively ill, the researchers designed two intervention programs (i.e., clinician based and lecture). These programs aimed to (a) decrease the impact of family and marital risk factors, (b) encourage the promotion of resilience-related behaviors and attitudes in the children through enhanced parental and family functioning, and (c) prevent the onset of depression or related psychopathology.

Eighty dual and single parent families were included in the study, all of whom had at least one parent who had experienced an episode of affective disorder in the past 18 months, and at least one child between the ages of 8 and 15 years who had never been treated for an episode of affective disorder. The families were largely Caucasian and middle class. Each family member was assigned to a different member of the assessment team and was given a diagnostic interview to assess psychopathology, as well as some self-report instruments, prior to participating in one of the intervention programs. Immediately following the completion of the intervention programs, families were reassessed for psychopathology, symptoms, family relationship status, and response to intervention; these same measures were readministered approximately 8 months later.

Families who were assigned to the clinician-based intervention participated in 6 to 10 sessions, generally over a 6-month period, in which a clinician from the project initiated meetings with the parents only, individual meetings with each child, and a family meeting. A refresher meeting with the parents (and children, if requested) was held 6 months after the final intervention session. The clinician-based intervention included the following core elements: (a) assessing all family members, (b) presenting psychoeducational material about affective disorders and about risks and resilience in children, (c) linking the psychoeducational material to the family's life experience, (d) decreasing feelings of guilt and blame in children, and (e) helping the children to develop relationships both within and outside of the family to facilitate their independent functioning in school and in activities outside of the home.

The lecture condition consisted of two separate 1-hour standardized lectures delivered within a month by Dr. Beardslee in a group format without children present. Although family discussion was encouraged and the psychoeducational material presented mirrored that presented in the clinician-facilitated condition, there was no attempt in the lecture condition to link the cognitive material presented to the family's individual illness experience. As in the clinician-facilitated condition, affective disorder was presented as a family experience, and parents were encouraged to talk to their children about their illness. However, in the lecture condition the parents decided whether to initiate such conversations with their children.

A study with a portion of the sample indicated that both intervention conditions resulted in improved communication about the illness between spouses, with children, and as a family (Beardslee, Salt, et al., 1997). In addition, both interventions were reported to reduce levels of parental guilt regarding the illness and to increase understanding of parental illness by the child. Participants in the clinician-facilitated condition reported significantly greater levels of assessor-rated and self-reported change than did participants in the lecture condition (Beardslee, Salt, et al., 1997; Beardslee, Versage, et al., 1997; Beardslee, Wright, et al., 1997).

The data that have been collected on 80 families participating in this study through the third assessment period support findings from a portion of the sample. In addition, within families reporting significant parental benefit from intervention (in terms of changes in illness-related behaviors and attitudes), children were rated as making significant global change, including enhanced understanding of parental illness and improved communication with parents. In addition, children whose parents were rated as making significant changes in behaviors and attitudes themselves reported that participation in this project enhanced their understanding of parental illness. Even after controlling for baseline scores, parental change was correlated significantly with these children's higher ratings by assessors on current global functioning, higher ratings by parents on a measure of participation in adaptive activities, and lower scores on a self-report measure of depressive symptoms. The data also indicate that providing parents with factual information regarding risk and resilience in children, and linking this factual information to family members' illness experiences, can result in behavioral and attitudinal changes among parents that ultimately translate into more optimal functioning among children.

A Group Intervention Program

Based on the social learning model of depression, Clarke and Lewinsohn (1995) developed the Coping with Stress (CWS) course, a manual-based psychoeducational group program that targets adolescents who are at risk for the development of significant depressive disorders. CWS is a modification of the Coping with Depression Course for Adolescents (CWDA; Clarke, Lewinsohn, & Hops, 1990), which was developed for use with clinically depressed adolescents. It aims to assist vulnerable adolescents in gaining control over negative moods, resolving conflicts that arise at home and with peers, and altering maladaptive thought patterns. The program, which targets adolescents aged 13 to 18, was designed to be administered by mental health professionals (e.g., psychologists, psychiatrists, social workers) with prior experience with cognitive behavioral treatments. A group rather than an individual format was used because it is more cost-effective, it provides opportunities for modeling and role-playing of interpersonal behaviors, and research suggests that the group setting may be beneficial during mid to late adolescence when peer relations are primary (e.g., Moreau, Mufson,

Weissman, & Klerman, 1993). Fifteen 1-hour sessions are conducted over an 8-week period in which adolescents are instructed in self-help and cognitive restructuring techniques and then role-playing and modeling exercises are used to help adolescents apply new information to real-world situations. In addition, sessions include time to review and assign homework exercises, and each session concludes with unstructured sharing time.

In the present study, Clarke and colleagues (2000) recruited adolescents with depressed parents who were enrolled in a program maintained by a health maintenance organization. Prospective adults (aged 30 to 65 with dependents aged 13 to 18 years) were identified if they had received two dispensations of an antidepressant medication in the past year, or if they had two mental health visits within the past year. Medical chart reviews revealed that about 66% of these adults had recorded depressive diagnosis and symptoms, and, after consultation with health care providers, letters were sent to 2,995 adults. Adolescent offspring were contacted to determine their interest in participating in this project. Five hundred fifty-one youth–parent dyads were interviewed for parent diagnosis, child diagnosis, symptoms and psychosocial functioning, and 472 adolescents were enrolled in the project.

Adolescents enrolled in the project were divided into three groups based on the severity of depressive symptoms they endorsed. Adolescents labeled *demoralized* were the focus of the present study, as they presented with subdiagnostic levels of depressive symptoms or earned an elevated score on a self-report measure of depressive symptoms. Adolescents labeled *depressed* met criteria for a diagnosis of major depressive disorder or dysthymia, and they participated in a separate treatment study. Likewise, *resilient adolescents* presented with no significant depressive symptoms and no history of depressive disorder, and they were not investigated further. Demoralized youth and their parents completed a battery of extensive assessments, including interview and self-report measures, at intake, posttreatment, and at follow-up assessments approximately 1 and 2 years later. Demoralized youth were then randomized to the experimental (n = 45) or to a usual care condition (n = 49).

In the experimental condition, adolescents participated in 15 one-hour sessions in groups of 6 to 10 people; each group was led by a masters level therapist trained in CWS, as described above. Adolescents assigned to both groups were permitted to continue any nonstudy related mental health services, and information regarding those services was collected from usual care participants as a representation of the comparison group. Parents of children in both groups were invited to three separate informational and psychoeducational meetings during the early, middle, and later sessions of the youth groups. Parents were informed about the general topics covered in the youth groups and were able to ask questions specific to their children. Parent groups did not address parental illness, and no individual or family sessions were conducted.

On measures of self-report depressive symptoms and on interview diagnostic assessments, adolescents assigned to the experimental condition generally reported less depression than did adolescents assigned to the usual care condition. Moreover, participants in the experimental group were less likely than those in the control group to develop an episode of diagnosable depression both immediately following group participation and throughout the 2-year follow-up interval. No significant effects of the parent groups were reported. Clarke and his colleagues have concluded that participation in their group intervention program brought the rate of depressive illness in demoralized offspring of depressed parents to a level consonant with the general rate of depression in community samples (i.e., in samples with no particular risk for illness).

Conclusions

The study of treatment and intervention with the offspring of depressed parents during adolescence highlights some important areas for consideration. First, whereas interventions appropriate for infants and toddlers focus primarily on depressed mothers and their behaviors toward their children, it appears that treatment and intervention programs that target children during adolescence may benefit from a more significant focus on the adolescents themselves. In fact, Beardslee and colleagues (1993) found that adolescents in families assigned to the lecture condition, which included intervention for parents only, reported less benefit from participation in the study than did adolescents who participated in the clinician-based intervention program. Moreover, research by Clarke and colleagues (2000) revealed significant effects from intervention on child outcome whether or not parents attended the informational sessions. It may be that during adolescence, when children are developing more complex and stable senses of themselves and are relying heavily on peer relationships as they separate from their families, successful treatment and intervention programs must target the adolescents and their interactions with significant others, rather than target the parents and their management of their psychopathology. Moreover, it may be that the Beardslee intervention program, which targets child outcome through parental and family intervention, is more appropriate for earlier adolescents, and the Clarke intervention program, which targets child outcome through group intervention with minimal parental involvement, is most appropriate for later adolescents.

Second, as discussed above, research on the connection between maternal depression and adolescent outcome generally does not delineate the direction of this relationship (i.e., whether maternal depression precedes poor adolescent functioning, or whether poor adolescent functioning precedes maternal depression). In a study designed to investigate the direction of this relation, Forehand and McCombs (1988) collected data from a variety of sources: self-reported maternal and child depressive symptoms, paper-and-pencil measures of adolescent behaviors (parent and teacher reported), and observational ratings of a mother–adolescent interaction. They found that maternal depression is likely the antecedent event in the relation between maternal depression and adolescent functioning and that maternal depression scores are associated with subsequent poorer functioning in multiple areas of adolescent outcome (e.g., internalizing, externalizing, prosocial, cognitive). Hammen, Burge, and Stansbury (1990), however, provided support for a structural equation model that includes a reciprocal causal relation between mother and adolescent functioning. They found that adolescents who had more negative self-concepts and who were critical in interactions with their mothers had mothers who functioned less adaptively. It is important that future research in this area consider the likelihood that the relationship between maternal and adolescent functioning is bidirectional in nature, so that the role of adolescent factors in families with parental depression is not overlooked.

Research on resilience indicates that not all adolescents who live with depressed parents develop depression. In fact, despite the high risk for depression and other forms of psychopathology in children of depressed parents, a number of studies have demonstrated that many youngsters who grow up with ill parents actually do well. These "resilient" individuals exhibit the ability to adapt successfully despite the presence of significant adversity. A number of studies have reported that the ability to work and engage in supportive and intimate interpersonal relationships contributes to resilient outcomes in children (Beardslee & Podorefsky, 1988; Garmezy, 1985; Rutter, 1987). These findings suggest that adolescents who manage to find the support they need to negotiate important developmental tasks outside of the home, through activities and through relationships with peers and other adults, may be protected from the potentially harmful impact of maternal depression on child outcome. Outcomes of studies of resilient youth may provide an important foundation for preventive intervention research.

IMPLICATIONS FOR CLINICIANS AND RESEARCHERS

The literature discussed above suggests that it may be necessary to intervene with children of depressed parents differentially and consistently throughout development. Specifically, given that the developmental issues pertinent to each age group vary and that the presentation of symptoms varies throughout development (e.g., insecurely attached toddlers may develop secure attachments, and previously securely attached toddlers may develop insecure attachments; Cicchetti et al., 1991; Egeland & Sroufe, 1981), it may be necessary to provide age-appropriate interventions to children of depressed parents at several points during their lives. For example, it may be necessary to work with mothers alone and in interactions with their infants to address early deficits in homeostatic and emotional regulation. Later, it may be necessary to provide individual and joint therapeutic sessions to these same families when the children become toddlers, in order to address the development of secure attachments and prosocial behaviors. As these same children reach middle childhood and early adolescence, treatments addressing their individual mental health and cognitive styles, and their positions within their families, may be most beneficial. During late adolescence, a group focus may be most appropriate, given the developmental task of separation that confronts later adolescents and the increased importance of peers during this life stage (see Dudley, 1997; Reynolds & Coats, 1986). Although this proposal may seem overly ambitious, the vulnerability of children of depressed parents suggests that a longitudinal approach may be necessary.

We are not aware of treatment or intervention literature that targets children of depressed parents during middle childhood. Several researchers have identified key developmental issues during this life stage, including the emergence of the self-concept, the development of modulated self-control, moral internalization, and the acquisition of peer relations skills (Damon & Hart, 1982; Goodman, 1992; Zahn-Waxler, Kochanska, et al., 1990). Moreover, deficits in these areas have been associated with dysfunction in children of depressed parents during middle childhood, who, relative to children of well mothers, have been judged to exhibit poorer peer relationship skills (Billings & Moos, 1985), have been rated as less popular (Goodman et al., 1993), and have been found to lack maturity in their response to hypothetical situations of interpersonal conflict (Zahn-Waxler, Kochanska, et al., 1990). Treatment and intervention programs clearly are required to address these issues in children of depressed parents during this developmental period or stage.

As noted above, most research on the impact of parental depression on child outcome has focused on the relation between maternal depression and child functioning. It is true that women are more likely to experience depression than men during adulthood (Nolen-Hoeksema, 1987) and that mothers are more likely to be their children's primary caregivers than are fathers. Yet Phares (1992; Phares, Duhig, & Watkins, chapter 9, this volume) has argued that fathers influence their children much like mothers do, and fathers' symptoms and characteristics are related to child and adolescent outcome. Moreover, research suggests that in families with one depressed parent, the second parent is likely to experience psychopathology as well (Coyne, 1976; Quinton, Rutter, & Liddle, 1984). Zahn-Waxler, Iannotti, and colleagues (1990) suggested that, when fathers are also depressed, marital discord is likely to evolve, and the genetic loading for psychopathology in offspring increases. Research on resilience suggests that healthy fathers may serve a protective role in families with maternal depression (Beardslee & Podorefsky, 1988). The few research groups that have addressed the role of fathers in families with maternal depression support the importance of considering fathers' mental health in the equation that explains the intergenerational transmission of dysfunction. Specifically, Goodman et al. (1993) reported that children whose mothers are depressed and who also have a father with a psychiatric disorder were found to be less skilled in interpreting social cues than were children with a depressed mother and a healthy father. Likewise, Compas, Howell, Phares, Williams, and Giunta (1989) reported a significant predictive relation between fathers' reports of psychological symptoms and adolescents' self-reported behavioral and emotional problems. Future research is needed to explore the additive and preventive effects of fathers' mental health status on outcome in children with depressed mothers.

To date, most of the research on depression in children and adolescents has focused on the design, implementation, and evaluation of tertiary treatment interventions (i.e., psychosocial responses to the diagnosis of depression in youth). Psychosocial treatments known to be effective with depressed adults have been adapted for adolescents (e.g., Clarke et al., 1990), and the results from studies testing these treatments generally have been positive (e.g., Birmaher, Ryan, Williamson, Brent, & Kaufman, 1996). Several controlled intervention studies have addressed specifically depression in youth, but all have targeted children and adolescents who present with current depressive symptoms, as identified by elevated scores on self-report measures or teacher report (e.g., Clarke et al., 1995; Jaycox, Reivich, Gillham, & Seligman, 1994; Moreau, Mufson, Weissman, & Klerman, 1991).

In response to mandates by the Institute of Medicine (1994) and the National Institute of Mental Health (1993), researchers recently have begun to examine the primary prevention of depression in youth. In fact, Lewinsohn and colleagues (1994) noted that, whereas most recent research on youth depression has focused on the etiology and correlates of depression, an important area for depression research involves the development of preventive intervention programs for children. Thus, in recent years, research on depression in youth has shifted from tertiary treatment efforts to primary prevention studies and from primary prevention approaches aimed at general, unselected populations to prevention programs that focus on "targeted" populations (i.e., populations identified as having an increased risk of future depression).

This chapter has provided significant support for the definition of children of depressed parents as a population that must be targeted for prevention. We believe that an important area for future research involves the development, implementation, and evaluation of primary prevention programs targeting children of depressed parents from infancy through adolescence. Given that depression in youth has been correlated with a number of psychiatric and interpersonal difficulties that persist through adolescence and into adulthood (Mufson, Moreau, Weissman, & Klerman, 1993), we believe that research programs preventing the onset of depression in at-risk samples are required.

SUMMARY

Children of depressed parents have been identified as a population at high risk for a variety of emotional problems, including depression and other forms of psychopathology. Parental depression affects children differentially at each developmental stage. During infancy, maternal depression has been found to interfere with children's internal and social goals and with their regulation of emotion and attention. During toddlerhood, maternal depression has been associated with insecure attachment and with deficits in socioemotional development. During adolescence, maternal depression has been associated with negative self-concept and with the use of poor interpersonal strategies. In this chapter, treatment and intervention research addressing these issues was reviewed and suggestions for further research were offered. Ultimately, we argued for the development of primary prevention programs targeting the children of depressed parents as they negotiate developmental tasks throughout childhood and adolescence.

REFERENCES

Beardslee, W. R., & Podorefsky, D. (1988). Resilient adolescents whose parents have serious affective and other psychiatric disorders: The importance of self-understanding and relationships. *American Journal of Psychiatry, 145,* 63–69.

Beardslee, W. R., Salt, P., Porterfield, K., Rothberg, P. C., van de Velde, P., Swatling, S., Hoke, L., Moilanen, D. L., & Wheelock, I. (1993). Comparison of preventive interventions for families with parental affective disorder. *Journal of the American Academy of Child and Adolescent Psychiatry, 32,* 254–263.

Beardslee, W. R., Salt, P., Versage, E., Gladstone, T. R. G., Wright, E., & Rothberg, P. C. (1997). Sustained change in parents receiving preventive interventions for families with depression. *American Journal of Psychiatry, 154,* 510–515.

Beardslee, W. R., Schultz, L. H., & Selman, R. L. (1987). Level of social–cognitive development, adaptive functioning, and *DSM–III* diagnoses in adolescent offspring of parents with affective disorders: Implications of the development of the capacity for mutuality. *Developmental Psychology, 23,* 807–815.

Beardslee, W. R., Versage, E. M., & Gladstone, T. R. G. (1998). Children of affectively ill parents: A review of the past 10 years. *Journal of the Academy of Child and Adolescent Psychiatry, 37,* 1134–1141.

Beardslee, W. R., Versage, E. M., Wright, E., Salt, P., Rothberg, P. C., Drezner, K., & Gladstone, T. R. G. (1997). Examination of preventive interventions for families with depression: Evidence of change. *Developmental Psychopathology, 9,* 109–130.

Beardslee, W. R., Wright, E., Salt, P., Drezner, K., Gladstone, T. R. G., Versage, E. M., & Rothberg, P. C. (1997). Examination of children's responses to two preventive intervention strategies over time. *Journal of the American Academy of Child and Adolescent Psychiatry, 36,* 196–204.

Billings, A. G., & Moos, R. (1985). Children of parents with unipolar depression: A controlled one-year follow-up. *Journal of Abnormal Child Psychology, 14,* 149–166.

Birmaher, B., Ryan, N. D., Williamson, D. E., Brent, D., & Kaufman, L. (1996). Childhood and adolescent depression: A review of the past 10 years. Part I. *Journal of the American Academy of Child and Adolescent Psychiatry, 35,* 1427–1439.

Bowlby, J. (1969). *Attachment and loss: Vol. 1.* New York: Basic Books.

Bowlby, J. (1973). *Attachment and loss: Vol. 2. Separation.* New York: Basic Books.

Bowlby, J. (1980). *Attachment and loss: Vol. 3. Loss, sadness, and depression.* New York: Basic Books.

Brazelton, T. (1973). *Neonatal Behavioral Assessment Scale* (Clinics in Developmental Medicine, No. 50). Philadelphia: Lippincot.

Brazelton, T., & Nugent, J. (1995). *Neonatal Behavioral Assessment Scale* (3rd ed.). London: MacKeith.

Campbell, S. B., Cohn, J. F., Flanagan, C., Popper, S., & Meyers, T. (1992). Course and correlates of postpartum depression during the transition to parenthood. *Development and Psychopathology, 4,* 29–47.

Campbell, S. B., Cohn, J. F., & Meyers, T. (1995). Depression in first-time mothers: Mother–infant interaction and depression chronicity. *Developmental Psychology, 31,* 349–357.

Cicchetti, D. (1987). Developmental psychopathology in infancy. *Journal of Consulting and Clinical Psychology, 55,* 837–845.

Cicchetti, D., Ganiban, J., & Barnett, D. (1991). Contributions from the study of high risk populations to understanding the development of emotion regulation. In J. Garber & K. A. Dodge (Eds.), *The development of emotion regulation and dysregulation* (Cambridge studies in social and emotional development, pp. 15–48). New York: Cambridge University Press.

Cicchetti, D., Rogosch, F. A., & Toth, S. L. (1998). Maternal depressive disorder and contextual risk: Contributions to the development of attachment insecurity and behavioral problems in toddlerhood. *Development and Psychopathology, 10,* 283–300.

Cicchetti, D., & Schneider-Rosen, K. (1986). An organizational approach to childhood depression. In M. Rutter, C. Izard, & P. Read (Eds.), *Depression in young people: Clinical and developmental perspectives* (pp. 71–134). New York: Guilford Press.

Cicchetti, D., & Sroufe, A. (1978). An organizational view of affect: Illustration from the study of Down's syndrome infants. In M. Lewis & L. Rosenblum (Eds.), *The development of affect* (pp. 309–350). New York: Plenum Press.

Cicchetti, D., Toth, S. L., & Rogosch, F. A. (2000). The effectiveness of toddler–parent psychotherapy to increase attachment security in offspring of depressed mothers. *Attachment and Human Development, 28,* 135–148.

Clarke, G. N., Hawkins, W., Murphy, M., Sheeber, L. B., Lewinsohn, P. M., & Seeley, J. R. (1995). Targeted prevention of unipolar depressive disorder in an at-risk sample of high school adolescents: A randomized trial of a group cognitive intervention. *Journal of the American Academy of Child and Adolescent Psychiatry, 34*, 312–321.

Clarke, G. N., Hornbrook, M., Lynch, F. R., Polen, M., Gale, J., Beardslee, W. R., O'Connor, E., & Seeley, J. (2000). *Offspring of depressed parents in an HMO: A randomized trial of a group cognitive intervention for preventing adolescent depressive disorder.* Unpublished manuscript, Kaiser Permanente Center for Health Research.

Clarke, G. N., & Lewinsohn, P. M. (1995). *Instructor's manual for the Adolescent Coping with Stress Course.* Unpublished work.

Clarke, G. N., Lewinsohn, P. M., & Hops, H. (1990). *Instructor's manual for the Adolescent Coping with Depression Course.* Eugene, OR: Castalia Press.

Compas, B. E., Howell, D. C., Phares, V., Williams, R. A., & Guinta, C. T. (1989). Risk factors for emotional/behavioral problems in young adolescents: A prospective analysis of adolescent and parental stress and symptoms. *Journal of Consulting and Clinical Psychology, 57*, 732–740.

Cooper, P. J., & Murray, L. (1997). The impact of psychological treatments of postpartum depression on maternal mood and infant development. In L. Murray & P. Cooper (Eds.), *Postpartum depression and child development* (pp. 201–220). New York: Guilford Press.

Coyne, J. C. (1976). Depression and the response of others. *Journal of Abnormal Psychology, 85*, 186–193.

Cutrona, C. E., & Troutman, B. R. (1986). Social support, infant temperament, and parenting self-efficacy: A mediational model of postpartum depression. *Child Development, 57*, 1507–1518.

Damon, W., & Hart, D. (1982). The development of self-understanding from infancy through adolescence. *Child Development, 53*, 841–864.

DeMulder, E., & Radke-Yarrow, M. (1991). Attachment with affectively ill and well mothers: Concurrent behavioral correlates. *Development and Psychopathology, 3*, 227–242.

Downey, G., & Coyne, J. C. (1990). Children of depressed parents: An integrative review. *Psychological Bulletin, 108*, 50–76.

Dudley, C. D. (1997). *Treating depressed children.* Oakland, CA: New Harbinger Publications.

Egeland, B., & Sroufe, L. A. (1981). Developmental consequences of maltreatment in infancy. In R. Rizley & D. Cicchetti (Eds.), *Developmental perspectives on child maltreatment: New directions for child development* (pp. 77–92). San Francisco: Jossey-Bass.

Field, T. (1992). Infants of depressed mothers. *Development and Psychopathology, 4*, 59–66.

Field, T. (1997). The treatment of depressed mothers and their infants. In L. Murray & P. Cooper (Eds.), *Postpartum depression and child development* (pp. 221–236). New York: Guilford Press.

Field, T., Dempsey, J., Hallock, N., & Schuman, H. (1978). The mother's assessment of the behavior of her infant. *Infant Behavior and Development, 1*, 156–167.

Field, T., Fox, N. A., Pickens, J., & Nawrocki, T. (1995). Relative right frontal EEG activation in 3- to 6-month-old infants of "depressed" mothers. *Developmental Psychology, 313*, 358–363.

Field, T., Grizzle, N., Scafidi, F., Abrams, S., Richardson, S., Kuhn, C., & Schanberg, S. (1996). Massage therapy for infants of depressed mothers. *Infant Behavior and Development, 19*, 107–112.

Field, T., Healy, B., Goldstein, S., & Guthertz, M. (1990). Behavior-state matching and synchrony in mother–infant interactions of nondepressed versus depressed dyads. *Developmental Psychology, 26*, 7–14.

Field, T., Pickens, J., Fox, N. A., Nawrocki, T., & Gonzalez, J. (1995). Vagal tone in infants of depressed mothers. *Development and Psychopathology, 7*, 227–231.

Forehand, R., & McCombs, A. (1988). Unraveling the antecedent–consequence conditions in maternal depression and adolescent functioning. *Behavioral Research and Therapy, 26*, 399–405.

Garmezy, N. (1985). Stress-resilient children: The search for protective factors. In J. E. Stevenson (Ed.), *Recent research in developmental psychology* (Journal of Child Psychology and Psychiatry Book Supplement No. 4, pp. 213–233). Oxford, England: Pergamon.

Goodman, S. H. (1992). Understanding the effects of depressed mothers on their children. In E. Walker, R. Dworkin, & B. Cornblatt (Eds.), *Progress in experimental personality and psychopathology research, Vol. 15* (pp. 47–109). New York: Springer.

Goodman, S. H., Brogan, D., Lynch, M. E., & Fielding, B. (1993). Social and emotional competence in children of depressed mothers. *Child Development, 64*, 516–531.

Hammen, C. (1991). *Depression runs in families*. New York: Springer-Verlag.

Hammen, C. (1992). Cognitive, life stress, and interpersonal approaches to a developmental psychopathology model of depression. *Development and Psychopathology, 4*, 189–206.

Hammen, C., Burge, D., & Stansbury, K. (1990). Relationship of mother and child variables to child outcomes in a high-risk sample: A causal modeling analysis. *Developmental Psychology, 26*, 24–30.

Harnish, J. D., Dodge, K. A., & Valente, E. (1995). Mother–child interaction quality as a partial mediator of the roles of maternal depressive symptomatology and socioeconomic status in the development of child behavior problems. *Child Development, 66*, 739–753.

Hart, S., Field, T., & Nearing, G. (1998). Depressed mothers' neonates improve following the MABI and a Brazelton Demonstration. *Journal of Pediatric Psychology, 23*, 351–356.

Hirsch, B. J., Moos, R. E., & Reischl, T. M. (1985). Psychosocial adjustment of adolescent children of a depressed, arthritic, or normal parent. *Journal of Abnormal Psychology, 94*, 154–164.

Institute of Medicine. (1994). *Reducing risks for mental disorders: Frontiers for preventive intervention research.* Washington, DC: National Academy Press.

Jacob, T. (1974). Patterns of family conflict and dominance as a function of child age and social class. *Developmental Psychology, 10,* 1–12.

Jaenicke, C., Hammen, C., Zupan, B., Hiroto, D., Gordon, D., Adrian, C., & Burge, D. (1987). Cognitive vulnerability in children at risk for depression. *Journal of Abnormal Child Psychology, 15,* 559–572.

Jaycox, L. H., Reivich, K. J., Gillham, J., & Seligman, M. E. P. (1994). Prevention of depressive symptoms in school children. *Behavior Research and Therapy, 32,* 801–816.

Kazdin, A. E. (1990). Childhood depression. *Journal of Child Psychology and Psychiatry, 31,* 121–160.

Kazdin, A. E. (1993). Adolescent mental health: Prevention and treatment programs. *American Psychologist, 48,* 127–141.

Kendler, K. S., Neale, M. C., Kessler, R. C., Heath, A. C., & Eaves, L. J. (1993). The lifetime history of major depression in women. *Archives of General Psychiatry, 50,* 863–870.

Lewinsohn, P. M., Roberts, R. E., Seeley, J. R., Rohde, P., Gotlib, I. H., & Hops, H. (1994). Adolescent psychopathology: II. Psychosocial risk factors for depression. *Journal of Abnormal Psychology, 103,* 302–315.

Lieberman, A. F. (1992). Infant–parent psychotherapy with toddlers. *Development and Psychopathology, 4,* 559–574.

Malphurs, J. E., Field, T. M., Larraine, C., Pickens, J., Pelaez-Nogueras, M., Yando, R., & Bendell, D. (1996). Altering withdrawn and intrusive interaction behaviors of depressed mothers. *Infant Mental Health Journal, 17,* 152–160.

Moreau, D., Mufson, L., Weissman, M. M., & Klerman, G. L. (1991). Interpersonal psychotherapy for depressed adolescents: Description of modification and preliminary application. *Academy of Child and Adolescent Psychiatry, 30,* 642–651.

Mufson, L., Moreau, D., Weissman, M. M., & Klerman, G. L. (1993). *Interpersonal psychotherapy for depressed adolescents.* New York: Guilford Press.

Murray, L., & Cooper, P. J. (1997). The role of infant and maternal factors in postpartum depression, mother–infant interactions and infant outcome. In L. Murray & P. Cooper (Eds.), *Postpartum depression and child development* (pp. 111–135). New York: Guilford Press.

Murray, L., Fiori-Cowley, A., Hooper, R., & Cooper, P. J. (1996). The impact of postnatal depression and associated adversity on early mother–infant interactions and later infant outcome. *Child Development, 67,* 2512–2526.

Murray, L., Kempton, C., Woolgar, M., & Hooper, R. (1993). Depressed mothers' speech to their infants and its relation to infant gender and cognitive development. *Journal of Child Psychology and Psychiatry, 34,* 1083–1101.

National Institute of Mental Health. (1993). *The prevention of mental disorders: A national research agenda.* Bethesda, MD: Author.

Nolen-Hoeksema, S. (1987). Sex differences in unipolar depression: Evidence and theory. *Psychological Bulletin, 101,* 259–282.

O'Hara, M. W., Neunaber, D. J., & Zekoski, E. M. (1984). Prospective study of post-partum depression: Prevalence, course, and predictive factors. *Journal of Abnormal Psychology, 93,* 158–171.

Pelaez-Nogueras, M., Field, T., Cigales, M., Gonzalez, A., & Clasky, S. (1994). Infants of depressed mothers show less "depressed" behavior with their nursery teachers. *Infant Mental Health Journal, 15,* 358–367.

Pelaez-Nogueras, M., Field, T. M., Hossain, Z., & Pickens, J. (1996). Depressed mothers' touching increases infants' positive affect and attention in still-face interactions. *Child Development, 67,* 1780–1792.

Phares, V. (1992). Where's poppa? The relative lack of attention to the role of fathers in child and adolescent psychopathology. *American Psychologist, 47,* 656–664.

Prince, S. E., & Jacobson, N. S. (1995). A review and evaluation of marital and family therapies for affective disorders. *Journal of Marital and Family Therapy, 21,* 377–401.

Quinton, D., Rutter, M., & Liddle, C. (1984). Institutional rearing, parenting difficulties, and marital support. *Psychological Medicine, 14,* 107–124.

Radke-Yarrow, M., Cummings, E. M., Kuczynski, L., & Chapman, M. (1985). Patterns of attachment in two- and three-year-olds in normal families and families with parental depression. *Child Development, 56,* 884–893.

Radke-Yarrow, M., Nottelmann, E., Martinez, P., Fox, M. B., & Belmont, B. (1992). Young children of affectively ill parents: A longitudinal study of psychosocial development. *Journal of the American Academy of Child and Adolescent Psychiatry, 31,* 68–77.

Reynolds, W. M., & Coats, K. I. (1986). A comparison of cognitive–behavioral therapy and relaxation training for the treatment of depression in adolescents. *Journal of Consulting and Clinical Psychology, 54,* 653–660.

Rubin, K. H., Both, L., Zahn-Waxler, C., Cummings, E. M., & Wilkinson, M. (1991). Dyadic play behaviors of children of well and depressed mothers. *Developmental Psychopathology, 3,* 243–251.

Rutter, M. (1986). The developmental psychopathology of depression: Issues and perspectives. In M. Rutter, C. Izard, & P. Read (Eds.), *Depression in young people* (pp. 3–30). New York: Guilford Press.

Rutter, M. (1987). The role of cognition in child development disorder. *British Journal of Medical Psychology, 60,* 1–16.

Rutter, M. (1990). Commentary: Some focus and process considerations regarding effects of parental depression on children. *Developmental Psychology, 26,* 60–67.

Seligman, M. E. P., Peterson, C., Kaslow, N. J., Tanenbaum, R. L., Alloy, L. B., & Abramson, L. Y. (1984). Attributional style and depressive symptoms among children. *Journal of Abnormal Psychology, 93,* 235–238.

Selman, R. L. (1980). *The growth of interpersonal understanding.* New York: Academic Press.

Selman, R. L., Beardslee, W., Schultz, L. H., Krupa, M., & Podorefsky, D. (1986). Assessing adolescent interpersonal negotiation strategies: Toward the integration of structural and functional models. *Developmental Psychology, 22,* 450–459.

Steinberg, L. D. (1981). Transformations in family relations at puberty. *Developmental Psychology, 17,* 833–840.

Sullivan, H. S. (1953). *The interpersonal theory of psychiatry.* New York: Norton.

Teti, D. M., Gelfand, D. M., Messinger, D. S., & Isabella, R. (1995). Maternal depression and the quality of early attachment: An examination of infants, preschoolers and their mothers. *Developmental Psychology, 31,* 364–376.

Tronick, E. Z. (1989). Emotions and emotional communication in infants. *American Psychologist, 44,* 112–119.

Whiffen, V. E., & Gotlib, I. M. (1989). Infants of postpartum depressed mothers: Temperament and cognitive status. *Journal of Abnormal Psychology, 98,* 274–279.

Zahn-Waxler, C., Iannotti, R. J., Cummings, E. M., & Denham, S. (1990). Antecedents of problem behaviors in children of depressed mothers. *Development and Psychopathology, 2,* 271–291.

Zahn-Waxler, C., Kochanska, G., Krupnick, J., & McKnew, D. H. (1990). Patterns of guilt in children of depressed and well mothers. *Developmental Psychology, 26,* 51–59.

Zahn-Waxler, C., Mayfield, A., Radke-Yarrow, M. R., McKnew, D. H., Cytryn, L., & Davenport, Y. B. (1988). A follow-up investigation of offspring of parents with bipolar disorder. *The American Journal of Psychiatry, 145,* 506–509.

Zahn-Waxler, C., McKnew, D. H., Cummings, M. E., Davenport, Y. B., & Radke-Yarrow, M. R. (1984). Problem behaviors and peer interactions of young children with a manic-depressive parent. *American Journal of Psychiatry, 141,* 236–240.

Zahn-Waxler, C., & Radke-Yarrow, M. (1982). The development of altruism: Alternative research strategies. In N. Eisenberg (Ed.), *The development of prosocial behavior* (pp. 109–137). San Diego, CA: Academic Press.

Zahn-Waxler, C., Radke-Yarrow, M., Wagner, E., & Chapman, M. (1992). Development of concern for others. *Developmental Psychology, 28,* 126–136.

13

TRANSMISSION OF RISK TO CHILDREN OF DEPRESSED PARENTS: INTEGRATION AND CONCLUSIONS

SHERRYL H. GOODMAN AND IAN H. GOTLIB

In a previous article (Goodman & Gotlib, 1999), we highlighted a number of theories that are relevant to understanding risk for psychopathology in children with depressed parents. Moreover, we proposed that each of these various theories could be used to explain different aspects or components of vulnerability to depression. The purpose of this book was to build on that formulation by giving experts in the field the opportunity to present focused and detailed perspectives on seven models of mechanisms and four models of moderators of risk for depression in children of depressed parents.

The authors of each of the chapters in Parts I (Mechanisms of Risk) and II (Moderators of Risk) presented a model that has guided their efforts to gain a better understanding of the risks to children of depressed parents. We encouraged the authors to present their theoretical models addressing how and why, or under what circumstances, parental depression increases children's risk for developing psychopathology. More specifically, the authors of the chapters in Part I focused on mediational models of a range of biopsychosocial processes that have strong empirical support. Similarly, the authors of the chapters in Part II discussed moderator models that might help to explain why, although many children with depressed parents develop psychopathology, a significant subset do not.

The study of children of depressed parents is particularly compelling because of the potential implications of research in this area for prevention and early intervention. In Part III of this book, Gladstone and Beardslee (chapter 12, this volume) provided a unique perspective, summarizing the empirical clinical work that has been conducted with offspring of depressed parents.

In this concluding chapter, we highlight the distinctive and overlapping elements of the different models. We both identify connecting points across models and underscore the unique contributions of each model. In this context, we focus on how different perspectives may help to explain the risk for particular outcomes, the specificity of risk, and the varying risk depending on several aspects of the child, the environment, or the parent's depression. In discussing these issues, we draw on these chapters to elaborate our integrative model of risk. Because such a broad model raises as many questions as it answers, in this final chapter we also outline what we believe are important questions that should guide future research in this area. Finally, we highlight implications for intervention that cut across models and suggest intervention designs that have the potential not only to help prevent or minimize the negative outcomes in the children, but also to test hypotheses that are generated by the models. We begin our discussion by identifying common themes that emerged in the presentations of mechanisms underlying the intergenerational transmission of risk for depression.

MEDIATORS: COMMONALITIES AND UNIQUE CONSIDERATIONS

Each of the seven chapters that discuss potential mechanisms through which depressed parents may impart elevated risk for psychopathology to their children describe distinct variables and paths through which they may operate. Nonetheless, five constructs cut across many of these diverse mechanisms: inadequate parenting, exposure to stress, exposure to negative cognitions, disrupted biological systems, and the interplay of nature and nurture.

Inadequate Parenting

Perhaps the single predominant theme that cuts across virtually all of the proposed mechanisms is inadequate parenting. Depression, by nature of its symptoms (such as emotional dysregulation) and correlates (such as stress), is likely to interfere with parent–child relationships (Lyons-Ruth, Lyubchik, Wolfe, & Bronfman, chapter 5, this volume; Radke-Yarrow & Klimes-Dougan, chapter 7, this volume). Inadequate parenting raises concerns because it increases the likelihood that several aspects of healthy development are disrupted, such as the following:

1. infants' needs for appropriate levels of stimulation to facilitate their development of emotional expression and regulation (Ashman & Dawson, chapter 3, this volume; Field, chapter 4, this volume):
2. the development of a secure attachment relationship between mother and infant (Lyons-Ruth et al., chapter 5, this volume); and
3. the acquisition of a healthy attributional style and self-efficacy beliefs (Garber & Martin, chapter 6, this volume).

Disruption in these normal developmental processes has been associated with risk for depression. Overall, these authors offered strong support from several perspectives for the thesis that maternal depression affects the quality of parenting, increasing children's vulnerability for the development of psychopathology.

Exposure to Stress

Another common theme across chapters was stress as a mechanism in the transmission of depression from parent to child. Stress was the primary focus of chapter 8 (Hammen) and chapter 10 (Compas, Langrock, Keller, Merchant, & Copeland), and it was also discussed by other authors. Stress is a central construct in the understanding of mechanisms of risk for psychopathology in children with depressed parents from several perspectives:

1. The depressed parents' illness-related behavior, which may be a large component of family stress (Hammen, chapter 8, this volume).
2. Other stressors are often a consequence of the parents' depression, for example, difficulties in social network relationships, occupational impairment, and related financial stresses (Hammen, chapter 8, this volume).
3. Depressed women are likely to marry men who themselves have psychopathology and to have conflictual marriages, two additional stressors for the children (Hammen, chapter 8, this volume; Garber & Martin, chapter 6, this volume; Radke-Yarrow & Klimes-Dougan, chapter 7, this volume).
4. In some families, maternal depression is one of multiple risk factors (including poverty, minority status, lack of education, chronic health problems, and, for some, adolescent parenthood) to which the children are exposed (Field, chapter 4, this volume; Hammen, chapter 8, this volume).

5. Coping processes may be compromised (Compas et al., chapter 10, this volume).

6. Children might experience their interactions with their depressed mothers as stressful (e.g., when a depressed mother does not respond to the infant's social initiation), regardless of other additional contextual stressors (Ashman & Dawson, chapter 3, this volume; Field, chapter 4, this volume; Garber & Martin, chapter 6, this volume; Lyons-Ruth et al., chapter 5, this volume; Compas et al., chapter 10, this volume).

7. Children with depressed parents also are exposed to stressors outside the family (e.g., peer conflicts and academic problems), some of which may be at least partly as a result of the behavior and characteristics of the children (Compas et al., chapter 10, this volume; Hammen, chapter 8, this volume).

8. Children's repeated and, especially, early exposure to stressors might lead to inadequate stress regulation later in their lives (Ashman & Dawson, chapter 3, this volume; Field, chapter 4, this volume; Lyons-Ruth et al. chapter 5, this volume; Hammen, chapter 8, this volume).

Hammen elegantly described the challenge of understanding the direct and indirect mechanisms by which these multiple stressors influence the emergence of psychopathology in the children.

Negative Cognitions

The role of cognitions was central to Garber and Martin's and Hammen's chapters (6 and 8, respectively), and it also was considered in the models proposed by the authors of several other chapters. Given the central role of negative cognitions in models of risk for the development of depression, it is particularly important to understand how children with depressed parents might acquire these beliefs. Several processes were implicated:

1. Depressed parents explain their children's behavior in terms of negative attributional styles, giving children the opportunity to learn depressogenic cognitions (Garber & Martin, chapter 6, this volume).

2. Depressed parents engage in negative exchanges with their children during which the parents' words (e.g., criticism, blaming) or actions (e.g., ignoring, punishing) convey negative ascriptions about the child or negative attributions about the causes of events, through which children learn negative beliefs about themselves and the world (Garber & Martin, chapter 6, this volume).

3. Depressed parents expose their children to more stressors than do nondepressed parents, which, if particularly traumatic, chronic, or uncontrollable, are likely to contribute to children's development of negative cognitions, including self-blame, helplessness, and hopelessness (Garber & Martin, chapter 6, this volume; Hammen, chapter 8, this volume).

4. Children struggle to make sense of their observations of their parents' symptoms and other depression-related behaviors; they blame themselves or decide to take on a caretaking role (Radke-Yarrow & Klimes-Dougan, chapter 7, this volume; Hammen, chapter 8, this volume).

Despite the strong support for the role of cognitions in the transmission of risk for depression, it is important to keep in mind Silberg and Rutter's (chapter 2, this volume) caveat. Silberg and Rutter argued that emotionality may be more central to models of risk for depression than is cognition. Exploration of the associations between emotionality and cognitive variables may yield valuable insights.

Disrupted Biological Systems

In several of the models proposed by the authors, biological systems were assumed to play an important role, either moderating or mediating the inadequate parenting. Authors emphasized biological systems related to emotional expression and regulation, including stress-related neuroendocrinology (e.g., elevated stress hormones), autonomic activity (e.g., lower vagal tone), and cortical activation (e.g., relative right frontal EEG activation). Developmental considerations are essential for this mechanism. In particular, early exposure is probably a necessary aspect of this mechanism. Even the distinction between whether the first exposure to parents' depression is prenatal or postnatal might set children on different developmental pathways (Ashman & Dawson, chapter 3, this volume).

Infants whose mothers were depressed during pregnancy are characterized by abnormalities in all three of these psychobiological systems, which could reflect both genetic influences and exposure to atypical neuroendocrine patterns during fetal development; Field (chapter 4, this volume) argued for the latter. In addition, depressed mothers' inadequate parenting may exacerbate the infants' biological vulnerabilities. Of particular concern is that infants born with these biological vulnerabilities could be less responsive, expressive, and attentive. Depressed mothers may be particularly challenged by the difficulties these babies bring to the mother–infant interaction, a point to which we return later.

Infants whose mothers experience postpartum depression that interferes with their caregiving may experience alterations in their neuroendocrine systems, specifically HPA axis functioning (Lyons-Ruth et al., chapter 5, this volume) and in the development of their frontal lobes (Ashman & Dawson, chapter 3, this volume). The frontal lobe region in particular is critical to emotional expression and regulation and to the development of stress regulation–response systems. In summary, therefore, whether as a function of prenatal exposure to depressotypic neurochemical abnormalities or inadequate early parenting, alterations in children's psychobiological systems related to emotion expression and regulation contribute to their risk for depression.

Nature–Nurture Interplay

The interplay of nature and nurture was another theme in several of the chapters. It was central to Silberg and Rutter's thesis (chapter 2, this volume), and many of the other authors elaborated on specific aspects of heritability or other biological factors that they deemed important within their model of risk. In general, the authors stressed the importance of considering not only the heritability of depression per se, but also the heritability of personal or environmental characteristics that increase the risk of developing depression. Offspring of depressed mothers may carry a genetic predisposition that

1. leaves them vulnerable to the effects of both environmental mechanisms, such as inadequate parenting, and biological mechanisms, such as abnormal intrauterine stress hormone levels (Field, chapter 4, this volume);
2. increases their tendency to experience stressful events (Hammen, chapter 8, this volume; although see Silberg & Rutter, chapter 2, this volume, for a recent failure to replicate this finding); or
3. increases their likelihood of developing depression-related cognitions or, more broadly, a tendency to experience neuroticism or negative emotionality (Garber & Martin, chapter 6, this volume, argued for the former).

Silberg and Rutter (chapter 2, this volume) argued persuasively that the usually small amount of variance accounted for by any single genetic or environmental influence necessitates that the most viable model of risk is one in which combinations of risk factors are considered. Silberg and Rutter elaborated on three aspects of the interplay between nature and nurture: passive gene–environment correlations, active–evocative gene–environment correlations, and gene–environment interactions. Moreover, they provided further support for the point, also raised by Field (chapter 4, this volume), that genetic liability may operate in part through increasing children's sensitivity to environmental stressors. Radke-Yarrow and Klimes-Dougan (chapter 7, this volume) added that one potential role of early stress may be in the emergence of neurobiological mechanisms that could trigger gene expression.

In summary, the authors offered strong support for the importance of considering correlations and interactions between genetic and environmental effects. It is clear from these chapters that, as is the case with biological factors other than genetics, these two sets of effects are not independent. Future studies using longitudinal designs, genetic studies, and molecular genetics hold promise for clarifying the complex interplay among environment, behavior, and biology.

MODERATORS OF TRANSMISSION OF RISK FOR DEPRESSION

Three chapters dealt with moderators of the association between parental depression and child outcomes. Our goal in inviting authors to contribute these chapters was to understand the factors associated with better or worse outcomes among children with depressed parents. Inherent in the emphasis on moderators is the notion of multiple risk factors, which is important for at least two reasons. First, it is unlikely that any single risk factor, including parental depression, accounts for large proportions of the variance in child outcomes. Second, studying parental depression as the single predictor ignores differences in the contexts within which children are developing as well as individual differences among children. Thus, three sets of moderators were given primary consideration: (a) the role of the family (Phares, Duhig, & Watkins, chapter 9, this volume); (b) children's coping processes and adaptation (Compas et al., chapter 10, this volume), and (c) gender (Sheeber, Davis, & Hops, chapter 11, this volume).

Role of the Family

In terms of family influences, authors argued that children with depressed parents are worse off under the following conditions:

1. Both parents are depressed (e.g., assortative mating), whether because of increased genetic or environmental risk or both.
2. Interparental conflict is high.
3. The depressed parent is less emotionally available (more self-focus) and engages in less expression of positive emotions (e.g., warmth) and greater expression of negative emotions (e.g., hostility).
4. One or more siblings have low levels of functioning and children have impaired relationships with their siblings, reducing the opportunity for support from siblings, contributing to

children's stress, and increasing the amount of conflict the children experience.

Consideration of each of these aspects of the family is needed to understand the extent to which children with depressed parents are at risk for psychopathology.

Children's Coping Processes and Adaptation

Compas et al. (chapter 10, this volume) provided an in-depth exploration of the role of children's coping responses in the association between parents' depression and the emergence of psychopathology in the children. They considered not only that parent-related stressors and children's particular coping responses might moderate the association between parents' depression and children's psychopathology, but also that children's coping responses may mediate the association between parent-related stressors and children's symptoms. Thus, in terms of Goodman and Gotlib's (1999) integrative model (see Figure 13.1), Compas et al. were testing the role of one of the vulnerabilities, children's coping responses, in the association between the mechanism of exposure to stressful environments and children's psychopathology. Their findings were consistent with that model and may be the first evidence of the vulnerability of children's particular coping processes as mediators of the association between stress and children's symptoms of disorder.

Gender

Sheeber et al. (chapter 11, this volume) proposed and supported the idea that vulnerability may be gender specific. They found modest support for the formulations that adolescent daughters, but not sons, of depressed mothers are at particular risk for depression and that gender-stereotypic socialization practices contribute to that specific risk. Sheeber et al. proposed a stress–diathesis model to explain, in part, the likelihood of depression in adolescent girls. That is, girls become vulnerable (the diathesis) as a function of having learned and having been differentially reinforced by their parents (and later, by others) for gender-typic behavioral patterns such as the expression of sadness, self-derogation, and ruminative styles of responding to stressors rather than active coping and problem-solving strategies. These patterns (depressogenic cognitive and interpersonal styles and inadequate skills) would then interfere with girls' ability to deal effectively with stressors. Consequently, when faced with the normative challenges of adolescence, girls would be more likely than boys to develop symptoms of depression. In this sense, both gender and developmental stage were proposed as moderators.

Adolescent girls may also be more vulnerable than boys to depression because they have more conflictual interactions with their mothers and may be more sensitive to disturbances in parent–child relationships. In addition,

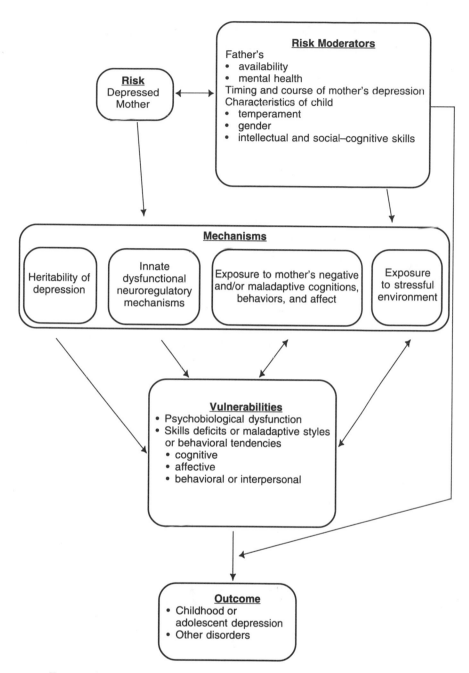

Figure 13.1. An integrative model for the transmission of risk to children of depressed mothers.

mothers' depressive interpersonal and cognitive styles may be particularly salient models for their same-sex children. Finally, maternal depression also functions to elicit caretaking behaviors and a sense of responsibility from the children, perhaps from girls in particular. These ideas encourage further exploration of the role of gender in enhancing risk or protecting children with depressed parents.

Age of Child

In addition to the three chapters focusing on specific moderators, several of the authors in Part I also mentioned moderators. The most common theme was developmental considerations. All of the authors stressed the importance in any model of risk of considering the concurrent and developing stage–salient needs of children. Radke-Yarrow and Klimes-Dougan (chapter 7, this volume) made a strong plea for developmental considerations in every aspect of a model. Other authors presented specific examples of the importance of considering development. For example, Garber and Martin (chapter 6, this volume) suggested that children's awareness of parents' cognitions, which sets the stage for modeling, varies developmentally. Similarly, Hammen (chapter 8, this volume) argued that considering developmental issues in stress exposure and stress processes is critical in gaining a better understanding of how parents' stressors affect children at different ages and of what might be an age-specific role of parent–child interactions in mediating that association. Stressors, both children's own and those affecting their parents, may affect children differently depending on their developmental stage. Hammen offers alternative hypotheses that should be tested.

Children's Personal Characteristics

Children's temperament and other personality characteristics as moderators were mentioned in several chapters. Garber and Martin (chapter 6, this volume) found that the association between life events and hopelessness was greater for children with low self-worth than for those with high self-worth. Children may be protected from any of the mechanisms of risk if they do not see the depressed parent as an attractive model; if they have high intelligence and good coping and problem-solving skills; if the parents' depression has fewer direct consequences for them; and if social support is available from other family members, peers, teachers, and others (Garber & Martin, chapter 6, this volume; Hammen, chapter 8, this volume). As with the other moderators, these ideas on possible protective mechanisms are important with respect to the development of effective preventive interventions, an issue to which we return in greater detail later in this chapter.

Severity and Chronicity of Parent's Depression

Radke-Yarrow and Klimes-Dougan (chapter 7, this volume) and others suggested another possible moderator in terms of qualities and characteristics of the parent's depression. Of particular concern is the severity and chronicity of the parent's depression. Radke-Yarrow and Klimes-Dougan suggested that these clinical characteristics be included in research studies in a dose-response manner. Although these indices could reflect greater genetic load, they may also represent tools for identifying the subset of children with depressed parents who are most at risk for the development of psychopathology.

DIVERSE OUTCOMES AND DEVELOPMENTAL PATHWAYS

Several authors took on the challenge of describing possible developmental pathways for the range of disorders for which children with depressed parents are at risk. Both Radke-Yarrow and Klimes-Dougan (chapter 7, this volume) and Silberg and Rutter (chapter 2, this volume) expounded on the developmental psychopathology concepts of *multifinality*, that multiple pathways that may diverge from common origins, and *equifinality*, that diverse developmental pathways may lead to a similar long-term outcome, such as the development of depression (Cicchetti & Rogosch, 1996). Radke-Yarrow and Klimes-Dougan encouraged readers to conceptualize outcome in terms of pathways and symptom patterns that unfold in a context of mutual influences, rather than as static diagnostic entities.

Silberg and Rutter (chapter 2, this volume) argued that the form of psychopathology exhibited by children of unipolar depressed parents is directly related to the relative extent of genetic and environmental mediation of transmission of risk. More specifically, they contended that genetic mediation is likely to be strongest for the development of children's anxiety or depressive disorders and weakest for externalizing types of childhood disorders, for which environmental mediation of risk was expected to be predominant.

In several chapters the authors described support for the importance of individual differences among depressed mothers and how those differences might relate to alternative pathways and outcomes in their children. Radke-Yarrow and Klimes-Dougan (chapter 7, this volume) described the potential contribution of comorbid, or co-occurring, personality disorders to differential child outcomes. They reported data indicating that depressed mothers' avoidant personality disorder, which may be reflected in uninvolved parenting, was associated with externalizing behavior in the children; in contrast, mothers' dependent personality disorder, which may be expressed in overinvolvement, was associated with recurrent disruptive or oppositional problems in the children.

Field (chapter 4, this volume) and Lyons-Ruth et al. (chapter 5, this volume) focused on another aspect of individual differences among depressed mothers: two contrasting maternal depression interaction styles, withdrawn and intrusive, and their potential for illuminating mechanisms underlying alternative pathways children may follow. In other writings, Hammen (1997) has also proposed two subtypes of manifestations of maternal depression: dysphoric withdrawn and hostile, each with unique implications for child outcomes. Similarly, Gelfand and Teti (1990) described two contrasting manifestations of maternal depression and elaborated on their implications for child discipline: one subtype predominantly showing "anger, rejection, and harsh, capricious discipline," and the other "characteristically apathetic, self-absorbed, tearful, and irresolute as a disciplinarian" (p. 342).

Lyons-Ruth et al. (chapter 5, this volume) grappled with the question of whether these two patterns characterize different subgroups of depressed parents or whether the same depressed parents alternate between the two patterns. In contrast to Field (chapter 4, this volume), Lyons-Ruth et al. argued that at least one subgroup of depressed parents is likely to display inconsistencies in the parenting behaviors. They theorized that these parents' own ambivalence about attachment would lead them to engage in contradictory caregiving strategies with their infants, who are then likely to develop disorganized insecure attachment styles. In contrast, other depressed mothers may relate to their infants in a fearful and withdrawn manner without the intrusive, rejecting behavior, and their infants are more likely to develop disorganized secure attachment styles with signs of apprehension and dysphoria. Following these two groups prospectively would help to determine whether the children of these two subgroups of depressed parents differ in their development of emotional or behavioral problems.

Compas et al. (chapter 10, this volume) also discussed the issue of the consistency of depressed parents' behaviors and, as a related issue, the children's perceptions and experience of the parents' behaviors. They found that depressed parents (mostly mothers) and their adolescent children reported that the depressed parents engaged in both withdrawal and intrusiveness. The adolescents reported that they found the depressed parents' behaviors associated with both of these styles at least moderately stressful and out of their control. Although Compas et al. found that all children were exposed to both styles, they were unable to determine whether children differed in the timing or amount of exposure to stressors related to withdrawal or intrusiveness. Their finding that withdrawal, but not intrusiveness, was related to concurrent parental reports of depressive symptoms suggests that intrusiveness may be a more stable aspect of depressives' parenting style than withdrawal.

Ashman and Dawson (chapter 3, this volume) were among the authors who noted that the adverse outcomes to children with depressed parents are not limited to depression, but include the full range of disorders as well as other problems in adjustment. If, as they argued, psychobiological systems involved in infants' emotion regulation are implicated in the development of disorder, then the children are at risk for developing not only depression but other emotional problems as well.

Hammen (chapter 8, this volume) took a different approach to considering differential outcomes. She interpreted the findings on children exposed to their parents' depression and other stressors to suggest that stress may set the stage for the development of other disorders in children. For example, children of depressed parents who also experience their parents' marital discord may be more likely to develop externalizing rather than internalizing disorders. Hammen recommended further study of the role of specific and general stressors that are associated with parental depression and that may lead to emotional difficulties in the children.

Phares et al. (chapter 9, this volume) and Sheeber et al. (chapter 11, this volume) raised the possibility that gender may help to explain differential outcomes of children. Phares et al. suggested that gender, and particularly the interaction of the gender of the depressed parent and the gender of the child, may help to account for particular outcomes in the children. For example, they found that adolescent daughters of depressed fathers tend to exhibit internalizing problems, whereas sons of depressed mothers tend to exhibit externalizing problems. Nevertheless, as a cautionary note, Sheeber et al. noted that, although there is modest support for the formulation that adolescent daughters of depressed mothers are at greater risk for depression than are adolescent sons, there is little evidence that prepubertal sons are at differential risk for conduct problems relative to daughters.

ROLE OF AN INTEGRATIVE MODEL

A compelling impression from the models of mechanisms and moderators presented by the authors is that the outcomes among children with depressed parents are determined by multiple variables interacting with developmental processes. Thus, there is no single risk factor, fixed developmental course, or single outcome for which children of depressed parents are at risk. Any one component of a model most likely both is multiply influenced and exerts multiple influences. Although each of the authors of chapters on mechanisms (Part I) emphasized a particular mechanism, they all drew connections to other mediating factors. For example, Hammen (chapter 8, this volume) made reference to neurobiological processes that may mediate the relation between stress and adverse outcomes among children of depressed parents, particularly when exposure to stress occurs early in development. Similarly, Radke-Yarrow and Klimes-Dougan (chapter 7, this volume) pointed out that the negativity that often characterizes depression in adults would affect the children by exposing them not only to negativity directed toward them (criticism, rejection), but also to a generally negative outlook on life (see also Garber and Martin, chapter 6, this volume). The children would also be exposed to the parents' negative interactions with each other and, as the family becomes more isolated from the outside world, the children would have less exposure to nondisturbed families and healthy peer relationships and fewer opportunities to receive support from others.

Radke-Yarrow and Klimes-Dougan (chapter 7, this volume) also provided support for a cumulative risk perspective, whether conceptualized in additive terms or taking into account the more complex transactional properties of multiply interacting factors. They found that individual risk factors such as family stress and severity of the parent's depression could account for moderate proportions of variance in children's problems; children who had both of these risks, particularly at adolescence, had significantly higher rates of depression. A more transactional model, as they illustrated with a case presentation, would take into account interactions among children's characteristics, mothers' symptoms, and developmental processes. For example, children's difficult temperament may only matter among those with highly symptomatic mothers, most likely as a function of reciprocal negative processes set into play early and accelerated over time. Hammen (chapter 8, this volume) expressed a similar idea in suggesting that children who develop psychological maladjustment early on, in association with maternal depression, may consequently have more problematic relationships with peers and, therefore, fewer opportunities to develop effective coping and problem-solving skills. This situation would be further exacerbated by the relative inability of the depressed parent to help the child.

Several of the authors observed that each of the key components of a model of risk is part of a set of components that are multiply and mutually influenced. For example, Garber and Martin (chapter 6, this volume) added a caveat that the correlation between parents' and children's cognitive style should not be assumed to reflect modeling, because stressors may have influenced both parents' and children's cognitions. Garber and Martin also elaborated on the multiple processes through which children's exposure to stressors might lead to the development of negative cognitions. In this context, Silberg and Rutter (chapter 2, this volume) noted that genetic influences are involved both in children's likelihood of experiencing stressful environments and also in the extent to which they are susceptible to the risk environments.

Numerous examples of transactional processes were provided in these chapters. For example, Hammen (chapter 8, this volume) drew on her stress-generation hypothesis in describing how the impaired functioning associated with depression contributes to stressful circumstances, which then further challenge the depressed person's coping capacities and exacerbate the disturbances. Although not specifically mentioned by Hammen, one likely scenario is the depressed mother who is characterized by inadequate parenting, resulting in a child who becomes increasingly fussy, demanding, and negative. These child difficulties and negativity further stress the depressed parent, setting the stage for reciprocal, spiraling negative consequences for both mother and child and for their relationship.

Hammen (chapter 8, this volume) also raised intriguing questions about stress, not only as an independent contributor to negative outcomes in children with depressed parents, but also as a moderator in a stress–diathesis model. In this model children of depressed parents are exposed to high levels of chronic and episodic stress. Hammen suggested that diatheses in these children could be genetic, neurobiological, or cognitive or that it may involve attachment insecurity or other risk factors. She presented support for two such diatheses in association with stress: children's negative cognitions about themselves and their high levels of sociotropic beliefs. In the latter case, the diathesis is expected to interact with a particular type of stressor (i.e., stressors with interpersonal content). Hammen also presented evidence that high levels of negative life events experienced by the children were associated with their depressive symptoms only if their mothers had been highly symptomatic during the preceding year. This interaction suggests that mothers who experience an episode of depression may not be able to effectively buffer their children against the adverse effects of stressful life events associated with the depressive episode.

Compas et al. (chapter 10, this volume) discussed the association between stress and coping at a cognitive level and the probable ramifications for children's physiological functioning. They described how children of depressed parents, faced with increased levels of both parent- and peer-related stressors, seem to be less able to control problematic involuntary stress responses. Thus, children with higher levels of stressors are more likely to respond with increased emotional and physiological reactivity. This maladaptive coping response, therefore, would likely further interfere with the children's ability to regulate both their behaviors and their emotions. Indeed, greater use of maladaptive coping responses was associated concurrently with higher levels of symptoms of depression and anxiety and behavior problems. An important next step would be to test this model prospectively at various developmental stages to determine whether coping responses predict the emergence of psychopathology differently at various stages of development. Developmental variation would be expected as a function of both the extent to which particular events related to the experience of having a depressed parent are experienced as stressful and the coping and stress responses that are available to the children.

Phares and her co-authors (chapter 9, this volume) emphasized the less complex but often overlooked bidirectional, reciprocal influences within families. In particular, parents influence their children and children also influence their parents. In general, difficult or symptomatic children may contribute to their parents' depression. At a more molecular level, children contribute to parent–child interactions with both their behavior and affect.

In summary, virtually all of the authors not only presented compelling evidence for a particular mediator or moderator, but also argued strongly for models involving interactions with factors that cut across the traditional boundaries that have separated discussions of genetic–biological and cognitive–interpersonal factors (see Goodman & Gotlib, 1999). Moreover, the authors also gave serious and creative consideration to developmental processes that are crucial to an understanding of the risk for the development of psychopathology in children of depressed parents. Integrating principles of developmental psychopathology into models of the intergenerational transmission of risk promises to enhance the effectiveness of efforts to prevent or intervene early in the emergence of psychopathology in children of depressed parents. We turn now to a discussion of these encouraging early efforts to intervene.

IMPLICATIONS FOR CLINICIANS

A number of themes emerged with regard to clinical implications of the theories and research on mechanisms of risk for psychopathology in children with depressed parents. Each of the authors included a section on clinical implications of their particular perspective, and Gladstone and Beardslee (chapter 12, this volume) provided a focused review of intervention in this area. Here, we highlight ideas that are particularly promising and that we encourage clinicians to pursue.

First and foremost is the importance of viewing adult depression from a family perspective. Although this idea may seem self-evident, it is often not put into practice. For example, one of us (Goodman) has frequently had the experience of meeting with clinicians who treat adults in hospitals, mental health centers, or large group private practice settings. In the context of making a presentation on clinical issues for depressed women who are parents, she would ask clinicians how many of the adults with depression whom they were treating had children. Typically, although each could respond anecdotally, most clinical settings had no systematic procedure for recording that information. This lack of information was symbolic of a neglect, not only of parenting issues for these depressed patients, but also of the potential needs of the children.

With respect to treatment, therefore, when a depressed adult who is a parent seeks help, there is a compelling need for two approaches: (a) to assess the spouse and children and (b) to educate the parents about the potential effects of their disorders on their children. Phares et al. (chapter 9, this volume) reminded us to include fathers, both as sources of information about the children and in the treatment process. With regard to assessment, Radke-Yarrow and Klimes-Dougan (chapter 7, this volume) pointed out that it may be particularly important to screen the children for symptoms that may not yet impair their functioning. Parents may not have noticed a problem or may not be concerned.

With respect to education, Beardslee's (e.g., Beardslee et al., 1997) interventions are the most developed and empirically supported. Gladstone and Beardslee (chapter 12, this volume) described two approaches to psychoeducation: a lecture format and a clinician-facilitated intervention. Although both were effective, the clinician-facilitated intervention produced greater levels of change. In particular, children demonstrated a better understanding of their parents' depression and had improved communication with parents. These interventions offer great potential for widespread use in a range of settings by clinicians of any orientation.

In addition to educational approaches aimed at improving knowledge of depression and communication within families, other approaches to marital and family therapy are consistent with many of the theories. For example, reducing marital conflict would minimize one of the stressors in the families. Any approach focused on enhancing communication would also reduce children's tendencies to blame themselves and acquire other negative cognitions. With structural family therapy, families with a depressed parent would benefit if the parents are supported for asserting their parenting roles and keeping the children from taking on the role of caregiver. Other approaches could be expanded to include interventions relevant to the theoretical models proposed in these chapters.

Behavioral family therapy is another approach with direct applications for children with depressed parents. Sheeber et al. (chapter 11, this volume) recommended helping parents recognize and stop any tendency to reinforce their children's (especially their daughters') depressive behavior and, conversely, to increase their reinforcement of their children's adaptive social and problem-solving behavior. Sheeber et al. also suggested that family behavioral interventions may be needed to reduce any inappropriate emotional reliance of depressed mothers on their children and to reduce mother–daughter conflict and replace it with prosocial behaviors.

Other suggested approaches are more skills based. In particular, given the emphasis on parenting as a mechanism, therapy for depressed parents should include assessment and, if necessary, intervention for the specific parenting skills that are required for the child's particular stage of development.

Silberg and Rutter's (chapter 2, this volume) discussion of the interplay of nature and nurture in the mechanisms of risk for psychopathology in children with depressed mothers has direct implications for clinicians who treat depressed parents. First, to the extent that disorders associated with the parents' depression contribute to the risk to the children, clinical interventions would benefit from a focus on treating not only the parent's depression but also the comorbid disorders. Second, given that children experience psychosocial risks because of certain aspects of the parents' behavior, it might be productive to think of interventions targeting the depressed parents' behaviors to reduce the creation of high-risk environments for their children.

In addition to traditional clinical assessments and interventions, the mechanisms of risk presented in these chapters have powerful implications for preventive approaches. Several authors emphasized the importance of approaches aimed at the prevention of difficulties in the children of depressed parents, which was the perspective strongly advocated by Gladstone and Beardslee (chapter 12, this volume).

The notion of preventive intervention is particularly compelling for depressed mothers of infants. Following Field's (chapter 4, this volume) model of maladaptive depressed parent–child relationships, it is important to match the intervention to the interactive style of individual patients. For example, Field described the effectiveness of interaction coaching, but only when the researchers matched the intervention strategy to the depression profile of the mother (e.g., withdrawn vs. intrusive).

Within the prevention field, it is important to identify individuals who are at risk for the development of psychopathology. One of the important observations made by many of the authors is that not all children with depressed parents are at risk for psychopathology. The chapters on moderators offered many suggestions for identifying those most likely to be at risk. For clinicians interested in preventive intervention approaches, it is important to use assessments to measure markers of risk. Ashman and Dawson (chapter 3, this volume) suggested that atypical EEG patterns and elevated cortisol levels could be considered as physiological markers of elevated risk among children with depressed mothers and, thus, could be used to identify those who might benefit most from preventive interventions. Although these techniques might be outside the range of possibilities for many clinicians, other measures could be used to assess exaggerated stress responses and inadequate affect regulation.

Children identified as having difficulty coping with stress or with regulating their affect might benefit from Sheeber et al.'s (chapter 11, this volume) suggestion that clinicians might modify the parenting behavior of depressed women and their partners. This would be important for two reasons: It would reduce the children's experience of stressors, and it would increase the parents' ability to help their children regulate their dysphoric affect and cope with stressors.

Clinicians who incorporate a cognitive perspective in their assessment and treatment also have important preventive work to do with families with depressed parents. Garber and Martin (chapter 6, this volume) described two types of prevention programs: those aimed at altering children's negative cognitions in order to prevent depression and those targeting at changing the dysfunctional patterns of parent–child interactions that give rise to negative cognitions in the children. Radke-Yarrow and Klimes-Dougan (chapter 7, this volume) also suggested a focus on cognitive factors, especially with respect to helping children understand their depressed parent's behavior.

Stress reduction and developing coping resources interventions are compatible with at least one of the mechanisms of risk. Hammen's (chapter 8, this volume) emphasis on stress led her to suggest intervention approaches that include teaching depressed parents how to resolve stressful situations, how to modify dysfunctional cognitions and behaviors that may contribute to the occurrence and maintenance of stressors (including parent–child difficulties), and how to help their children to resolve their own stressors. Based on their findings concerning the importance of examining children's coping responses, Compas et al. (chapter 10, this volume) emphasized the potential utility of interventions aimed at teaching children more effective ways of coping with the often uncontrollable stressors associated with their parents' depression.

Silberg and Rutter (chapter 2, this volume) were optimistic that interventions can be designed that would minimize the extent to which children with depressed parents are exposed to high-risk environments, thereby interrupting the interacting and correlated genetic impact of environmental risks. Nevertheless, they cautioned that risk factors that are highly genetically mediated (and thus carry little environmentally mediated risk) are not likely to be effective targets for intervention.

Although we are enthusiastic about the potential for preventive intervention approaches, we take note of the cautions concerning the practical implementation of preventive interventions expressed by several authors. In particular, because parental depression exerts its effects early and quickly, it may be difficult to implement truly preventive interventions. For example, Sheeber et al. (chapter 11, this volume) expressed concern that the gender-specific socialization practices that were a focus of their recommended intervention start very early in children's lives, making prevention efforts difficult.

One theme of this volume was intervention in a developmentally sensitive manner. Compas et al. (chapter 10, this volume) cautioned that interventions for children with depressed parents that focus on teaching children to cope with stress must be developmentally sensitive to the children's coping capacities. Thus, strategies to teach children to cope would likely need to be paired with interventions to reduce the levels of stressors, such as modifying the depressed parent's style of interacting with the child. Gladstone and Beardslee (chapter 12, this volume) used a developmental perspective to organize their review of the literature on empirically based clinical interventions for children with depressed parents. They delineated targets of intervention that are most strongly warranted by the research on mechanisms, moderators, and outcomes. The results were encouraging, with clinically significant outcomes having been reported for interventions designed to prevent depression in children of depressed parents from infancy through adolescence. Gladstone and Beardslee also made several cogent suggestions for further use of empirical tests of preventive interventions for children with depressed parents.

We underscore the potential value of using preventive intervention designs to test hypotheses derived from the models of risk for psychopathology in children with depressed parents described in the chapters in this volume. Each of the chapter authors offered a number of suggestions concerning causal risk processes and explanations for some of the variability in susceptibility to risk in offspring of depressed parents. Certainly, each of these suggestions could be the focus of a prevention or intervention study. Inevitably, the more accurate our understanding of the causal mechanisms becomes, the more effective our preventive interventions derived from that understanding.

REFERENCES

Beardslee, W. R., Salt, P., Versate, E., Gladstone, T. R. G., Wright, E., & Rothberg, P. C. (1997). Sustained change in parents receiving preventive interventions for families with depression. *American Journal of Psychiatry, 154*, 510–515.

Cicchetti, D., & Rogosch, F. (1996). Equifinality and multifinality in developmental psychopathology. *Development and Psychopathology, 8*, 597–600.

Gelfand, D., & Teti, D. (1990). The effects of maternal depression on children. *Clinical Psychology Review, 10*, 329–353.

Goodman, S. H., & Gotlib, I. H. (1999). Risk for psychopathology in the children of depressed parents: A developmental approach to the understanding of mechanisms. *Psychological Review, 106*, 458–490.

Hammen, C. (1997). Children of depressed parents: The stress context. In S. A. Wolchik & I. N. Sandler (Eds.), *Handbook of children's coping: Linking theory and intervention. Issues in clinical child psychology* (pp. 131–157). New York: Plenum.

AUTHOR INDEX

Numbers in italics refer to listings in the reference section.

Cutrona, C. E., 124, 141, *145, 146,* 279, *301*
Cytryn, L., *305*

D'Onofrio, B., 15, *35*
Dabholkar, A. S., 40, *56*
Dadds, M. R., 208, *219*
Dahl, R. E., *36, 223*
Daleiden, E. L., 231, *249, 251*
Daley, S., 185, *196*
Daley, S. E., 17, *29*
Damasio, A. R., 40, *51, 52*
Damasio, H., 40, *51*
Damon, W., 290, 297, *301*
Daniels, D., 214, *219*
Dansky, L., 180, *198, 204, 222*
Davalos, M., 43, *56,* 63, 67, 69, 71, 74, *85*
Davenport, Y., 166, 167, *172*
Davenport, Y. B., 17, *29,* 287, *305*
Davidson, R., 71, *84*
Davidson, R. J., 39, 40, *52–54,* 63, 66, 77, *85*
Davies, P., 156, 167, 168, *171,* 211, 213, *219,* 228, 229, 235, 236, 245, *249, 253, 269*
Davies, P. T., 4, 8, 70, *83,* 135, *145,* 175, 177, *178, 196,* 256, 262, *269*
Davila, J., *29,* 185, *196,* 227, *250*
Davis, B., 263, 266, *269, 273*
Davis, G., 94, *115*
Dawson, G., 38–40, 43–45, 49, *53,* 55, 66, *83*
De Jong, A., 106, *119*
de Wilde, E. J., 16, *29*
Deater-Deckard, K., 23, *32*
DeCasper, A. J., 65, 69, *83*
Deering, C. G., 203, *221*
DeFries, J. C., 66, *86*
del Valle, C., 42, *55*
DelValle, C., 62, 84, *86*
Demetrikopoulos, M. K., 73, *87*
Dempsey, J., 282, *302*
DeMulder, E., 163, 167, *172,* 287, *301*
DeMulder, E. K., 92, 93, 106, *115,* 133, *146*
Denham, S., 287, *305*
Denham, S. A., 41, 42, *53*
Dennig, M. D., 231, *251*
Dent, J., 124, *153*
Depue, R. A., 204, *222*
Devlin, J. B., 210, *222*
Diamond, A., 40, *53*
Dickstein, L. J., 218, *219*

Dickstein, S., *119, 199*
Diekstra, R. F. W., 16, *29*
Dierker, L. C., 209, *219*
Dieter, J., 64, *83*
DiLallo, J., 113, *117*
Dinger, T. M., 208, *219*
Dino, G. A., 257, *269*
Diorio, J., *54,* 90, *115*
DiPietro, J. A., 66, *83*
Dixon, J. F., 125, *146*
Dobson, K. S., 124, *152*
Dodge, K., 189, *198,* 253, *270*
Dodge, K. A., 139, *145,* 277, *302*
Donnelly, B. W., 215, 216, *224*
Donovan, W. L., 43, *53*
Dorer, D., *248*
Dorer, D. J., *173, 198, 222,* 263, *273*
Doussard-Roosevelt, J. A., 46, *57*
Downey, G., 13, 17, *29,* 37, *53,* 93, 94, 111, *115,* 125, 133, *146,* 156, 158, *172,* 175, 182, *196,* 204, 209, *220,* 235, *249,* 266, *269,* 277, *285, 301*
Doyle, A., 261, *273*
Drezner, K., 194, *195, 299*
DuBois, D. L., 139, *149*
Dubow, E., 232, *248*
Dudley, C. D., 297, *301*
Duggan, C., 15, *29*
Duhig, A. M., 217, *220*
Dumas, J. E., 111, *115,* 263, *269*
Duncan, S. F., *219*
Dunn, G., *28*
Dunn, J., 214, *220*
Dusek, J. B., 134, *150*
Dweck, C. S., 139, *146*
Dyck, M., 123, *148*
Dykman, B. M., 134, *151*

Eales, M. J., 15, *28*
Easterbrooks, M. A., 110, *117*
Eaton, W., 14, *32*
Eaton, W. W., 98, *115*
Eaves, G., 124, *146*
Eaves, J., 66, *85*
Eaves, L., 18, 20, *31, 34, 35*
Eaves, L. J., 15, 18, 19, *29, 31, 34, 35,* 278, *303*
Ebert, M. H., 75, *85*
Eccles, J. S., 259, *269*
Eckenrode, J., *119,* 260, *272*
Edelbrock, T., 69, *82*
Edelman, G. M., 41, *54*

Sternberg, C. R., 41, *52*
Stetela, B., *57*
Stevenson, J., 15, 19, *29*
Stevenson-Hinde, J., 107, *120*
Stewart, M., *115*
Stewart, S., 28, *30*
Stewart-Berghauer, G., *151*
Stoneman, Z., 214, *219*
Stoolmiller, M., 23, *35*
Storer, D., 163, *171*
Straus, A. M., 39, *54*
Strauss, J., 163, *172*
Streer, R. A., 234, *248*
Strickland, B. R., 260, 264, *272*
Stringer, S., 79, *84*
Studd, J. W. W., 76, *84*
Suchecki, D., 47, *58*
Suess, G., 106, *120*
Sullivan, H. S., 291, *305*
Sullivan, K. T., 204, *220*
Sullivan, P. F., 16, 19, *35*
Suomi, S., 90, *114*
Susman, A., 177, *199*, 260, *272*
Suster, A., *115*
Svejda, J., 41, *56*
Swain, A. M., 76, *86*
Swatling, S., *144*, *299*
Szatmari, P., 209, *219*

Tal, M., *196*
Talbot, C. J., 20, *35*
Tanenbaum, R. L., *304*
Tarullo, L., 163, *172*
Taylor, E., *34*, *87*
Taylor, L., 126–128, *152*
Teasdale, J., 122, *144*
Teasdale, J. D., 26, *35*, 124, *153*
Teichman, M., 215, *224*
Teichman, Y., 215, *224*
Tesman, J. R., 42, *57*
Teti, D., 133, *153*, 156, *172*, 229, 234–236, *249*, 318, *326*
Teti, D. M., 92, 107, 109, 112, *120*, 277, 287, *305*
Thapar, A., 15, 19, 23, *35*, 66, *86*
Theakston, H., *84*
Thelen, M. H., 257, *269*
Thomas, A. M., 204, *224*, 256, *273*
Thompsen, A. H., 231, 232, *251*
Thompson, M. P., 217, *221*
Thomsen, A. H., 230, *248*, *249*
Thornton, L. M., 16, *31*

Tiggemann, M., 134, *153*
Tildesley, E., 266, *269*
Todak, G., *223*
Tonge, W. L., 163, *171*
Topolski, T. D., 19, *35*
Toth, S., 113, *115*
Toth, S. L., 121, *145*, 215, *219*, 287, 288, *300*
Tranel, D., 40, *51*
Tronick, E., 94, 112, *120*, 133, *145*, 177, *196*
Tronick, E. Z., 42–44, *52*, *58*, 61, 62, 69–71, 74, *82*, *83*, *87*, 133, *145*, 279, 280, *305*
Troughton, E., 21, *28*, *115*
Troutman, B. R., 141, *146*, 279, *301*
Truett, T. R., *29*
Tucker, D. M., 40, *58*
Tupling, H., 17, *32*
Turk, E., 131, 132, *153*
Turnbull, J., *196*
Turner, J. E., 127, *153*
Turner, S. M., 94, *120*

Uytdenhoef, P., 40, *58*

Vaillant, G. E., 24, *29*
Valente, E., 189, *198*, 253, *270*, 277, *302*
Valle, C., *221*
van Berkel, C., 47, *57*
van de Velde, P., *144*, *299*
van den Oord, J. C. G., 22, *33*
Van Egeren, L. A., 134, *146*
van IJzendoorn, M., 107, *119*
van IJzendoorn, M. H., 89, 90, 92, 93, 107, *120*
Van Slyke, D. A., 232, *252*
Vasey, M. W., 231, *249*, *251*
Velez, C. N., 255, *273*
Versage, E., *114*, *248*, *299*
Versage, E. M., 204, *218*, 277, 293, *299*
Versate, E., *326*
Vize, C., 185, *197*
Vodde-Hamilton, M., *223*
von Baeyer, C., 141, *152*
von Eye, A., 262, *272*
Voydanoff, P., 215, 216, *224*

Wadsworth, M., 232, *251*
Wadsworth, M. E., 230–232, *248*, *249*, *252*
Wagner, E., 286, *305*
Wahler, R. G., 70, *86*

Zigler, E., 162, *173*
Zimmerman, E., *54*
Zimmerman, E. A., *84*
Zoll, D., 97, *118*

Zoll, D. L., 70, *85*
Zuckerman, B., 63, 69, *88*
Zupan, B., *149, 303*
Zuroff, D. C., 134, *150*

SUBJECT INDEX

Gender, 15
    as risk factor, 314–316
    and vulnerability to depression in children of depressed mothers, 253–268
Gene—environment correlations
    active (evocative), 21, 23–24
    passive, 21–23
Gene—environment interactions, 21–22, 24–25
Generalized anxiety disorders, 15
Genetic studies, 18–20, 141–142
Girls, depression in, 253–267
    clinical implications of, 265
    future research, directions for, 266–268
    and risk created by maternal depression, 262–265
    socialization mechanisms related to, 256–262
    vulnerability to depression, 255–256
Glucocorticoid levels, 47

Heart rate, 46, 66
Helplessness model, 122
Helpless parenting, 91
Hopelessness theory of depression, 122
Hostile parenting, 91
Hypothalamic-pituitary-adrenal (HPA) axis, 46–49, 90, 312

Inadequate parenting, 308–309
Infant depression, 60, 63–64
Infant(s), 279–286
    interactions of mother with, 61–66, 70–74
    interventions targeting emotional regulation in, 281–284
    interventions targeting homeostatic regulation in, 280–281
    longer-term outcome studies involving, 68–70
    maternal depression and prefrontal cortex activity in, 42–45
    relative right frontal EEG activation in, 66–67
    vagal tone in, 67–68
Instrumentality, 261–262
Internalizing coping, 232
Interparental conflict, 211
Intrusive mothers, 70–71, 74, 78
IQ, 69, 140
Irritability, 177–178

Lum Emotional Availability of Parents (LEAP) Scale, 213

MABI (Mother's Assessment of the Behavior of her Infant), 282
MacArthur preschool classification system, 93
Major depressive disorder (MDD), 233
Marital difficulties (as stressor), 182–183
Massage therapy, 76–78, 281
Maternal depression, 17, 37–51, 59–82
    and caregiving behaviors, 106–111
    clinical implications of, 50–51, 75–80
    and dysregulations in early stages of infancy, 66–70
    and effect of interaction style on infant, 70–74
    and heuristic model of interaction styles, 74–75
    and interactions between mother and infant, 61–66
    and prefrontal cortex development/activity, 42–45
    and prefrontal cortex development/functioning in children, 38–45
    prenatal vs. postnatal, 44–45
    research on effects of, 37–38, 60–61
    and risk for depression in girls, 262–265
    and role of fathers, 140
    and stress response in children, 46–50
Maternal Depression and Infant Disturbance (Tronick and Field, eds.), 62
MDD (major depressive disorder), 233
Molecular genetic studies, 19–20
Monozygotic (MZ) twins, 18, 20, 22, 24, 141
Mood alteration techniques, 76–77
Mother, depression in. *See* Maternal depression
Mother's Assessment of the Behavior of her Infant (MABI), 282
Mutual regulation model, 43, 62, 74
MZ twins. *See* Monozygotic twins

National Institute of Child Health in Human Development (NICHD) study, 92
Nature—nurture interplay in depressive disorders, 21–28
    active (evocative) gene—environment correlations, 23–24
    clinical implications of, 25–28

gene—environment interactions, 24–25

passive gene—environment correlations, 22–23

Neonatal Behavior Assessment Scale (NBAS), 63, 74, 279, 282

Neuroticism, 141

Newborns, 63–64. *See also* Infant(s)

NICHD (National Institute of Child Health in Human Development) study, 92

Norepinephrine, 73, 78

Ontogenetic sculpting, 41

Parasympathetic nervous system, 46

Parental depression
    and child attachment. *See* Child attachment
    chronic stress associated with, 179–184
    in father. *See* Paternal depression
    in mother. *See* Maternal depression
    and negative cognitions, 129–132. *See also* Cognitive vulnerability to depression
    and offspring disorders. *See* Development of offspring
    as risk factor for child psychopathology, 228–229
    as stressor, 176–179, 228

Paternal depression, 203–205, 207–211

Personality disorders, 16

Prefrontal cortex, 38–45
    development of, 40–41
    and emotional regulation/expression, 38–40
    environmental influences on, 41–42
    and maternal depression, 42–45

Pregnancy massage, 77–78

Primary control coping, 231

Psychobiological attunement, 62, 74

Puberty, 15

Raising Healthy Children Project, 232–244

Rats, 47

Relaxation therapy, 76–77

Responses to Stress Questionnaire (RSQ), 237, 238, 241, 244

Rhesus macaques, 47–48

RSQ. *See* Responses to Stress Questionnaire

Sadness, 42, 62

Schizophrenia, 138

SCID (Structured Interview for DSM IV), 181

Secondary control coping, 231

Sensitization, stress, 191–192

Serotonin, 70, 72

SES. *See* Socioeconomic status

Siblings, 213–214

Socialization
    and emotional expression/regulation, 41–42
    gender-differentiated, 258–259
    and vulnerability to depression, 256–262

Socioeconomic status (SES), 60, 99–102, 105–106, 189–190

Squirrel monkeys, 46–48

State—Trait Anxiety Inventory (STAI), 64

Stress, 175–195
    and child attachment, 104–105
    from children's own life events, 186
    from children's perception of parental depression, 176–179, 228
    chronic, 179–184, 186
    clinical implications of, 193–194, 244–245
    coping as mediator of, 230–244
    and dysfunctional coping skills, 190–191
    episodic, 184–186
    from family environment, 164, 165
    hormonal responses to, 46–48
    and interpersonal processes, 192–193
    from life events, 135–138
    and maternal depression, 49
    as mediator of parental depression and child psychopathology, 229–230
    and parent—child relationship, 188–190
    as precipitant of children's symptoms, 187–188
    sensitization to, 191–192
    and vulnerability to depression, 135–138

Structured Interview for DSM IV (SCID), 181

Substance abuse, 15, 138–139

Suicide rates, 15–16

TDT. *See* Transmission disequilibrium test

Toddler-parent psychotherapy (TPP), 288–289

Toddlers, 286–290

TPP. *See* Toddler-parent psychotherapy

Transmission disequilibrium test (TDT), 19–20

Transmission of risk for depression, 307–326
clinical implications of, 322–326
and developmental pathways, 317–319
from disruption of biological systems, 311–312
from exposure to stress, 309–310
from inadequate parenting, 308–309
integrative model explaining, 319–322
moderators of, 313–317
and nature—nurture interplay, 312–313
from negative cognitions, 310–311
and transmission of depression from parent to child, 309–310

Twin studies, 18, 20, 22–24, 141

UCLA Family Stress Project, 177–178, 180, 184, 186–190

Vagal tone, 46, 67–68, 70

Vermont Kaiser Permanente Family Health Care, 233

Virginia Twin Study of Adolescent Behavioral Development (VTSABD), 23

Vulnerability to depression
cognitive. *See* Cognitive vulnerability to depression
gender and, 255–256

"Weak model" of relations between parental depression and child maladaptation, 95–97

Withdrawn mothers, 71

Withdrawn parents, 102, 104

Youth Self-Report (YSR), 234, 236, 238, 241

ABOUT THE EDITORS

Sherryl H. Goodman received her PhD in clinical psychology in 1978 from the University of Waterloo. She is a professor in the Department of Psychology and the Department of Psychiatry and Behavioral Sciences at Emory University in Atlanta, Georgia, where she is also director of the Clinical Training Program in Psychology. Her research interests center around the field of developmental psychopathology and, more specifically, the mechanisms by which depression may be transmitted from mothers to their children. Dr. Goodman is also interested in the epidemiology of child and adolescent psychopathology, with a particular focus on risk and protective factors. She is currently directing research on: mother–infant interaction in association with mothers' treatment for postpartum depression; children's understanding of sadness in others; the development of a measure of children's perception of parental sadness; the role of fathers in families with depressed mothers; and maternal depression as an early life stress for infants. Dr. Goodman is a Fellow of the American Psychological Association and associate editor of the *Journal of Family Psychology*.

Ian H. Gotlib received his PhD in clinical psychology in 1981 from the University of Waterloo. He is a professor in the Department of Psychology at Stanford University in Stanford, California, and is director of the Stanford Mood and Anxiety Disorders Laboratory. In general, Dr. Gotlib's research examines information-processing styles of depressed children, adolescents, and adults; patterns of brain activation of depressed individuals in response to different emotional stimuli, and the emotional, cognitive, physiological, and behavioral functioning of children of depressed mothers. Dr. Gotlib is currently overseeing a project examining the mechanisms of transmission of risk factors for depression and anxiety from mothers to daughters and the identification and psychobiological assessment of depressed individuals who are characterized by strong negative biases in their cognitive functioning. Dr. Gotlib is a Fellow of the American Psychological Association, the American Psychological Society, and the American Psychopathological Association.